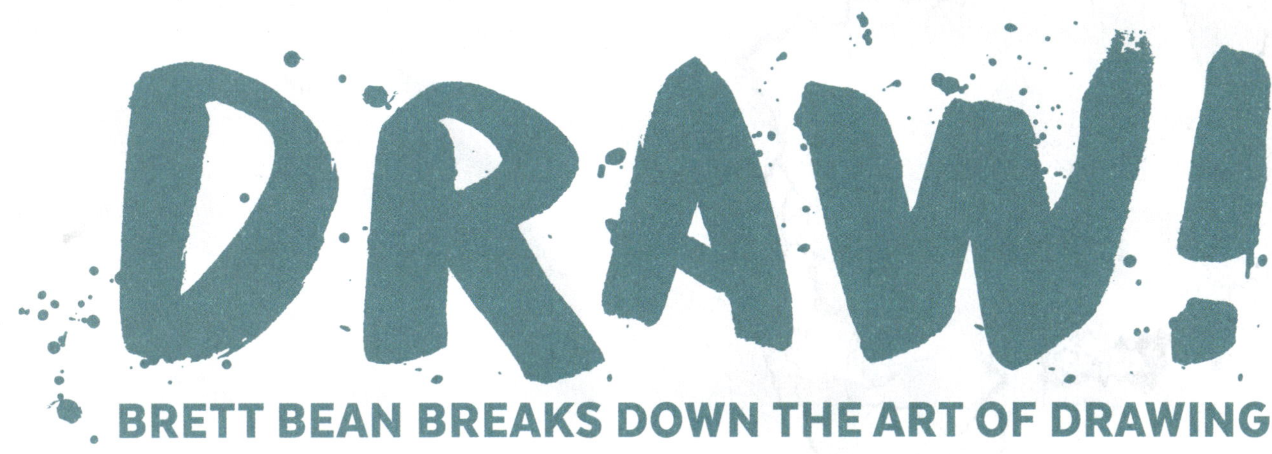

DRAW!

BRETT BEAN BREAKS DOWN THE ART OF DRAWING

3dtotal Publishing

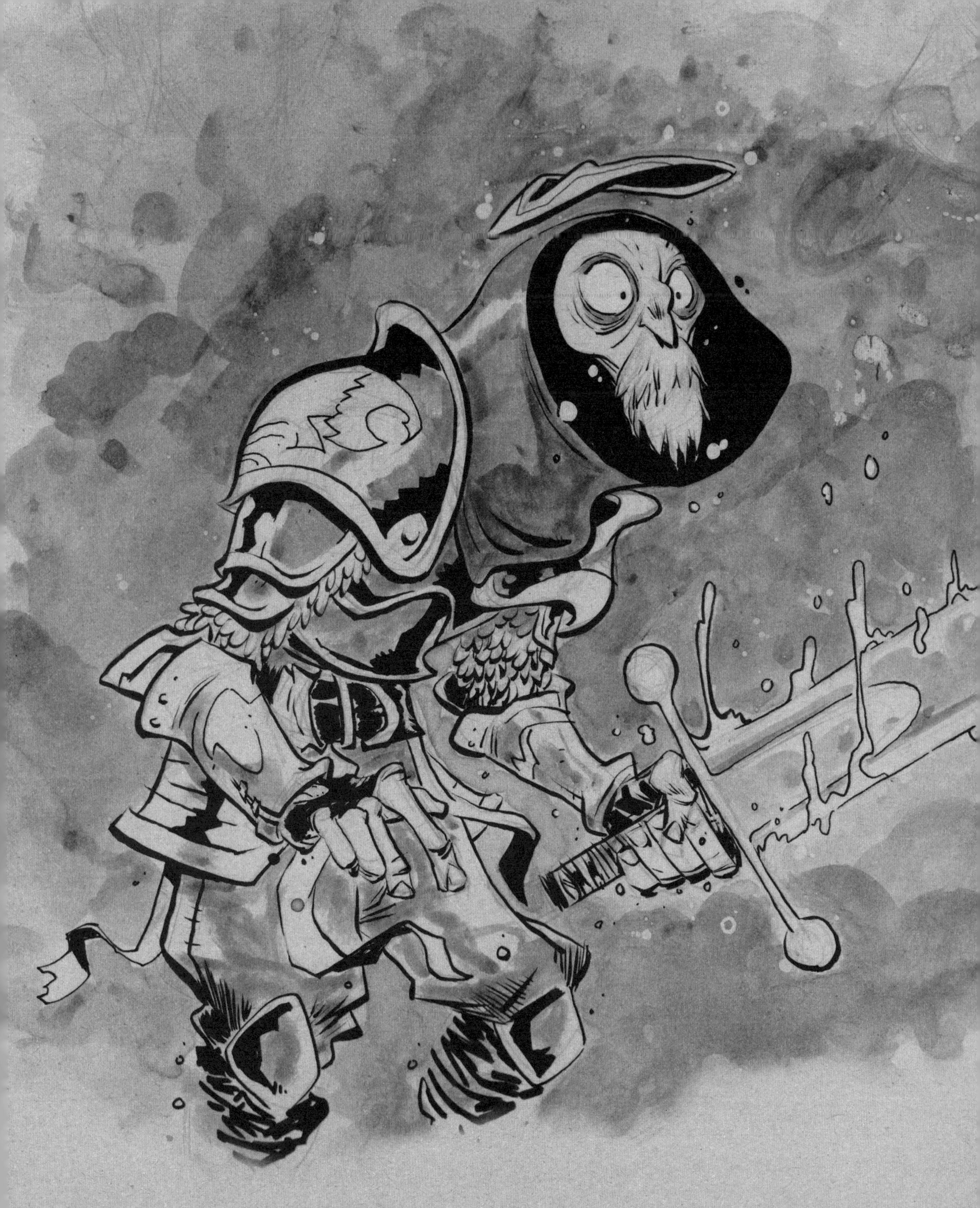

DRAW!

BRETT BEAN BREAKS DOWN THE ART OF DRAWING

3dtotalPublishing

3dtotalPublishing

Correspondence: publishing@3dtotal.com
Website: store.3dtotal.com

First published in the United Kingdom, 2024, by 3dtotal Publishing.

Address: 3dtotal.com Ltd,
29 Foregate Street, Worcester,
WR1 1DS, United Kingdom.

Soft cover ISBN: 978-1-912843-78-7

Printed and bound in China
by C&C Offset Printing Co., Ltd

Visit store.3dtotal.com for a complete list of available book titles.

Editor: Philippa Barker
Designer: Matthew Lewis
Lead Editor: Samantha Rigby
Lead Designer: Joseph Cartwright
Studio Manager: Simon Morse
Managing Director: Tom Greenway

All content © Brett Bean

Thank You Kobe font © Rpiclinez Studio

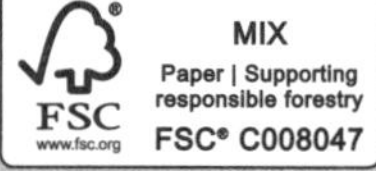

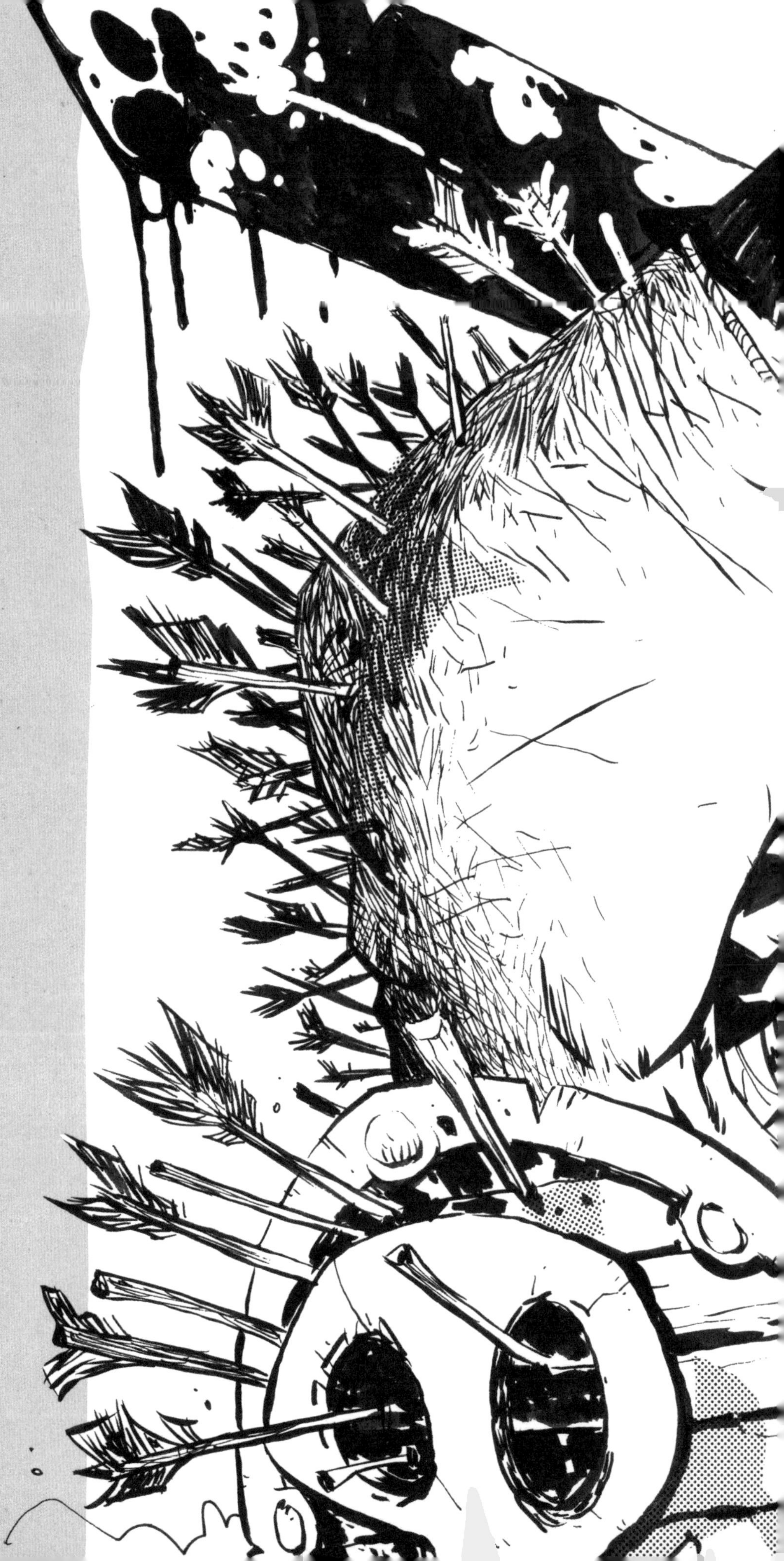

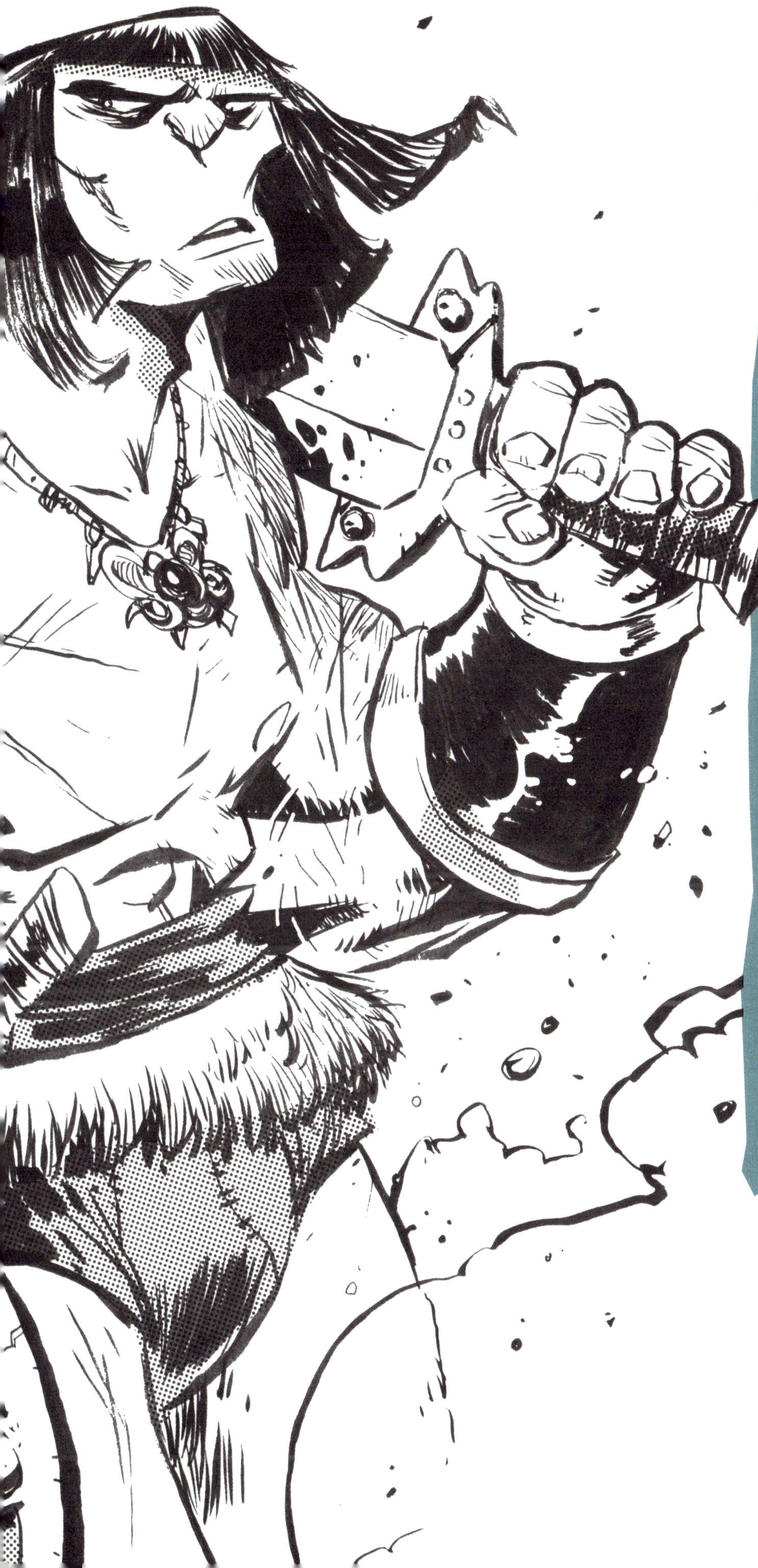

50%
of net profits donated
TO CHARITY

In 2022, 3dtotal Publishing became successful enough to make a pledge to donate 50% of its net profits to charity. This continues to be possible due to the incredible support from all our customers, employees, and partners. At the time of printing, we have donated over $1.3 million (USD) to charity.

We focus our giving on three charitable areas: environmental, humanitarian, and animal welfare. We use organizations such as Effective Altruism and Founders Pledge to guide who we help within these causes. Some ways of doing good are over 100 times more effective than others, so donating this way hugely increases the impact of our contributions.

See **3dtotal.com/charity** for full details.

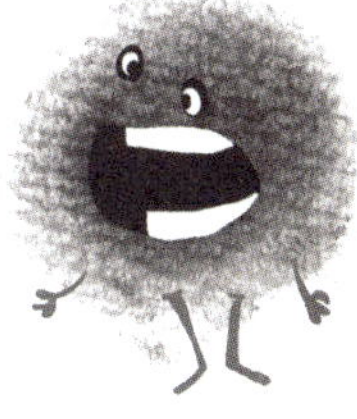

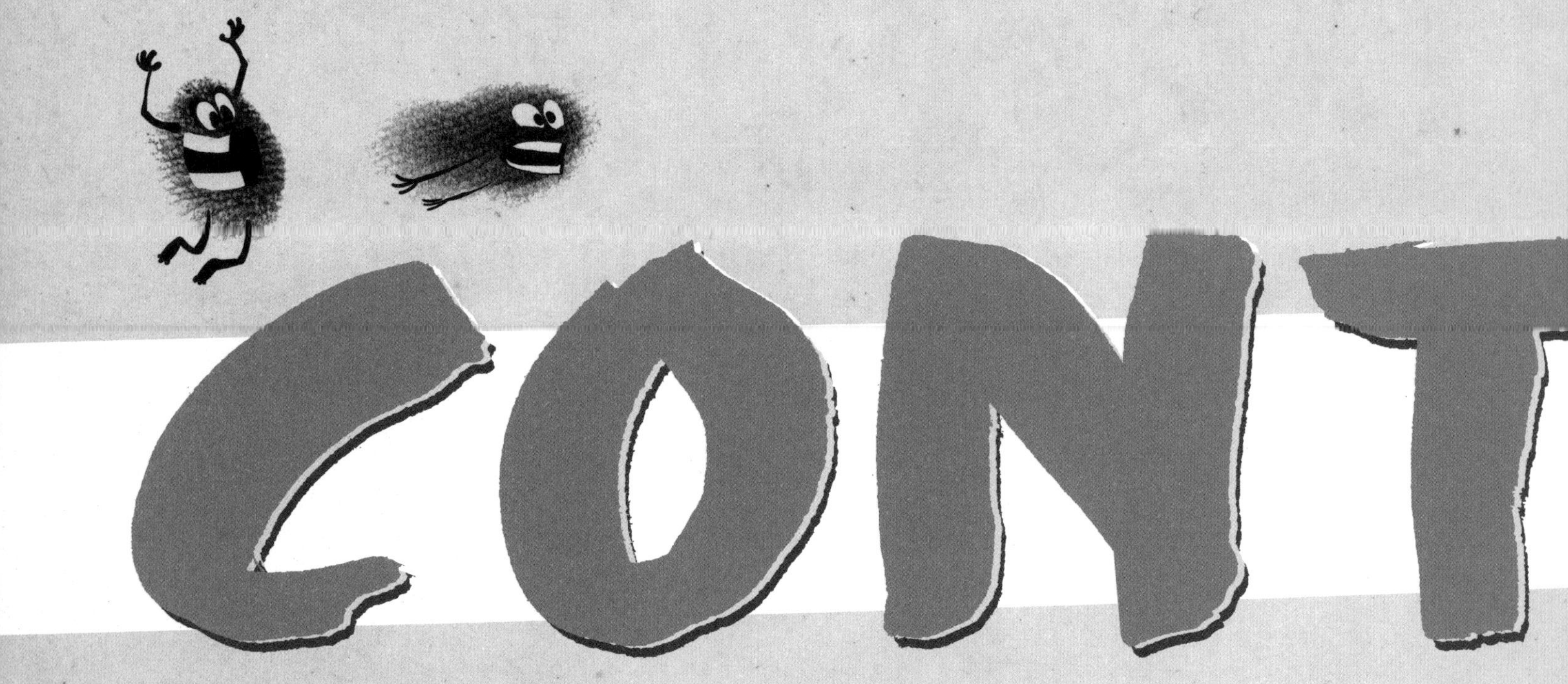

CONT[ENTS]

ENTS

EXERCISES

At the end of some of the chapters you'll find pages of exercises to complete. Use tracing paper to draw over these pages, or take a photo/scan them in to complete digitally. You can also print them out and draw on them as many times as you like by downloading them as PDFs here:

store.3dtotal.com/resources

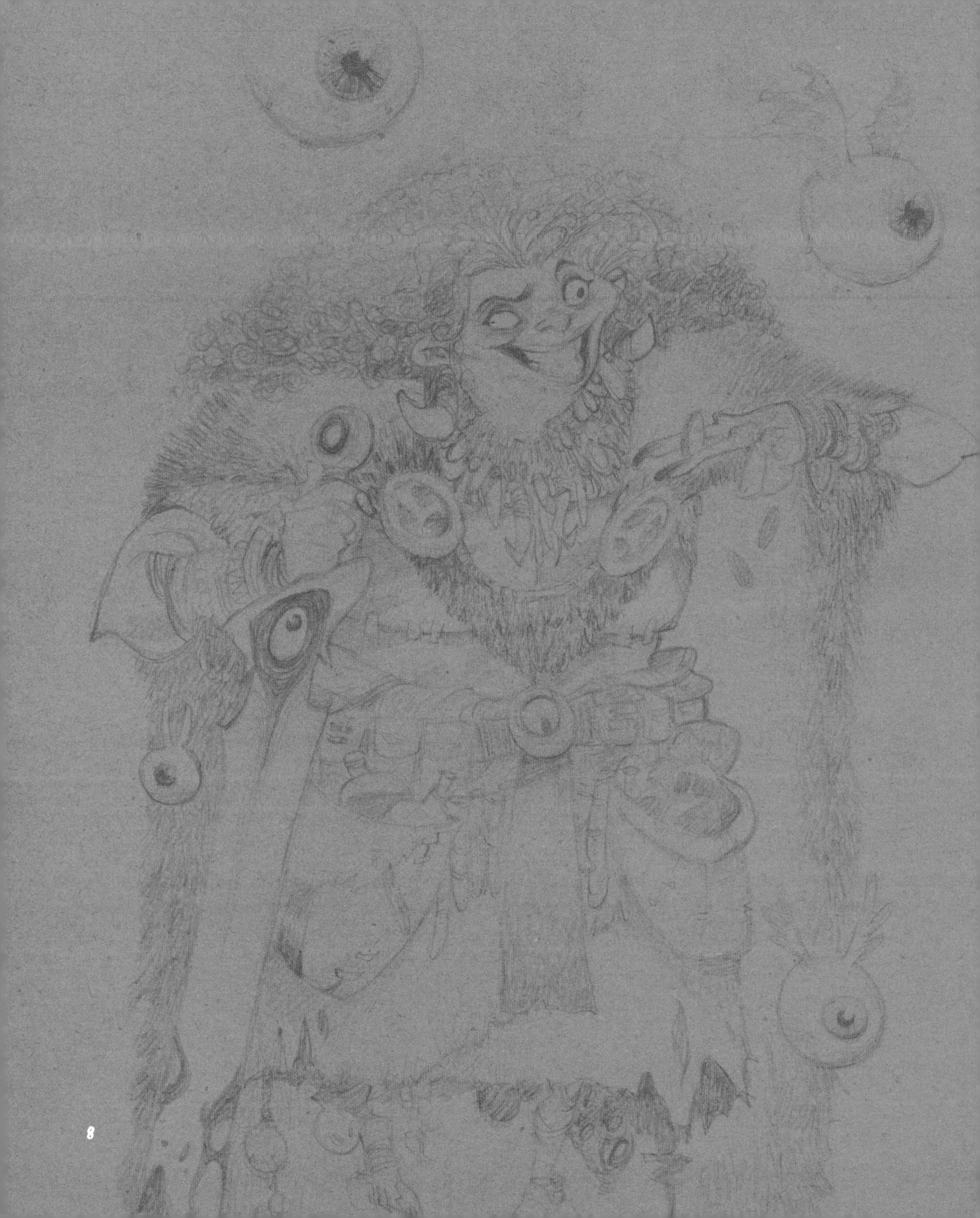

CHAPTER 01

HOW TO USE THIS BOOK

Drawing can be that miraculous place where practice and ability meets improvisation and meaning. And drawing **IS** improv if you do it for a living. One day you'll show up with your skill set and ability to think for yourself when the company 'genius' runs in and spews forth a string of nonsensical words you must commit to paper.

No one wakes up and thinks 'Today will be the day I'm asked to draw a mangy nardvark duelling a synth-devil-child on a speeding bullet train.' But it will happen. Even when working for yourself, you may have a big idea in your head, but it's a one-line-at-a-time, work-as-you-go kind of life when drawing. If that's not improvisation, I don't know what is!

This is why I've attempted to make the book I wish someone had given to me in high school, college, in my thirties, and even into my forties, to help guide people to draw with creativity, fun, and purpose.

Any way is possible if it gets your point across. That's true of any subjective medium. If you find an audience, you nailed it! For every 'Do it this way' instruction in this book, I've seen it successfully achieved another way. The practice of thinking 'what' and 'how' in drawing is just as important as the drawing mileage for your hand-eye coordination. But only one truth remains in this art form: did your intentions translate from vision to actuality?

...DUCTION

It's up to you to figure out the parts that work for you and to throw out the rest. Let these lessons blend and merge into whoever you end up becoming as an artist. Drawing is just one way to explore who you are.

Anything worth pursuing is hard in some way, so let's agree that you'll go easy on yourself during our time together. Set goals that you can realistically reach. Never put your hopes in someone else's hands with goals such as 'I'm going to work for ______', 'I'll be as famous as ______', or 'I've got to get to one million views on ______'. You don't get to decide that, but you **CAN** set targets such as practising drawing every week, learning to draw hands and feet, or finishing a sketchbook by the end of the year. Remember that goals without a plan are nothing but dreams.

Like a runner, you wouldn't start by running a marathon. Talk about leg cramp on the first lap! You would start with short five-minute jogs, before working up to fifteen-minute paced runs, then over time building up your ability to run that marathon! Drawing is no different. You're setting yourself up for a marathon, starting now.

Enjoy the journey, not just the destination!

Let's get started...

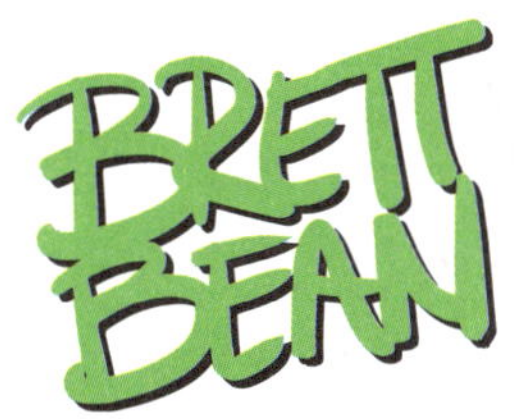

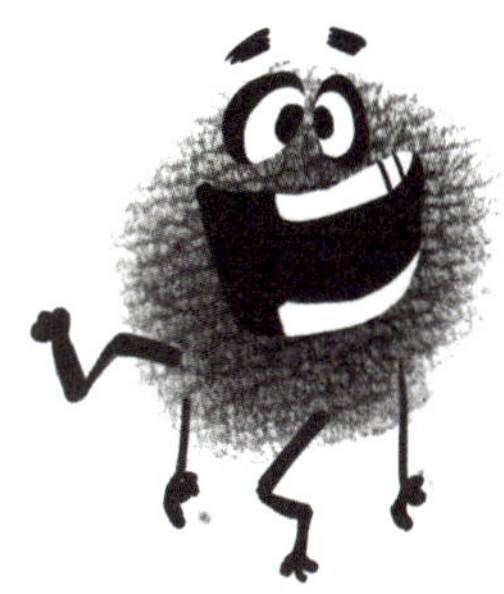

VISUAL COMMUNICATION

ART is the tool we have used to visually communicate ever since cavemen began daubing paint on cave walls.

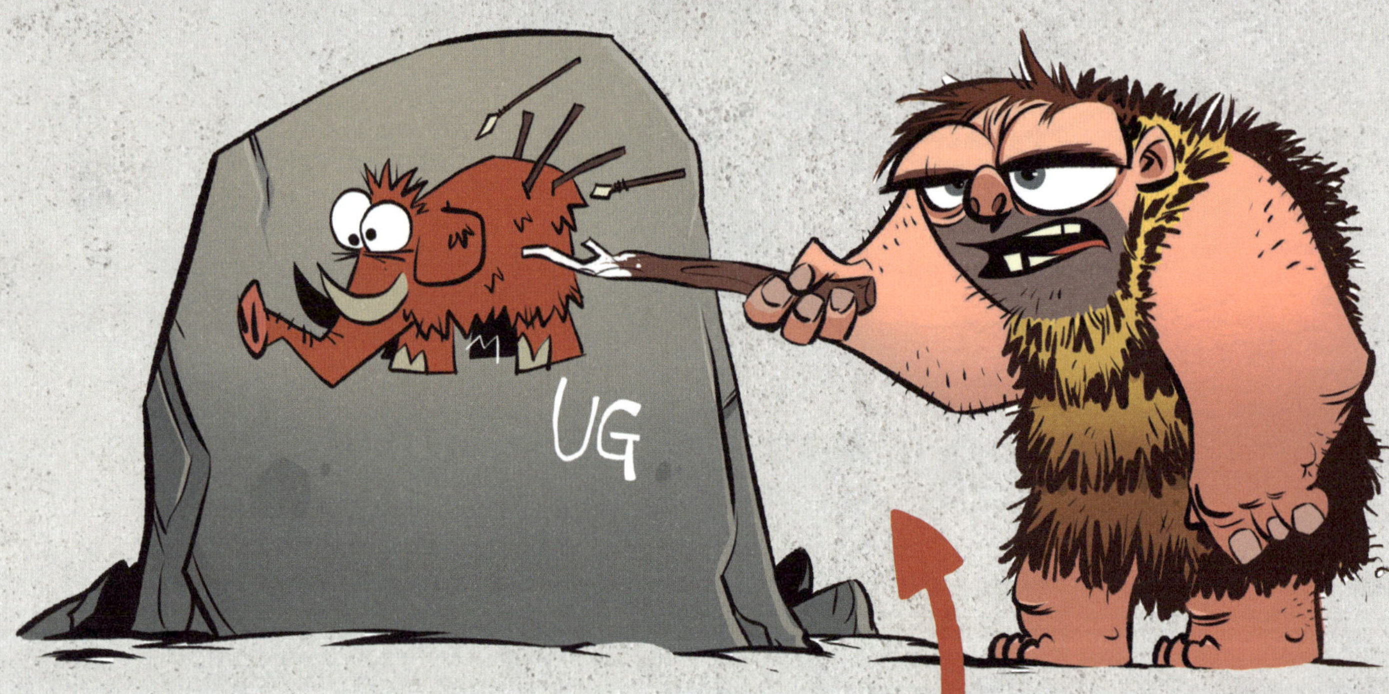

Nowadays it's much easier to do this on the internet. Cave walls don't get very good natural light! The internet doesn't give off natural light either, but you get what I mean...

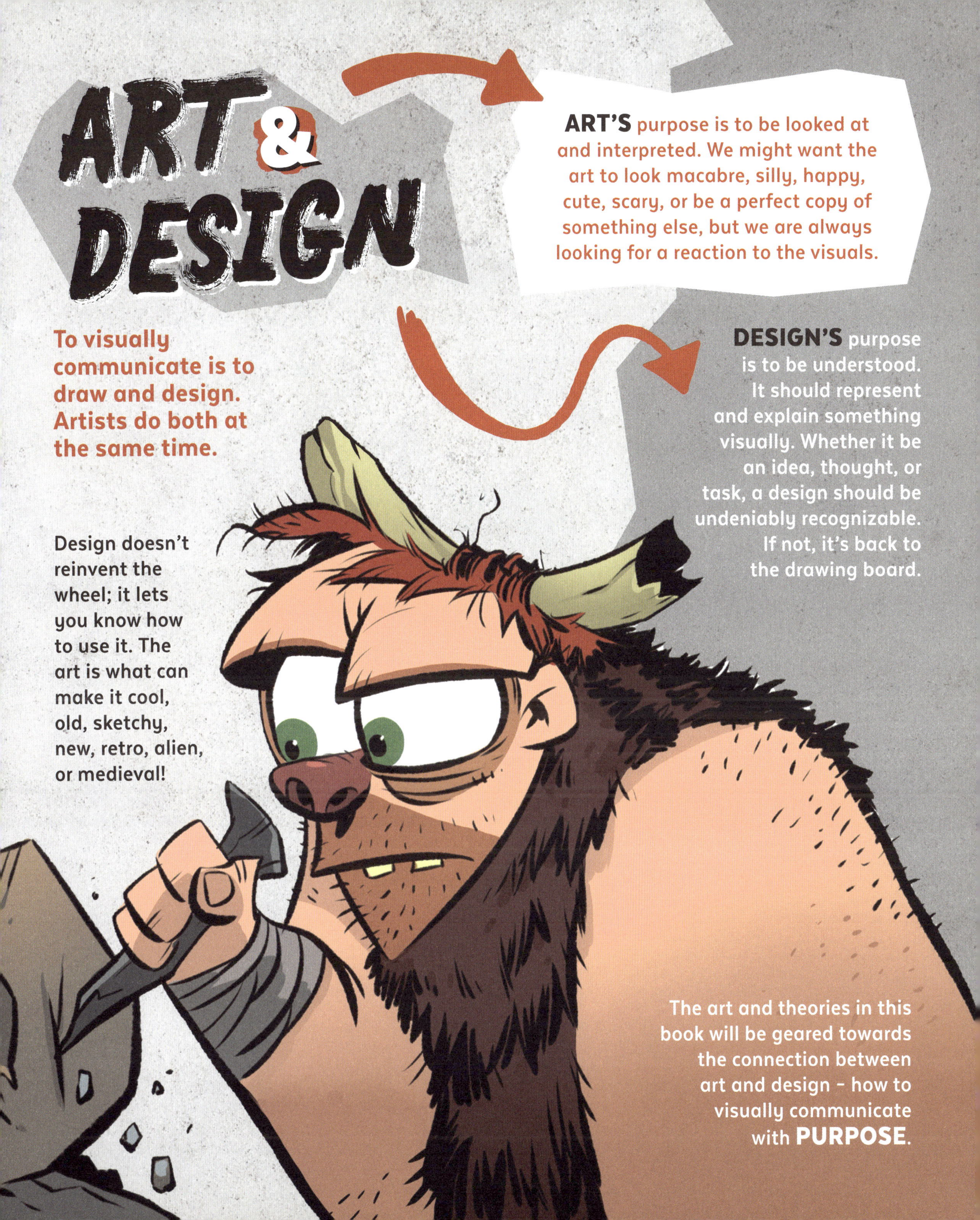

ART & DESIGN

ART'S purpose is to be looked at and interpreted. We might want the art to look macabre, silly, happy, cute, scary, or be a perfect copy of something else, but we are always looking for a reaction to the visuals.

To visually communicate is to draw and design. Artists do both at the same time.

DESIGN'S purpose is to be understood. It should represent and explain something visually. Whether it be an idea, thought, or task, a design should be undeniably recognizable. If not, it's back to the drawing board.

Design doesn't reinvent the wheel; it lets you know how to use it. The art is what can make it cool, old, sketchy, new, retro, alien, or medieval!

The art and theories in this book will be geared towards the connection between art and design – how to visually communicate with PURPOSE.

DRAWING lets us convey our ideas, information, and thoughts in many ways!

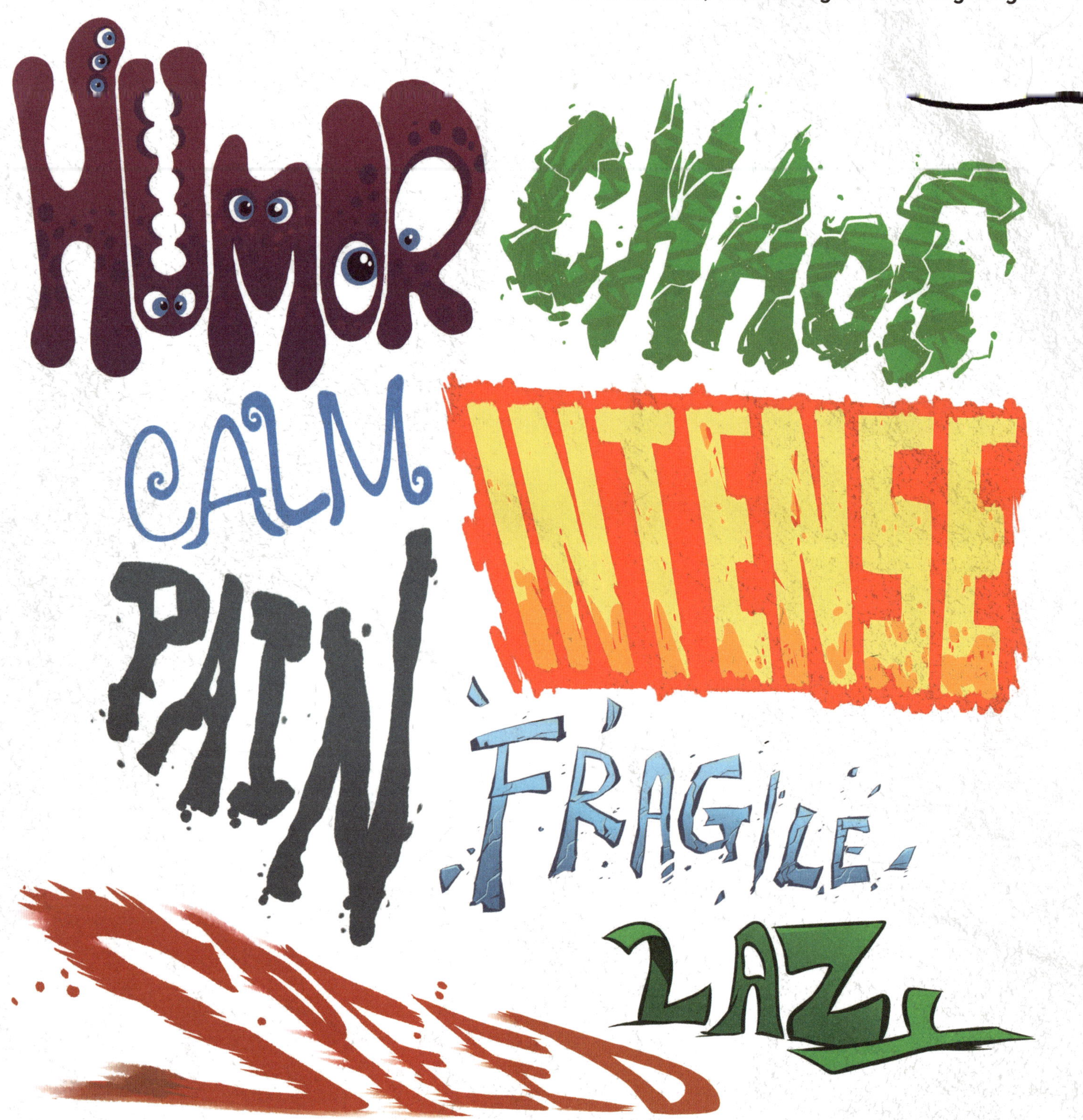
HUMOR
CHAOS
CALM
INTENSE
PAIN
FRAGILE
LAZY

Your personal journey as an artist will be shaped by your goals, aspirations, physical abilities, disabilities, likes, dislikes, financial situation, time constraints, and life pressures.

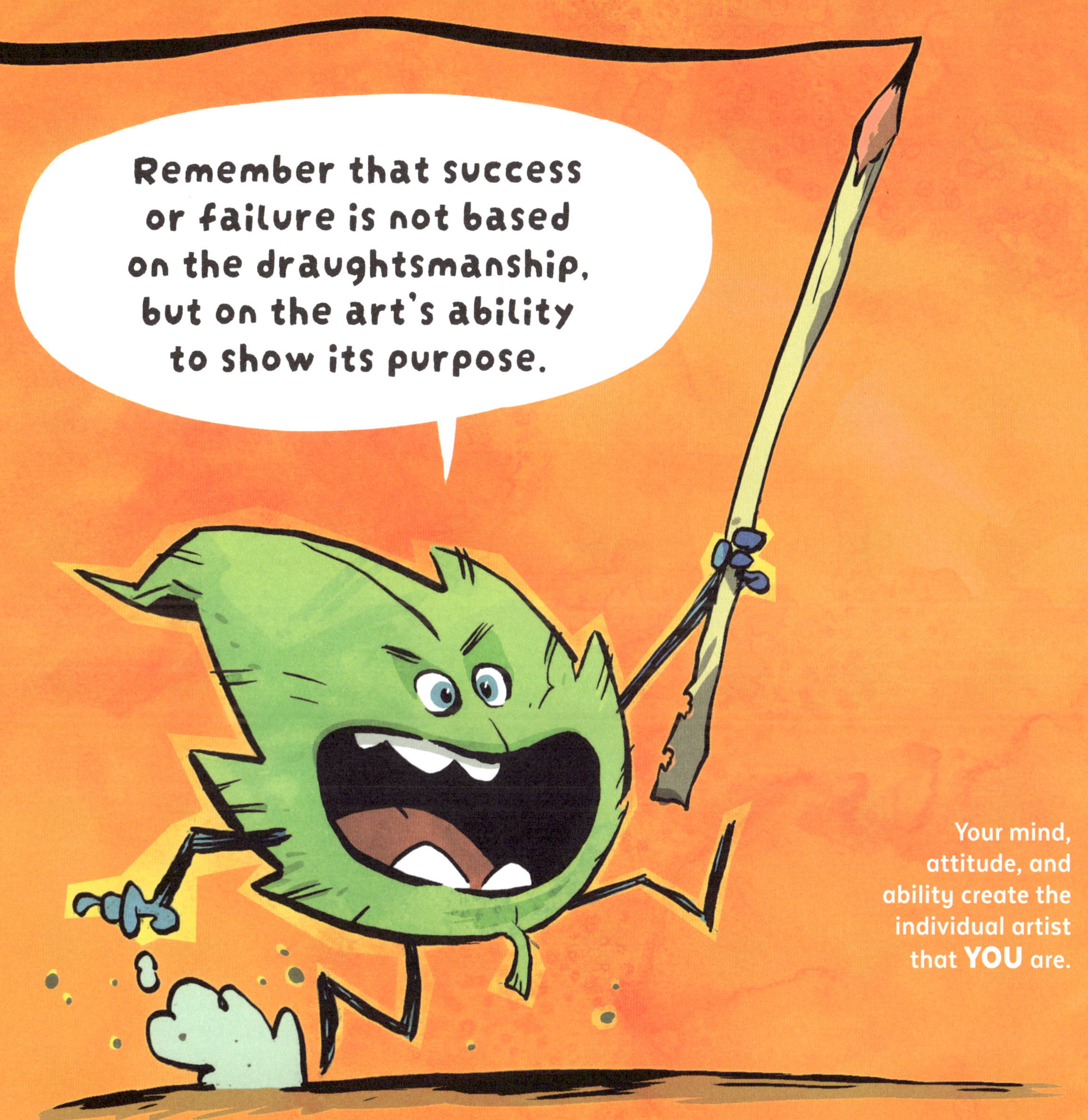

Your mind, attitude, and ability create the individual artist that **YOU** are.

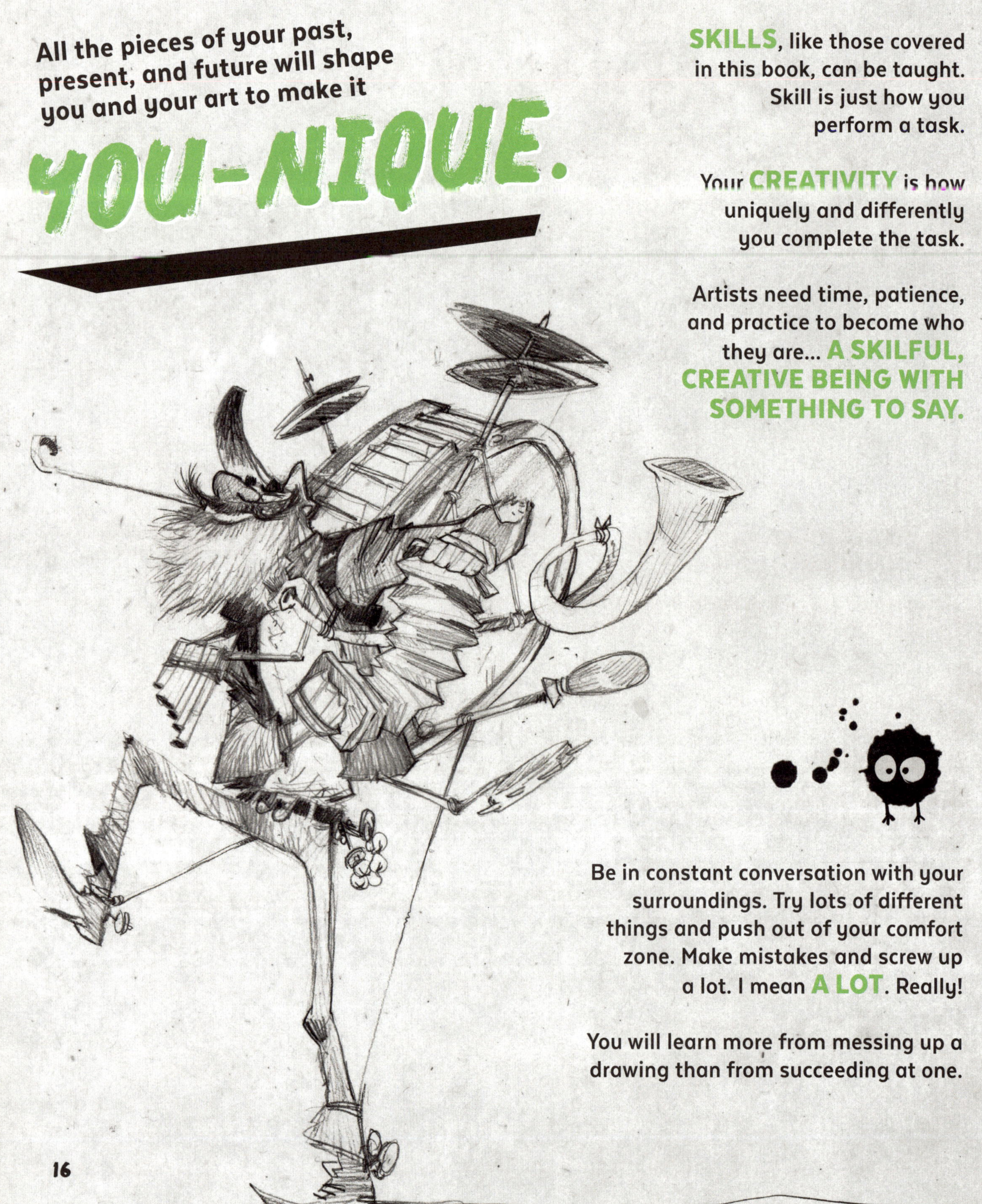

All the pieces of your past, present, and future will shape you and your art to make it

YOU-NIQUE.

SKILLS, like those covered in this book, can be taught. Skill is just how you perform a task.

Your **CREATIVITY** is how uniquely and differently you complete the task.

Artists need time, patience, and practice to become who they are... **A SKILFUL, CREATIVE BEING WITH SOMETHING TO SAY.**

Be in constant conversation with your surroundings. Try lots of different things and push out of your comfort zone. Make mistakes and screw up a lot. I mean **A LOT**. Really!

You will learn more from messing up a drawing than from succeeding at one.

There is no 'talent fairy' choosing who gets to be an artist. If that were true, there would be no reason to make this book.

Your personality and ability to work with others will far outweigh your artistic skills.

The grass is always greener on the other side.

People in life either add, subtract, multiply, or divide. Yourself included. Choose wisely.

You only get one reputation, so treat it, and others, with respect.

Don't take criticism from someone you wouldn't take advice from.

Create more than you consume.

There is no straight line to success.

HERE ARE SOME OF THE THINGS I'VE LEARNED

If you complain, you remain. Be a problem solver.

You can do anything, but not everything. Pick your battles.

Style will find you over time.

Be passionate about something besides art.

And **NEVER** pick your nose after cutting jalapeños...

Stand up more than you get knocked down.

Go outside, exercise, and drink water.

If art becomes a job, find a new hobby.

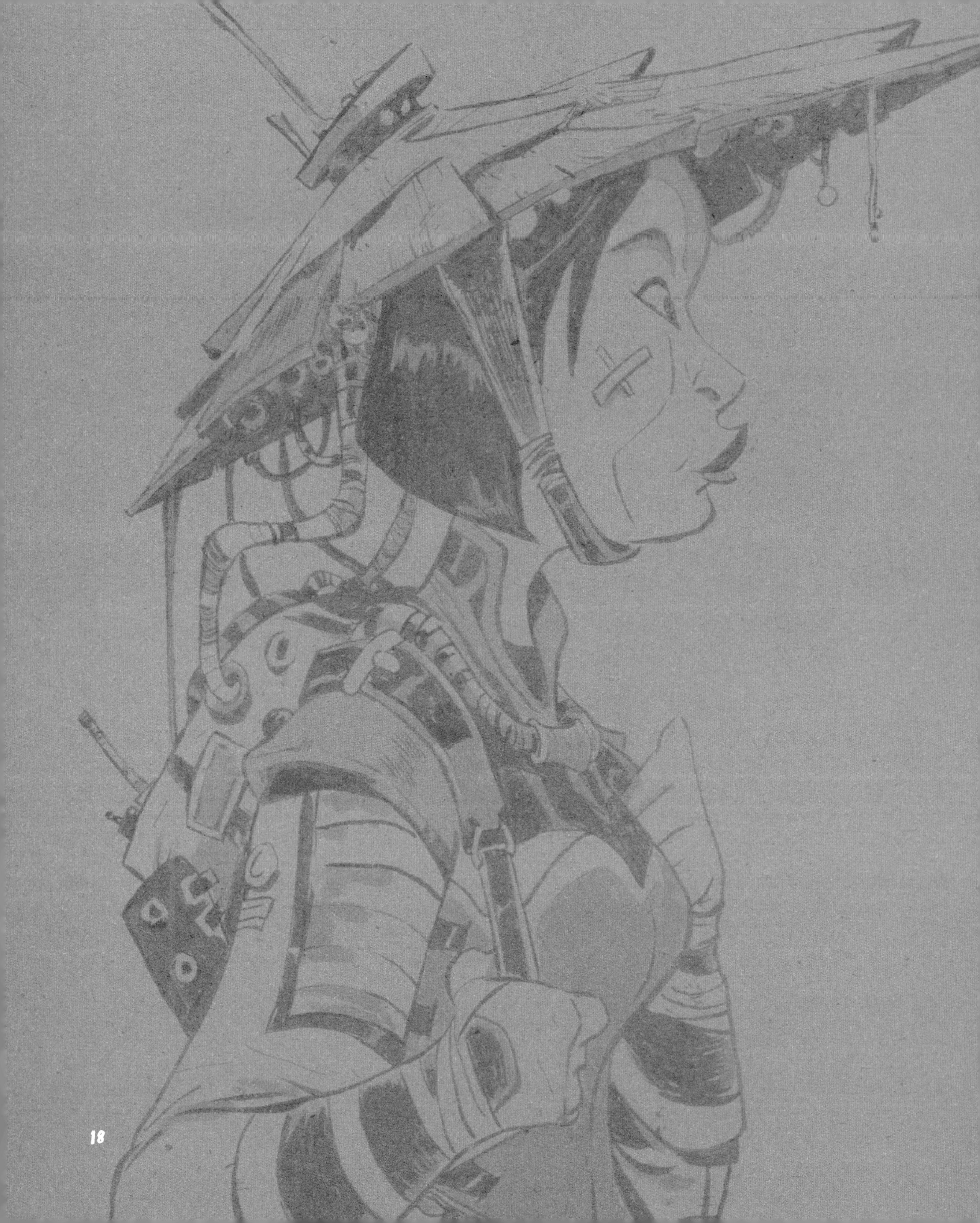

AN ARTIST'S SUPPLIES

EQUIPMENT & SUPPLIES

Before we get too far along, let's talk about the equipment and supplies artists typically use for drawing. These chapters won't cover everything, but you should try to make use of **ANYTHING** and **EVERYTHING** available to you.

Don't feel confined to the tools explored in this book. Draw with crayons and pastels, coffee and syrup... Create with fingerpaints, glitter guns, or your mom's ballpoint pen! Go on and **MIX THAT MEDIA!**

But because it would be silly to make nine chapters detailing all of the random items you **CAN** draw with, let's start with what artists **NORMALLY** use and see where it takes us.

This chapter will explore some of the physical items you would typically need when drawing.

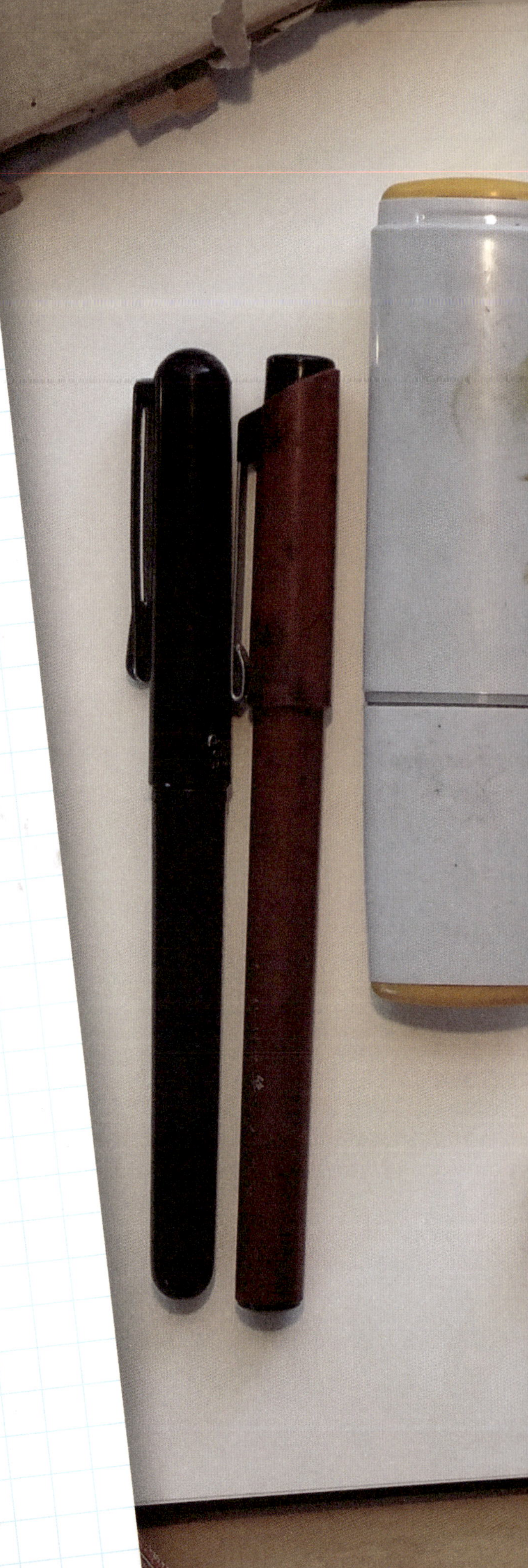

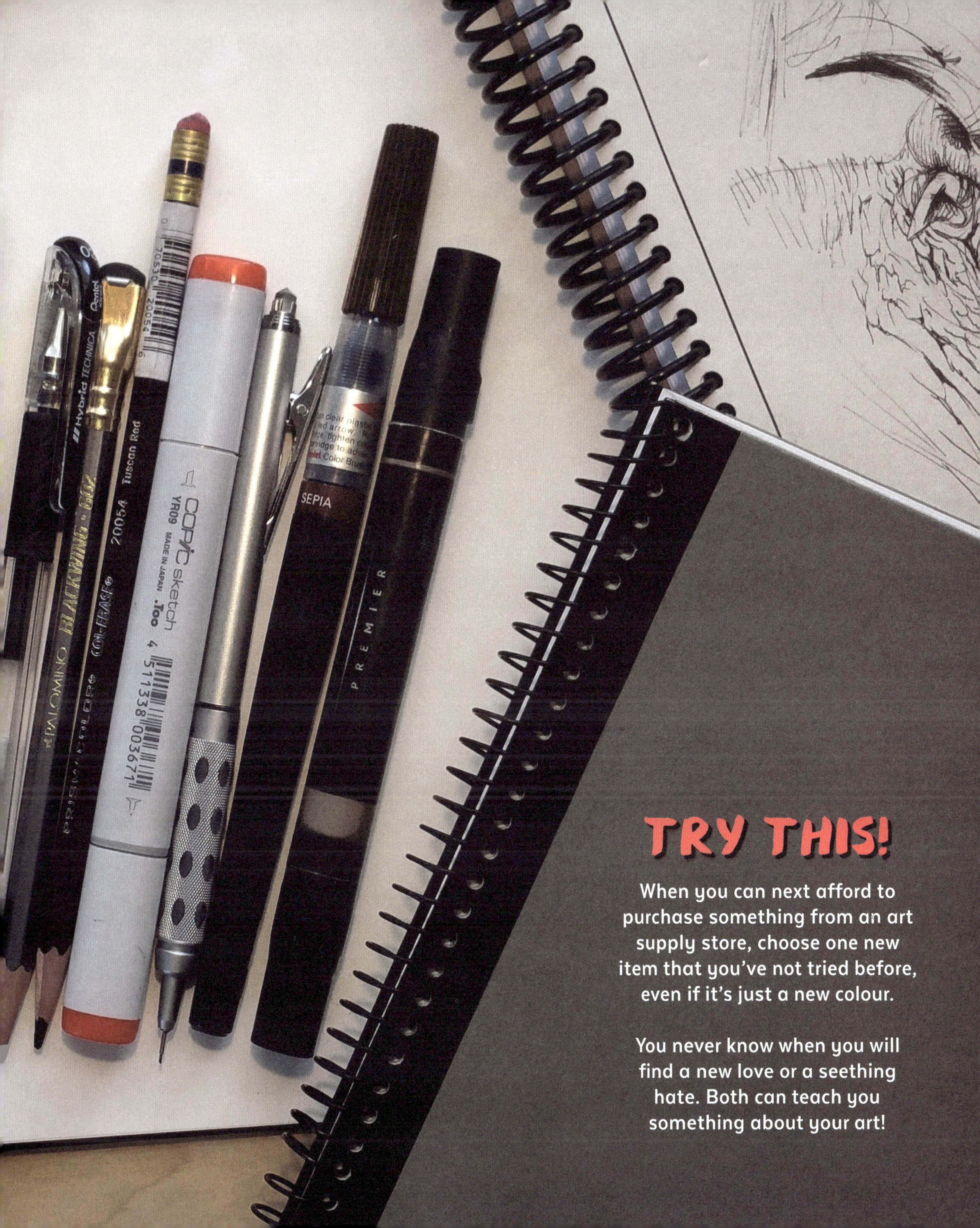

TRY THIS!

When you can next afford to
purchase something from an art
supply store, choose one new
item that you've not tried before,
even if it's just a new colour.

You never know when you will
find a new love or a seething
hate. Both can teach you
something about your art!

PENCILS

Mechanical, graphite, blue, charcoal, H, 2B or not 2B, coloured, and everything in between.

What can I say about pencils that hasn't been said a million times already? Pencils are an artist's bread and butter. They can also be used to spread butter onto bread, but not very well... I had one lodged in my palm at an early age and still have the mark from it. I bet that's something you didn't know about pencils until today...

OTHER RANDOM FACTS ABOUT PENCILS:

THE AVERAGE PENCIL CAN BE SHARPENED SEVENTEEN TIMES.

A PENCIL CAN BE USED UNDERWATER, IN SPACE, AND UPSIDE DOWN.

A SINGLE PENCIL CAN DRAW A THIRTY-FIVE-MILE-LONG LINE.

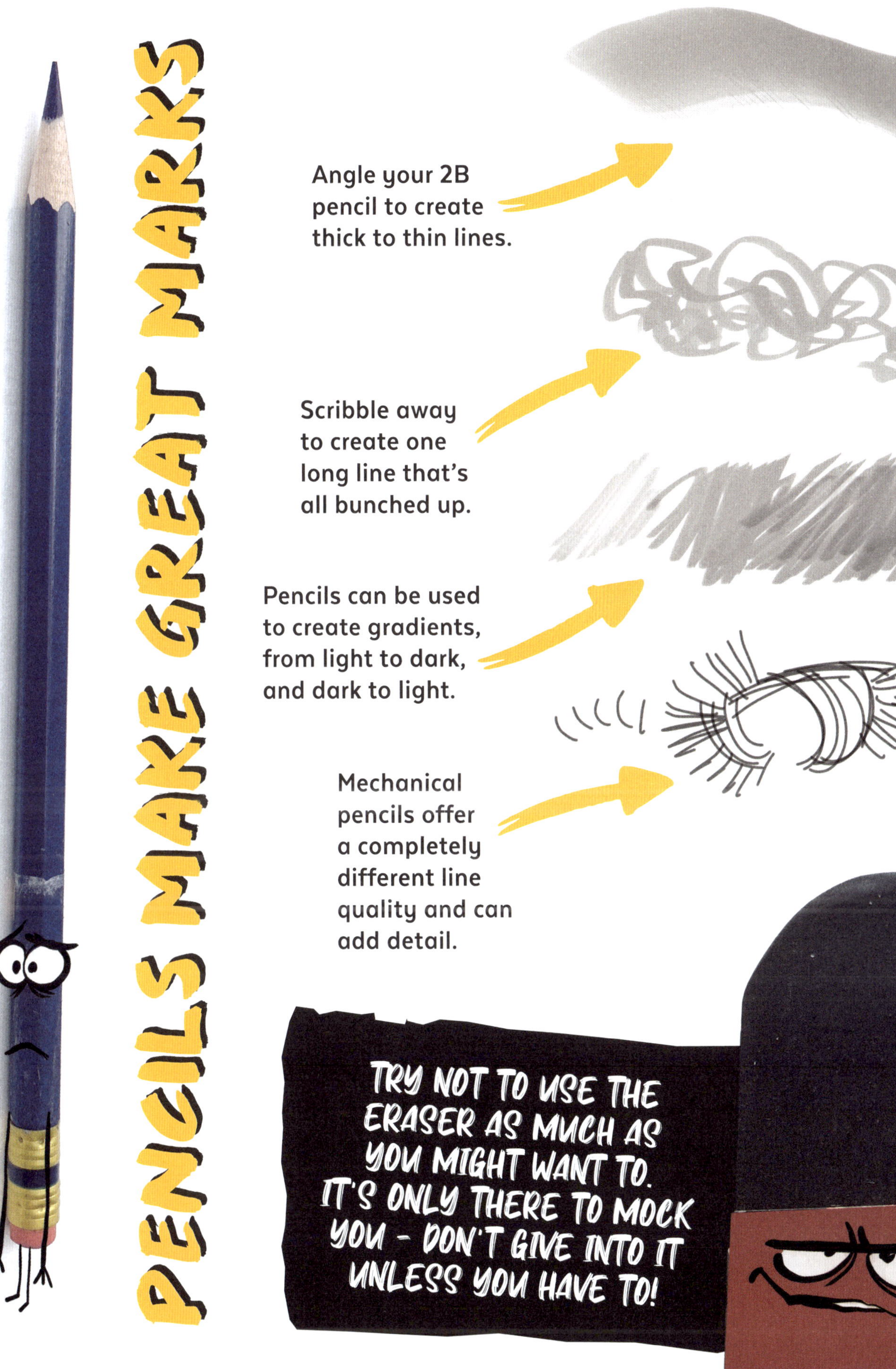
PENCILS MAKE GREAT MARKS
Angle your 2B pencil to create thick to thin lines.
Scribble away to create one long line that's all bunched up.
Pencils can be used to create gradients, from light to dark, and dark to light.
Mechanical pencils offer a completely different line quality and can add detail.
TRY NOT TO USE THE ERASER AS MUCH AS YOU MIGHT WANT TO. IT'S ONLY THERE TO MOCK YOU - DON'T GIVE INTO IT UNLESS YOU HAVE TO!

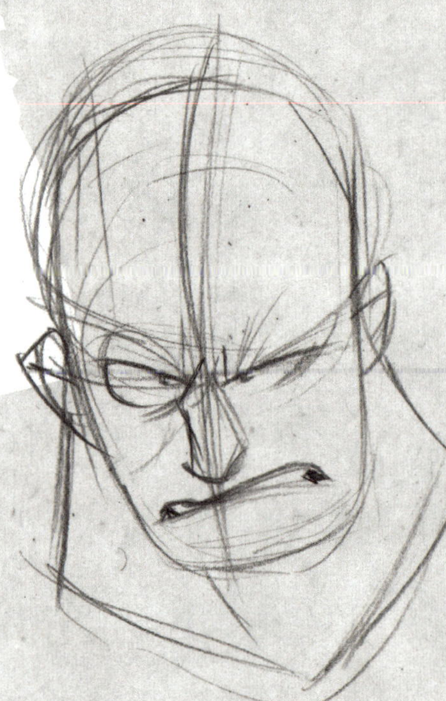

Using a light hand and concentrating on bigger shapes and concepts, sketches allow you to quickly explore lots of ideas without spending too much time on any one.

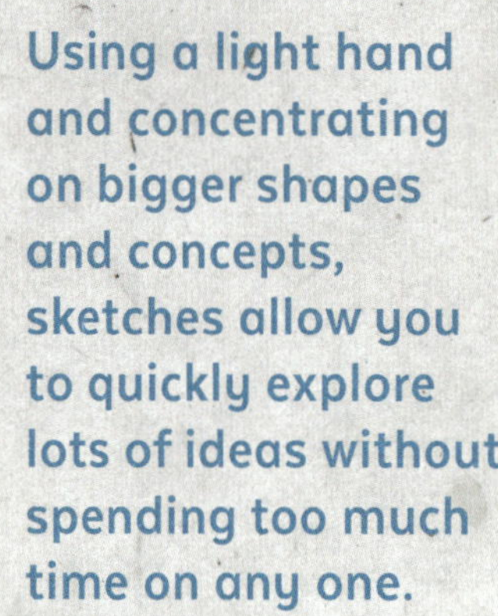

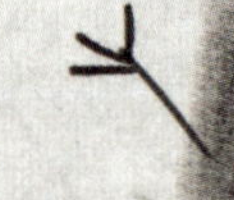

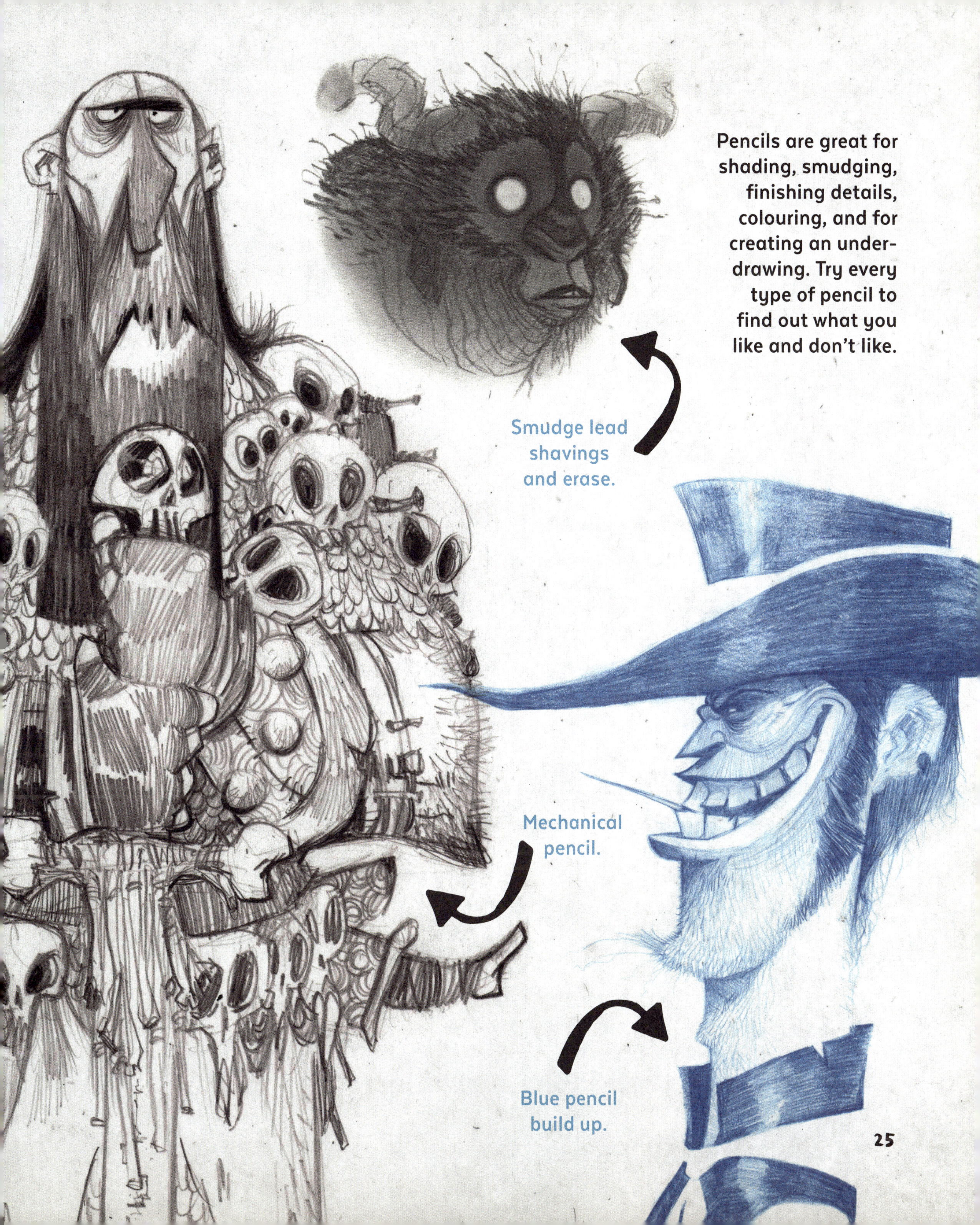

Pencils are great for shading, smudging, finishing details, colouring, and for creating an under-drawing. Try every type of pencil to find out what you like and don't like.

PENS & INKS

Brush pens, nibs, ink, fineliners, ballpoints, and more...

I'm totally biased here because I think pens are awesome. I like pens because they force you to leave the line where it is and move on. There's no going back!

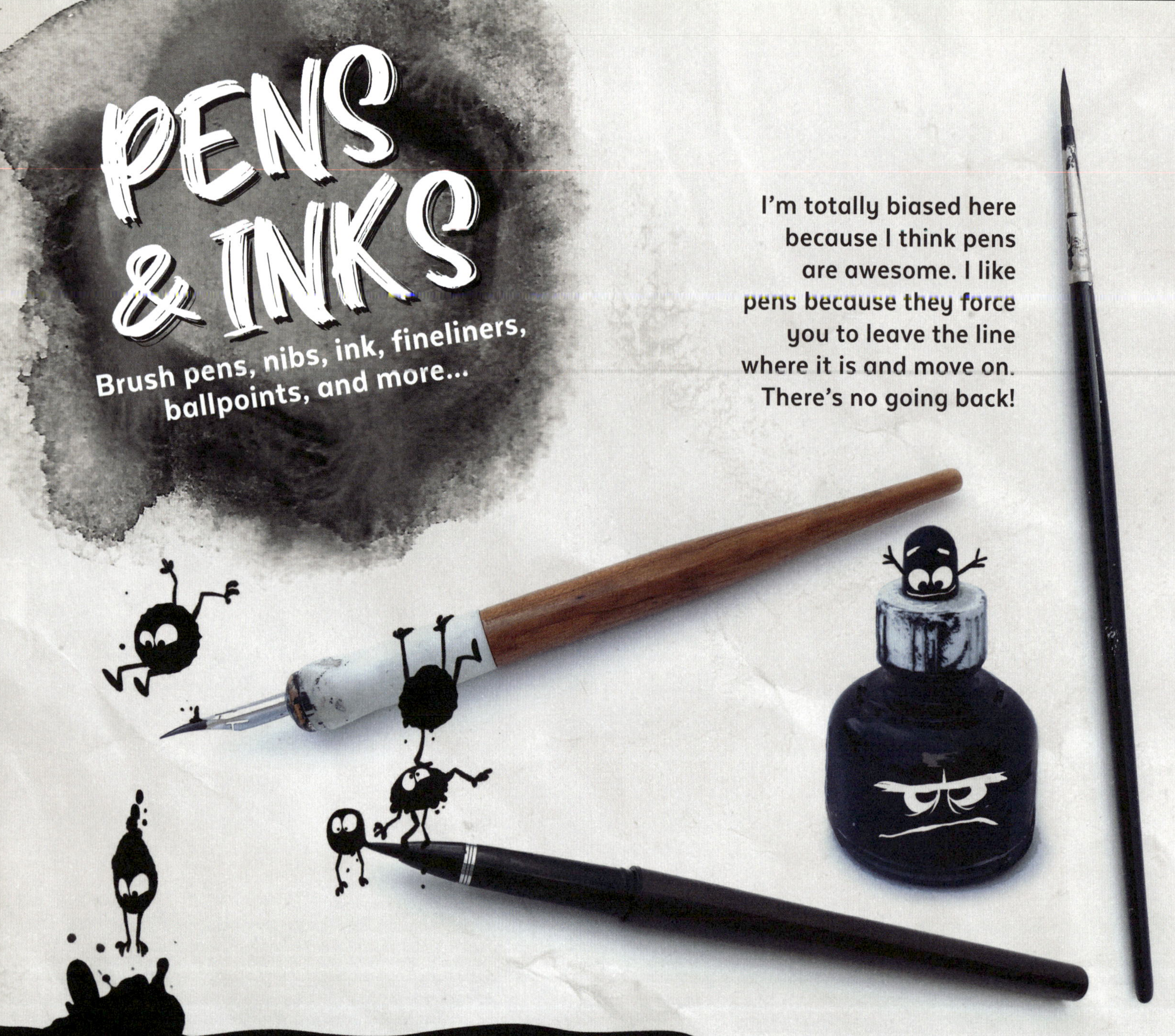

When I was just starting out as an artist, I always used pencil first, but now I often begin with ink. Not only does it save you time by skipping the pencil phase, but it makes you **REALLY** concentrate on where you want to put the next line. It can help to train your hand-eye coordination and grow your confidence over time.

Just not at first. At first you will feel like a newborn giraffe trying to ice skate while knitting a sweater.

PEN & INKS ARE IDEAL FOR LINE WEIGHT

Line weight is the visual lightness, darkness, or heaviness of a line within a drawing. In any drawing, from a sketch to a finished piece, the different line weights will communicate depth, importance, and proximity.

DEPTH

Where are the shadows?

DENSITY

How visually or physically heavy is it?

PROXIMITY

How close is it?

OUTLINE SURFACES

How do they relate to other lines?

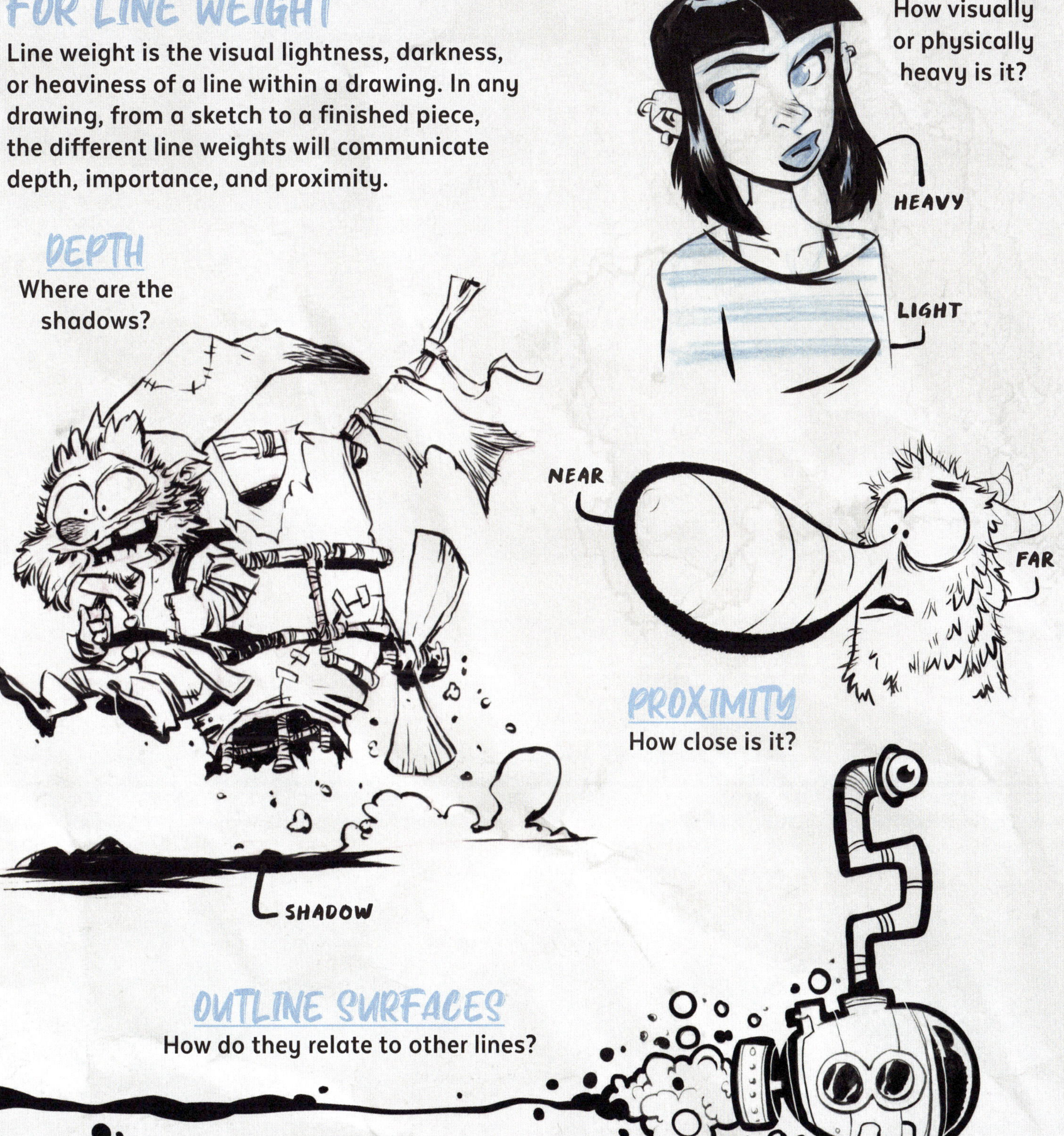

A FEW EXAMPLES OF HOW TO USE PEN & INKS

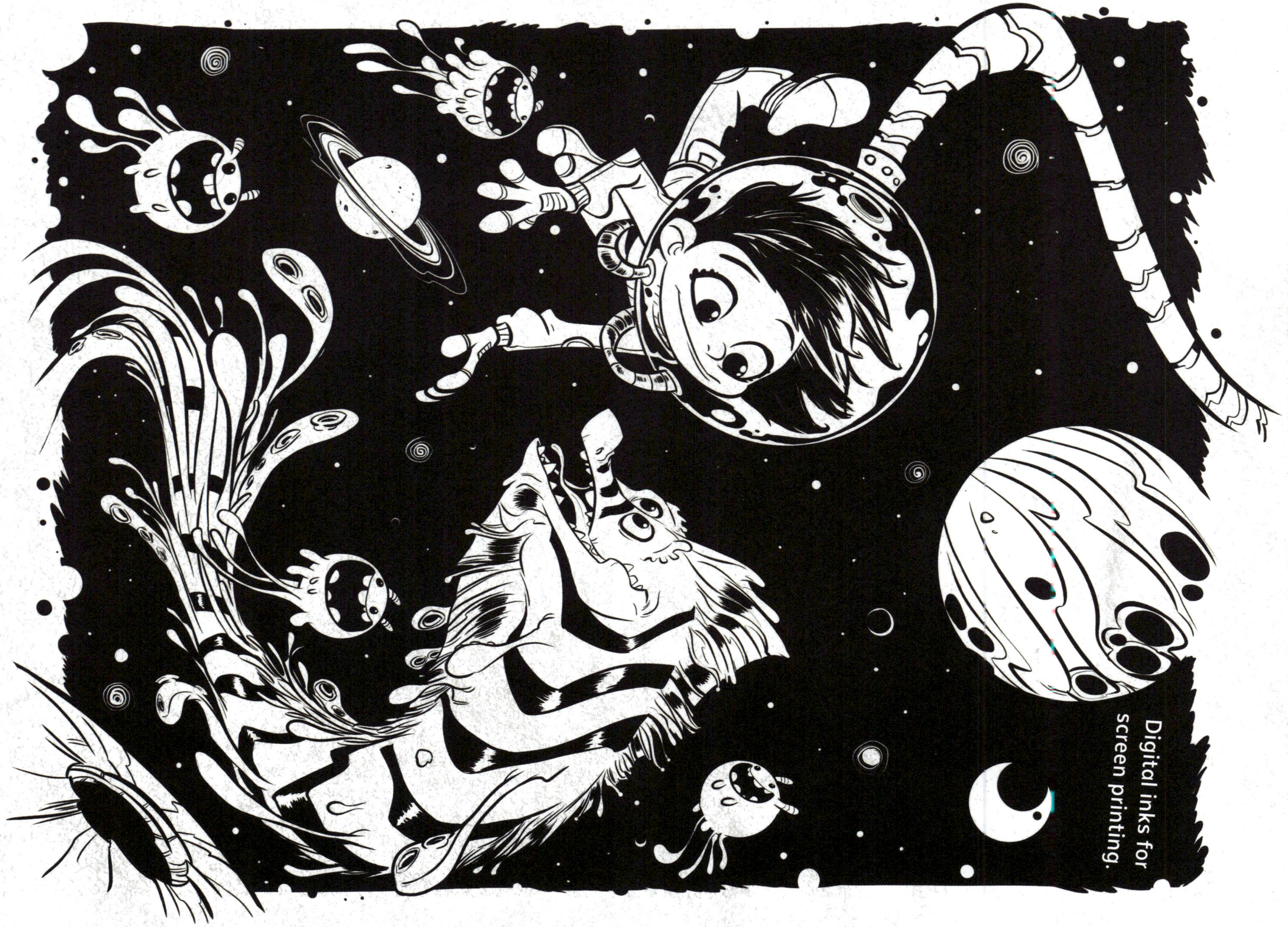

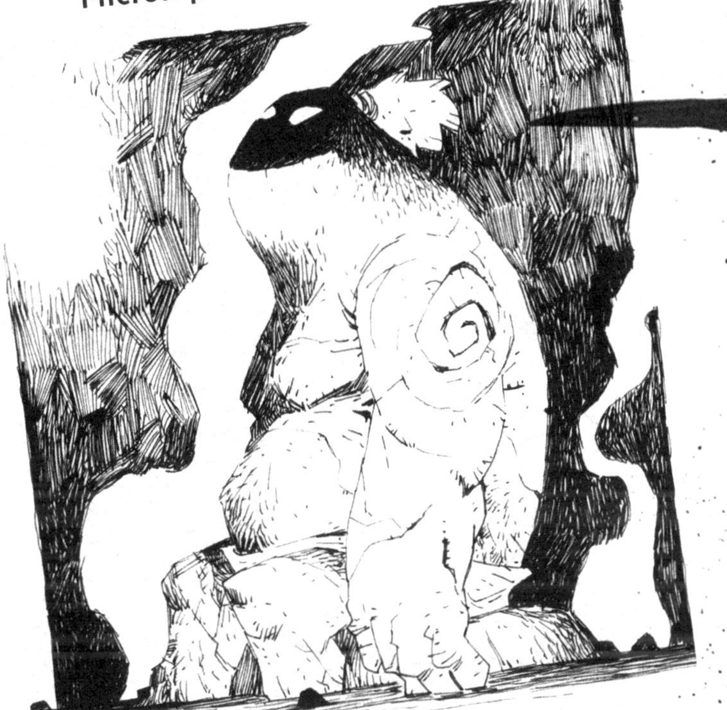

Brush pen and white gel pen.

Micron pen and hatching.

Ink splatters and brush.

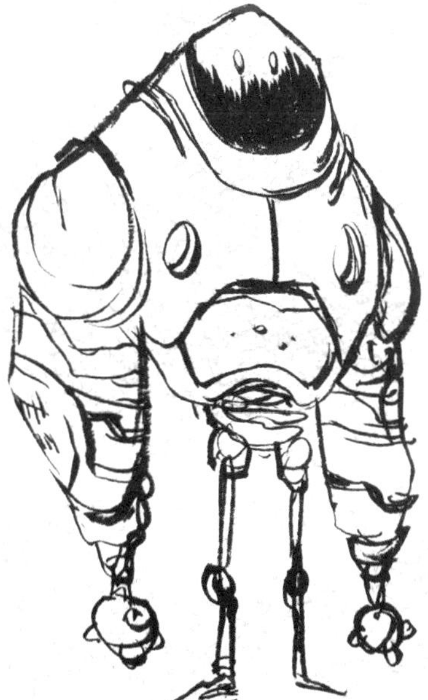

Quickly find a shape and feeling using fineliner pens!

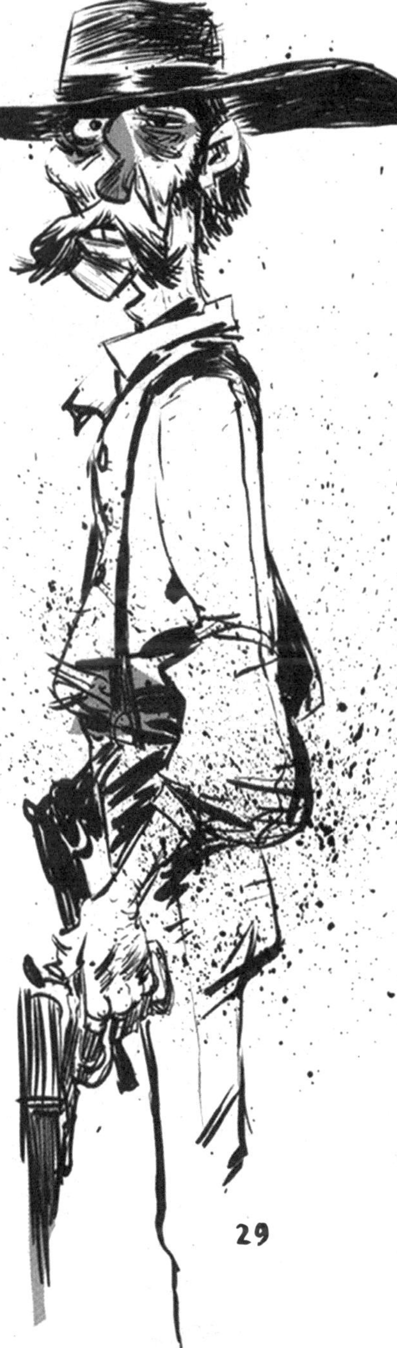

TRY THIS!

Try using an old toothbrush to flick ink. Or a chisel-tipped pen to create hard edges. Use correction fluid or acrylic white paint to add or remove details.

MARKERS

Along with coloured pencils, watercolours, and mixed media.

Many professional artists prefer to colour digitally, as they just can't quit that beautiful Undo button. In real life, the Undo button would be a time machine! But since no old grey-haired version of me with an awesome eyepatch has ever zapped in to warn me about all the mistakes I've made, including that bad egg I ate in ninth grade before gym class, I assume it's still not been invented. But I digress...

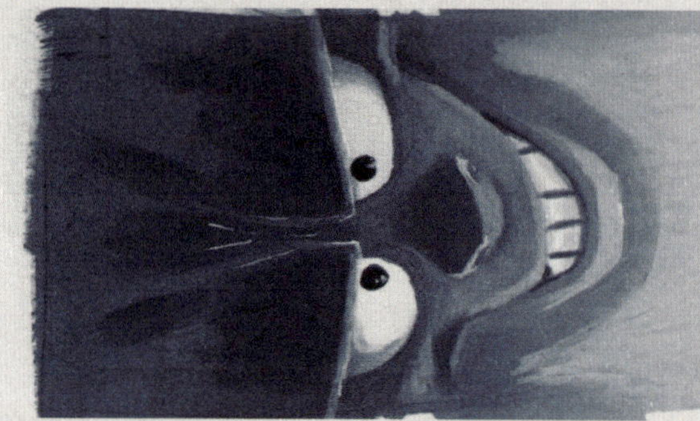

Greyscale and colour markers are used to give designs form, shape, style, and even better visual communication.

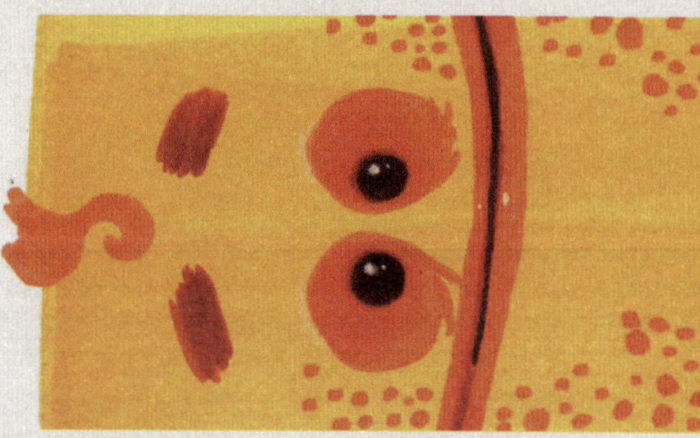

They can lead the eye, produce important details and textures, create contrast, and inform lighting!

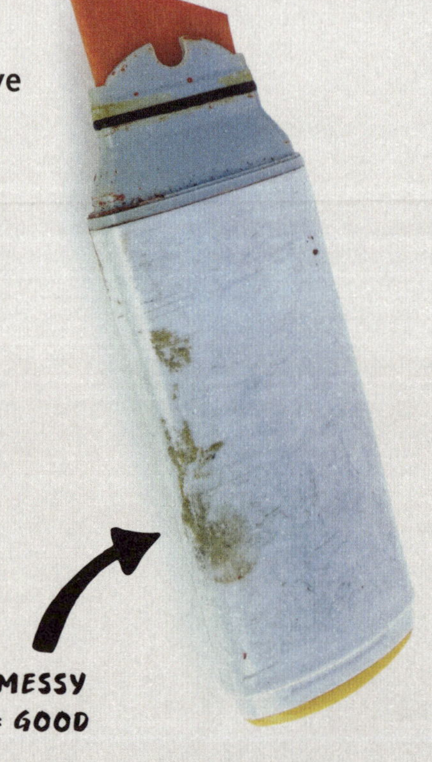

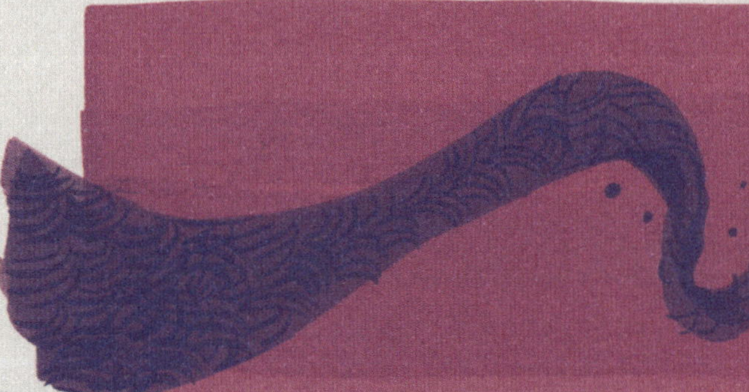

I treat markers like watercolours, building up my marker work from light to dark.

Try sticking to one colour to begin with. Choose a colour, then use the tonal values* of that one colour and see how much range you can create.

*TONAL VALUE IS THE IDEA THAT ALL HUES HAVE A SCALE FROM DARK TO LIGHT.

Don't forget that shapes become forms when depth is added.

If you begin on grey or brown paper, you're already starting with a midtone and it's easier to go lighter and darker from there.

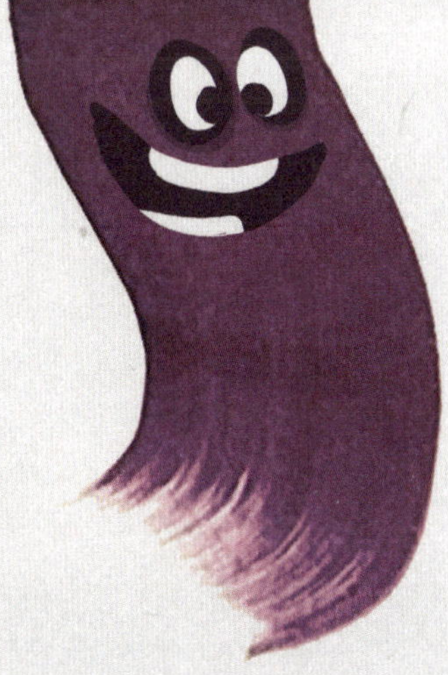

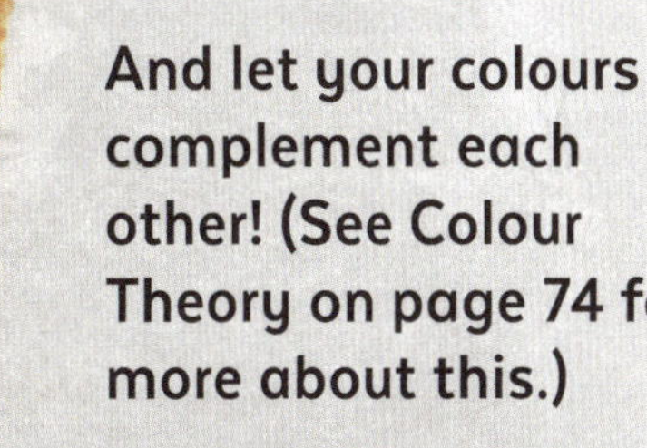

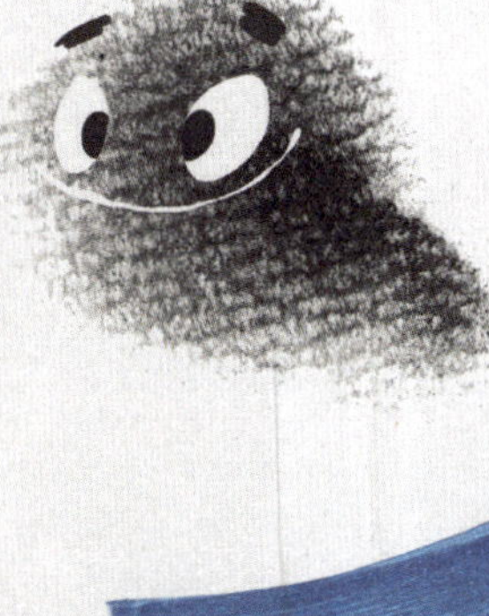

And let your colours complement each other! (See Colour Theory on page 74 for more about this.)

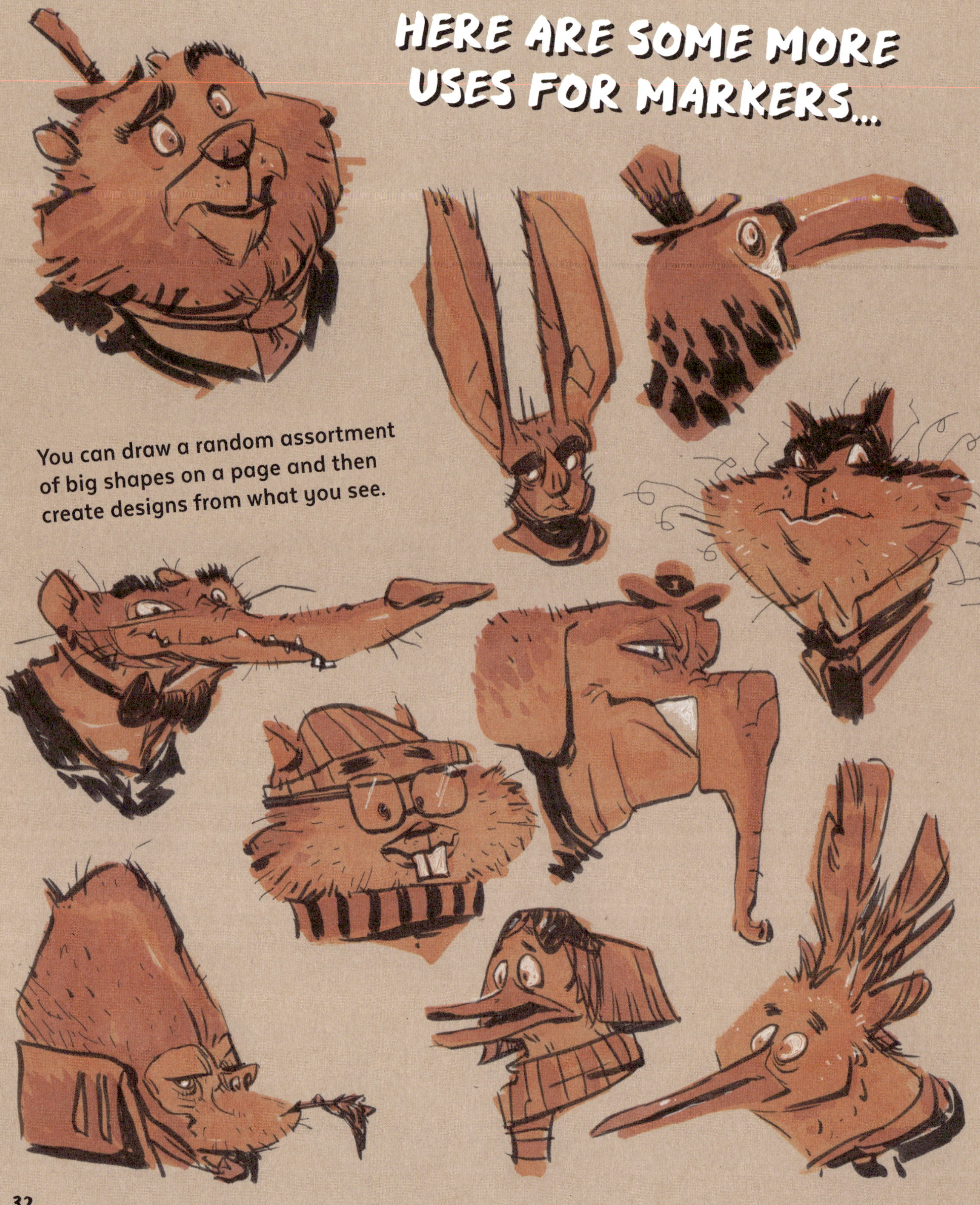

You can draw a random assortment of big shapes on a page and then create designs from what you see.

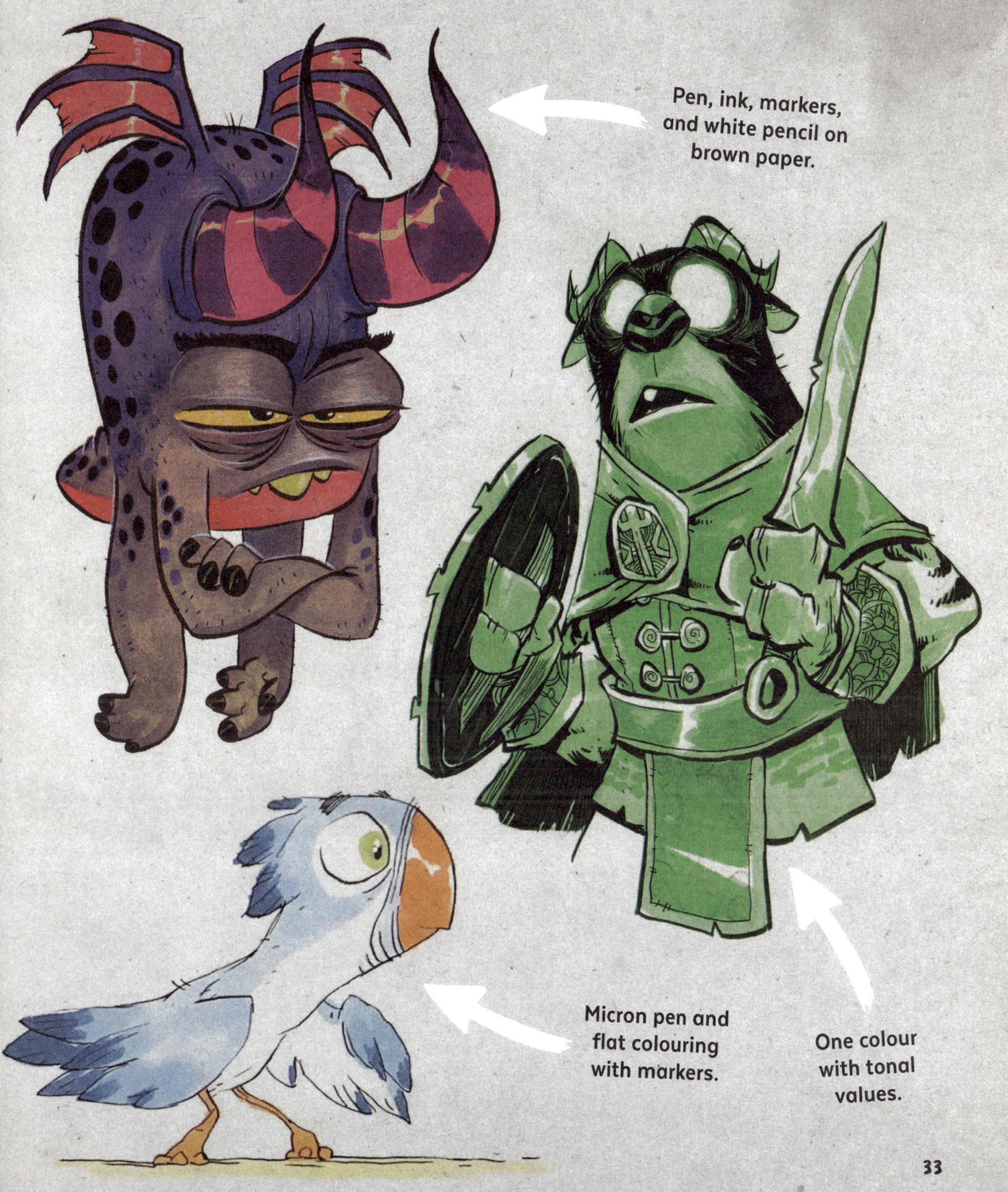

Pen, ink, markers, and white pencil on brown paper.

Micron pen and flat colouring with markers.

One colour with tonal values.

PAPER & SKETCHBOOKS

Get into the habit of drawing on **ANYTHING** and **EVERYTHING**. Paper and sketchbooks are just supplies, as is a computer screen, digital tablet, canvas, human body, paper napkin, or even a tree! When I visited Africa, the kids I met drew on the inside of tree bark. And it worked – I could see and understand everything they wanted to show me.

If it gets your idea out, go for it! Just remember, it's very hard to scan a tree...

I use animation paper on a clipboard because I love smooth paper. I like using brown paper for colour work and Bristol Smooth 11 x 17 paper for inking comic work.

Some of my favourite drawings were created on scraps of my kid's homework, mostly because there was no fear of screwing up.

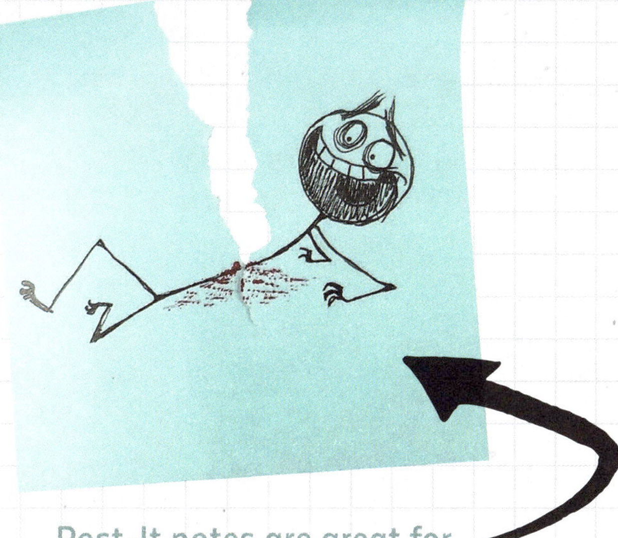

Try drawing on a rock.

Post-It notes are great for capturing quick ideas.

CARRY TWO SKETCHBOOKS WITH YOU.

Use one for practice (drawing from life, observational studies of things like hands and feet, or any other forms you need to practise sketching).

Use the other sketchbook for your thoughts (drawing out designs, ideas, and characters). This second one has nothing to do with draughtsmanship, but everything to do with generating **CREATIVITY**. It's important to care less about this sketchbook needing to 'look good' – that will only slow your ideas down. Never fear, you can always revisit your best ideas later!

Lined, recycled, smooth, textured, coloured, old, new... Use it all!

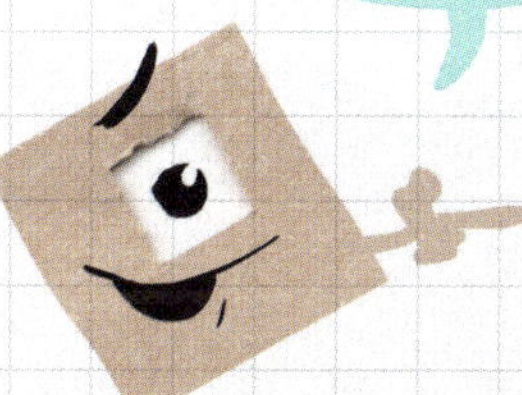

Share your art #3dtDRAW

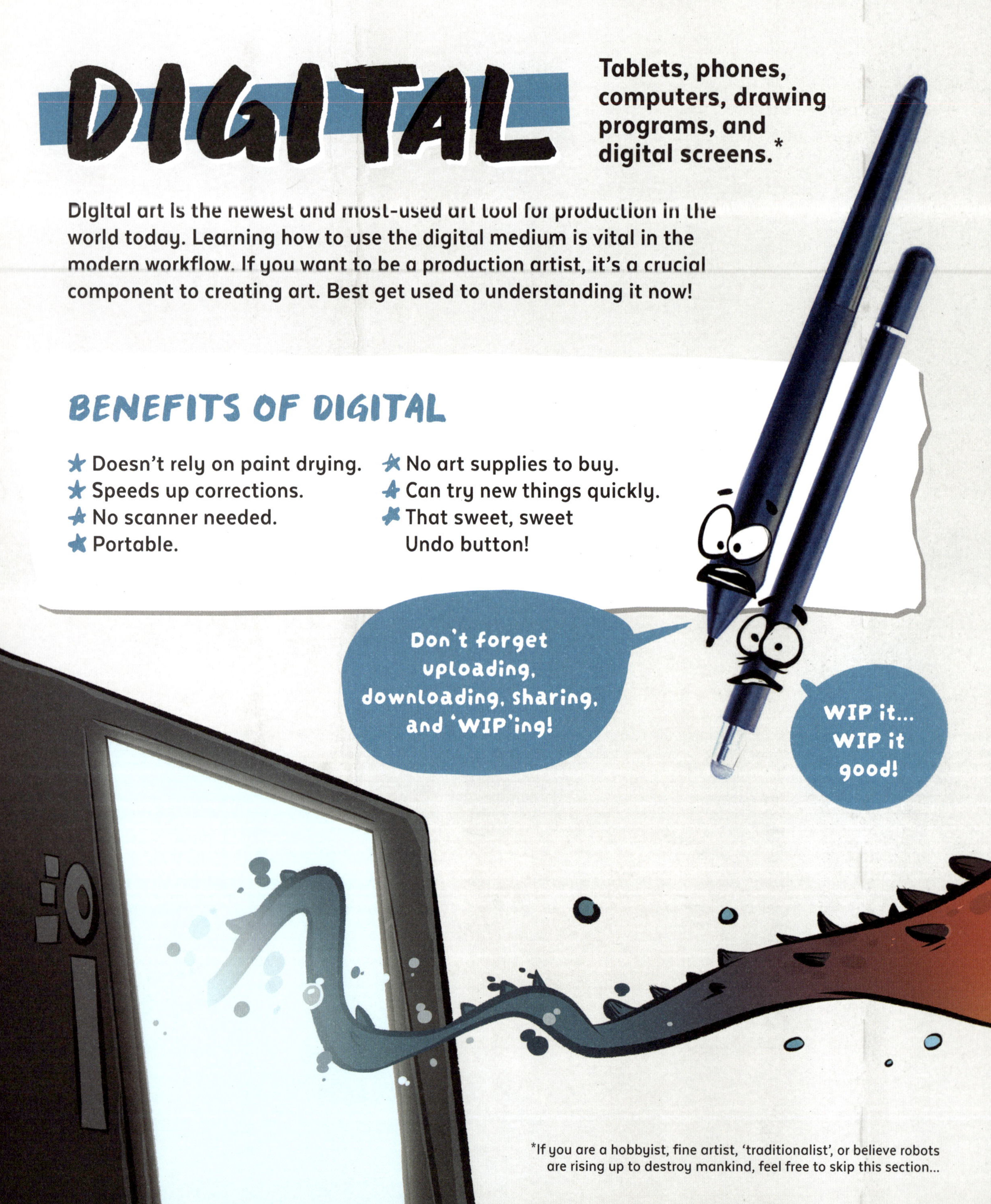

DIGITAL

Tablets, phones, computers, drawing programs, and digital screens.*

Digital art is the newest and most-used art tool for production in the world today. Learning how to use the digital medium is vital in the modern workflow. If you want to be a production artist, it's a crucial component to creating art. Best get used to understanding it now!

BENEFITS OF DIGITAL

- ★ Doesn't rely on paint drying.
- ★ Speeds up corrections.
- ★ No scanner needed.
- ★ Portable.
- ★ No art supplies to buy.
- ★ Can try new things quickly.
- ★ That sweet, sweet Undo button!

*If you are a hobbyist, fine artist, 'traditionalist', or believe robots are rising up to destroy mankind, feel free to skip this section...

As important and powerful as digital is, it also has its issues...

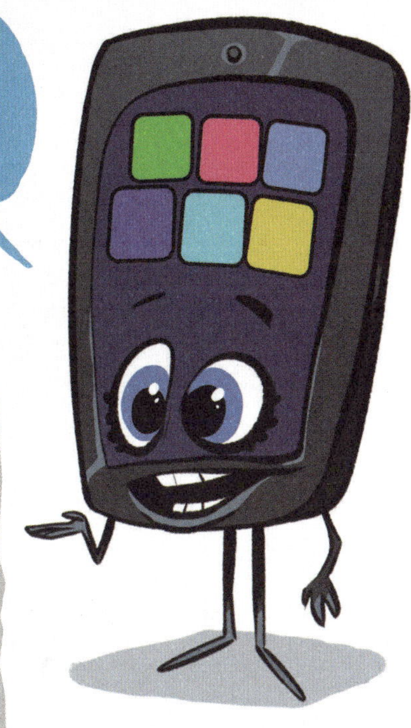

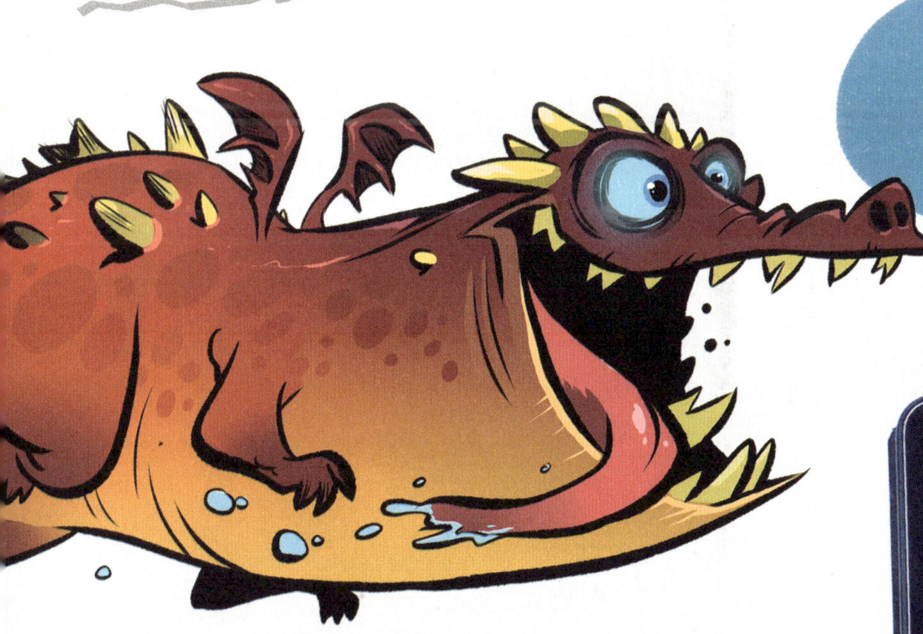

*...And if you ARE the robot uprising, remember, I was always on your side.

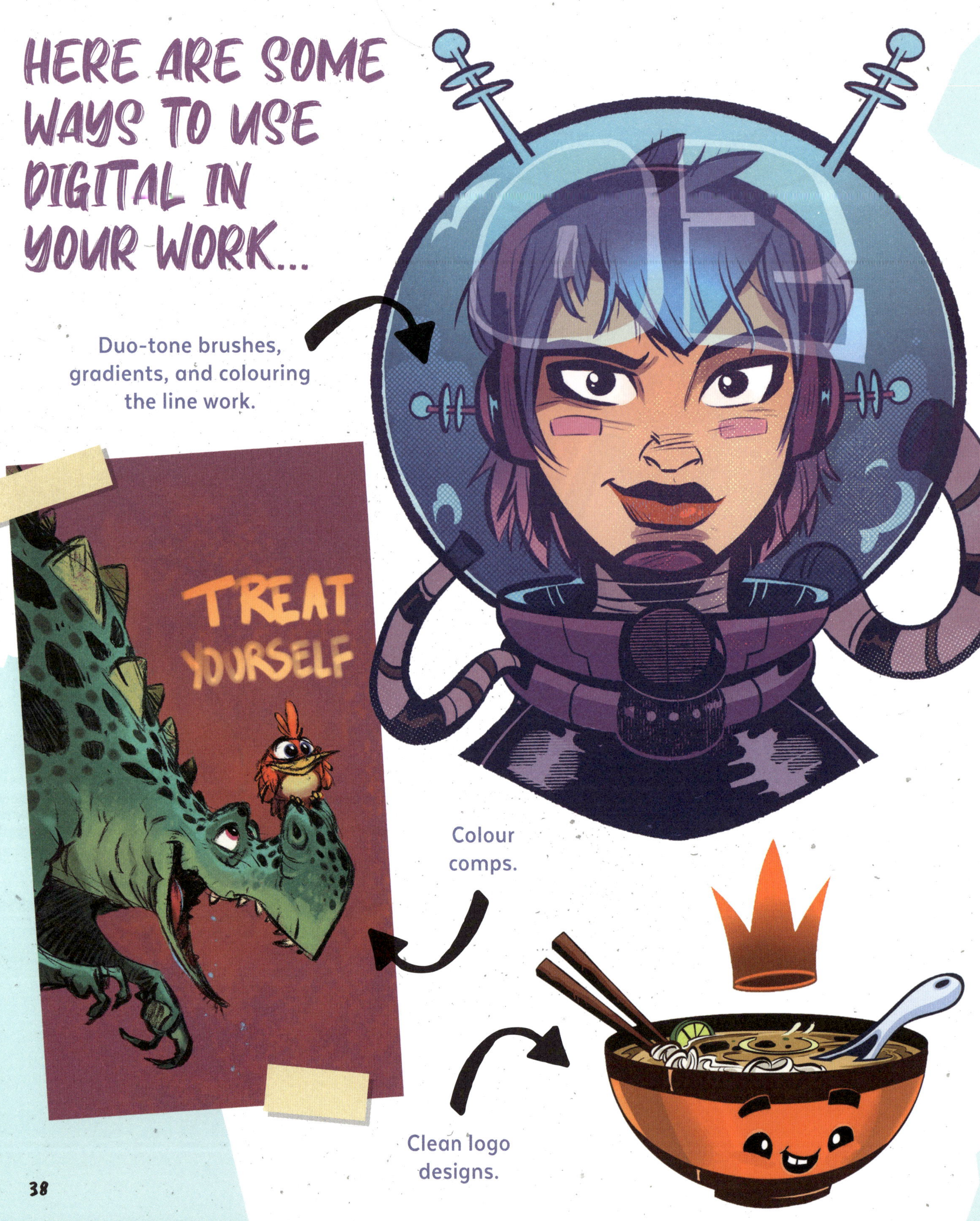
HERE ARE SOME WAYS TO USE DIGITAL IN YOUR WORK...

Duo-tone brushes, gradients, and colouring the line work.

TREAT YOURSELF

Colour comps.

Clean logo designs.

38

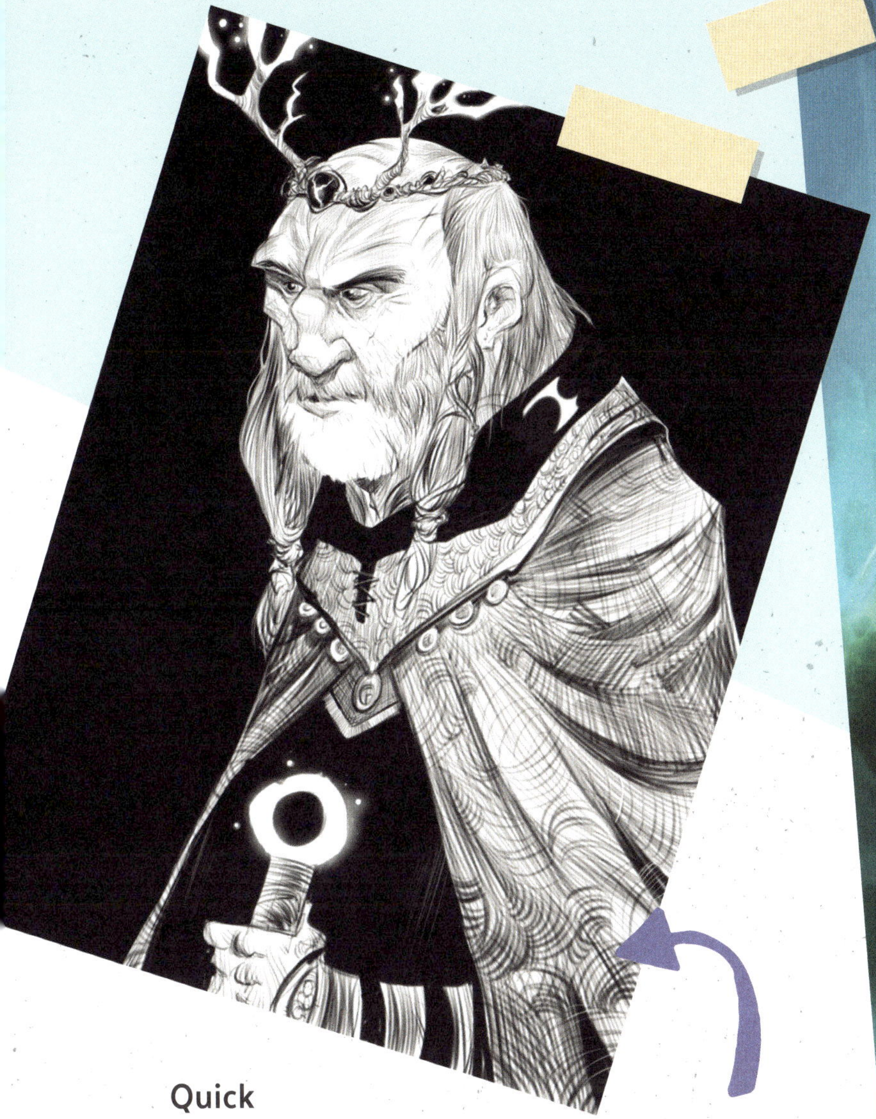

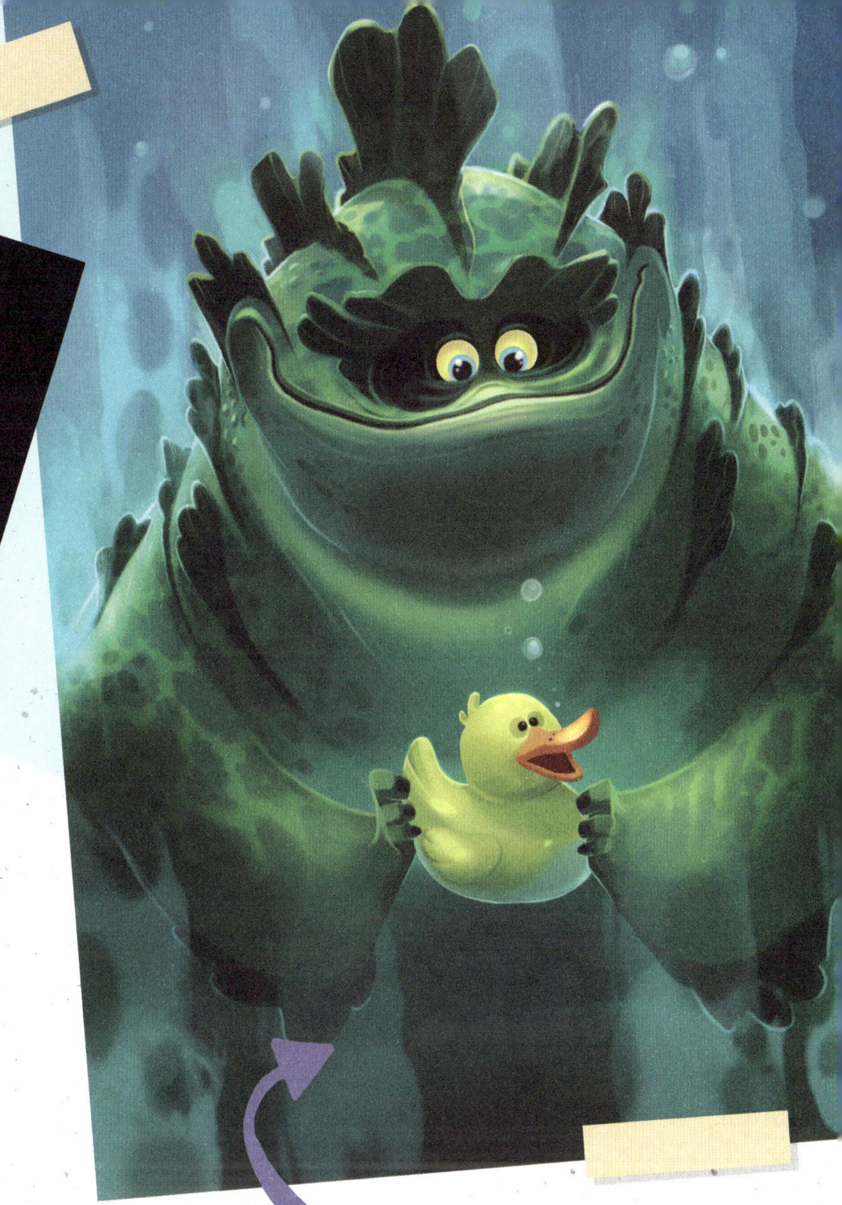

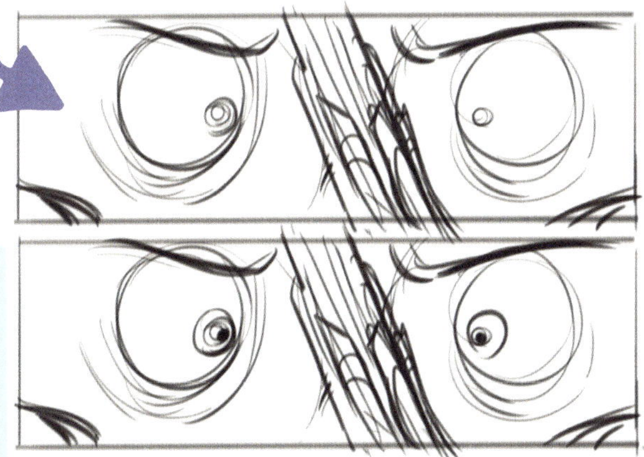

Quick
storyboards.

Pencil
under-drawings.

Painting with shapes.

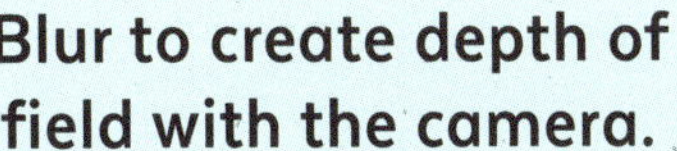

Blur to create depth of
field with the camera.

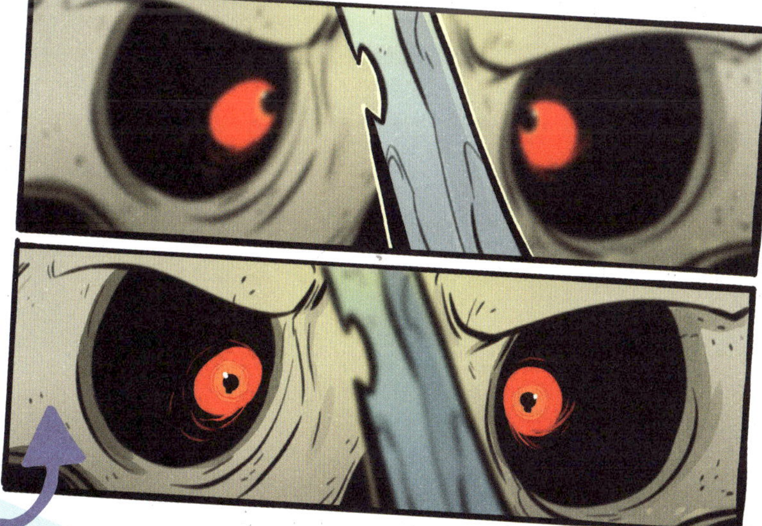

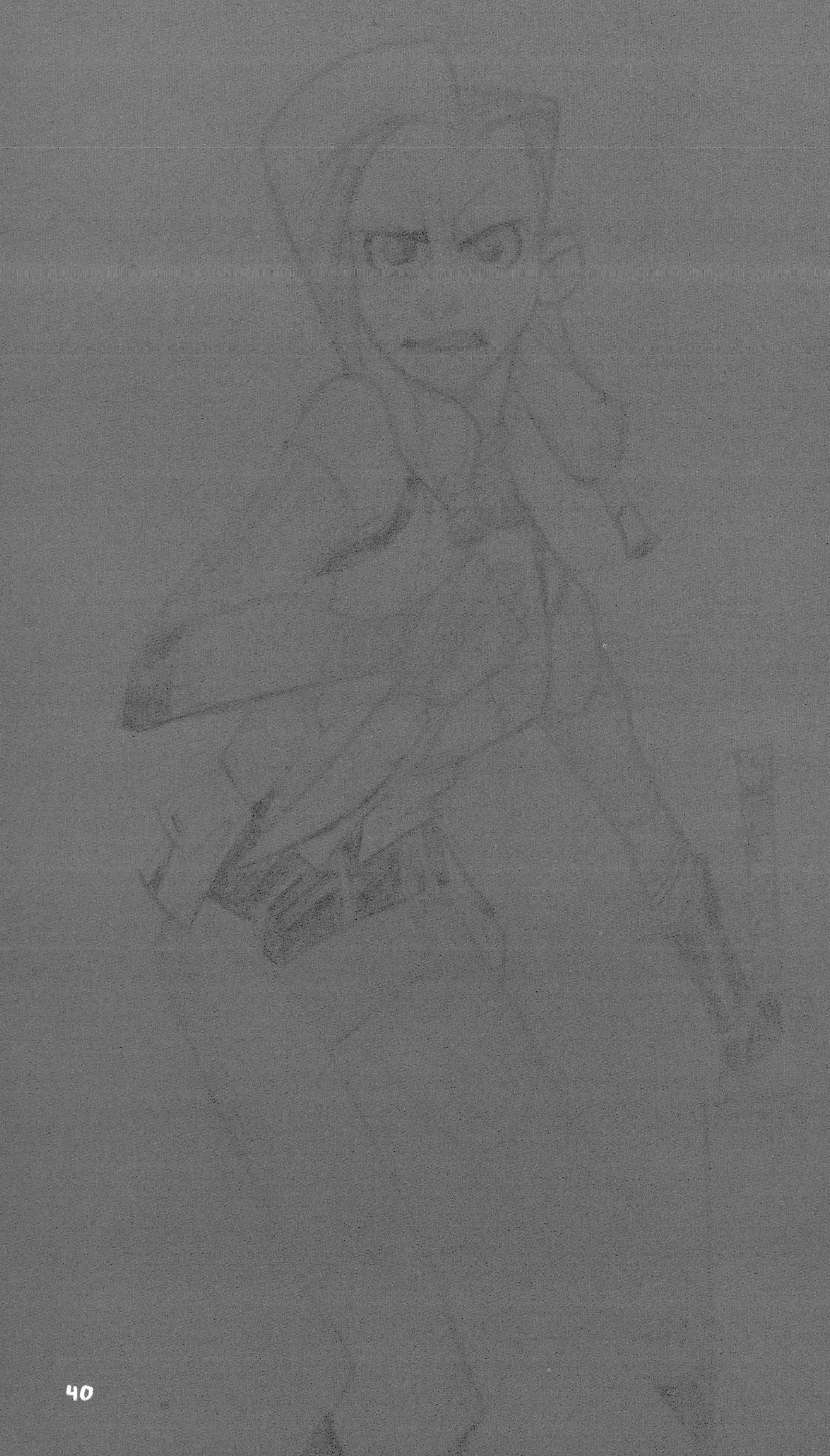

CHAPTER 03

THE TOOLS WE USE

TOOLS

The tools we use to create are an integral part of art and design. We use them to facilitate our vision of the world, whether it be on paper, canvas, sculpt, or screen.

Using these tools can make art complicated, or strip it down to its simplest forms.

What you choose **NOT** to use is just as important as what you keep. What to add or subtract are essential decisions to make.

Learning to use these techniques effectively will help you to translate emotions, objects, environments, and ideas to paper.

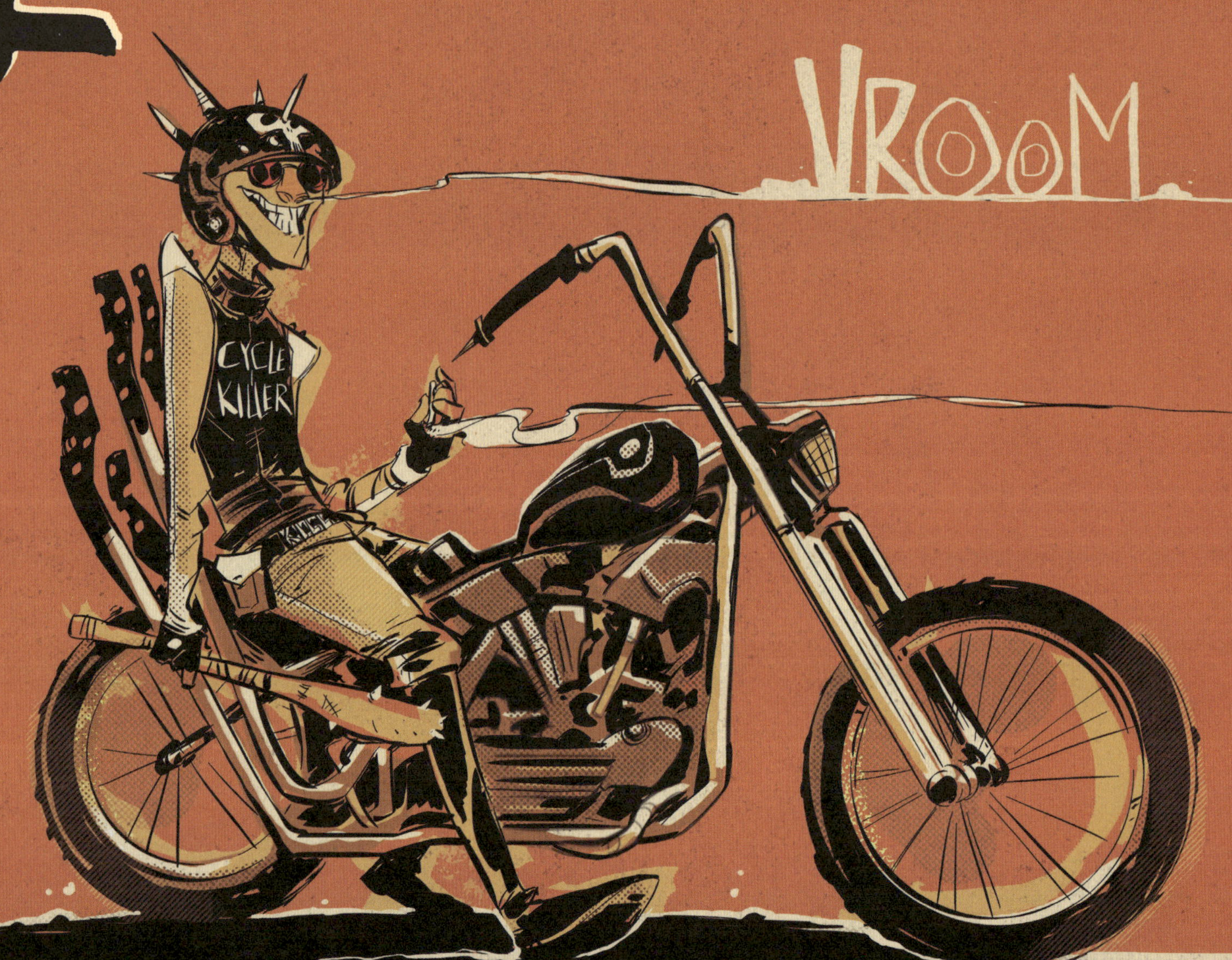

Some artists will concentrate on how to recreate what they literally see – to accurately describe the world and what's in it. Lighting and shadows, perspective, and how colours mix are important to those who wish to represent life as it is. The real world has no lines.

Some artists see a different world in their mind's eye, where the sky is purple and unicorns fart rainbows. No matter how often they are told to quit dreaming, this will manifest itself through vibrant colours, little concern for theories, or how many fingers humans are 'supposed' to have.

Many artists sit in between, are not quite ready to decide yet, or are just now waking up to the possibilities of a creative life.

None of these artists are 'wrong'...
Just different.

The tools you use will come down to **PURPOSE, PERSONALITY,** and **PERSPIRATION**. They should change depending on the current problem you have to solve. You may find yourself using only one, some, or all of them.

Learning any of these tools of the trade in-depth will never harm you. Continuing your education will provide you with more range and greater control over **WHEN** you decide to use them.

How to 'see' and 'feel' a motorcycle will differ from artist to artist. I draw in my own way, so try to look beyond the art to the thoughts behind the tools. They can be wielded by any type of artist and in many more ways than I have thought of here.

The world is wide open with choices to make, so let's rev the engines and go forth!

VROOM
VROOM

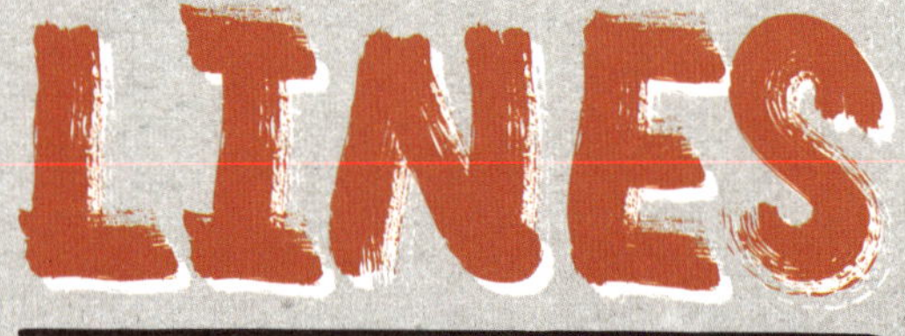

LINES

Lines aren't just for getting into expensive theme parks or buying macchiatos. Mark-making and lines can be used in all sorts of ways.

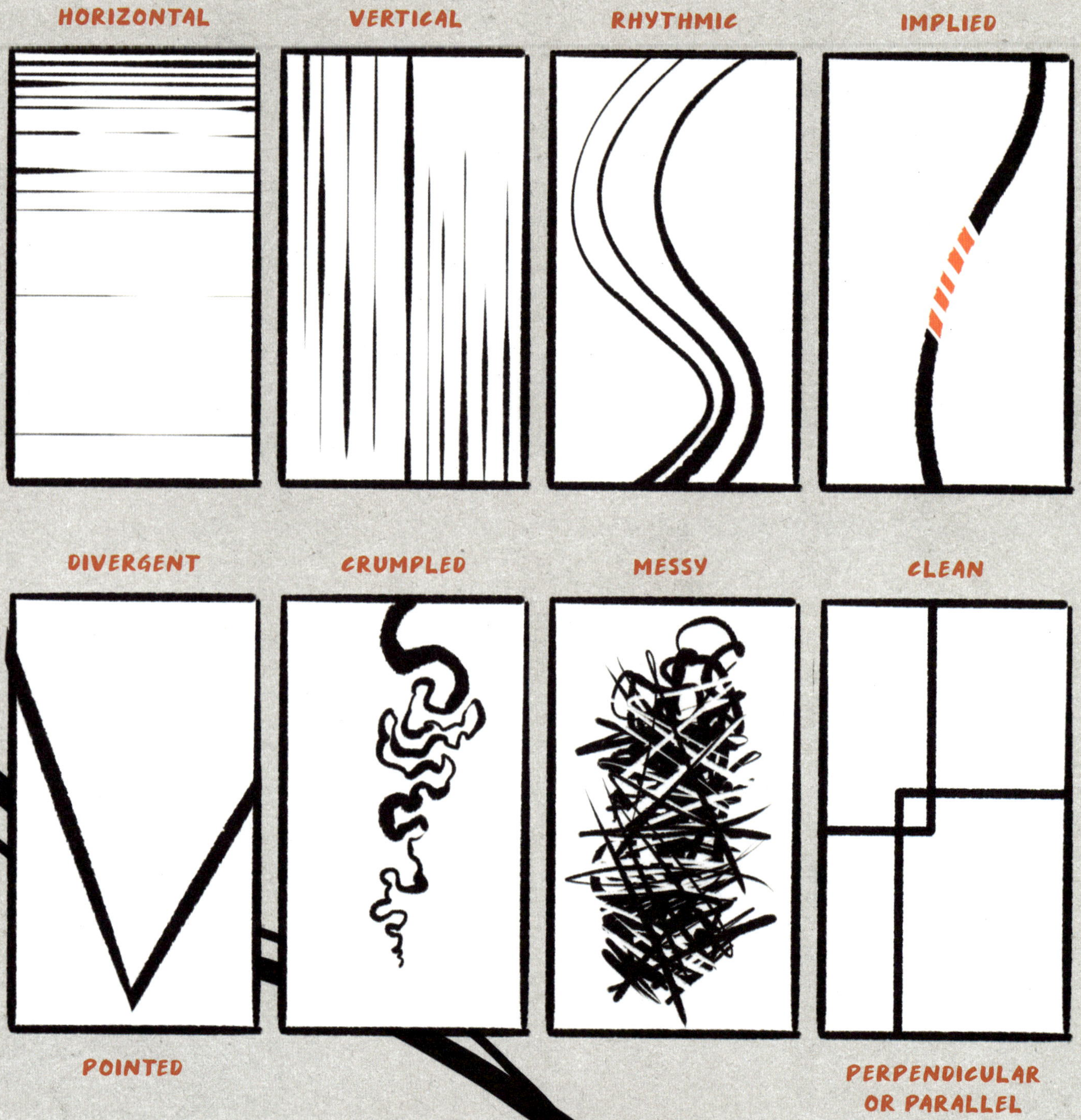

HORIZONTAL

VERTICAL

RHYTHMIC

IMPLIED

DIVERGENT

CRUMPLED

MESSY

CLEAN

POINTED

PERPENDICULAR OR PARALLEL

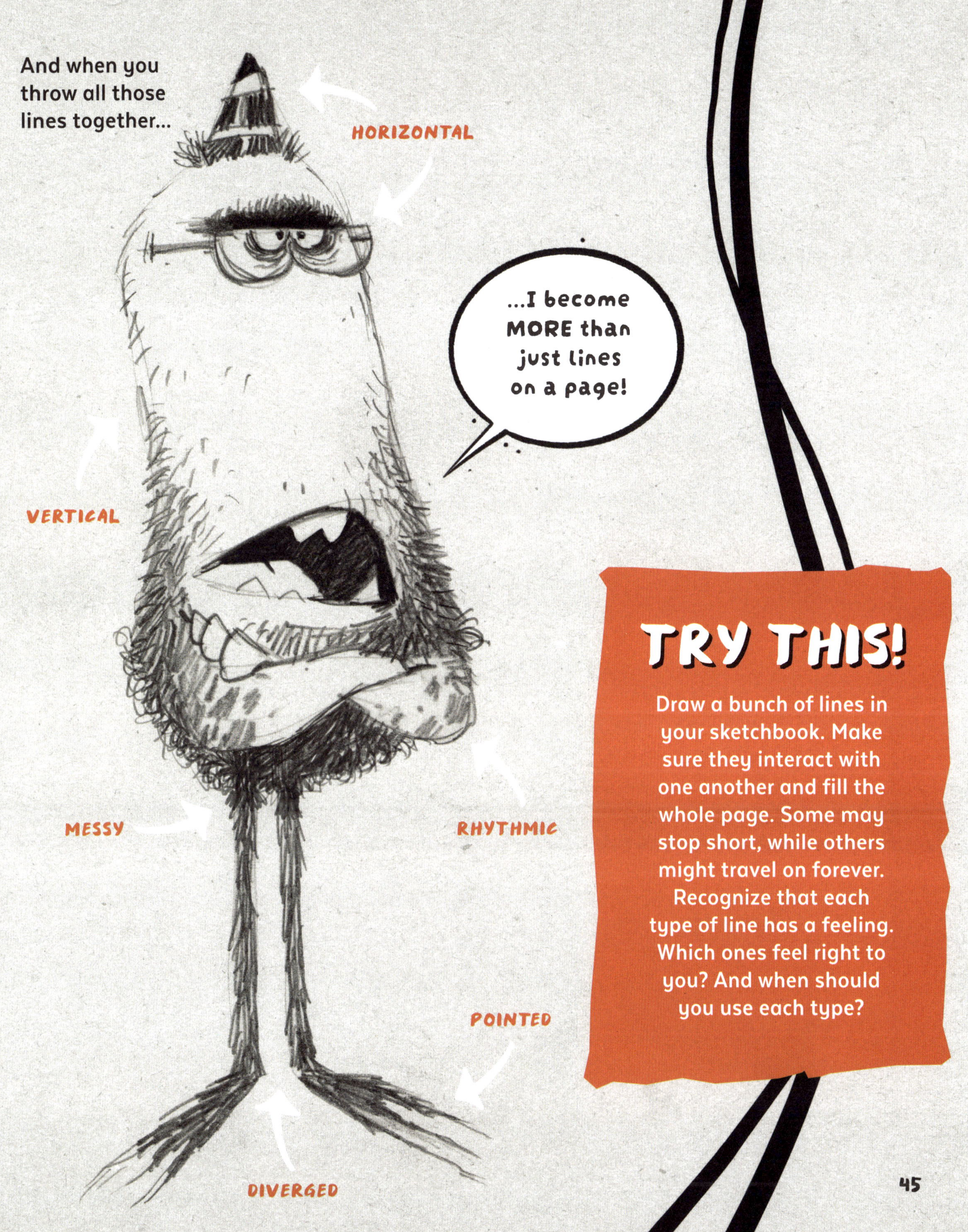

And when you throw all those lines together...
HORIZONTAL
...I become MORE than just lines on a page!
VERTICAL
MESSY
RHYTHMIC
POINTED
DIVERGED

TRY THIS!

Draw a bunch of lines in your sketchbook. Make sure they interact with one another and fill the whole page. Some may stop short, while others might travel on forever. Recognize that each type of line has a feeling. Which ones feel right to you? And when should you use each type?

CONTOURS

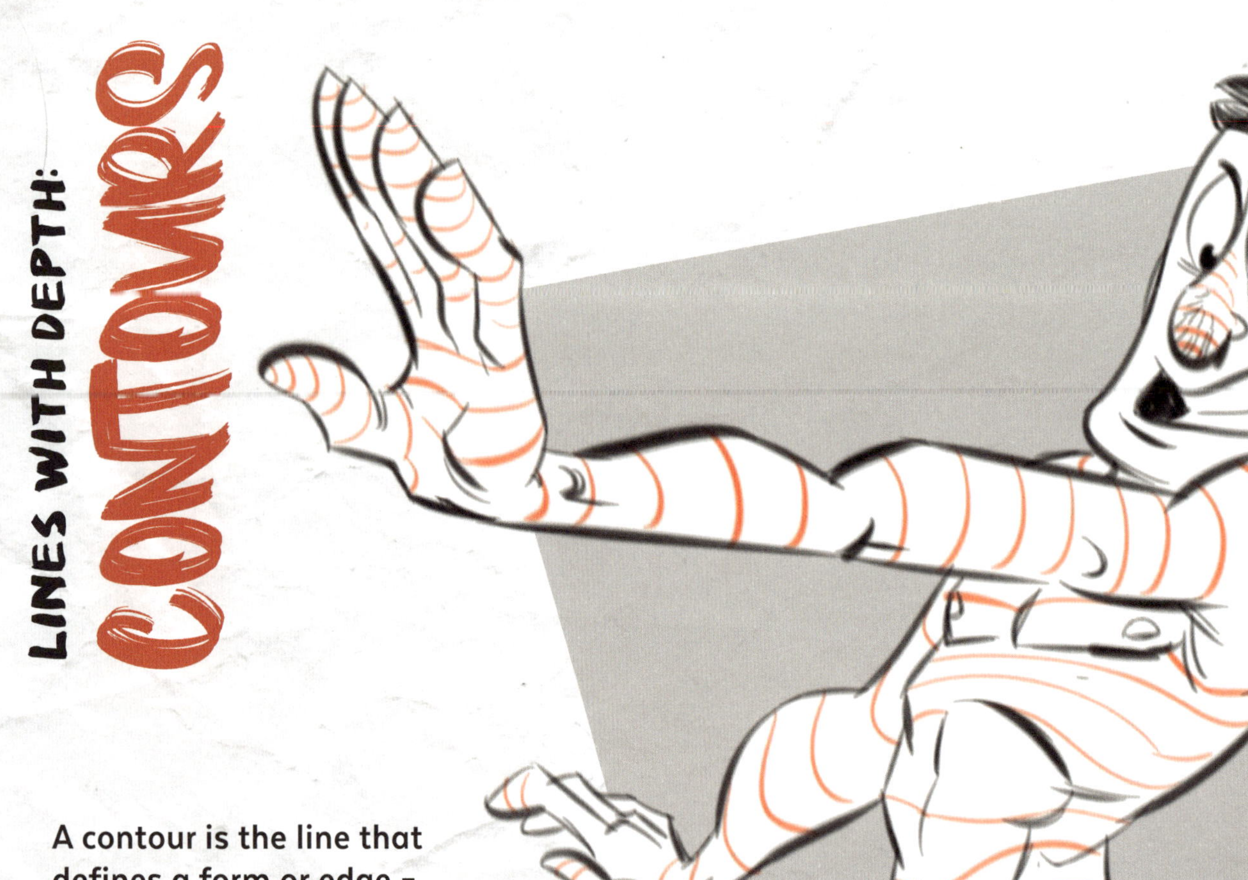

A contour is the line that defines a form or edge – it uses lines to show how objects turn in space. Make sure to follow the visible edges of a shape as well as dramatic changes within the form.

Put simply, contour lines are outline drawings.

FORESHORTENING

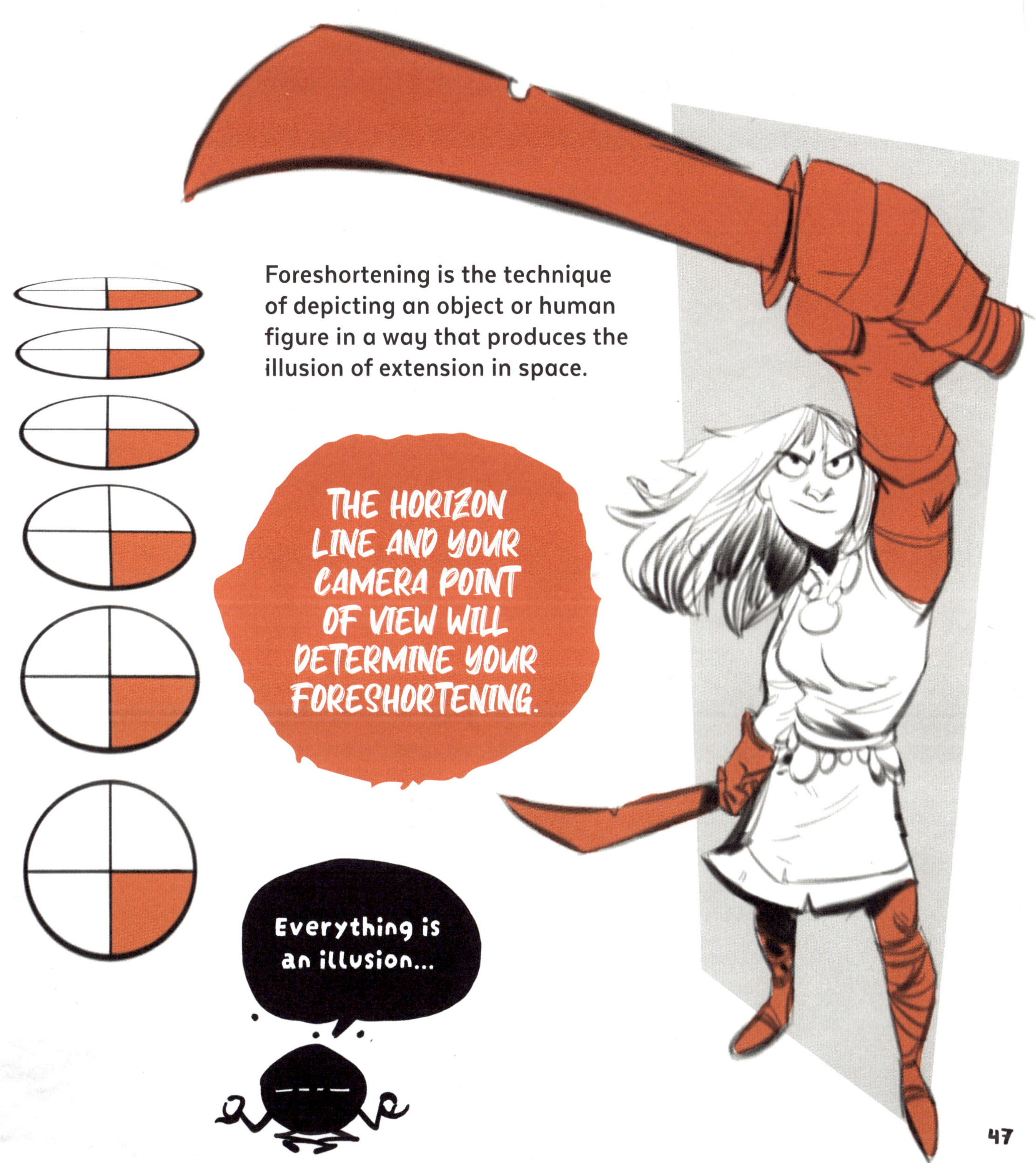

Foreshortening is the technique of depicting an object or human figure in a way that produces the illusion of extension in space.

SHADOW & LIGHT

Hatching is an artistic technique used to create shading effects by drawing closely spaced lines to produce depth. When you create shadows, you inherently suggest a light source too.

HATCHING

CROSS-HATCHING

Shadows help to ground your character, prop, or object in space.

48

LINES WITH DEPTH:
OVERLAP

The technique of overlapping is where all of the elements in a drawing, painting, or photograph overlap each other to help create a three-dimensional illusion.

Without overlap there is no depth.

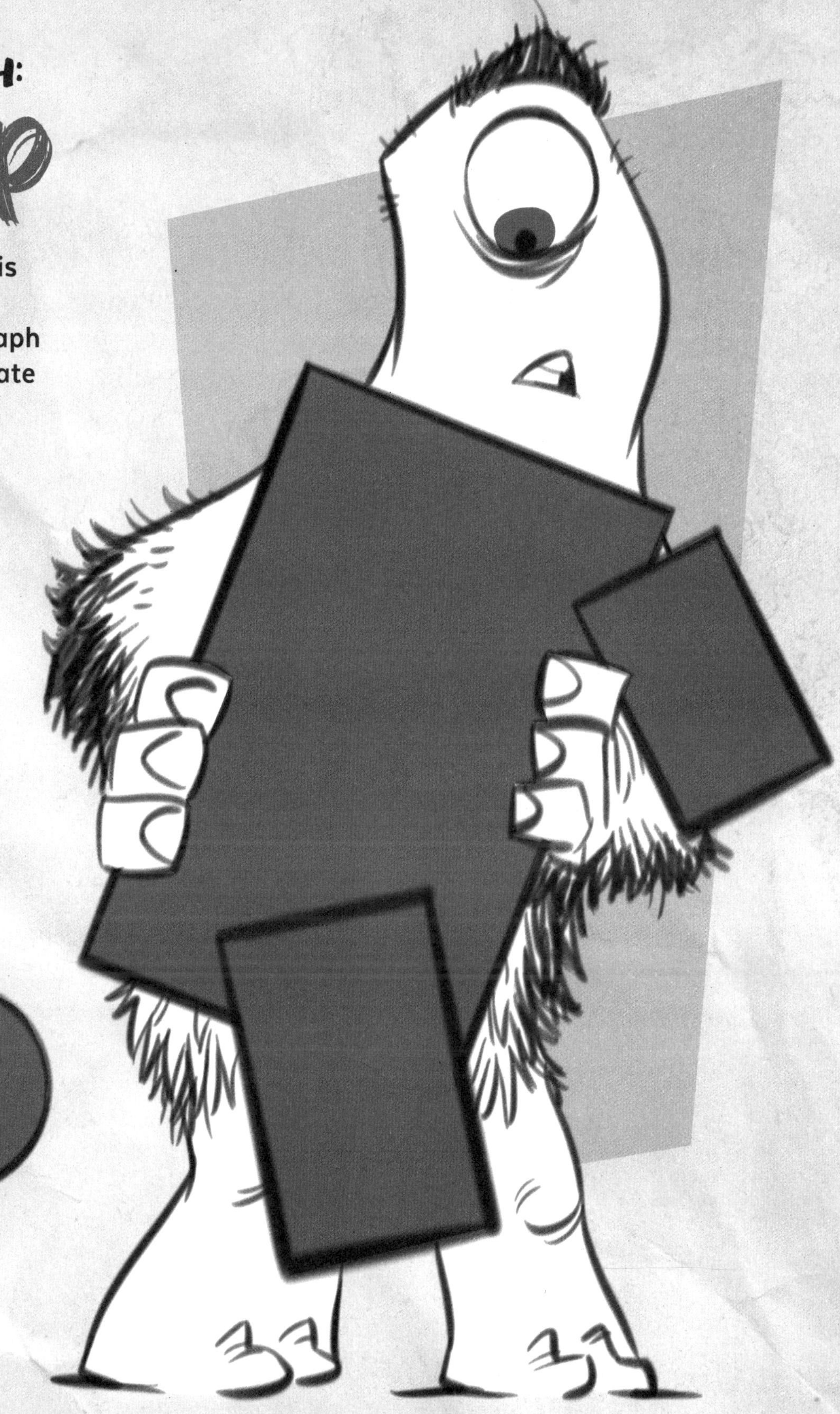

Now the circles are overlapping, we can see which is in front!

SHAPES

Shapes are the external form or appearance of someone or something – the outline of an area or figure. They are the physical state of an object or person – an outside shell that reflects what's inside.

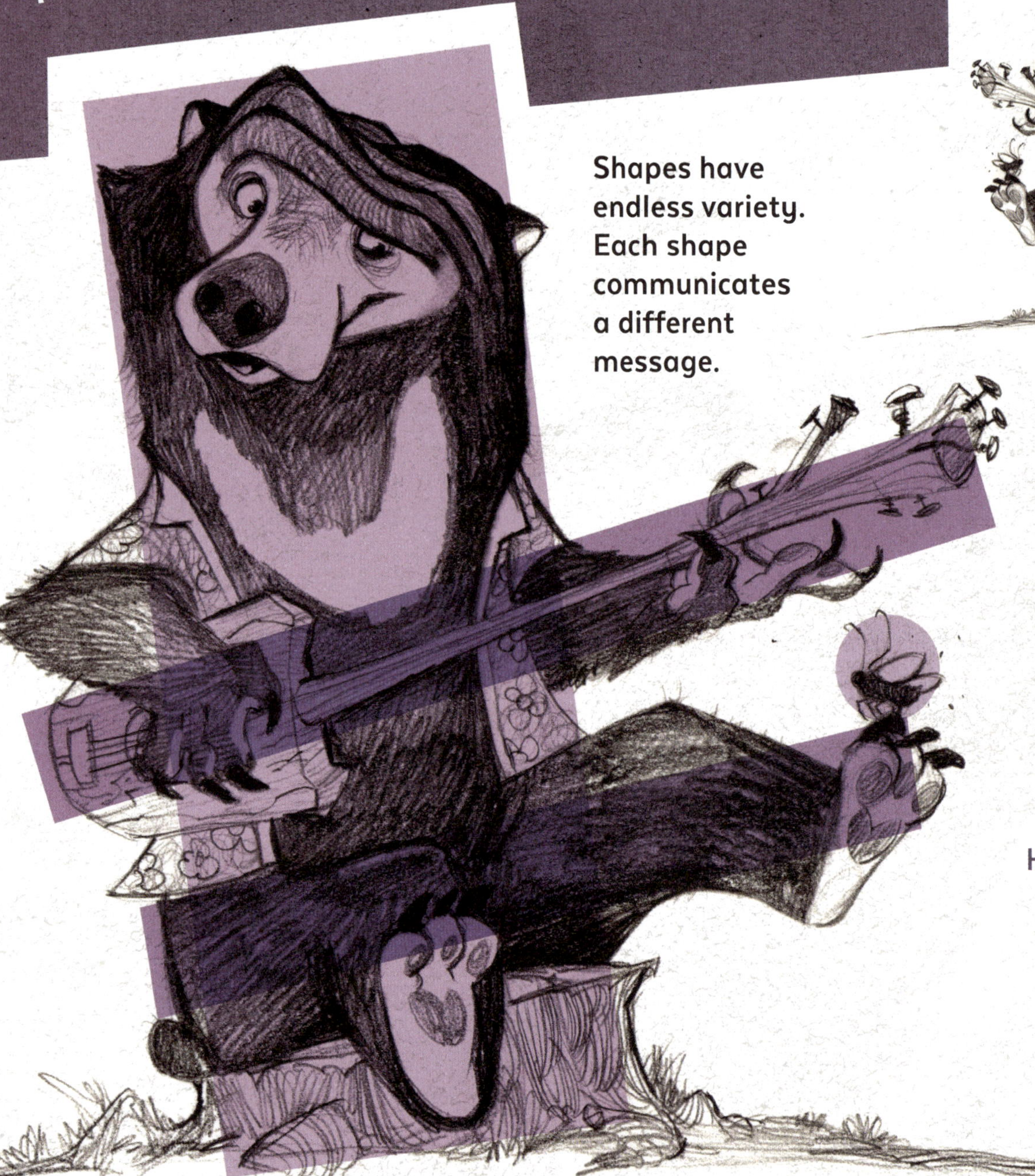

Shapes have endless variety. Each shape communicates a different message.

How you use shapes will influence how they enhance or detract from what your art means to someone else.

GEOMETRIC

These are what most people think of as shapes. They are recognized by most from a very young age and carry the most information (that you therefore don't have to provide to the audience).

ORGANIC

These are irregular yet pleasing to the eye (for the most part). Freeform and asymmetrical, they can represent shapes found in nature, such as leaves, trees, rocks, and clouds.

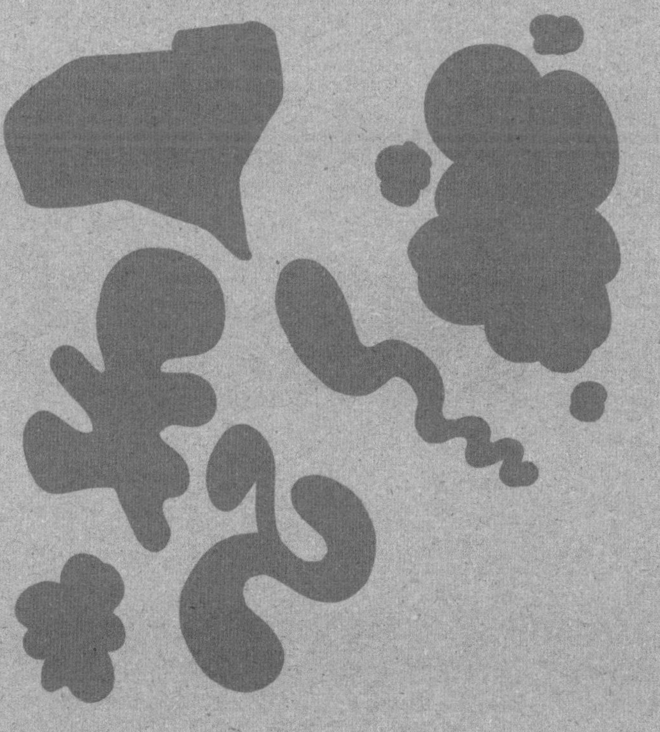

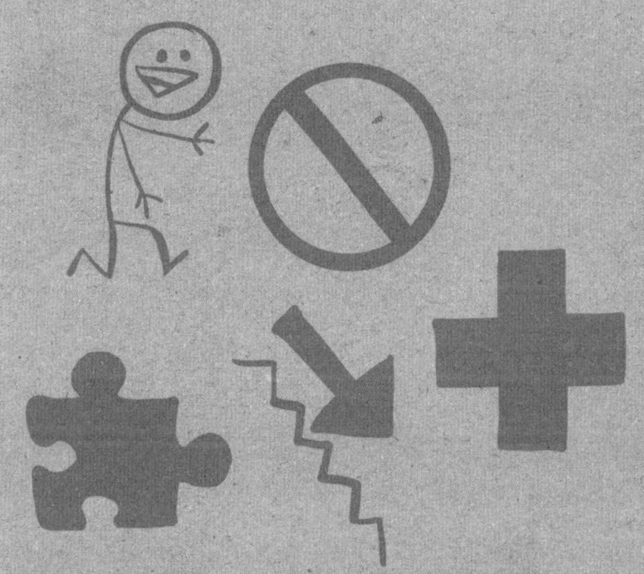

ABSTRACT/SYMBOLIC

These have a recognizable form and are stylized or simplified shapes. They often represent ideas and concepts. Even these words are symbolic shapes!

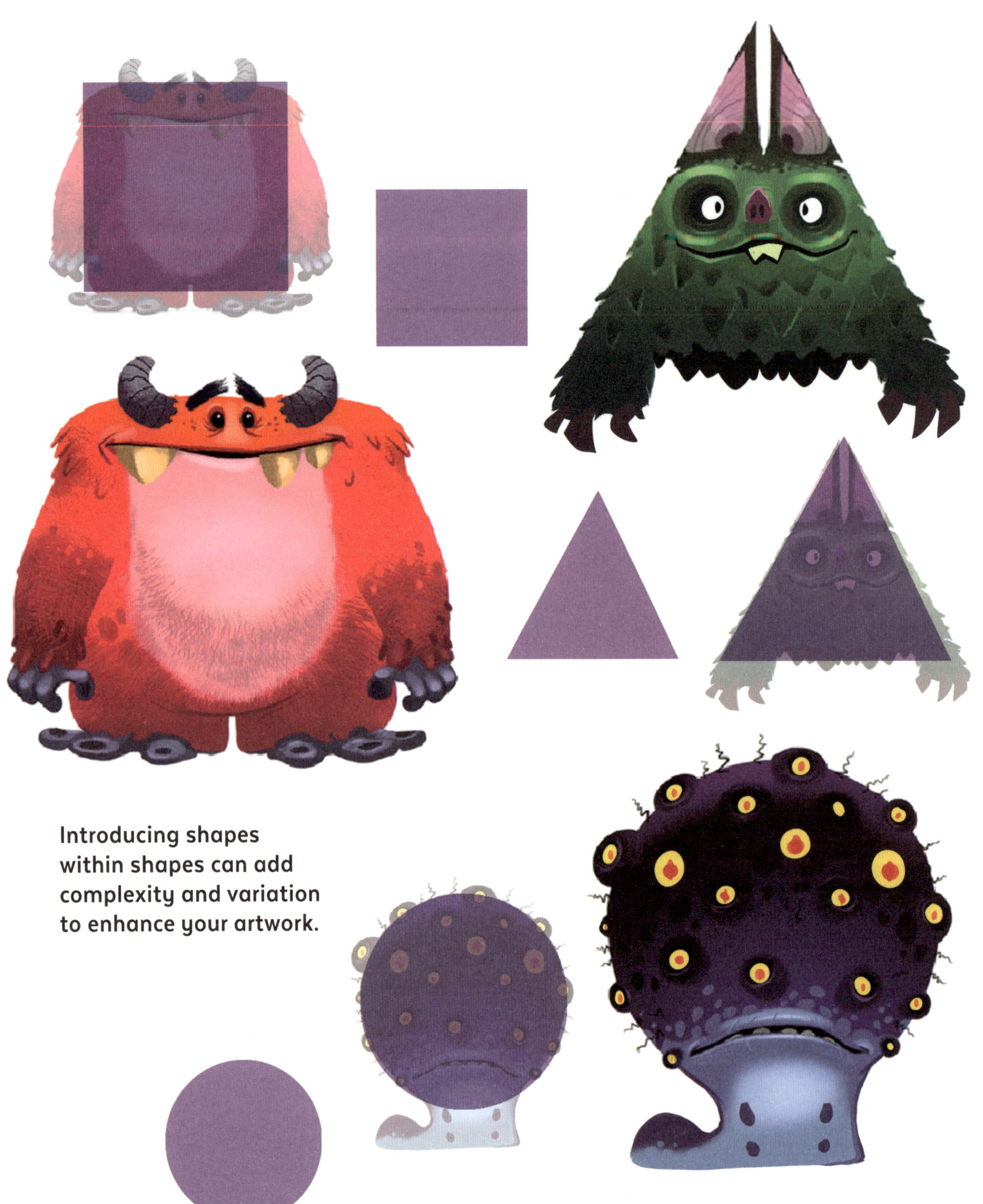

Introducing shapes within shapes can add complexity and variation to enhance your artwork.

I like to let one dominant shape guide the rest. All the other decisions regarding shapes, lines, and colours should follow, leading to one overall idea and purpose.

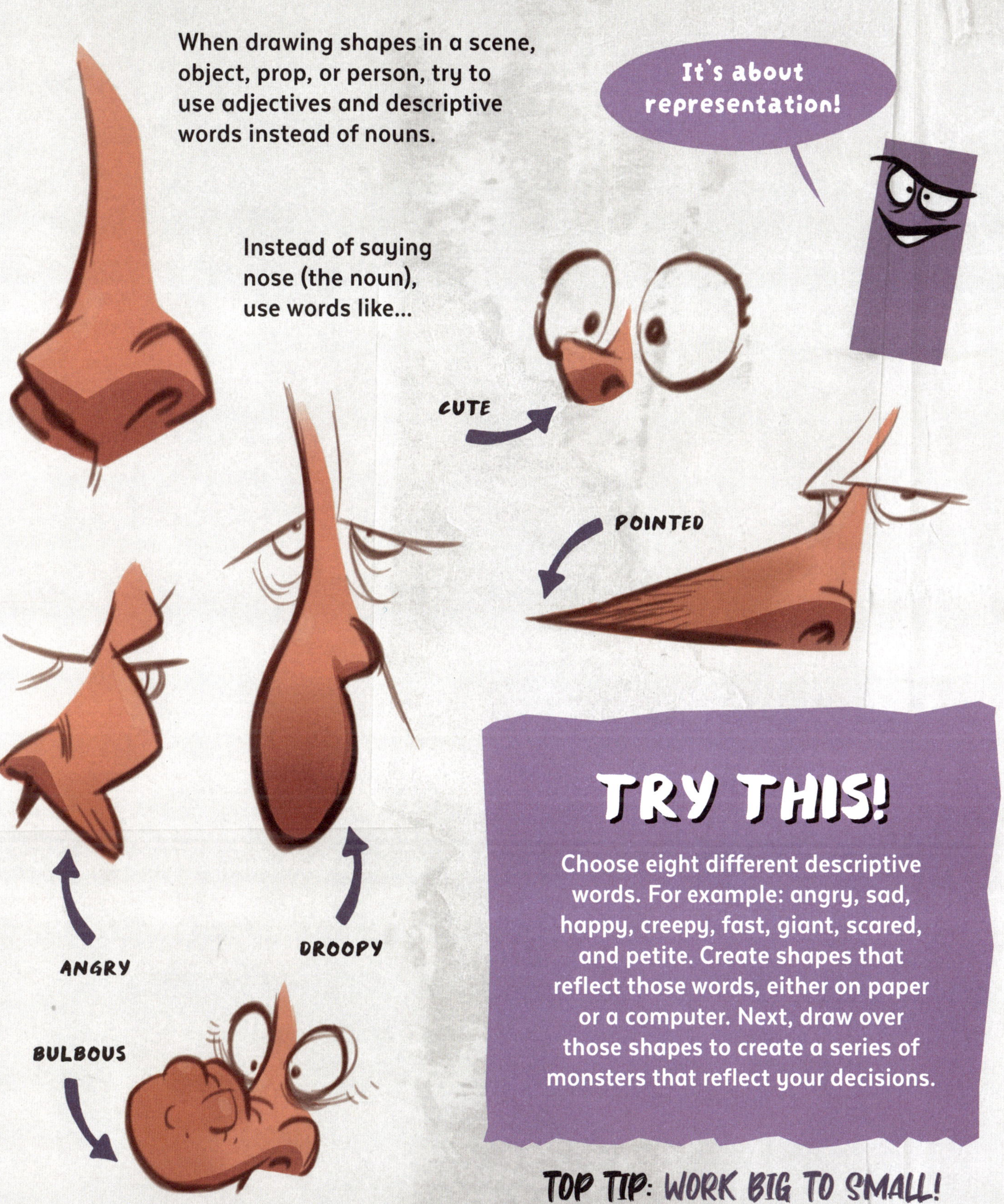

When drawing shapes in a scene, object, prop, or person, try to use adjectives and descriptive words instead of nouns.

Instead of saying nose (the noun), use words like...

It's about representation!

CUTE

POINTED

ANGRY

DROOPY

BULBOUS

TRY THIS!

Choose eight different descriptive words. For example: angry, sad, happy, creepy, fast, giant, scared, and petite. Create shapes that reflect those words, either on paper or a computer. Next, draw over those shapes to create a series of monsters that reflect your decisions.

TOP TIP: WORK BIG TO SMALL!

AN EXERCISE IN SHAPE STUDY

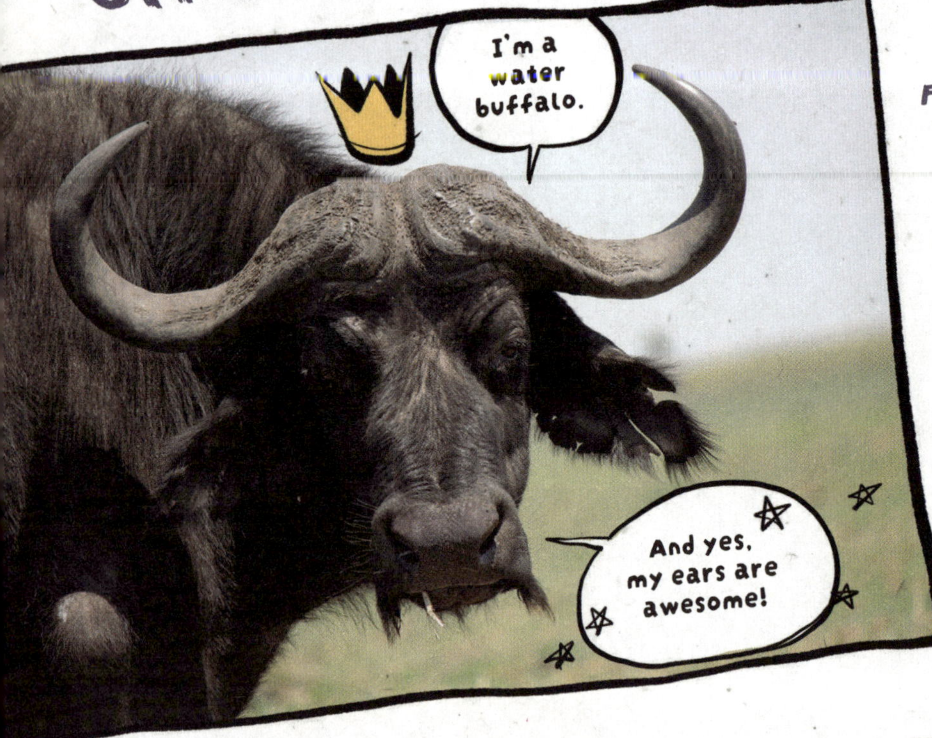

First, let's identify the features (shapes) and the words you think best describe them.

FLOPPY EARS

DISTINCT HORN SHAPE

MOUTH AND NOSE COMBO

Next, sketch some quick studies and try to break down the shapes to help you understand them better. Study the textures and details too. This stage is for observing and analysing the subject.

TRY TO FIND YOUR OWN ANSWERS RATHER THAN RELYING ON DECISIONS OTHER ARTISTS HAVE ALREADY MADE.

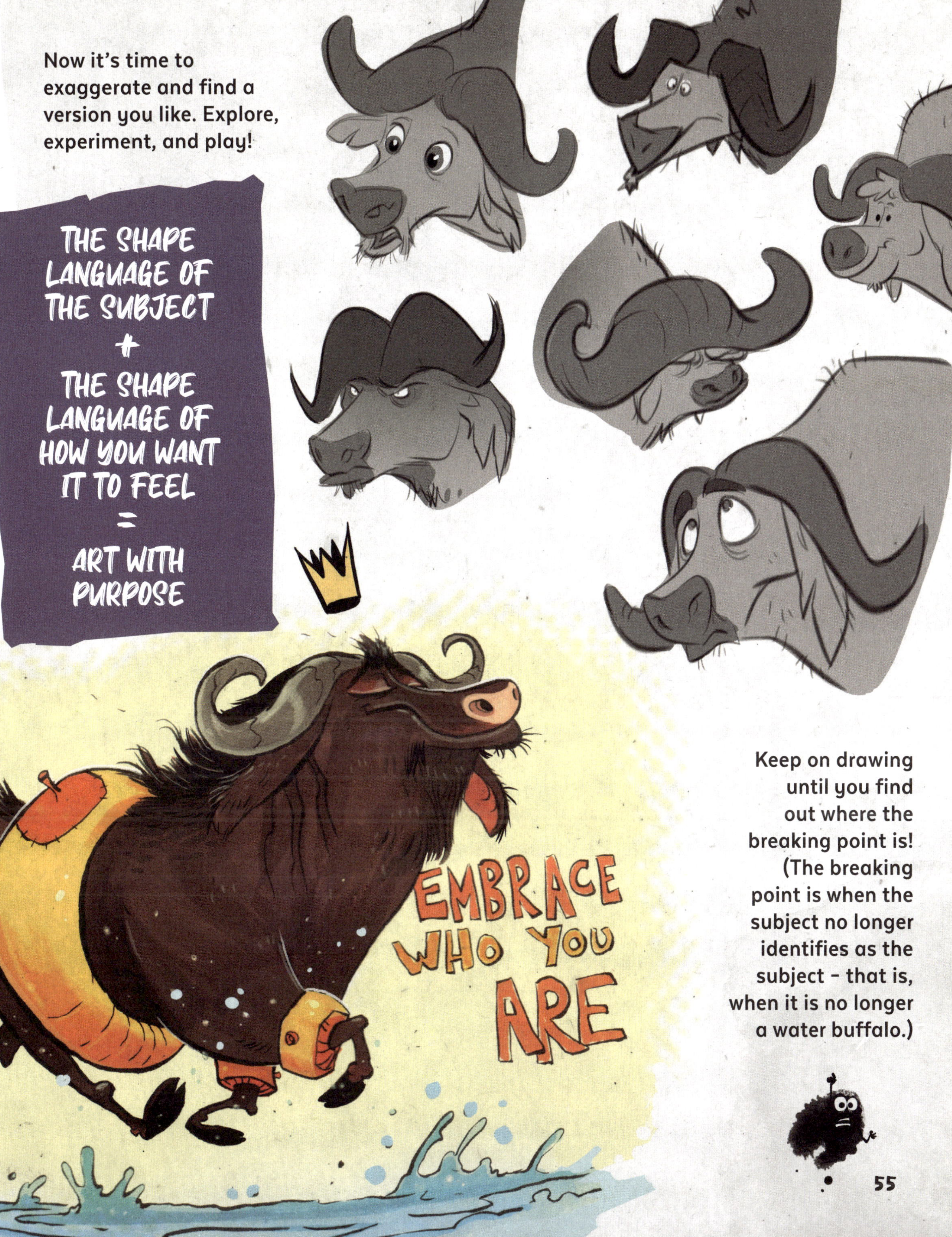

Now it's time to exaggerate and find a version you like. Explore, experiment, and play!

THE SHAPE LANGUAGE OF THE SUBJECT

+

THE SHAPE LANGUAGE OF HOW YOU WANT IT TO FEEL

=

ART WITH PURPOSE

Keep on drawing until you find out where the breaking point is! (The breaking point is when the subject no longer identifies as the subject - that is, when it is no longer a water buffalo.)

55

NEGATIVE SPACE

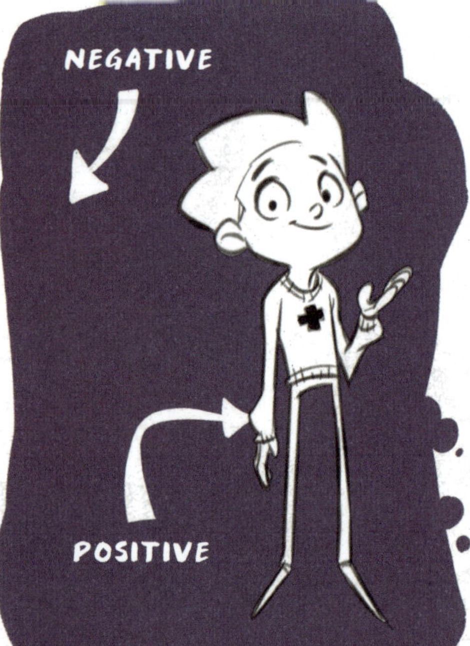

To understand any object, the negative is just as important as the positive!

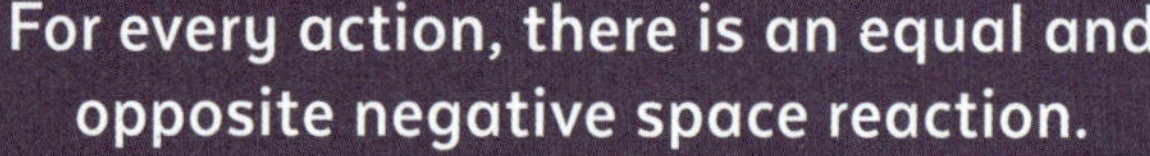

For every action, there is an equal and opposite negative space reaction.

When creating shapes within shapes, negative space can provide many options. For example, in the faces below, the nose, eyes, and mouth are all the same size, only the spaces **BETWEEN** them have changed!

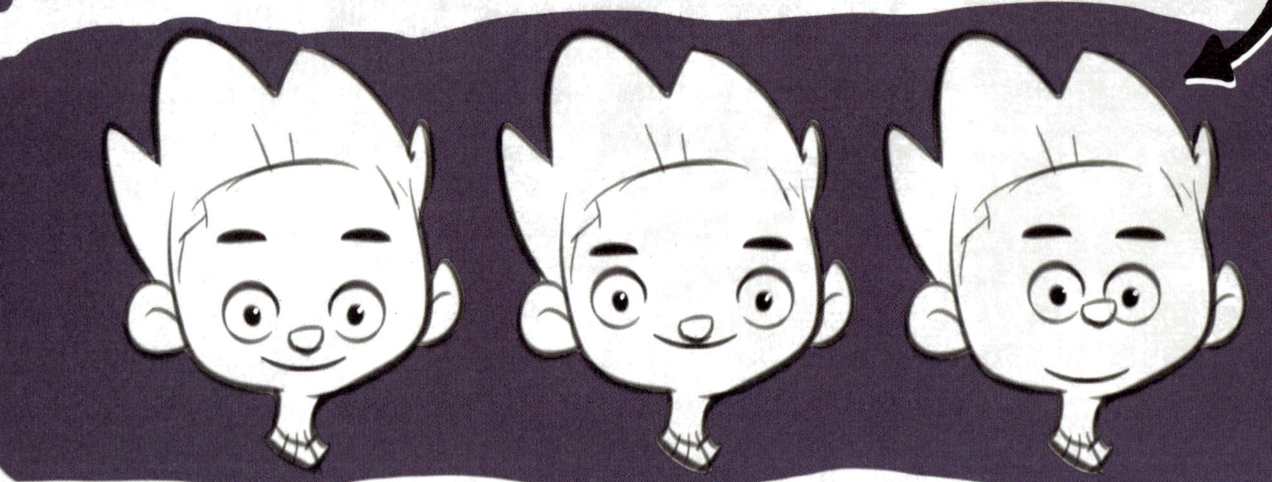

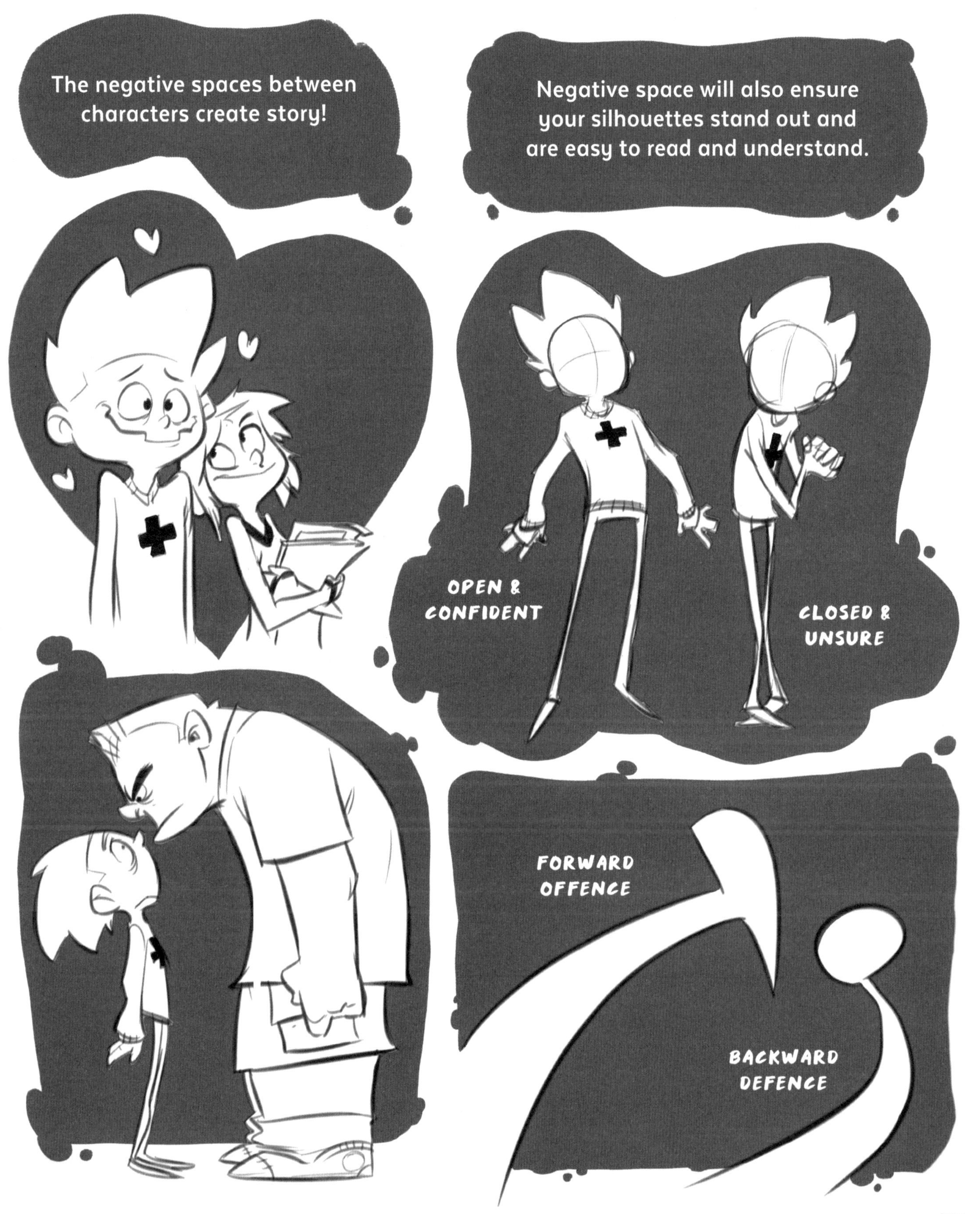

The negative spaces between characters create story!
Negative space will also ensure your silhouettes stand out and are easy to read and understand.
OPEN & CONFIDENT
CLOSED & UNSURE
FORWARD OFFENCE
BACKWARD DEFENCE

FROM SIMPLE TO BUSY

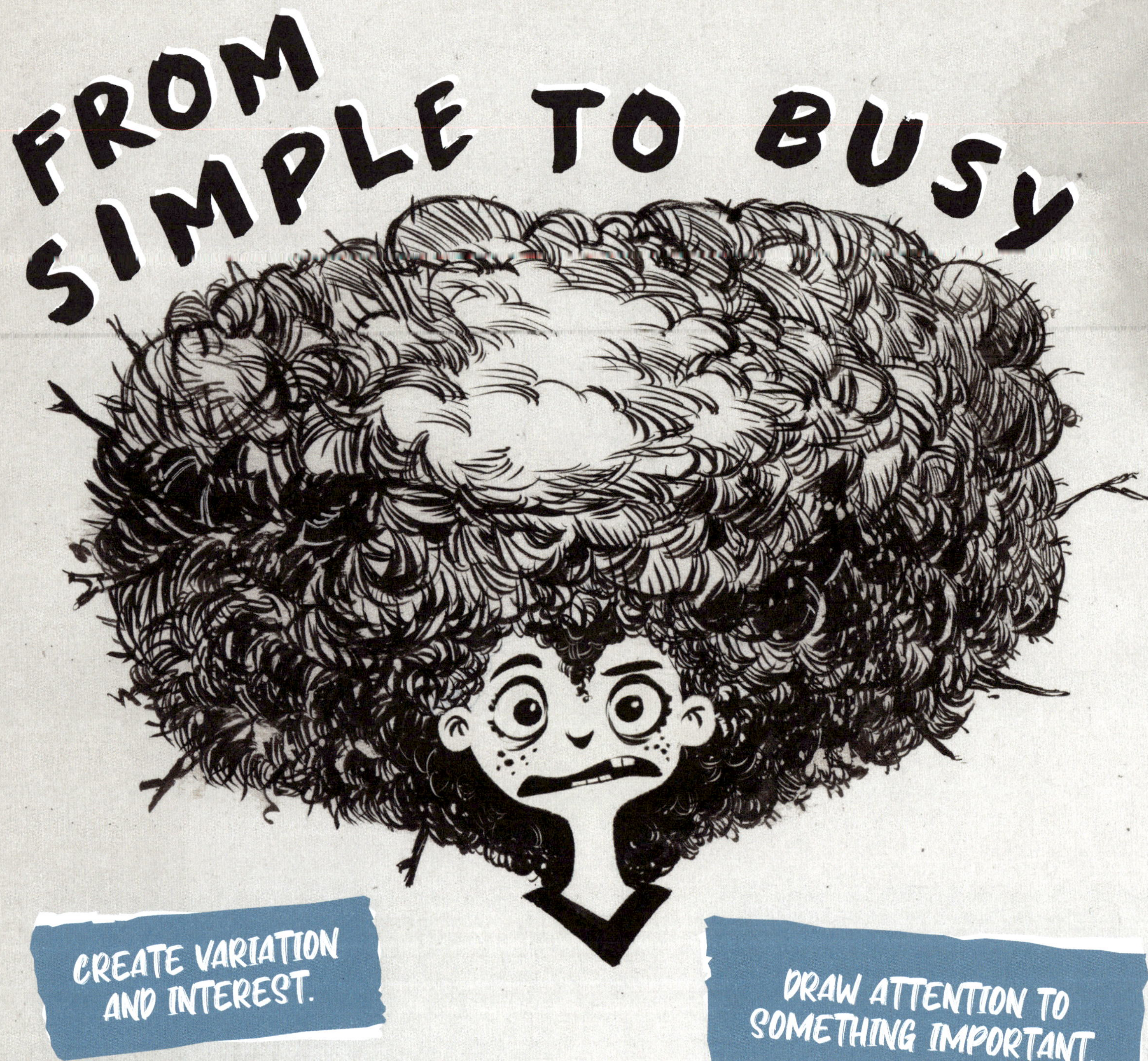

CREATE VARIATION AND INTEREST.

DRAW ATTENTION TO SOMETHING IMPORTANT.

PROVIDE THE EYE WITH A RESTING SPOT.

EXPLAIN DIRT, GRIME, SPOTS, PATTERNS, MECHANICAL GREEBLES, AND MORE!

BRING FOCUS IN A SCENE.

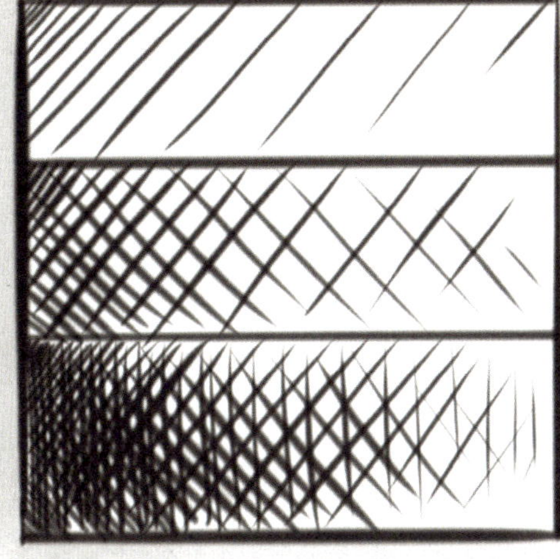
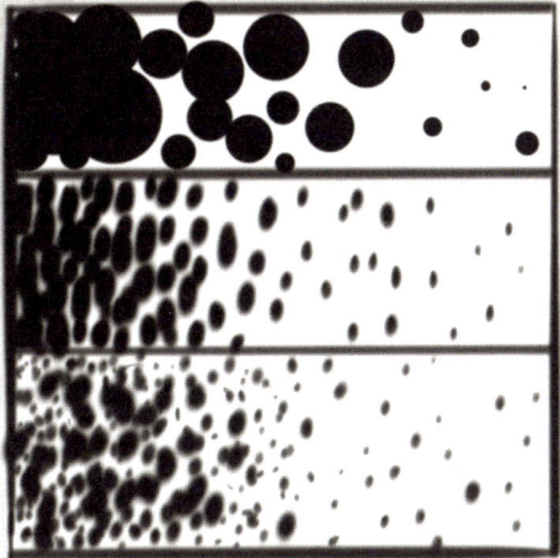
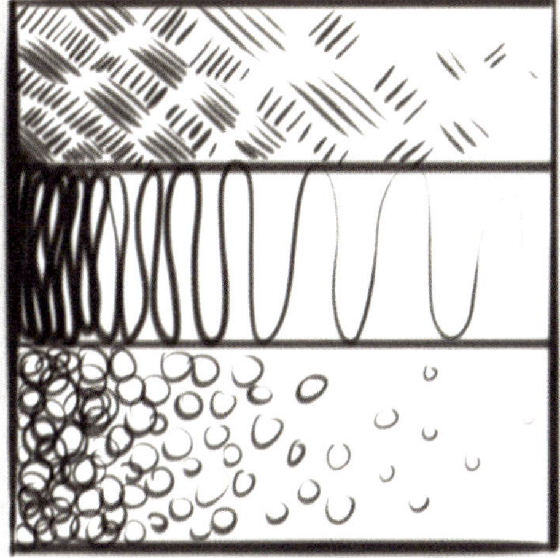
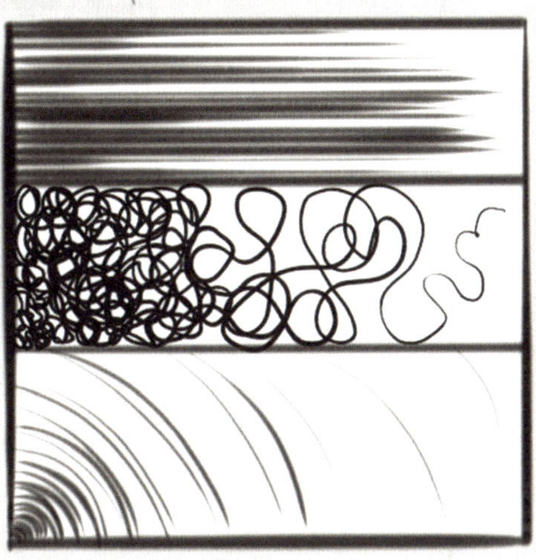
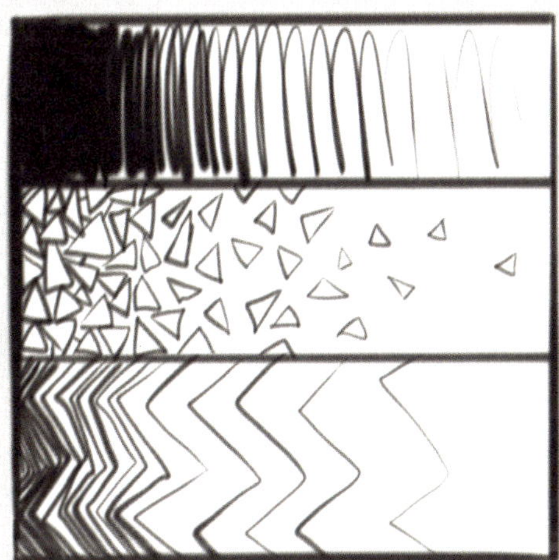
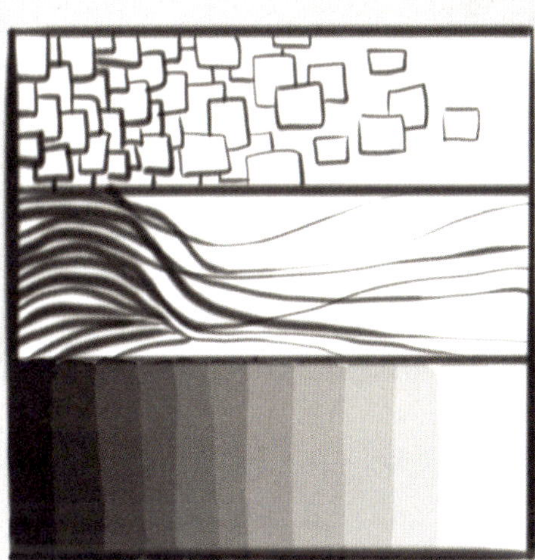

TRY THIS!

Practise how patterns and lines can create **VISUAL INTEREST**.

Draw a series of rectangles, then use circles, cross-hatches, lines, squiggles, squares, or anything you like to explore **SIMPLE** to **BUSY** marks on the page!

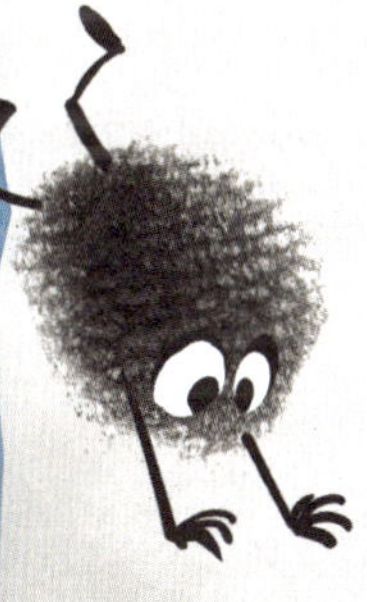
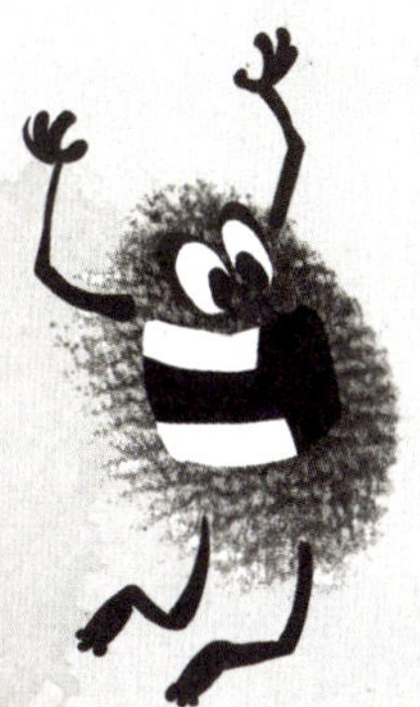

RHYTHM & FLOW

Remember when we discussed implied lines? Here they are again. Flow is the use of lines, shapes, colours, and details to move focus from one element to another. You can use it for storytelling, composition, and any other time you want your audience to focus on something in an image.

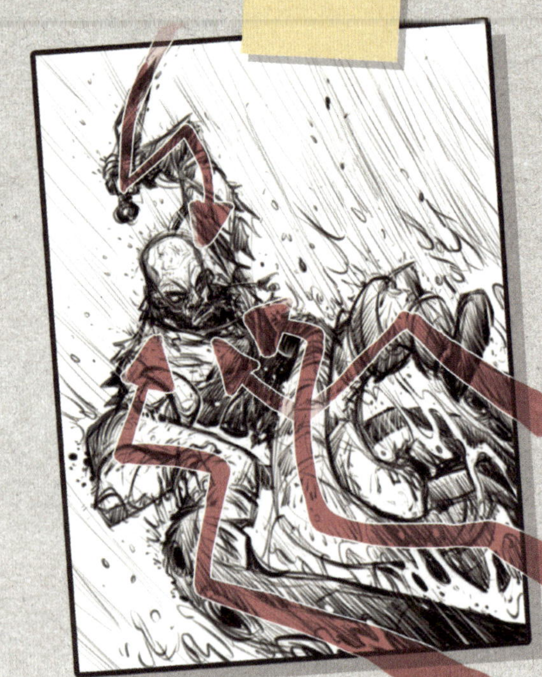

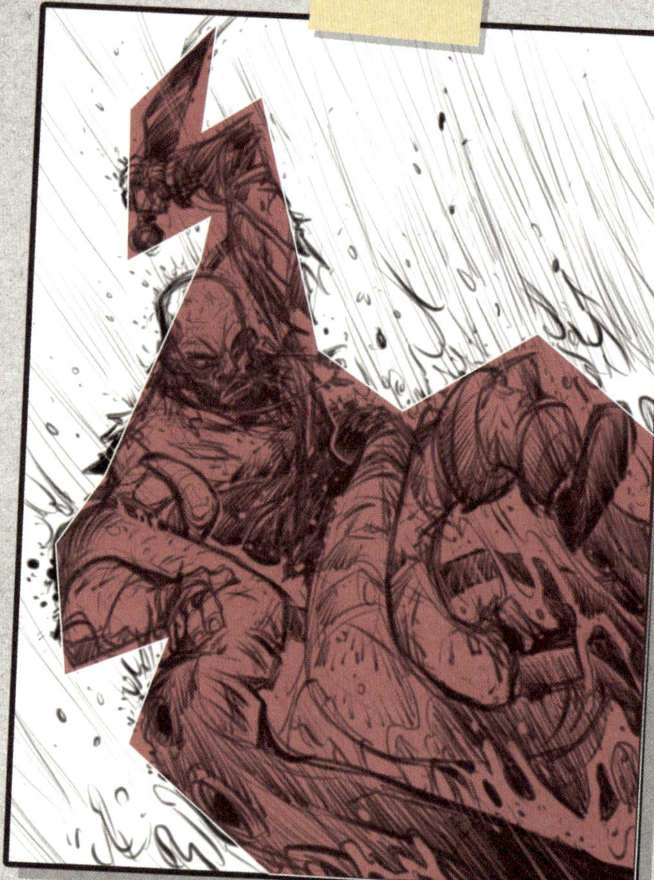

When all these lines are put together, they make shapes. Using straight lines alongside curved lines will feel more dynamic.

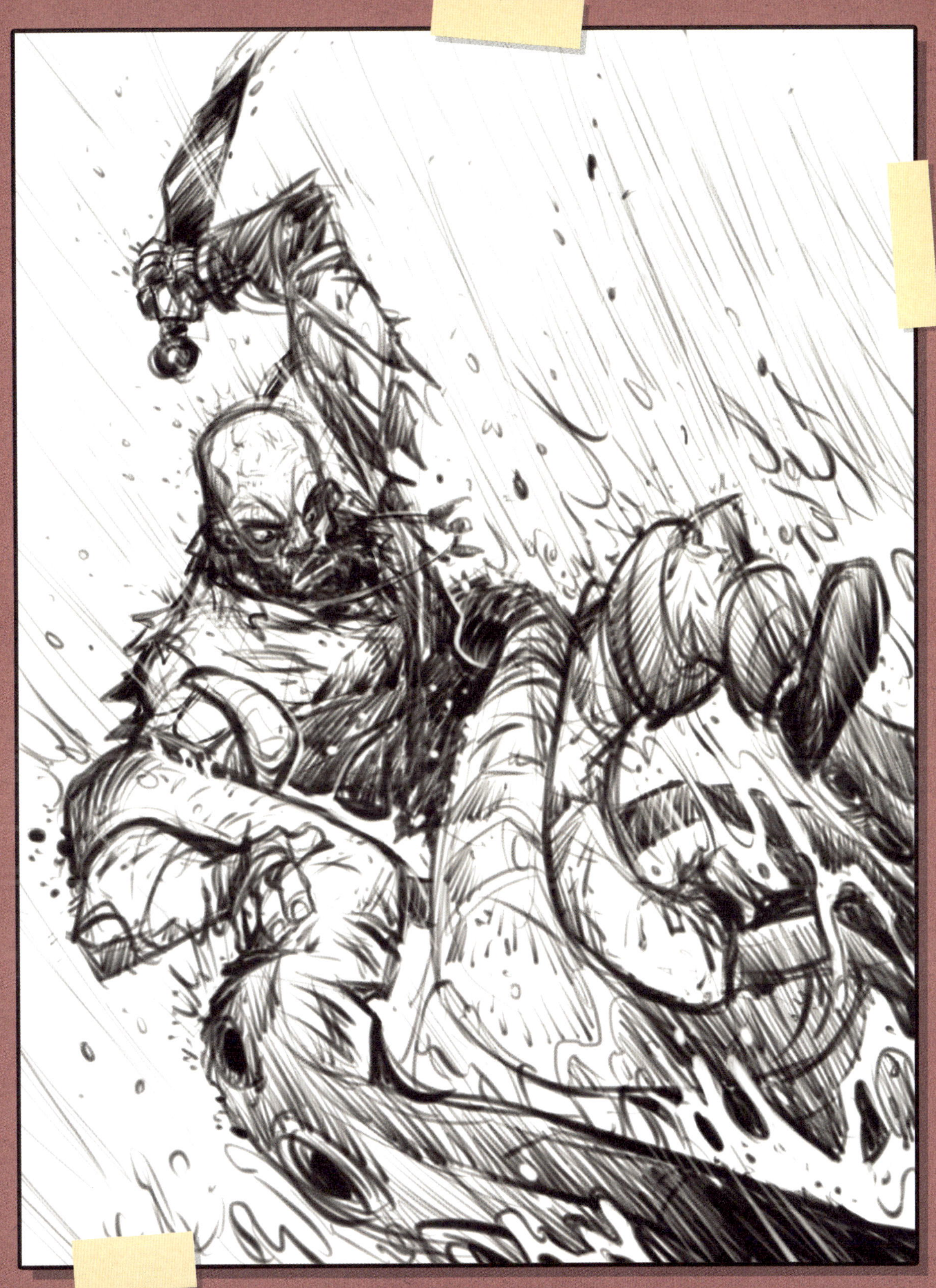

PATTERNS

Patterns are designs created by repeating a motif or symbol in a predictable combination. **SHAPES** are also valuable patterns.

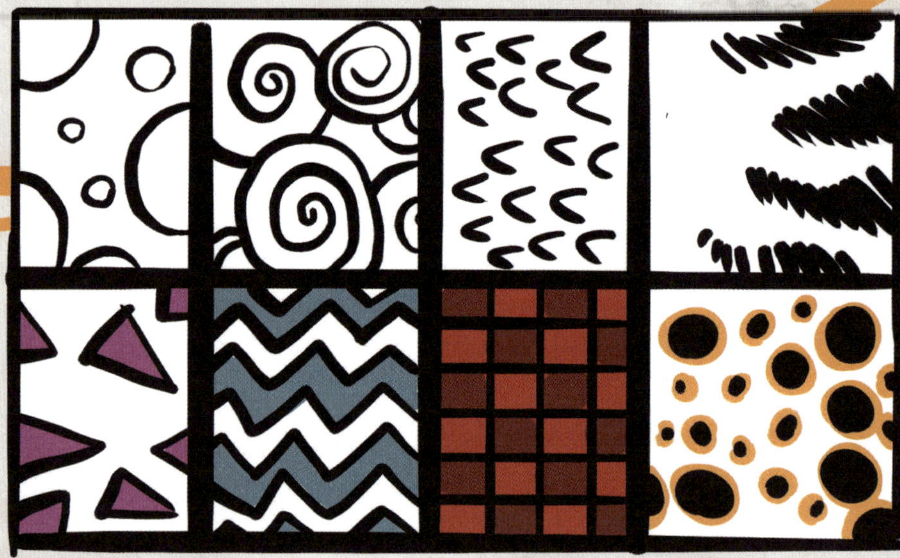

A **MOTIF** can be thought of as units of a pattern or shape.

In visual art, they are bounded areas, or volumes, that contain designs or elements such as textures, tiles, colours, shapes, or any other combination that repeats.

Motifs and shapes can be copied and arranged multiple times to create unified designs. This can be referred to as **REPETITION**. It's best to let one shape or pattern element dominate. If they're all important, none of them are.

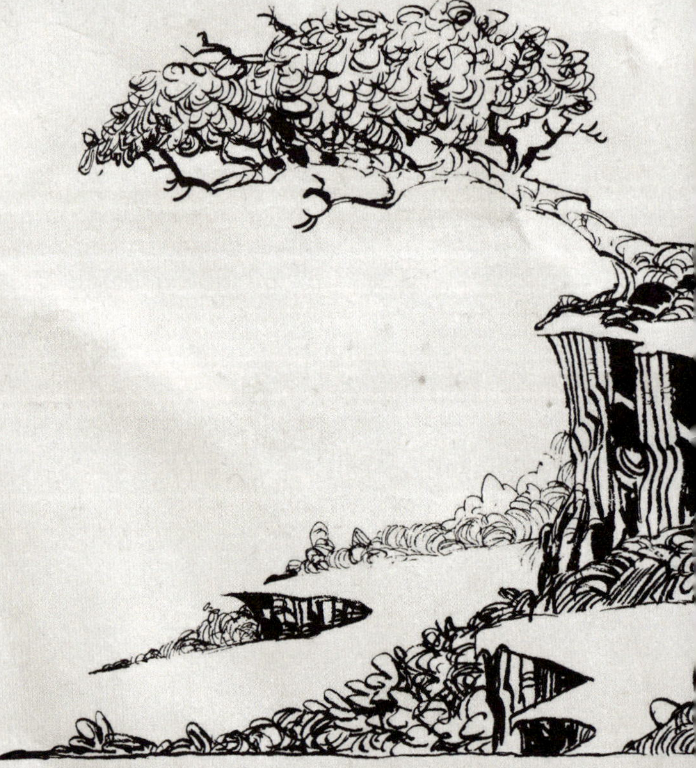

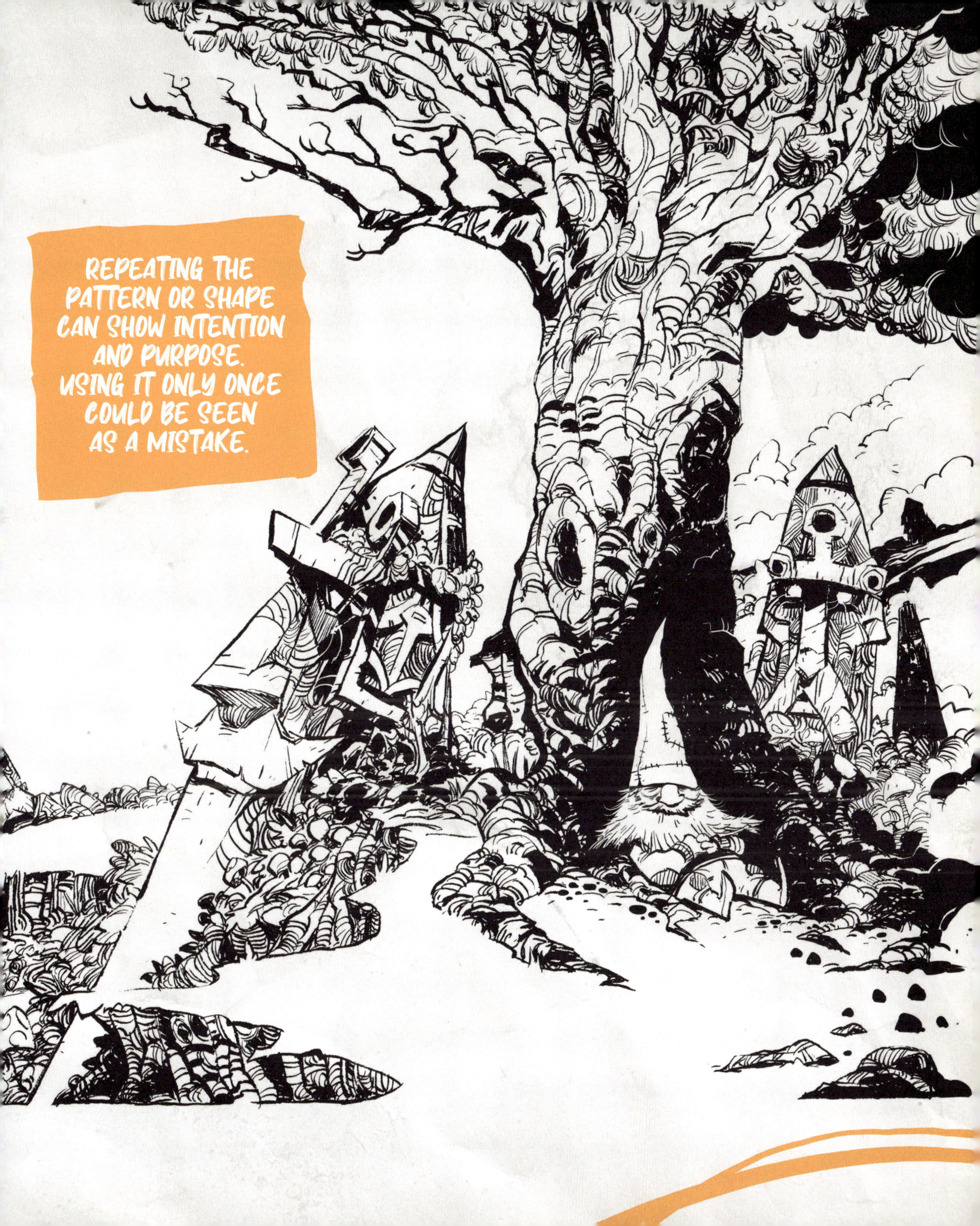

REPEATING THE PATTERN OR SHAPE CAN SHOW INTENTION AND PURPOSE. USING IT ONLY ONCE COULD BE SEEN AS A MISTAKE.

TEXTURES

Texture is the implied visual feel of a surface. Think about downy animal fur, soft bird feathers, smooth polished glass, or speckly sand on a beach.

Textures can also be the actual feel of paper, screen tones, and the build-up of paint or ink.

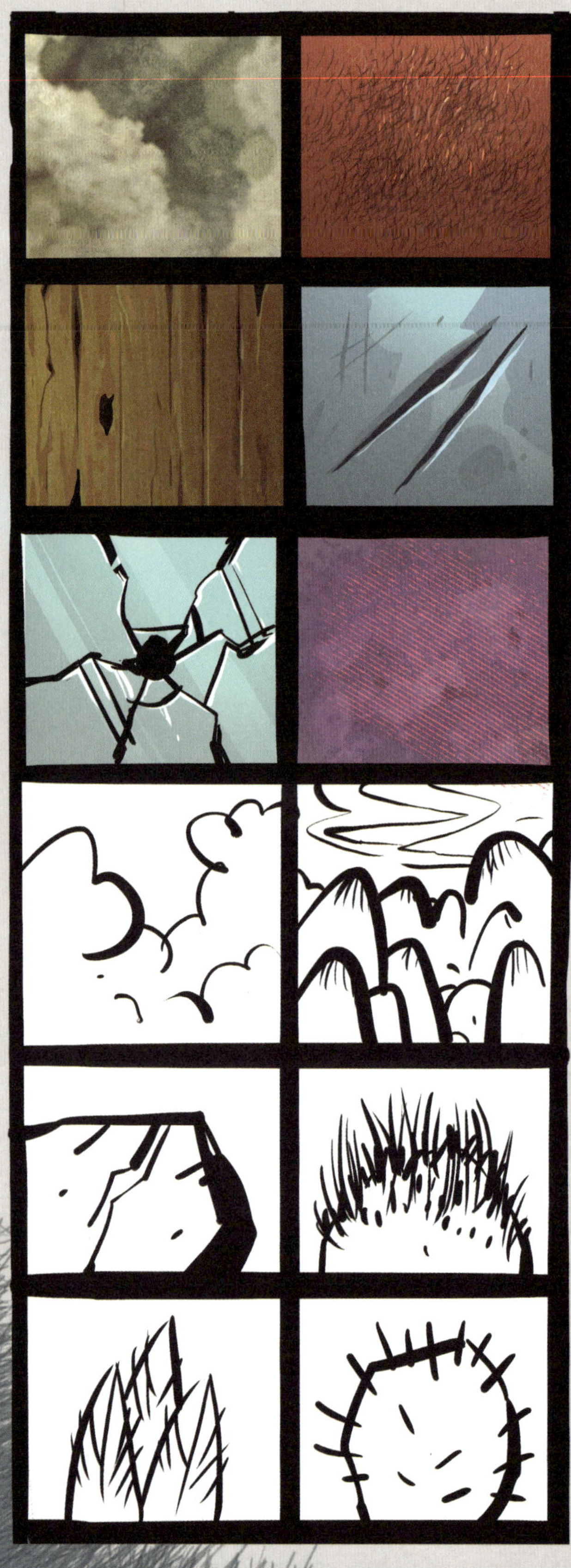

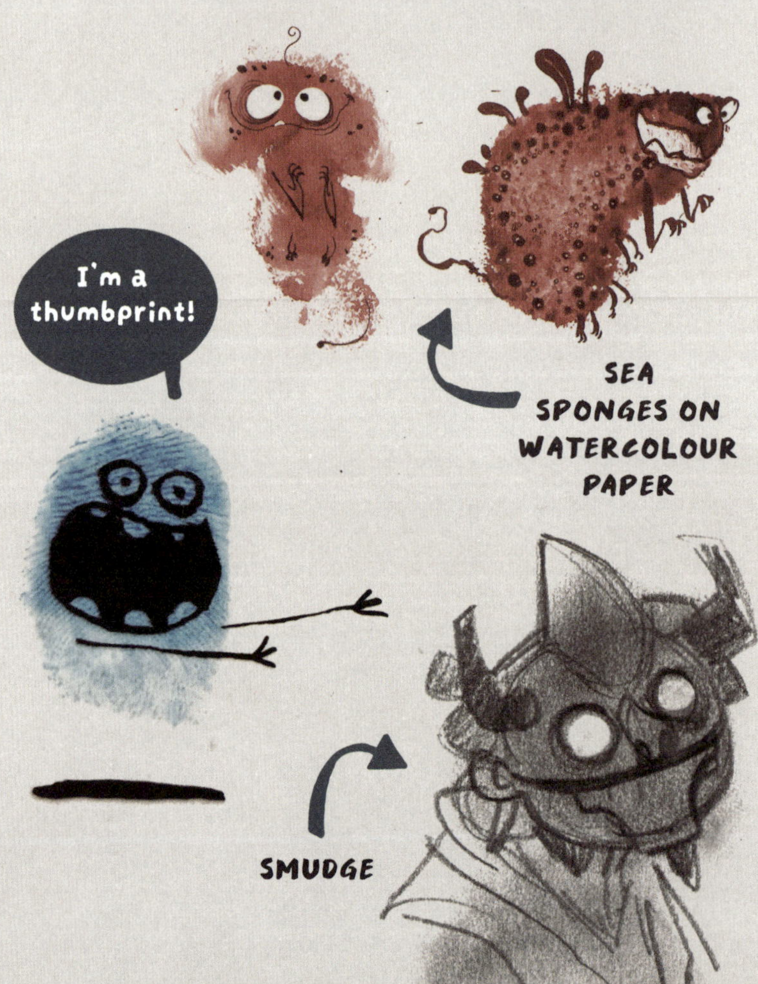

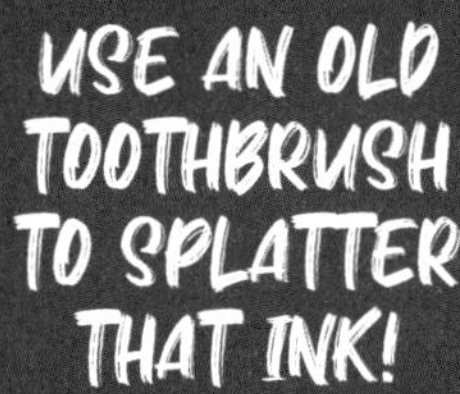

WHEN DRAWING TEXTURES...

They can be **ROUGH** or **SMOOTH**,

ACTUAL or **IMPLIED**,

SOFT or **SHARP**,

IRREGULAR or **REGULAR**,

HARD, HAIRY, BUMPY, or **ROUGH**,

STITCHED, WOVEN, or **LEATHERED**,

WEATHERED and **WORN**, or **SHINY** and **NEW**.

STAY INTERESTED AND TRY TO OBSERVE NATURE AND YOUR SURROUNDINGS WHEREVER YOU ARE. FEEL THE ROCK. HUG A TREE!

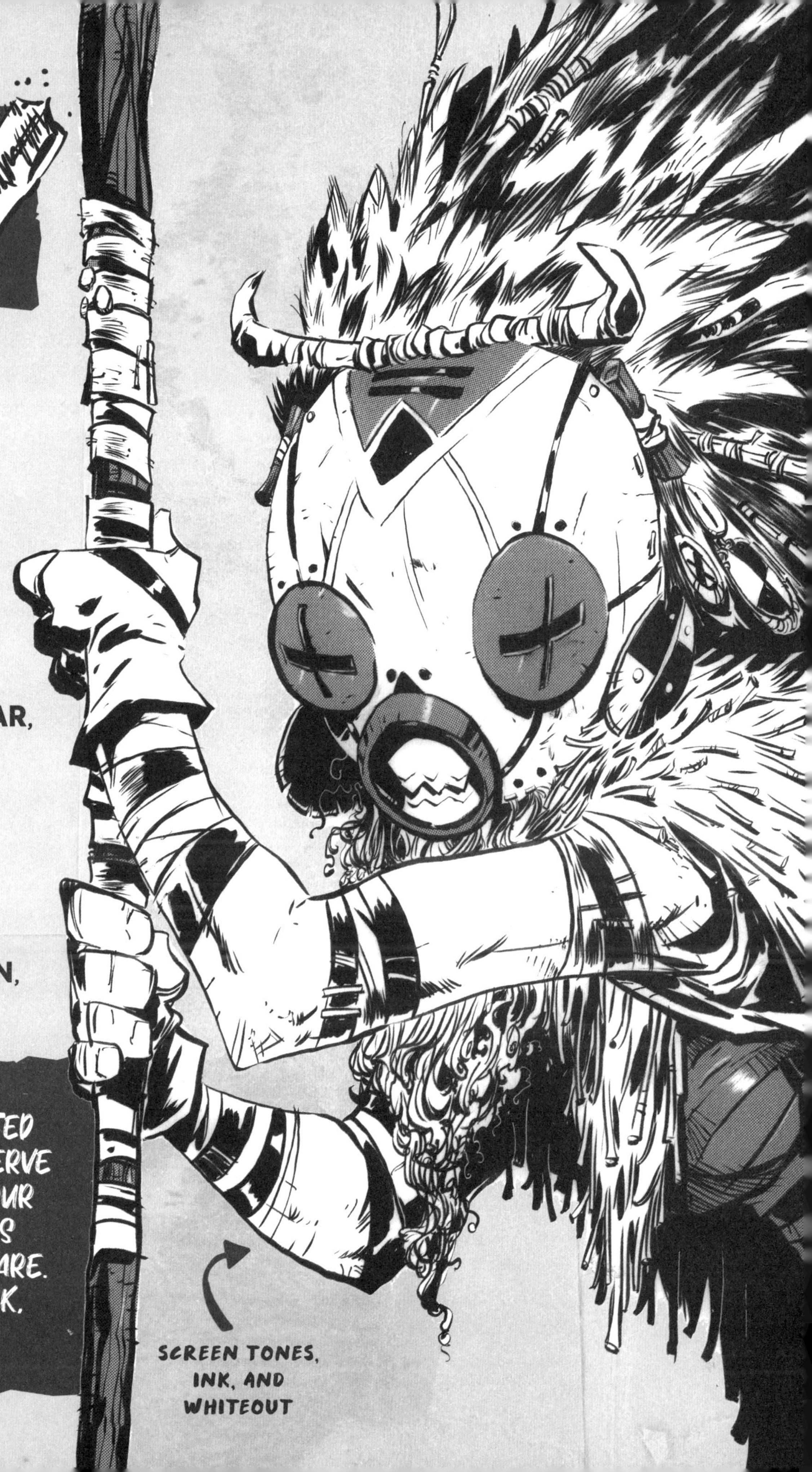

SCREEN TONES, INK, AND WHITEOUT

CONTRAST

Contrast is the noticeable difference between people, objects, or details in an image. You can use line, light, colour, or any combination of these to show contrast. Its best use is for clarity and understanding.

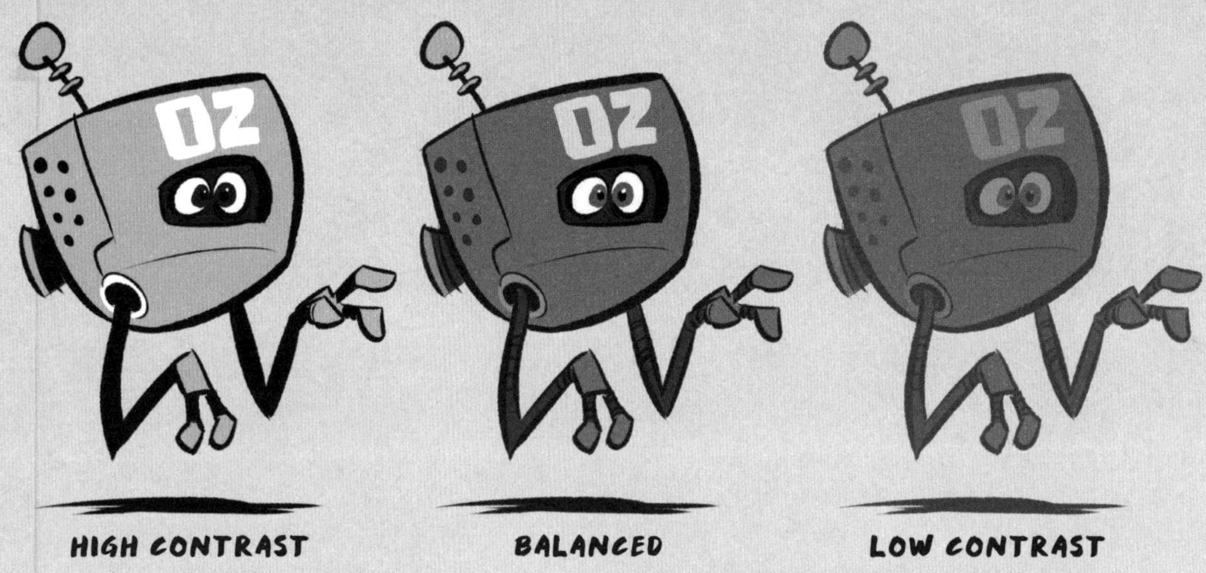

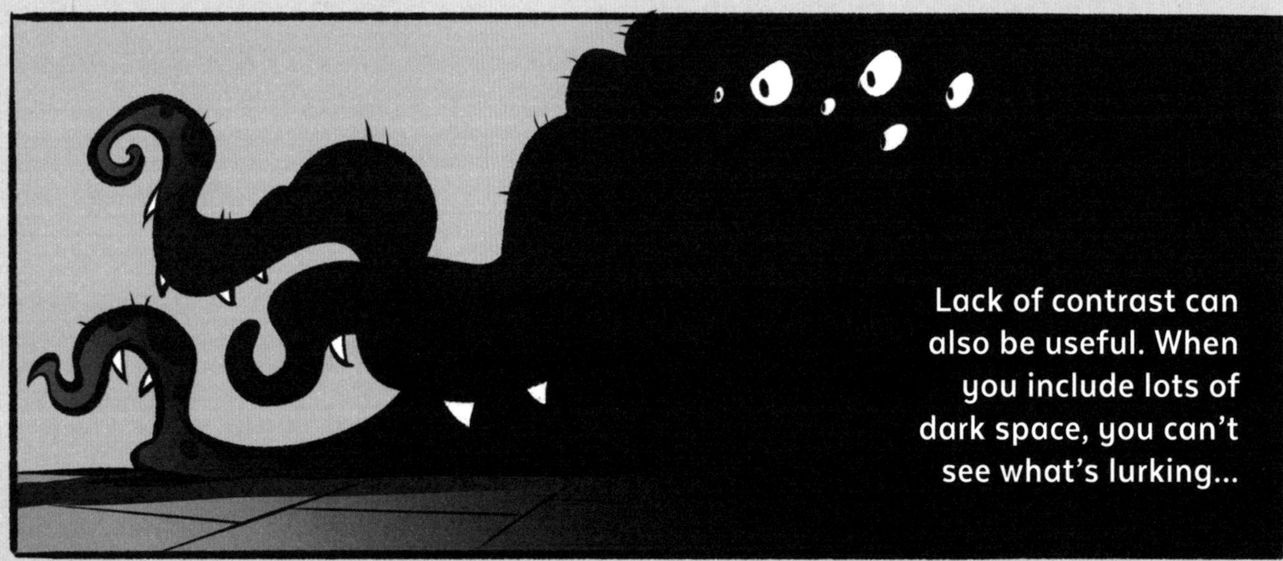

Viewers will focus on the most extreme point of contrast in your artwork, so save it until you need it.

INFORMAL BALANCE

Informal balance happens when the visual weight of the elements, shapes, details, and designs in an image is not equal, but still balanced.

SYMMETRY

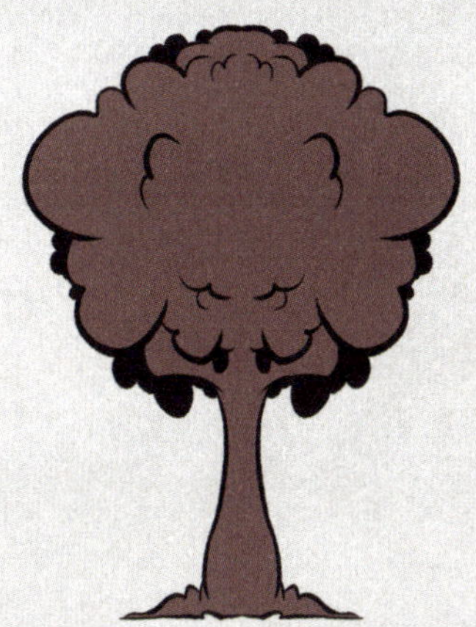

Elements arranged evenly around a central point.

* Healthy
* Clean
* Ordered
* Uptight
* Even
* Still

ASYMMETRY

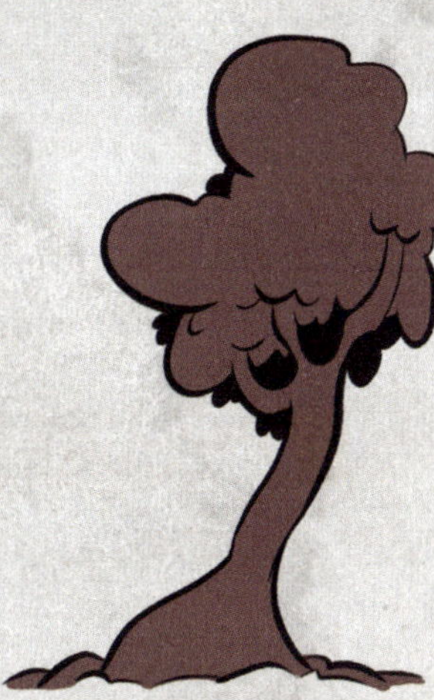

Elements arranged unevenly throughout.

* Dishevelled
* Disorder
* Dynamic
* At ease
* Natural
* Moving

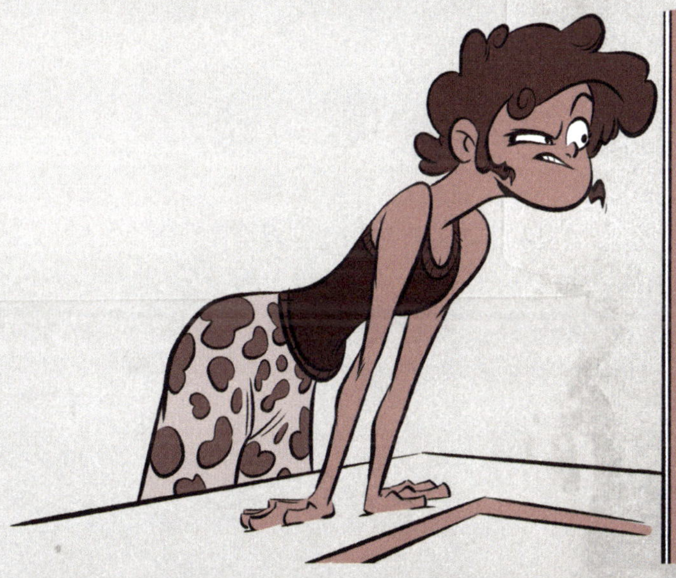
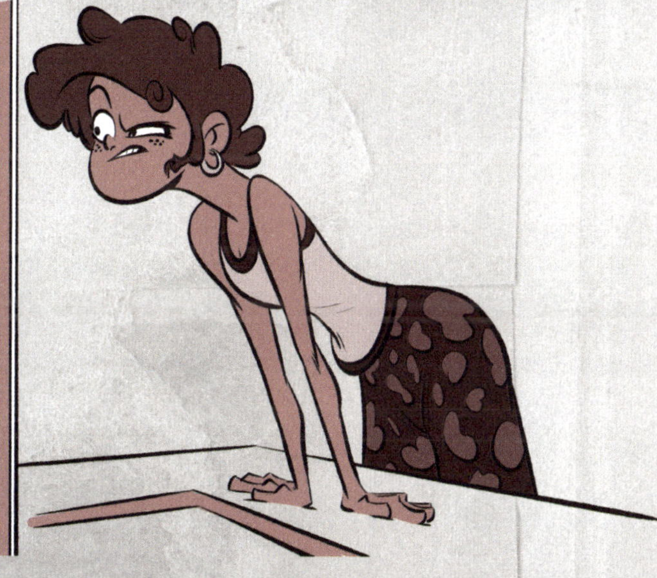

KNOWING HOW AND WHEN TO USE INFORMAL BALANCE WILL GIVE YOU A RANGE OF OPTIONS IN YOUR ART. TRY TO USE BOTH SYMMETRY AND ASYMMETRY TO FIND THE BALANCE YOU WANT.

TONAL VALUES

Let's find value in your art...
See what I did there?

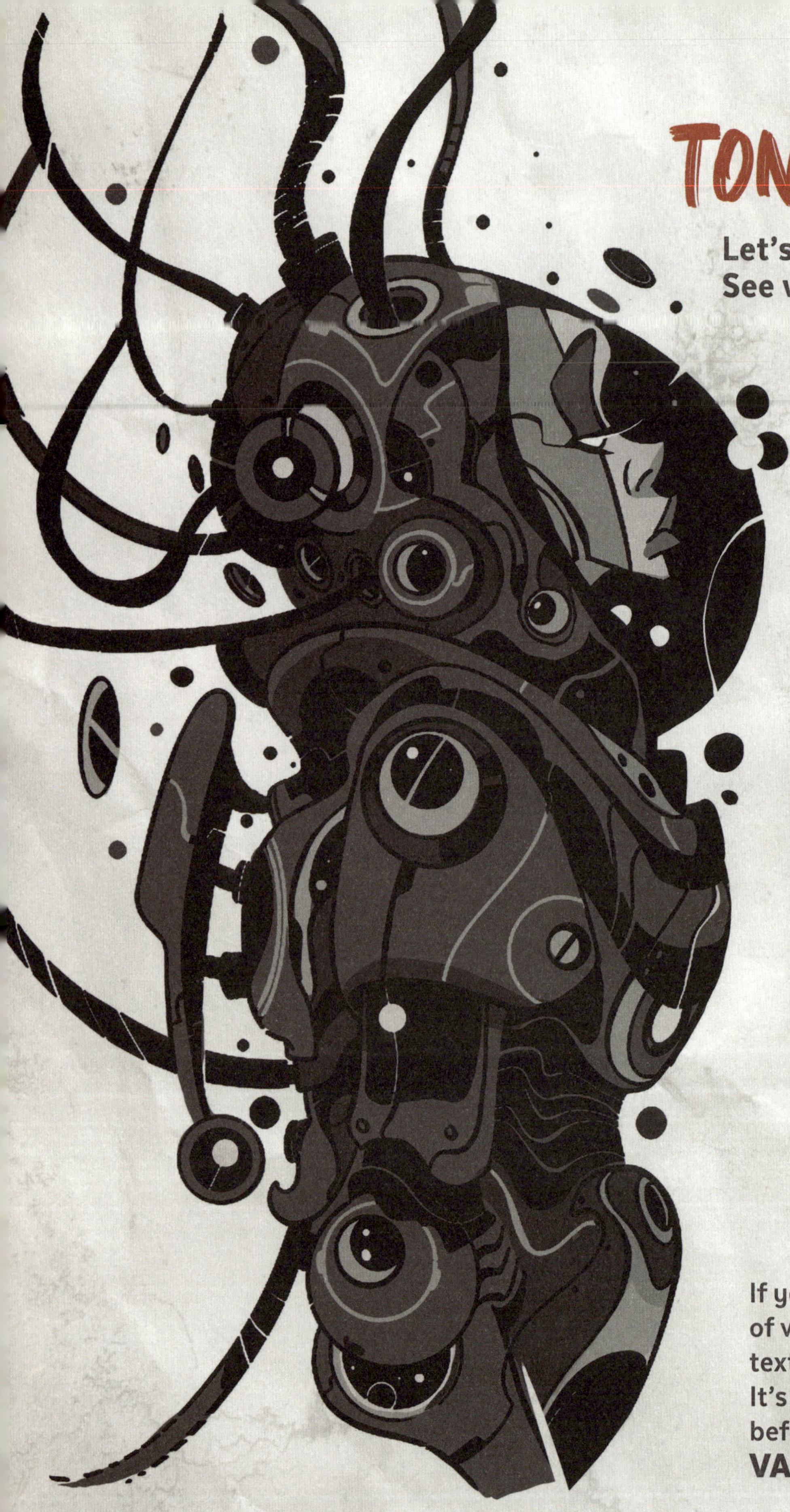

Value refers to the degree of lightness and darkness of an area. We only see things because of the light that reflects off objects and bounces into our eyes.

If your design has a poor arrangement of values, there is very little that colour, texture, or lines can do to save it. It's important to plan out your tones before starting on colours, because **VALUES DOMINATE HUE**.

Tonal gradations, from light to dark, help the eye to understand and move along a shape, because value largely determines our perception of form.

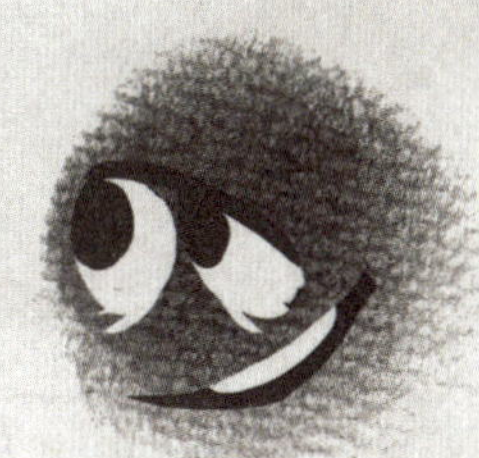

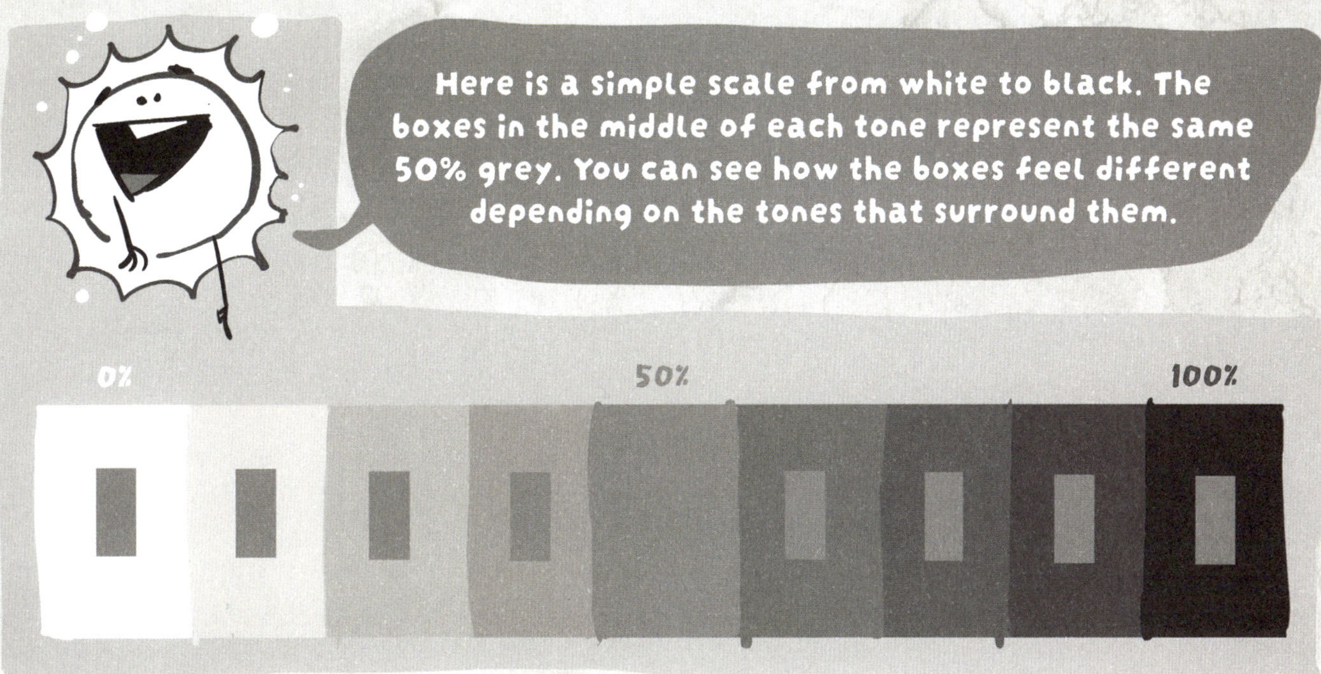

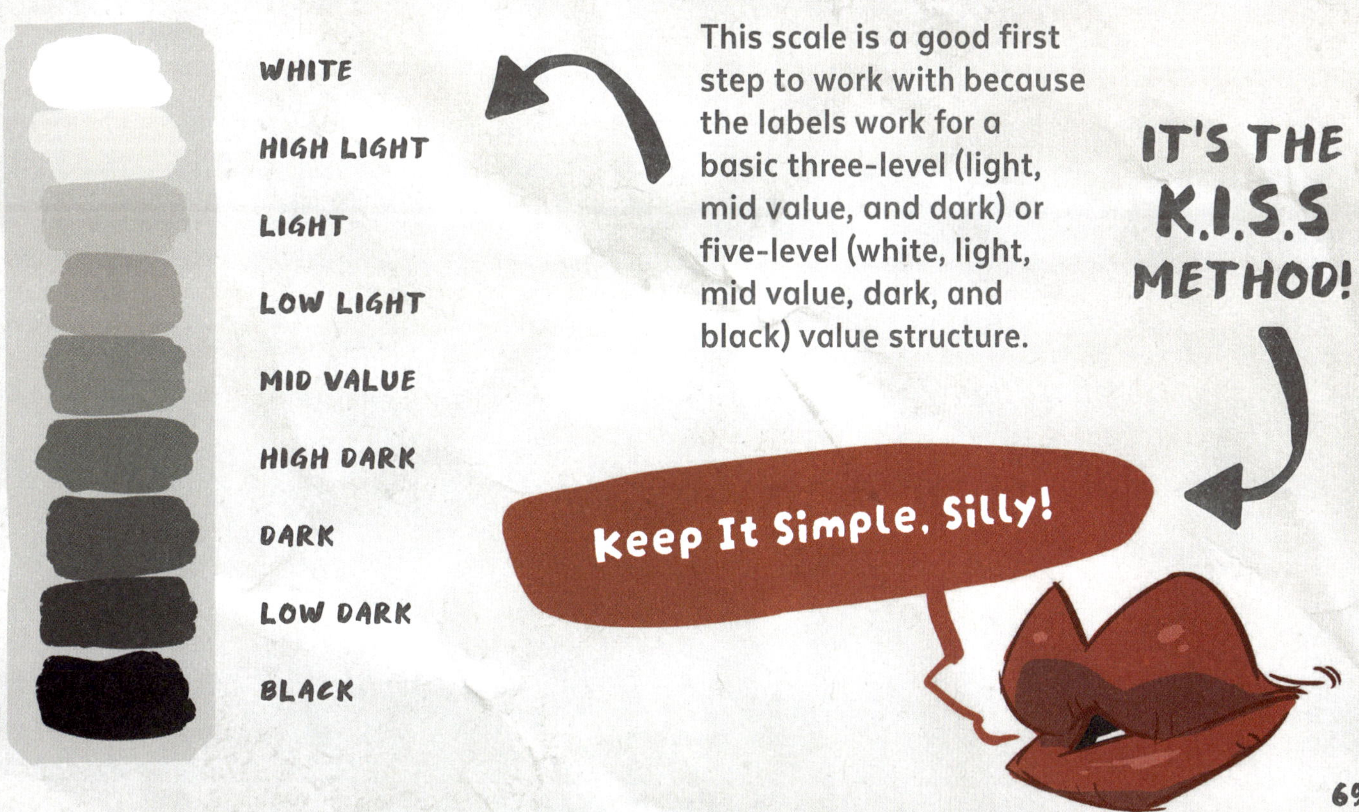

This scale is a good first step to work with because the labels work for a basic three-level (light, mid value, and dark) or five-level (white, light, mid value, dark, and black) value structure.

TONAL CLARITY

A good first design rule is to keep your design, or composition, to only 10% in the low dark/black and high light/white. The eye is naturally drawn to the highest level of contrast in a design, illustration, or pattern. Save those extreme contrasts for where you want your viewer to look first.

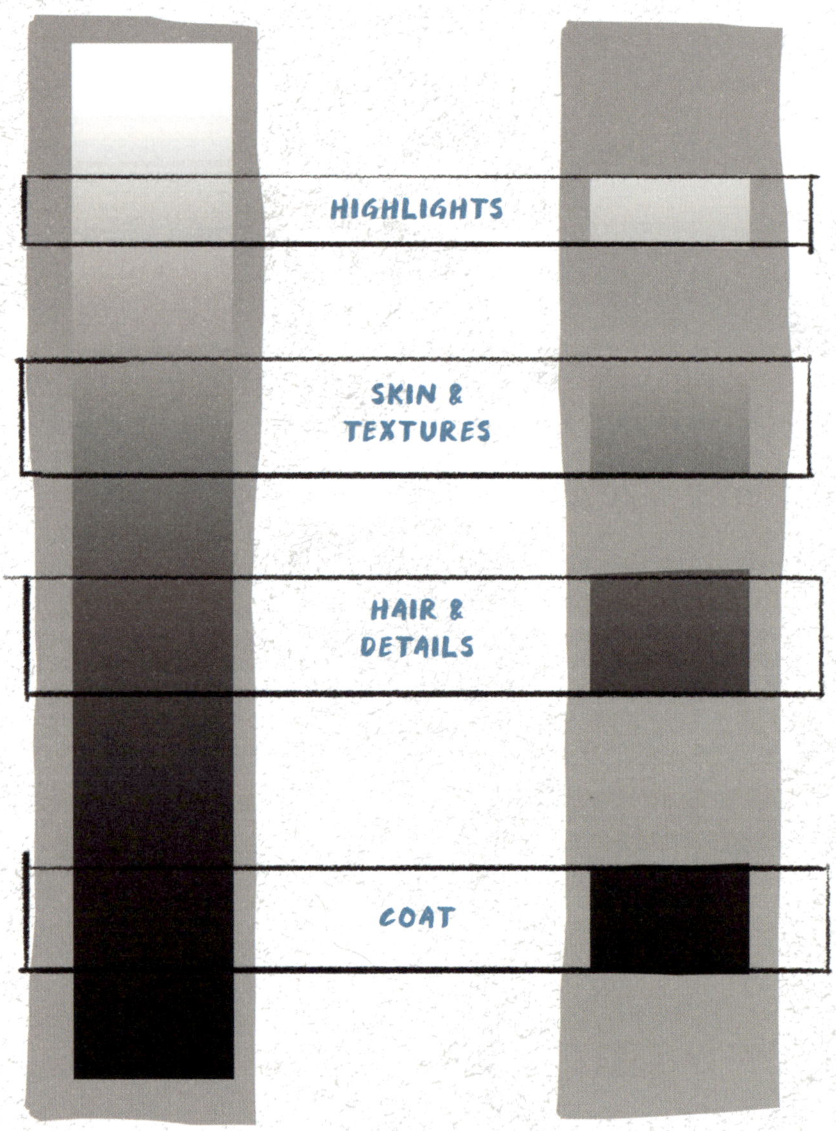

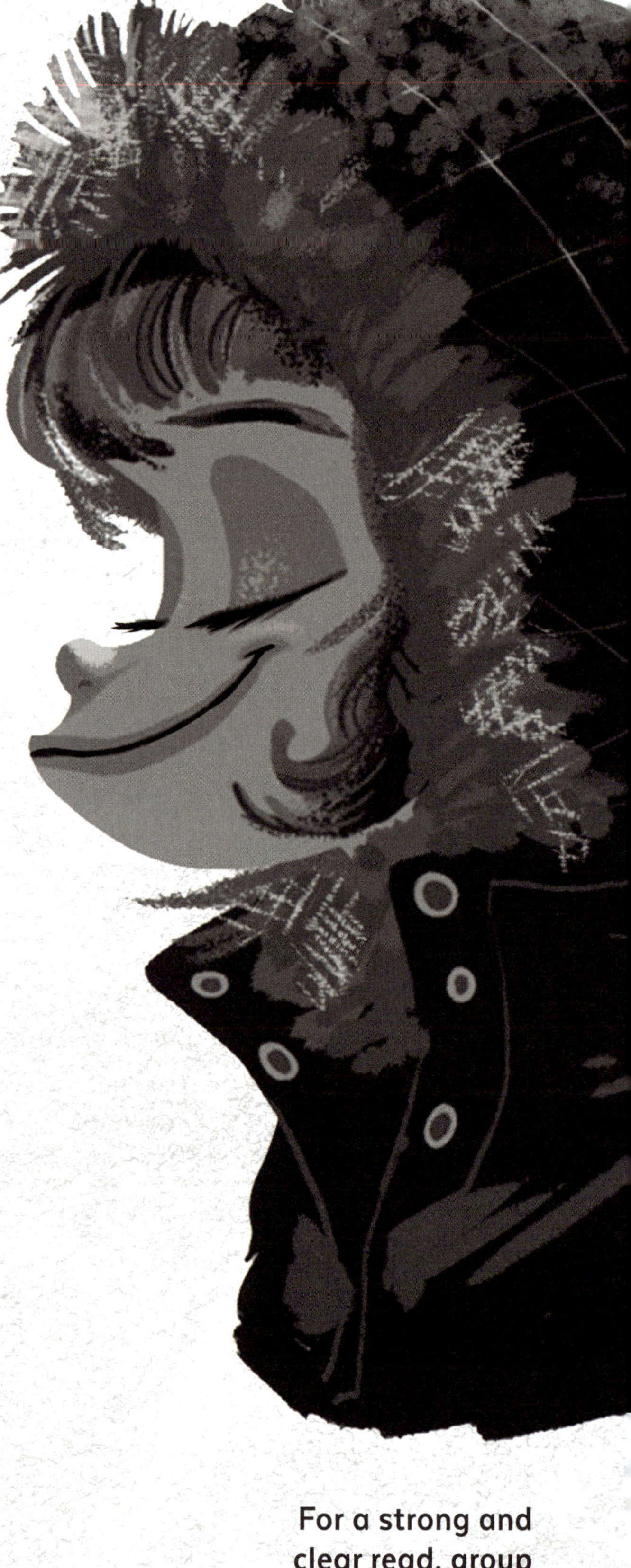

For a strong and clear read, group your tones.

MAJOR KEYS

The major keys aim to create a greater value contrast between shapes. They all contain both black and white, with changes in proportion, quantity, and/or dominance of the values.

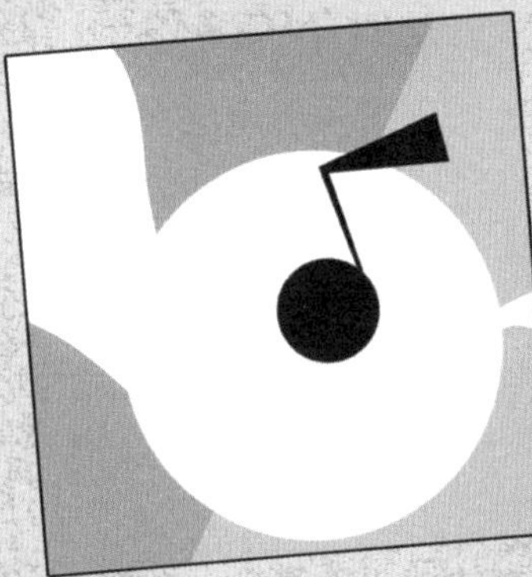

HIGH MAJOR

Dominant high/ light values.

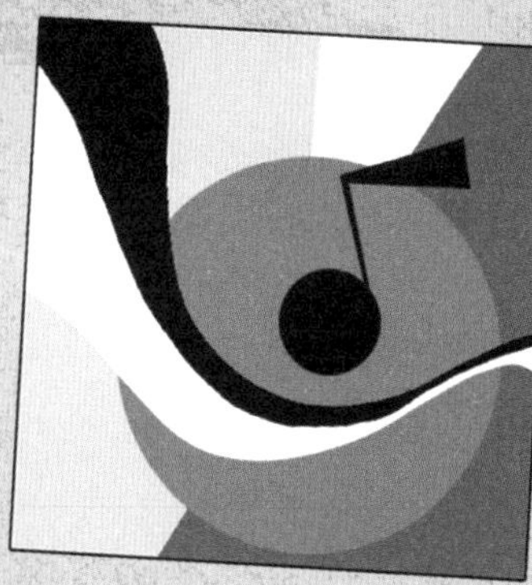

MIDDLE MAJOR

Equal amounts of black and white.

LOW MAJOR

Dominant low/ dark values.

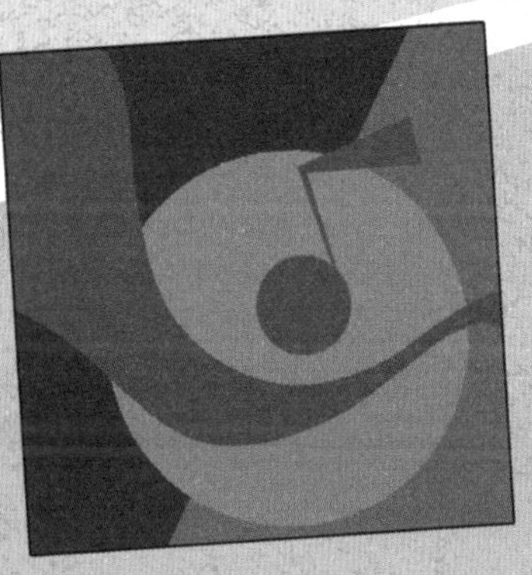

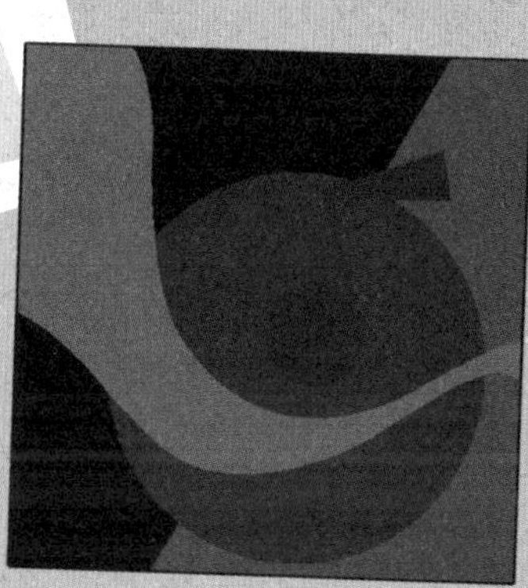

MIDDLE MINOR

All values from 40-60%.

LOW MINOR

All values from 75-100%.

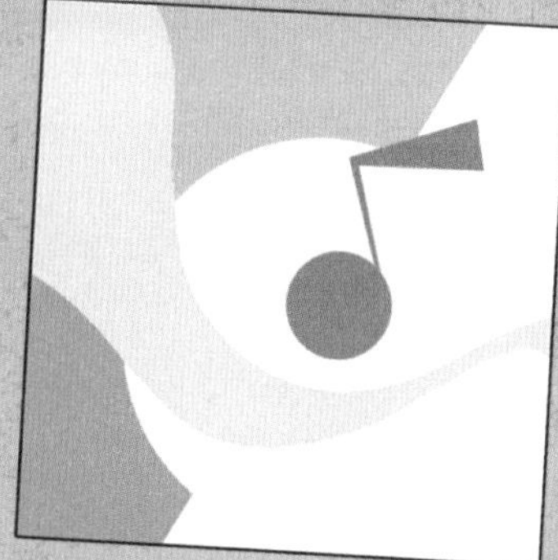

HIGH MINOR

All high/light values, no black.

MINOR KEYS

With closer value distances and less contrast between intervals, the minor keys don't include the entire value scale. The keys consist of groups of closely related values within a limited range.

TONE WITH LINE

Here are just a few ways to add value using lines.

Most of these values are created by how close the shapes are together.
The closer the lines, the darker the value is perceived to be.

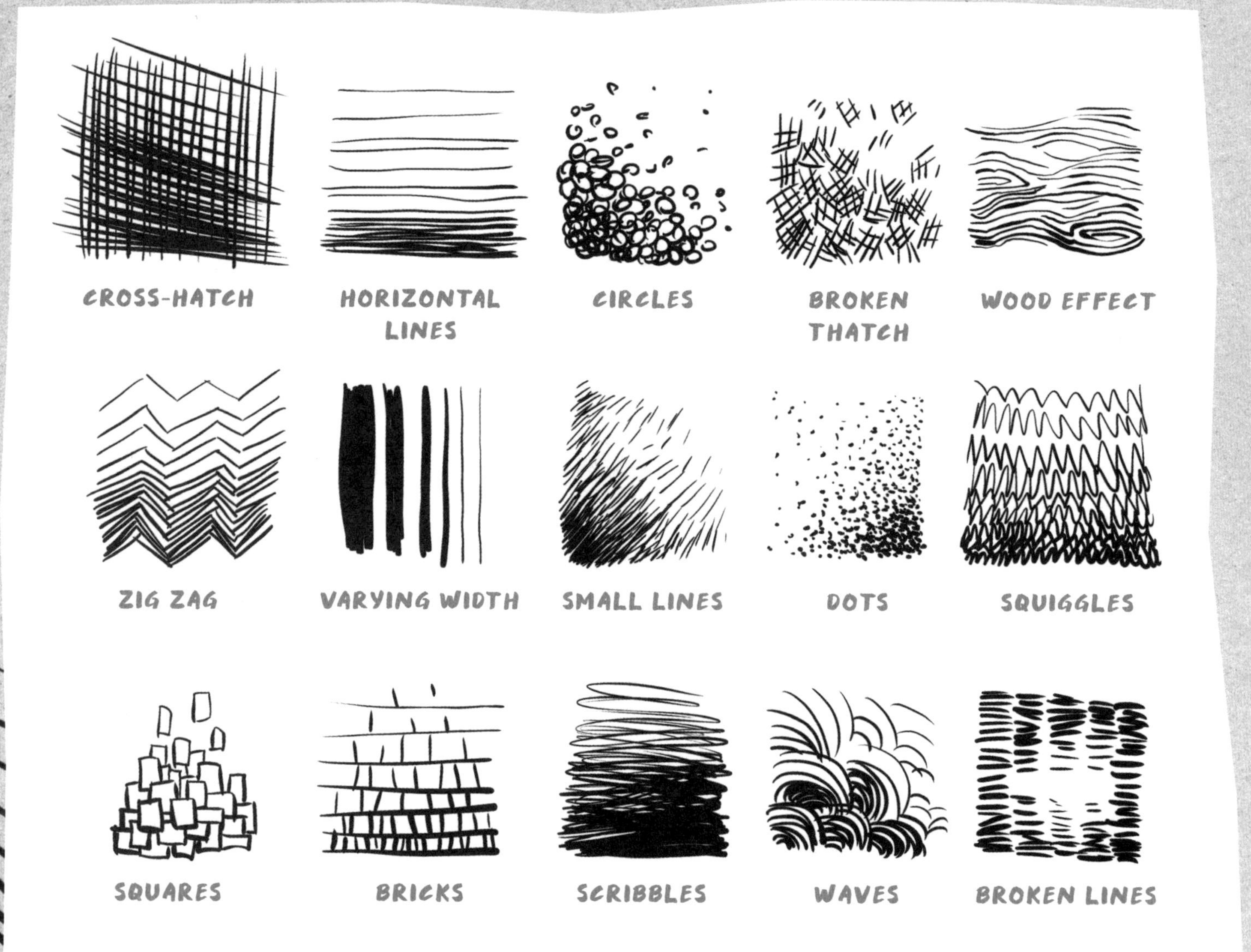

CROSS-HATCH   HORIZONTAL LINES   CIRCLES   BROKEN THATCH   WOOD EFFECT

ZIG ZAG   VARYING WIDTH   SMALL LINES   DOTS   SQUIGGLES

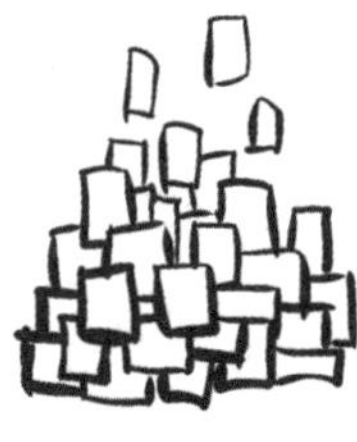 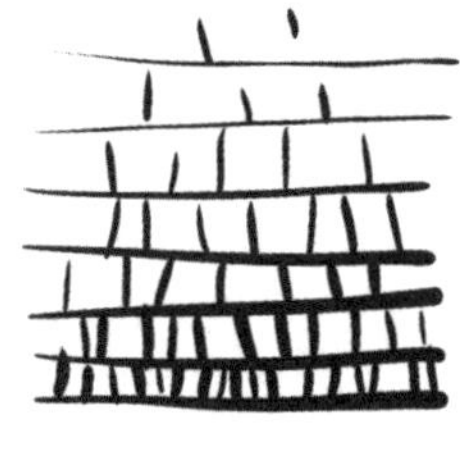 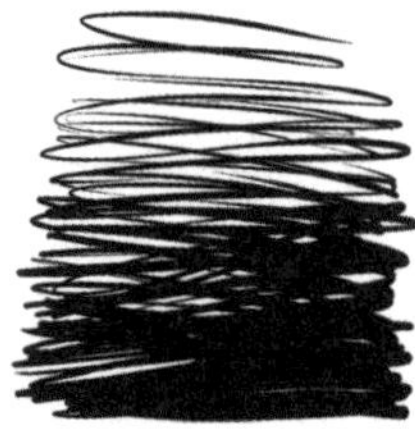 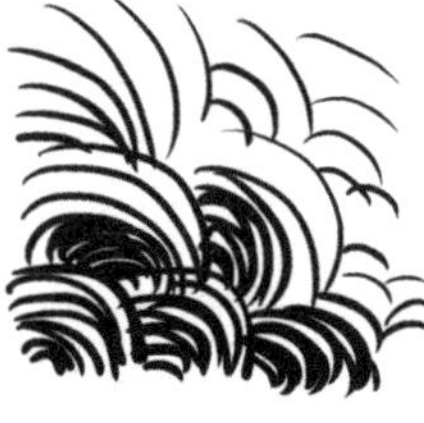 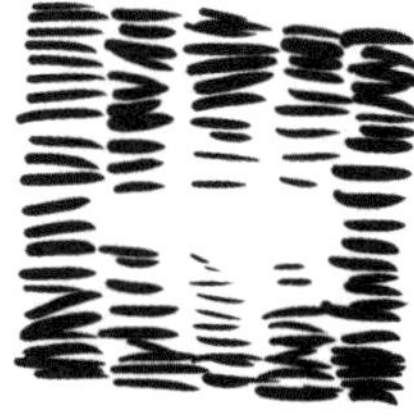

SQUARES   BRICKS   SCRIBBLES   WAVES   BROKEN LINES

It's vital to consider the light and how it falls on elements within a scene. This is all about **CLARITY** and **READABILITY**.

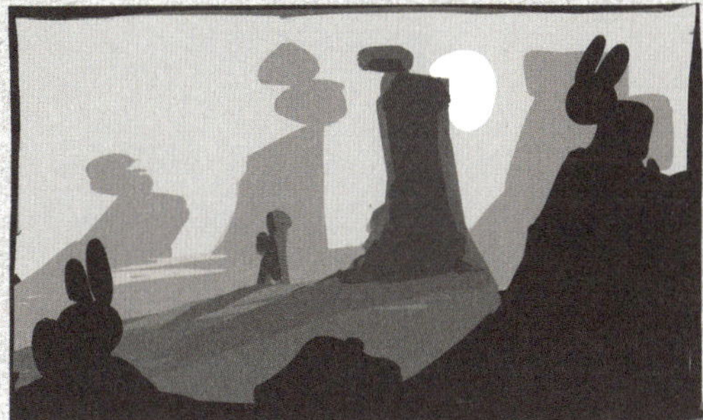

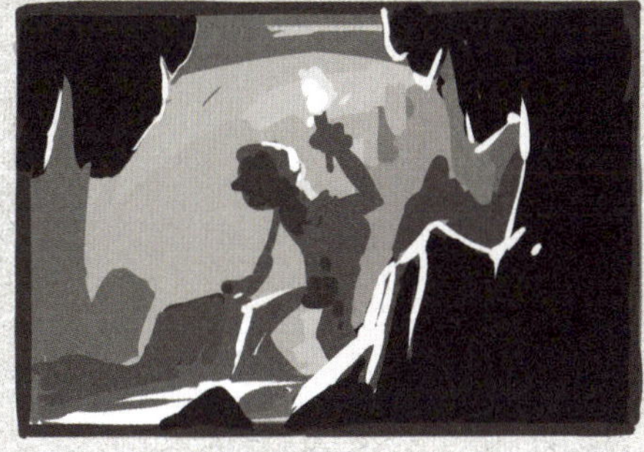

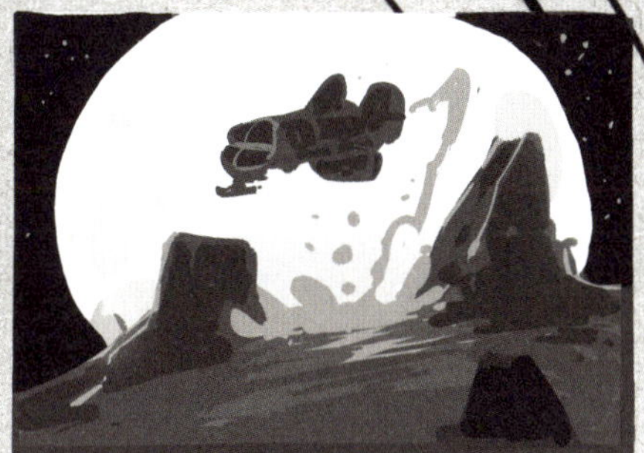

We can understand about five elements at once in an illustration. To prevent the number of tones from appearing overwhelming, try to group them so only a few dominate.

The centre of interest will be the area of greatest contrast. Grouping your tones will help to convey that hierarchy.

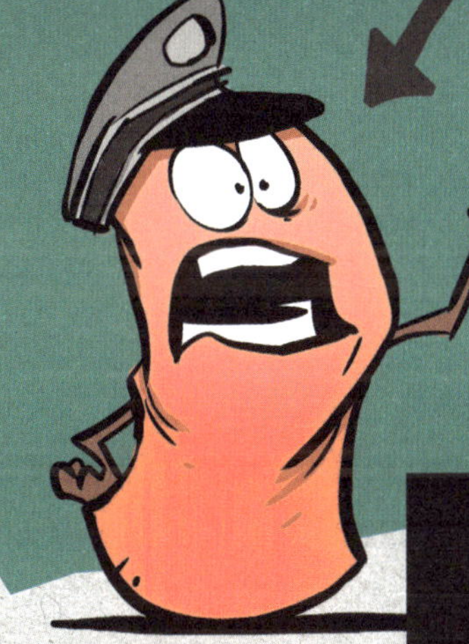

USE VALUE TO DIFFERENTIATE BETWEEN THE FOREGROUND, MIDDLE GROUND, AND BACKGROUND.

Including dark values in harmony with light values in your artwork will appear pleasing to the eye.

COLOUR THEORY

The colour wheel has been around since 1666 when Sir Isaac Newton discovered the visible spectrum of light. Artists and designers use the colour wheel for mixing and to create palettes and harmonies.

Mixing all three primaries or secondaries, two complementary colours, or all colours, will create a neutral colour, such as grey or brown.

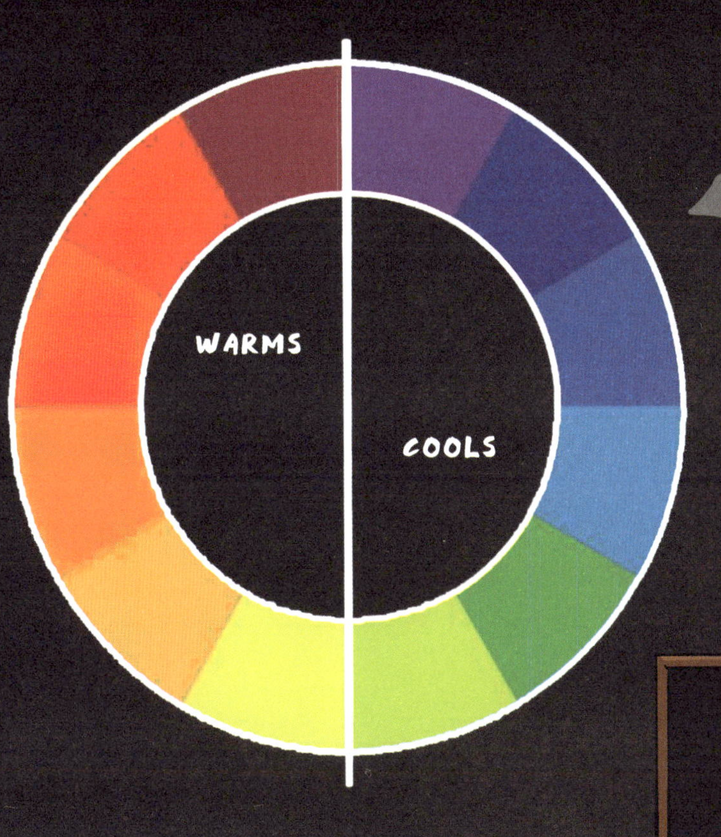

If we draw a line through the centre of the wheel, you will see the separation between the warm colours (reds, oranges, and yellows) and the cool colours (blues, greens, and purples).

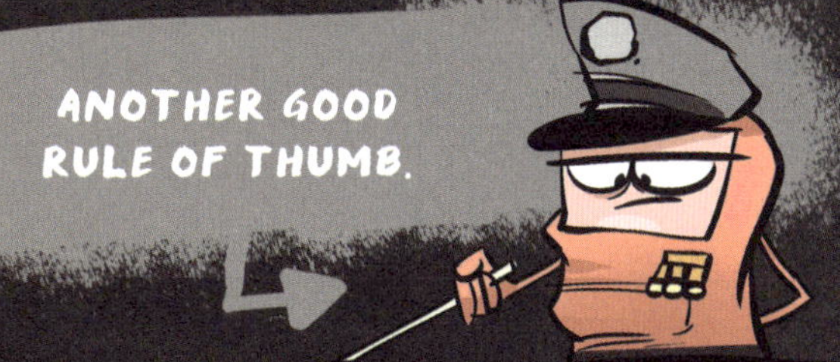

WARMER COLOURS ARE VIVID AND ENERGETIC, AND ADVANCE IN SPACE.

COOLER COLOURS TEND TO FEEL CALM AND SOOTHING, AND RECEDE IN SPACE.

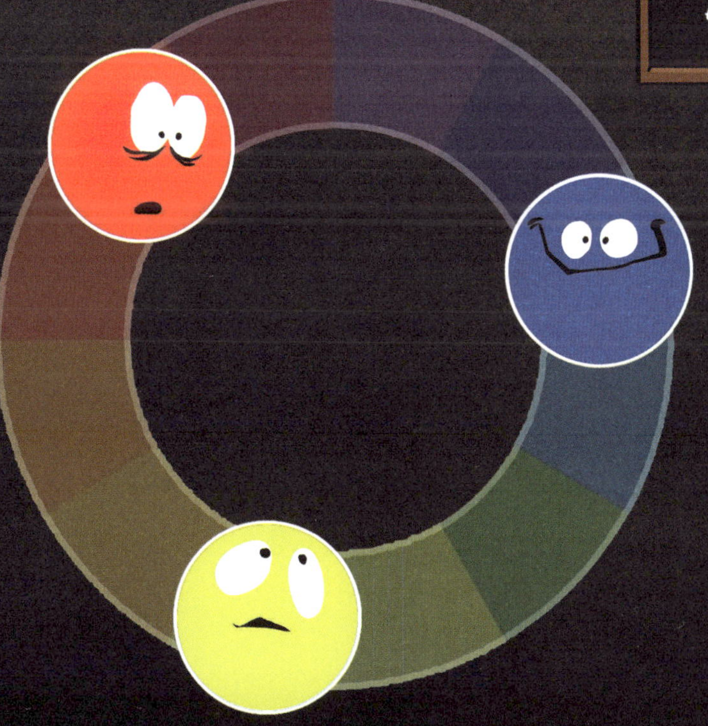

PRIMARY COLOURS

The wheel consists of three primary colours. These colours are mixed to create **ALL** other colours.

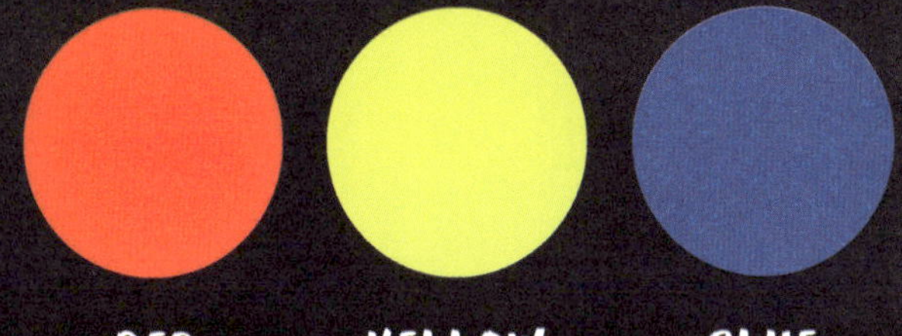

SECONDARY COLOURS

These are created when primary colours are mixed together.

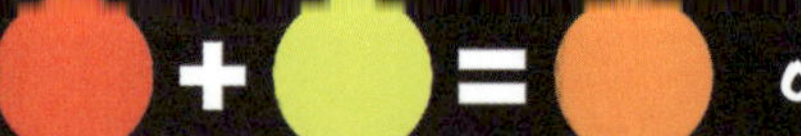

🔴 **+** 🟡 **=** 🟠 ORANGE

🟡 **+** 🔵 **=** 🟢 GREEN

🔵 **+** 🔴 **=** 🟣 PURPLE

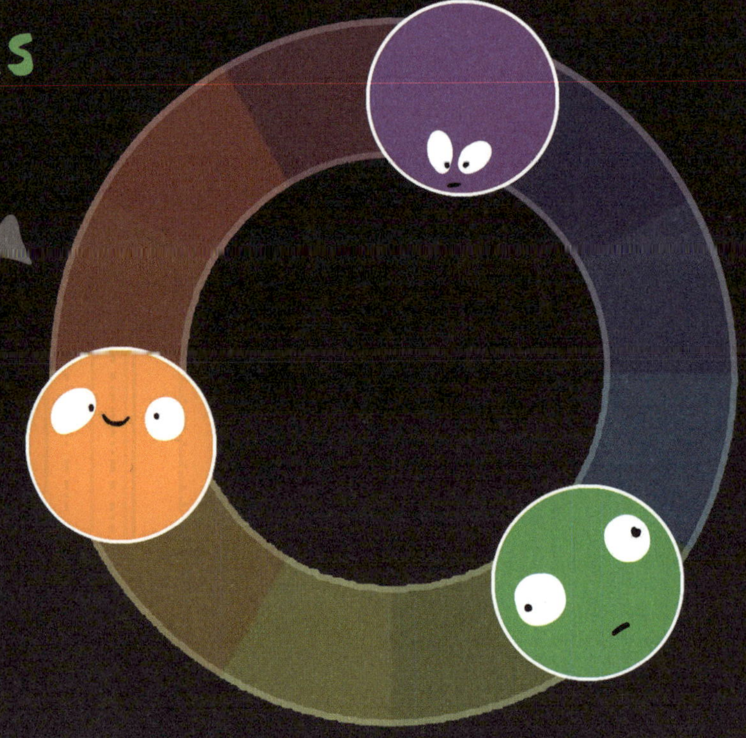

TERTIARY COLOURS

These are made by combining primary and secondary colours.

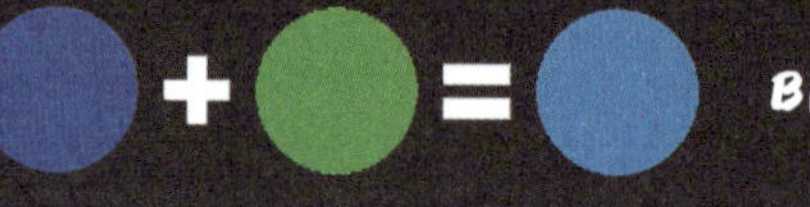

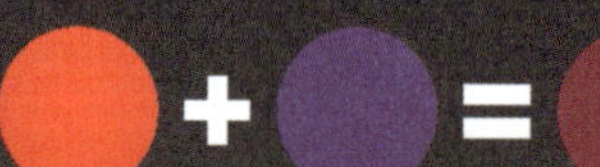
🔵 **+** 🟢 **=** 🔵 BLUE GREEN

🔵 **+** 🟣 **=** 🔵 BLUE VIOLET

🔴 **+** 🟣 **=** 🔴 RED VIOLET

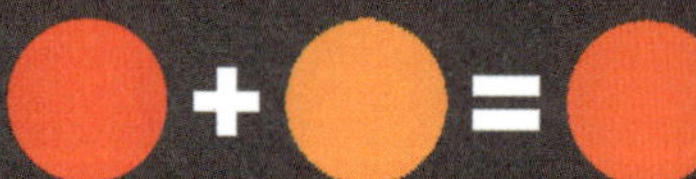
🔴 **+** 🟠 **=** 🔴 RED ORANGE

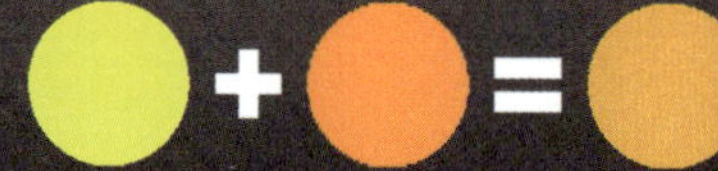
🟡 **+** 🟠 **=** 🟠 YELLOW ORANGE

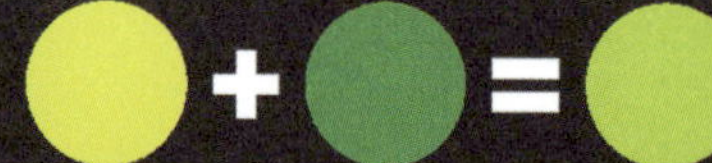
🟡 **+** 🟢 **=** 🟢 YELLOW GREEN

COLOURS CAN SYMBOLIZE DIFFERENT MOODS & FEELINGS

PASSION
ANGER
BLOOD
RAGE
DANGER
IMPULSIVE

CREATIVE
OPTIMISTIC
AGGRESSIVE
IMPULSIVE
CAUTIOUS
EXPRESSIVE

FUN
HUMOUR
SUN
WARM
PLAYFUL
CHILDLIKE

GROWTH
NATURE
FRESH
YOUNG
NEW
HEALTHY

CALM
PEACE
SKY OR WATER
EMOTIONAL
DEPTH
POSITIVE

INTUITION
IMAGINATION
MEDITATION
TRANQUILLITY
ARTISTIC

LIGHT
SPIRITUALITY
PURE
COLD

MYSTERIOUS
DARK
HEAVY
DEPTH
SHADOW
UNKNOWN

EARTH
SOIL
NEW BEGINNING
DIRT
DEAD

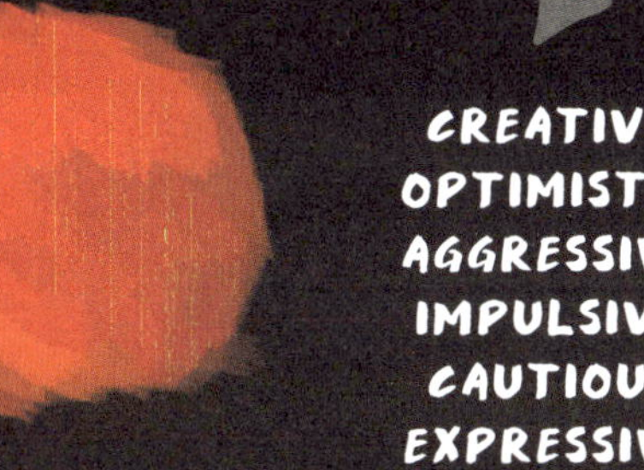
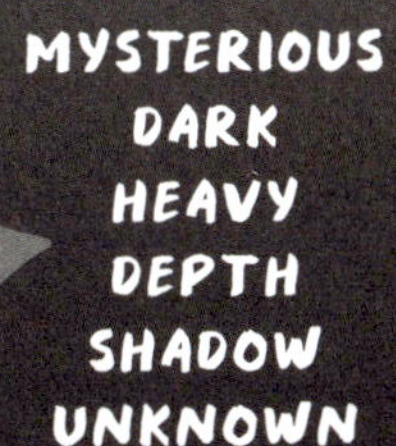

HUE

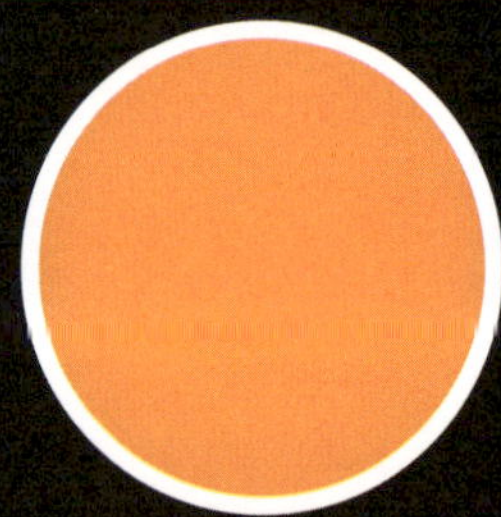

★ Hue is also known as 'pure colour'.

★ All tints, tones, and shades are variations of that hue.

★ Intensity is the brightness, or saturation, of that colour. A colour is at full intensity only when pure and unmixed.

TINT

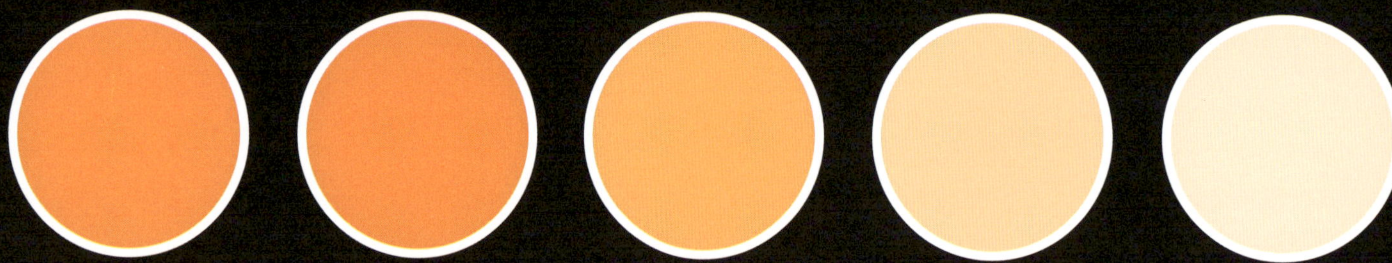

★ Tint is adding white to a hue.

★ The more white you add, the higher the colour will appear on the value scale.

★ This will make the colour high key.

TONE

★ Tone is adding grey to a hue.

★ The more grey you add, the darker the hue will be.

★ This will make the colour subtler and less intense.

SHADE

★ Shade is adding black to a hue.

★ The more black you add, the lower the colour will appear on the value scale. This will make the colour low key.

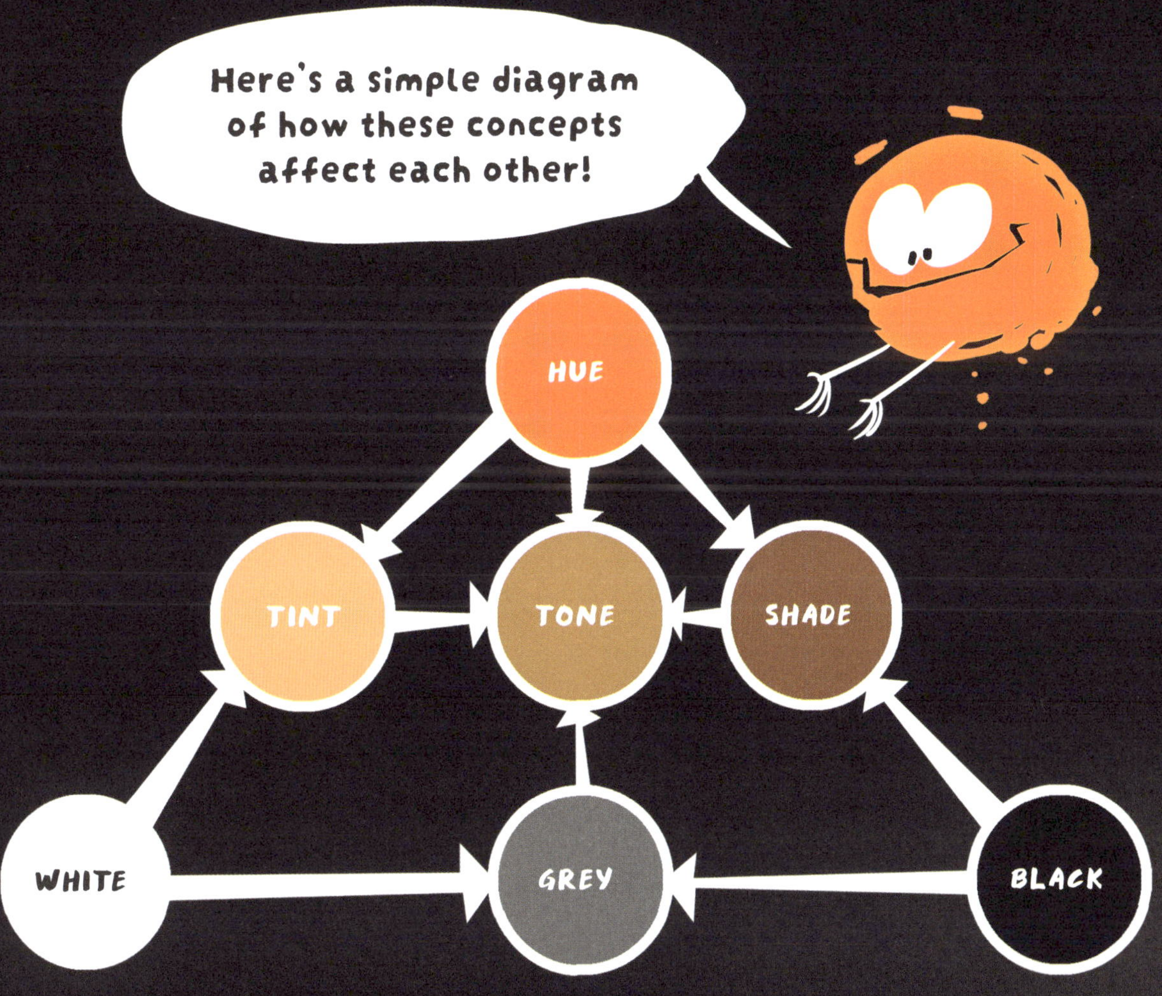

COLOUR SCHEMES

Colour schemes are combinations of colours used in a design. Different combinations will evoke different moods.

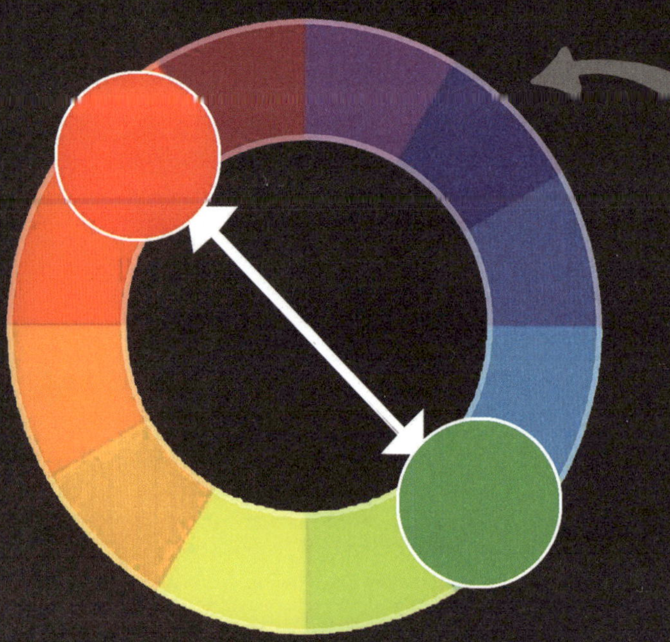

COMPLEMENTARY

★ Opposites on the colour wheel, such as **RED** and **GREEN** or **BLUE** and **ORANGE**.

★ When placed next to each other, they intensify each other's brightness.

★ The high contrast of complementary colours creates a vibrant look, especially when used at full saturation.

★ Complementary colour schemes work well when you want something to stand out.

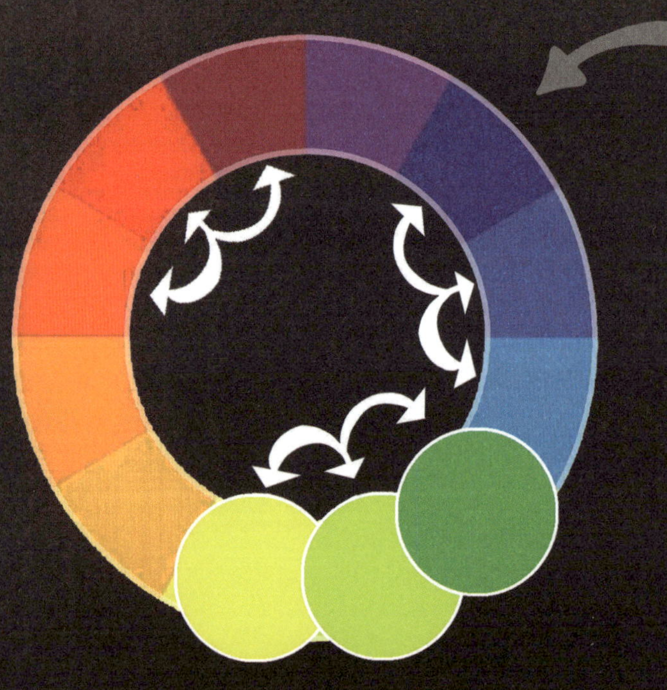

ANALOGOUS

★ Analogous colours sit next to (or near) each other on the colour wheel.

★ One colour should dominate, one will support, and one will accent.

★ They usually match well and create comfortable designs.

★ Often found in nature, they are harmonious and pleasing to the eye.

★ Make sure you have enough contrast when choosing an analogous colour scheme.

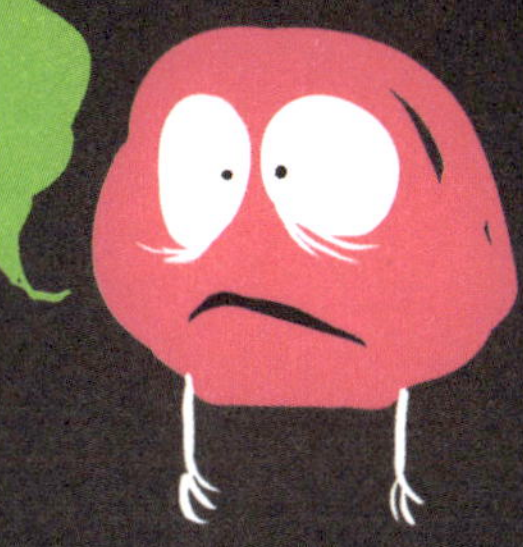

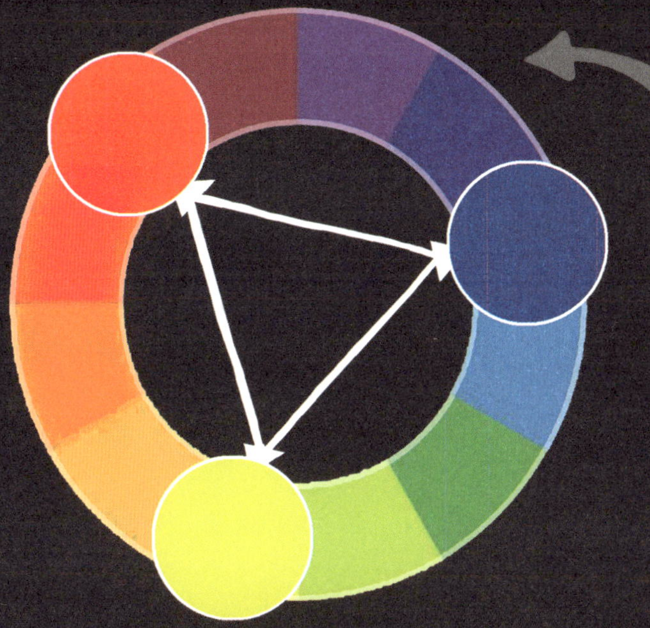

TRIADIC

★ Colours that are evenly spaced around the colour wheel.

★ Triadic colour schemes tend to be quite vibrant and dynamic, even if you use unsaturated versions of the hues.

★ Let one colour dominate and use the other two as accents.

★ Creates visual contrast and harmony.

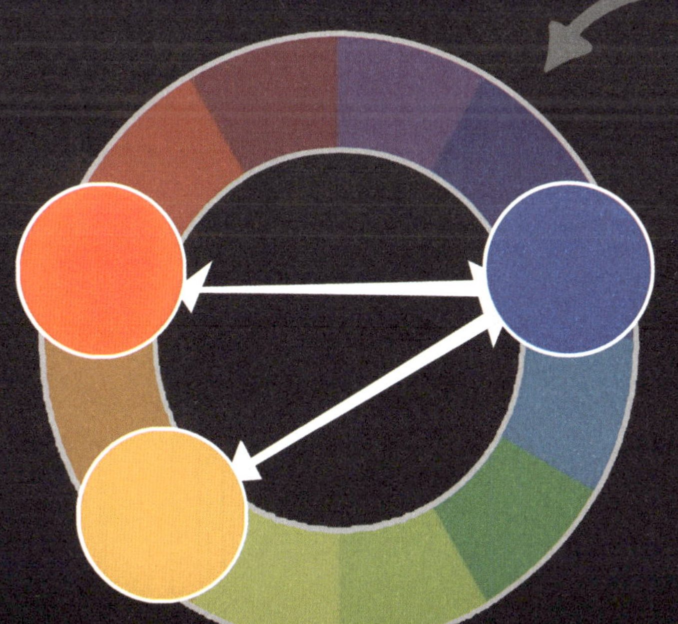

SPLIT COMPLEMENTARY

★ A variation of the complementary colour scheme. In addition to the main base colour, it uses the two colours adjacent to its complementary colour.

★ It has strong visual contrast and harmony.

★ The split complementary colour scheme is often a good choice for beginners, because it is difficult to mess up.

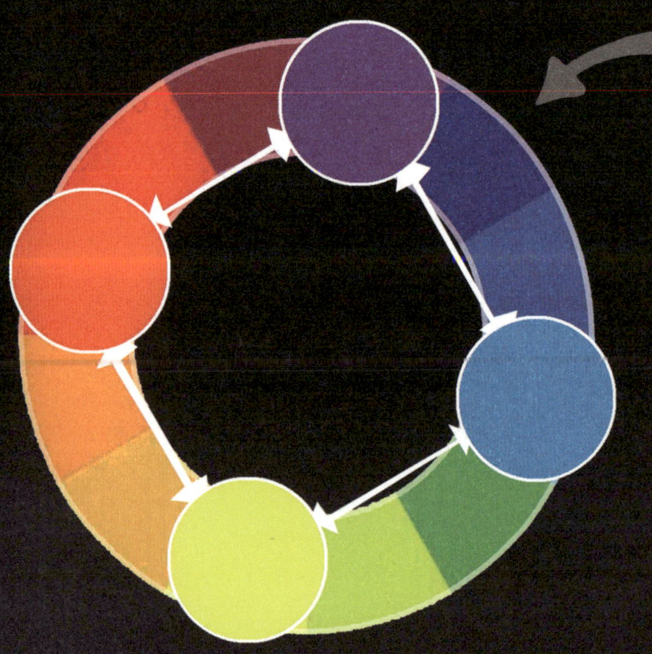

SQUARED OFF

- ★ All four colours are spaced evenly around the colour wheel.

- ★ Let one colour be dominant.

- ★ You should also pay attention to the balance between warm and cool colours in your design.

RECTANGLE VARIATION

- ★ Uses four colours arranged into two complementary pairs.

- ✹ This rich colour scheme offers plenty of possibilities for variation.

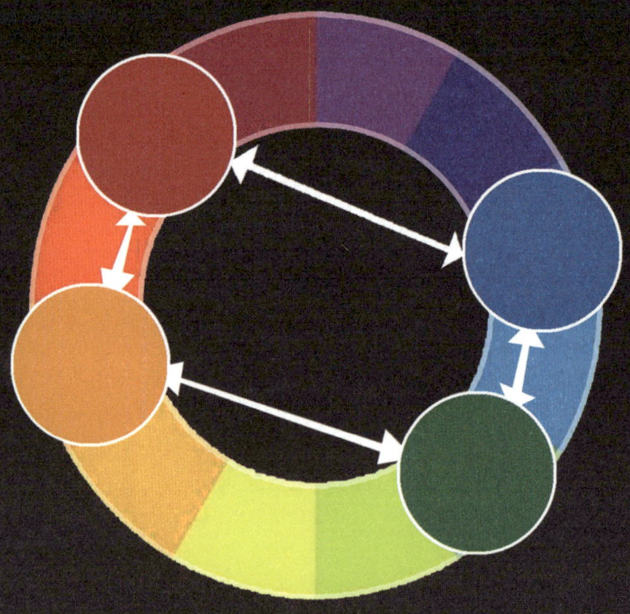

MONOCHROMATIC

- ★ Shades and/or tint variations of the same hue.

- ★ Unity is one of the benefits.

- ✹ Using sharp contrast can help keep the design interesting.

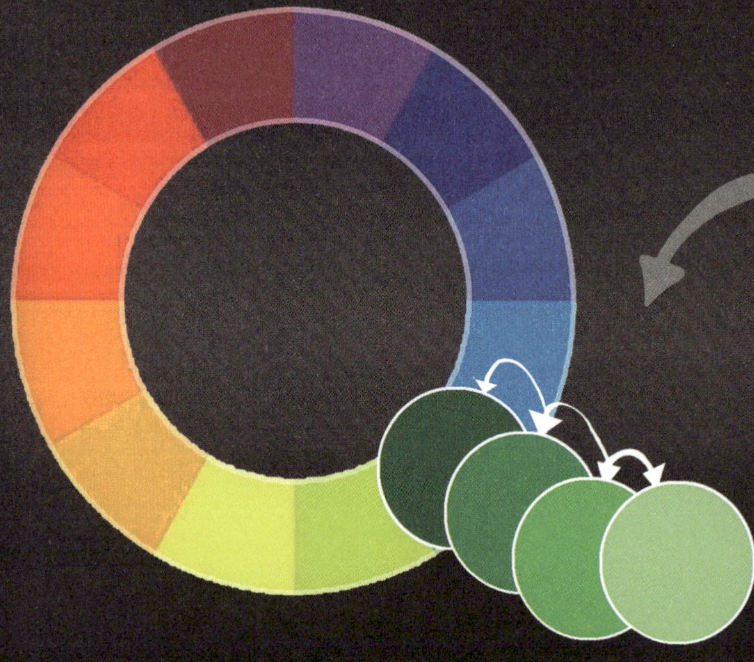

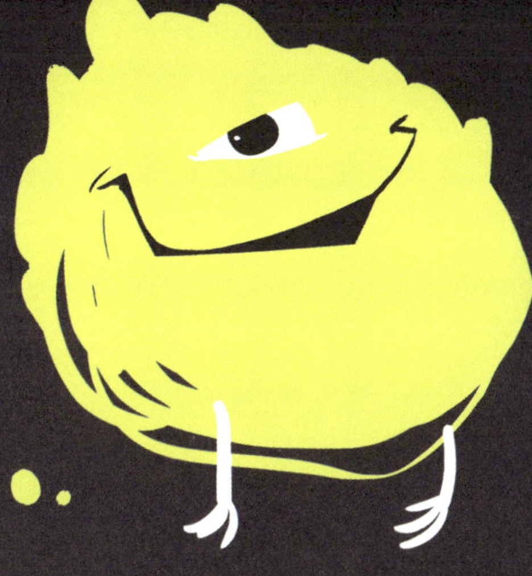

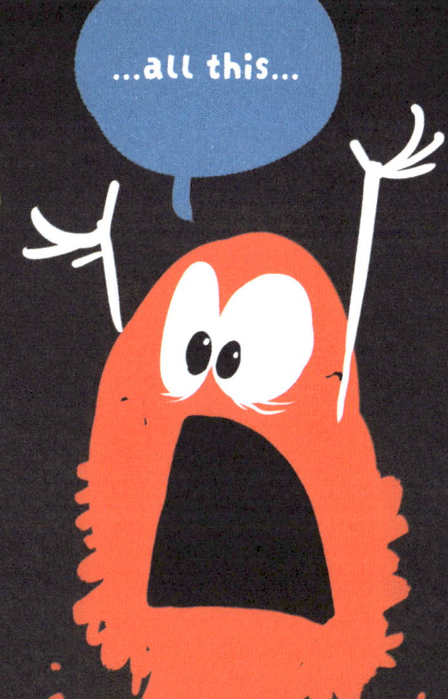

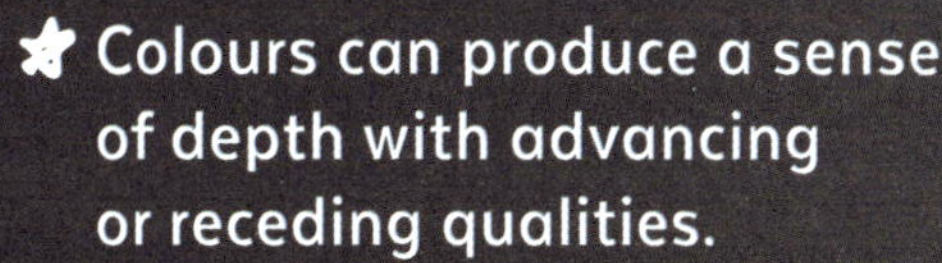

★ Colours can be purely subjective or objective, depending on how they are used.

*SUBJECTIVE is when the artist imparts a mood or feeling through colours.

*OBJECTIVE is to render as close to reality of what appears to the eye.

★ Artists can use any colour arbitrarily.

★ Colour can be used as emphasis, to steer the viewer to one specific part of a painting or design, or to guide the eye through the design as a whole.

★ Colours can produce a sense of depth with advancing or receding qualities.

*In terms of spatial illusion, dust in the earth's atmosphere breaks up the colour rays from distant objects and makes them appear bluish. As objects recede, colours become more neutral and bluish.

★ Objects that are closer possess more contrasting colours than those that are further away.

★ Colour discord is when two colours are used together in an attempt to make the viewer feel uneasy.

PERSPECTIVE

This is the art of making 2D art look 3D.
It's also a way to live life...

TERMINOLOGY

OBSERVER/CAMERA

Every image is seen from a point of view.
In still life, we are essentially seeing the
scene through the artist as observer.

In film, TV, storyboards, and comics, the
observer is usually a camera, and we
view scenes from all sorts of angles!

THE PICTURE PLANE

The picture plane sits out in front of the
observer. It's normally the physical surface
of the painting or an imaginary piece of
glass that follows where your eyes look.

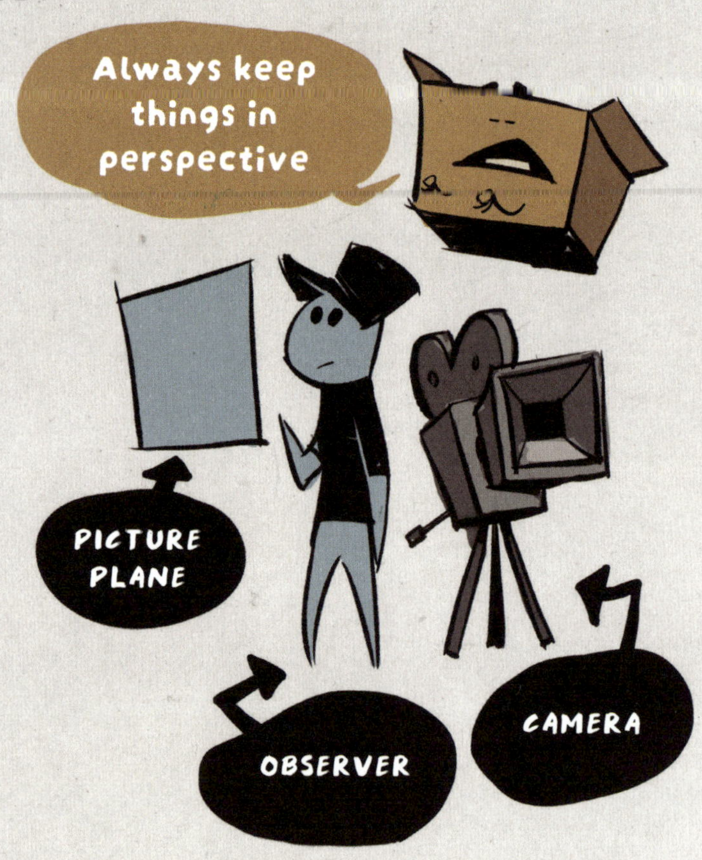

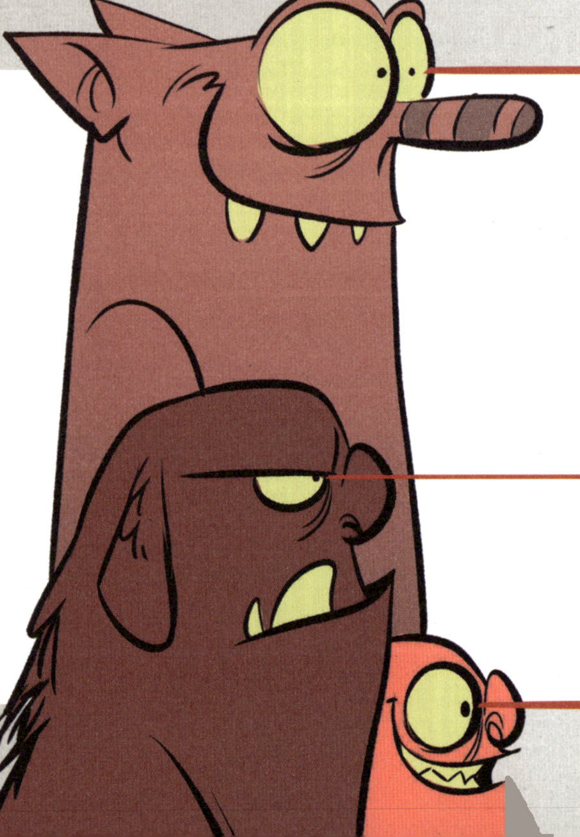

THE HORIZON LINE

The horizon line is the imaginary line that
extends from the plane of your eyes to where
the earth meets the sky. Eye level is the height
of the observer's eyes from the ground.

The horizon line helps guide us with objects.

If an object sits below the horizon line, you will see
the top of it. If an object sits above the horizon
line, you will see beneath it. And if it's sitting in
the middle, you won't see either its top or base.

THE VANISHING POINT

The vanishing point is where all parallel lines appear to move towards one spot, or convergence point, which can sit anywhere on the horizon line.

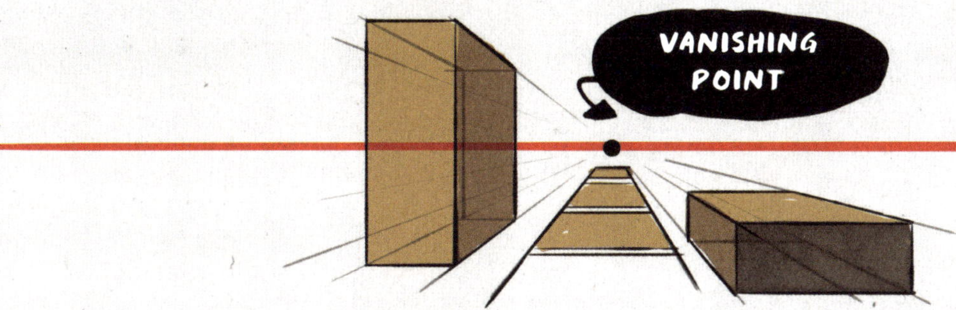

Objects grow smaller as they get further away, until they all appear to fit into a single point. This is what we call the 'vanishing point'.

Objects further away from you will appear smaller and closer together than those nearer to you.

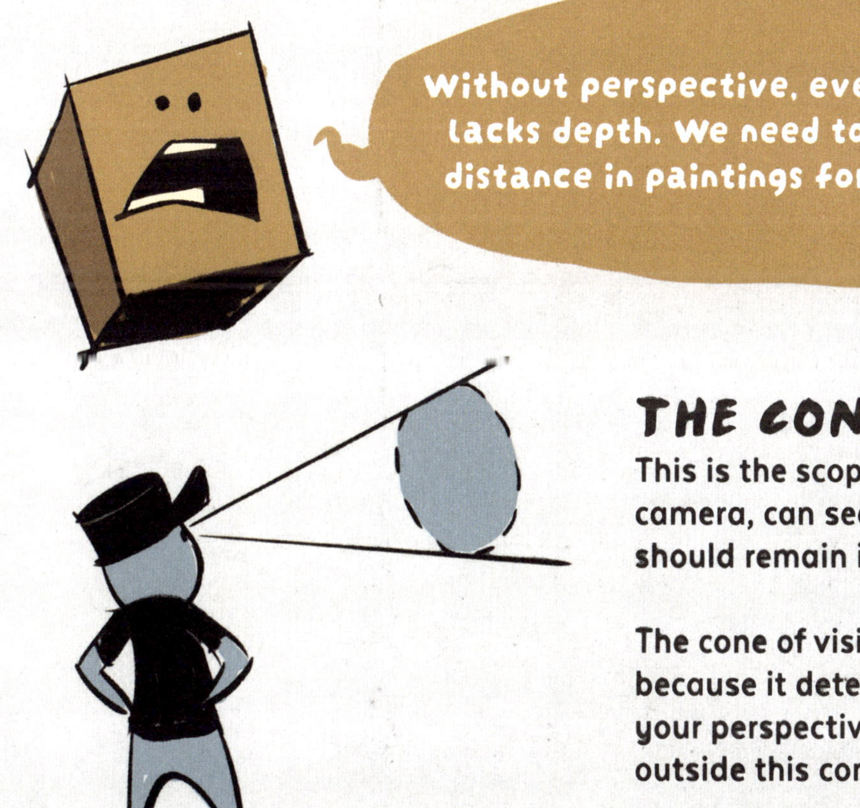

THE CONE OF VISION

This is the scope of what the observer, or camera, can see clearly. Your cone of vision should remain in your picture plane.

The cone of vision is important because it determines what will be in your perspective drawing. Drawing outside this cone creates distortion.

ONE-POINT PERSPECTIVE

One-point perspective is when you have a single vanishing point in a drawing. You can only draw an object in one-point perspective if the object is near (or in the middle of) the observer's field of vision. If the object begins to stray too far outside of the cone of vision's centre, the object will begin to appear in two-point or three-point perspective instead.

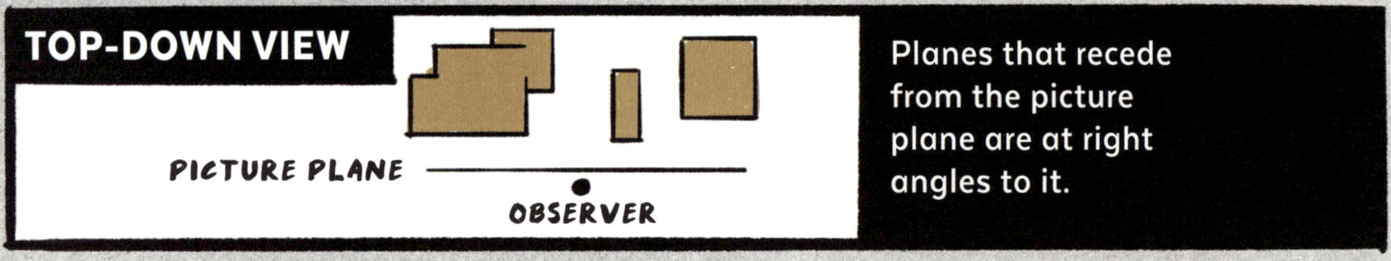

Each image shows the horizon line (**HL**) and vanishing point (**VP**).

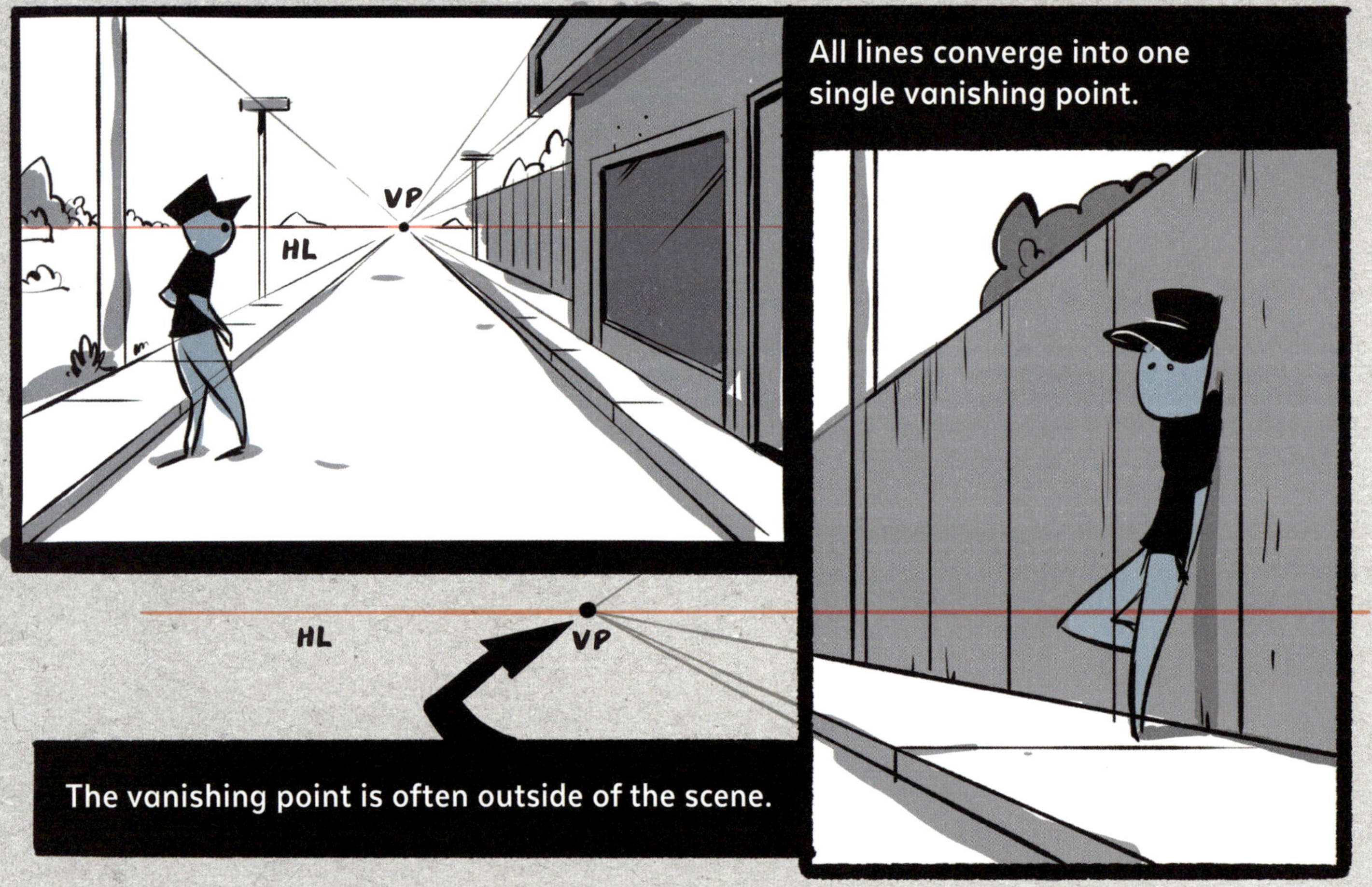

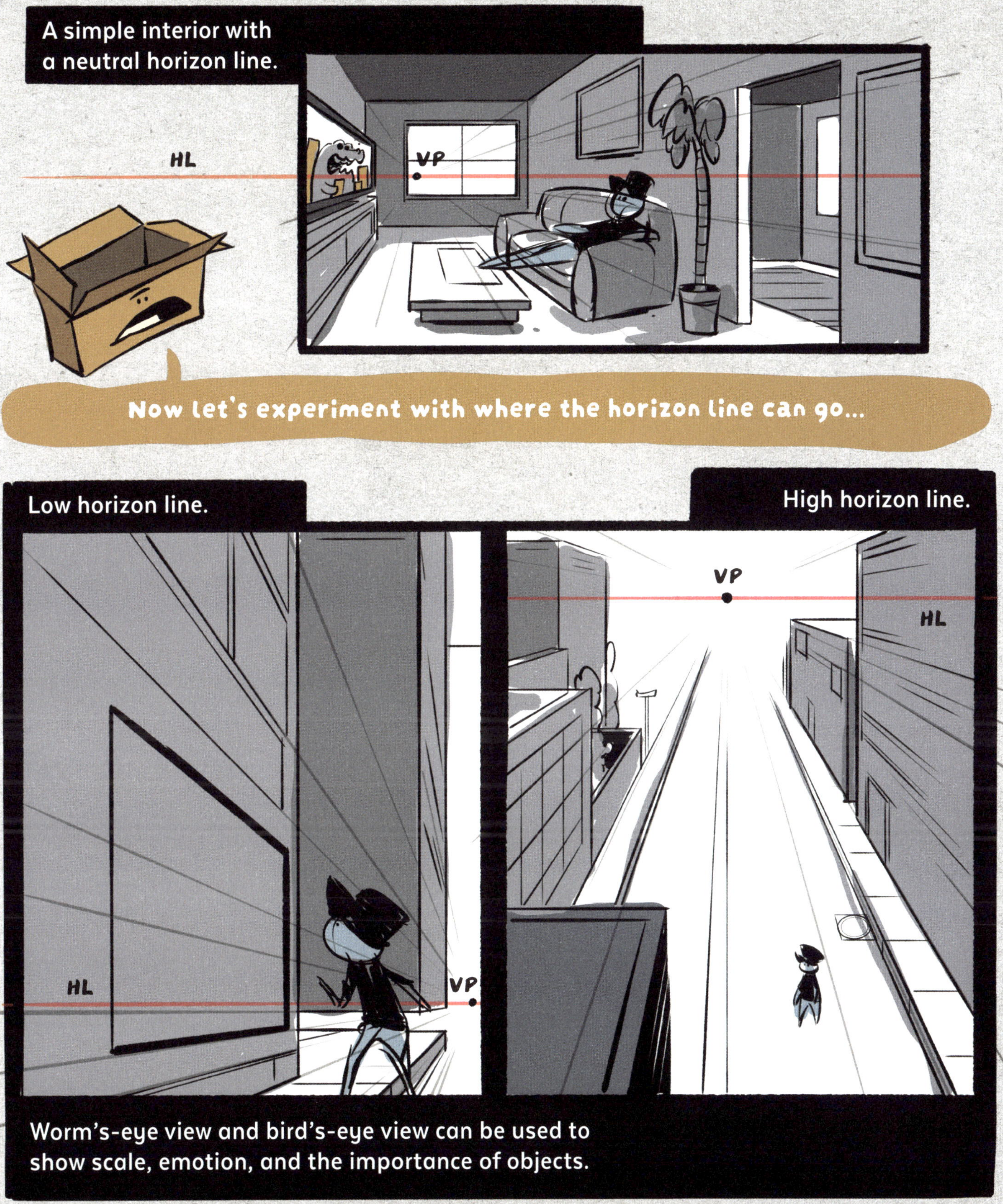

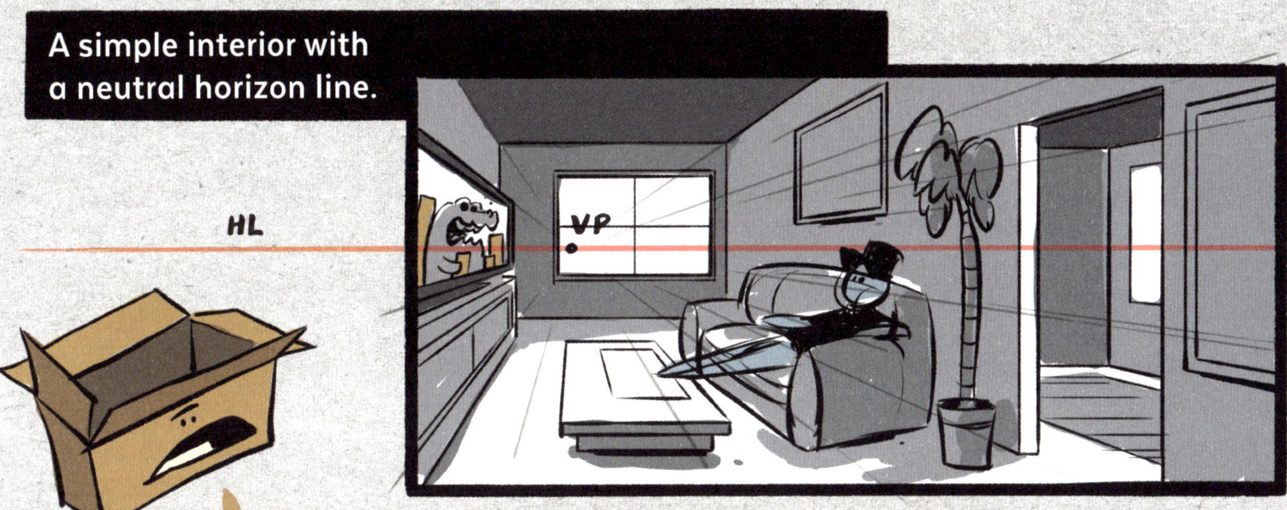

Low horizon line.

High horizon line.

Worm's-eye view and bird's-eye view can be used to show scale, emotion, and the importance of objects.

TWO-POINT PERSPECTIVE

Two-point perspective, also called angular perspective, is when two vanishing points are placed on the horizon line. The perspective lines run in two different directions, or angles, to these vanishing points. This is used when the angles of objects require more than one vanishing point.

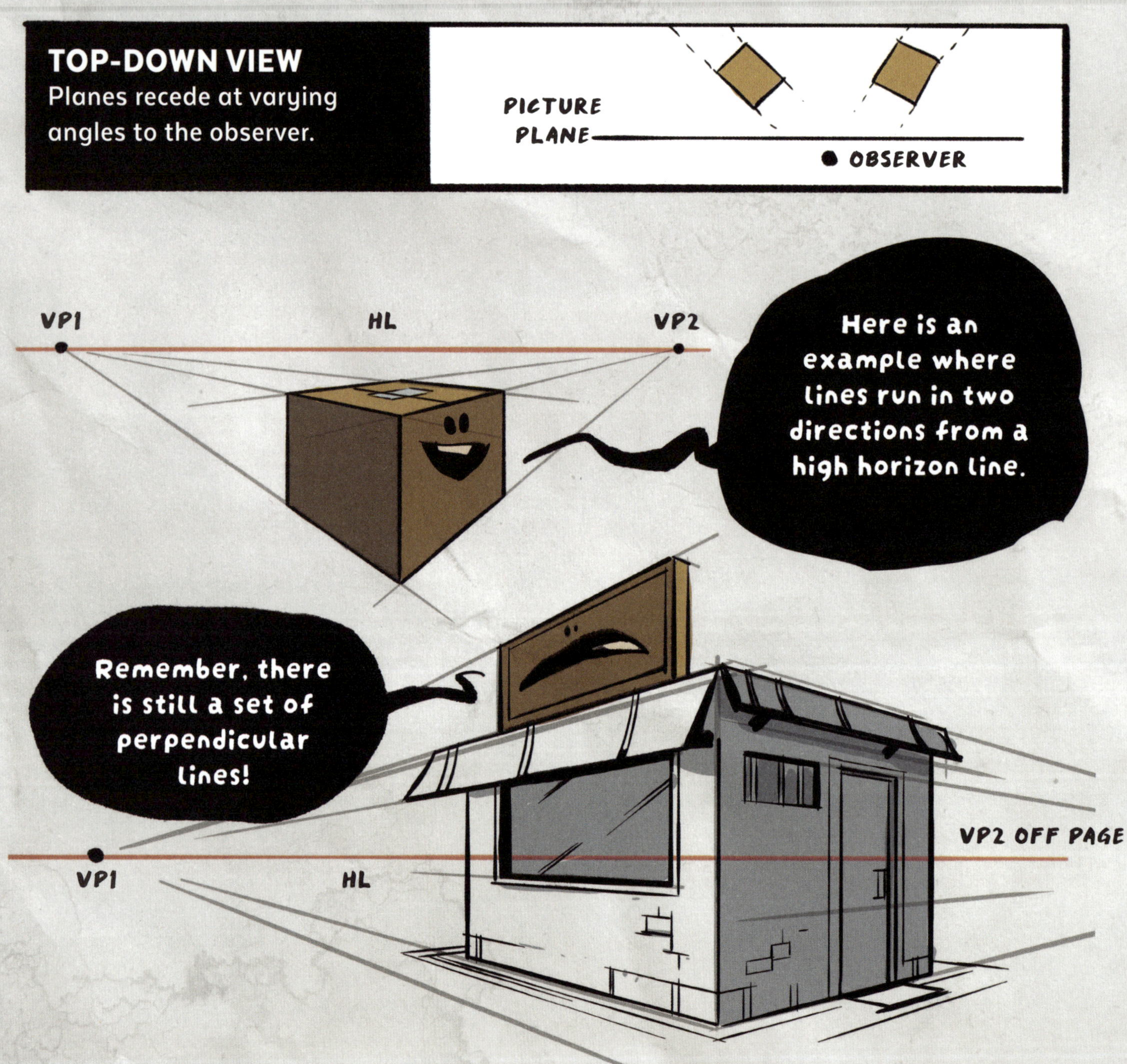

THREE-POINT PERSPECTIVE

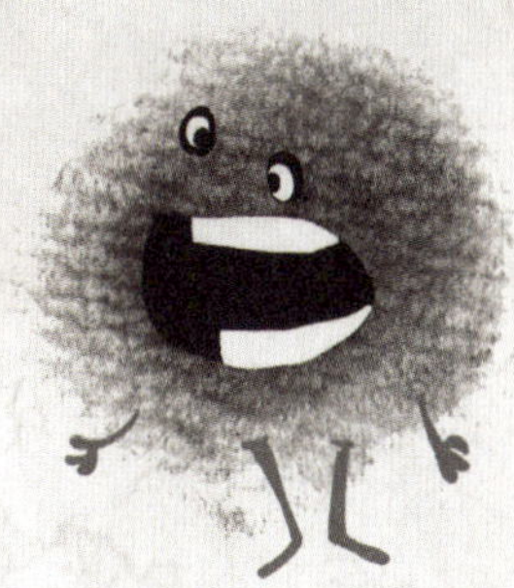

Three-point perspective has, you guessed it, three vanishing points.
Two sit on the horizon line, just like two-point, while the third
vanishing point is located either above or below the horizon line.

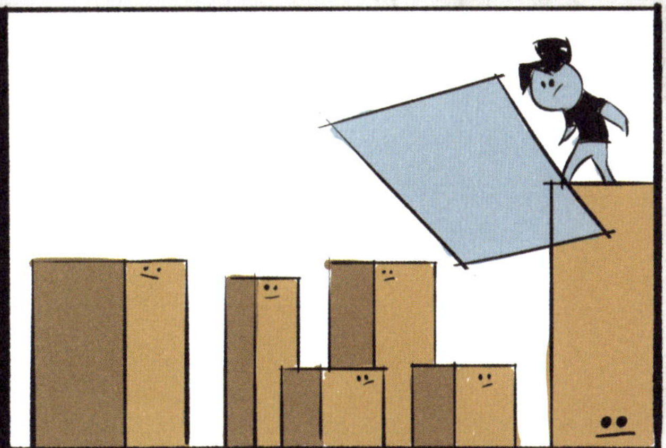

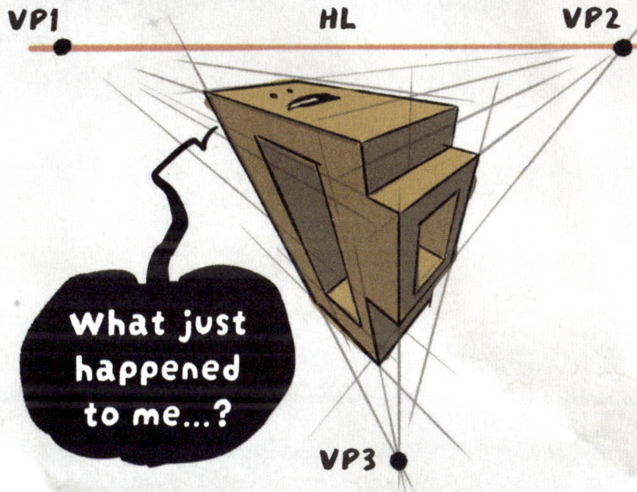

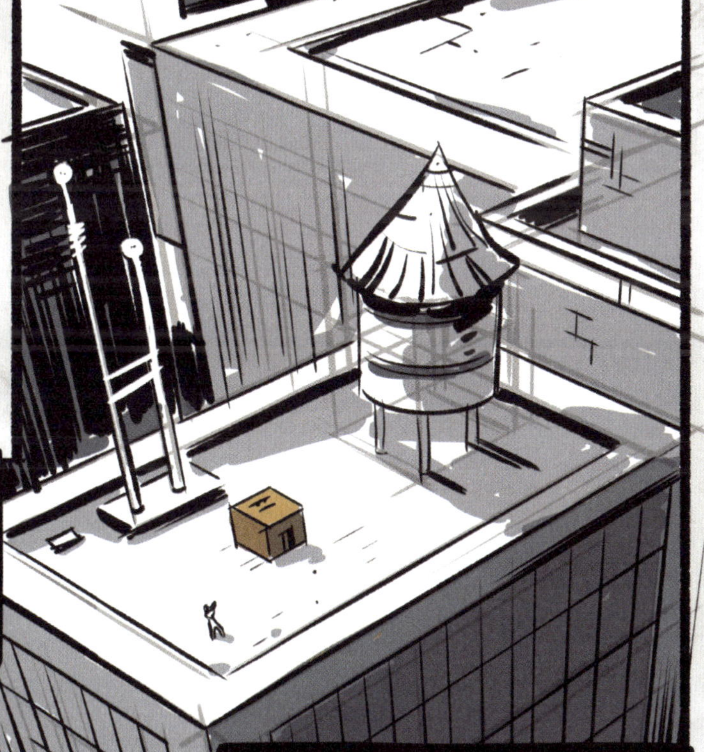

FINAL THOUGHTS

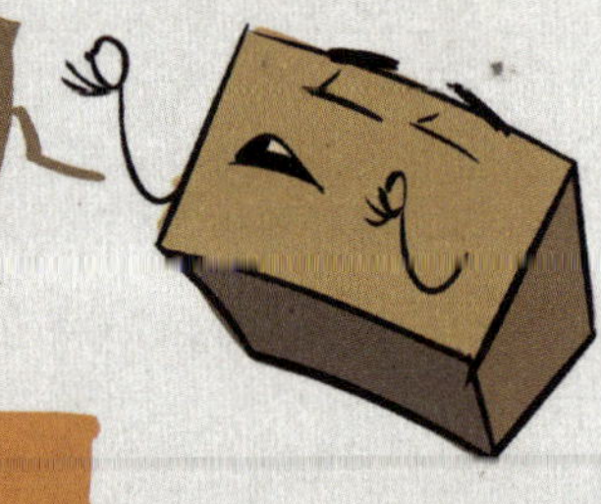

VP1   HL

VP2

TREES & FOLIAGE

Just like all objects, trees and foliage appear in perspective, but they can be very complex and irregular.

Try designing and editing vegetation like any other design. Break it down into simple shapes and find contours above and below your horizon line.

Creating basic contour grids and remembering the general area of the horizon line will allow you to stay loose and organic, the way nature intended.

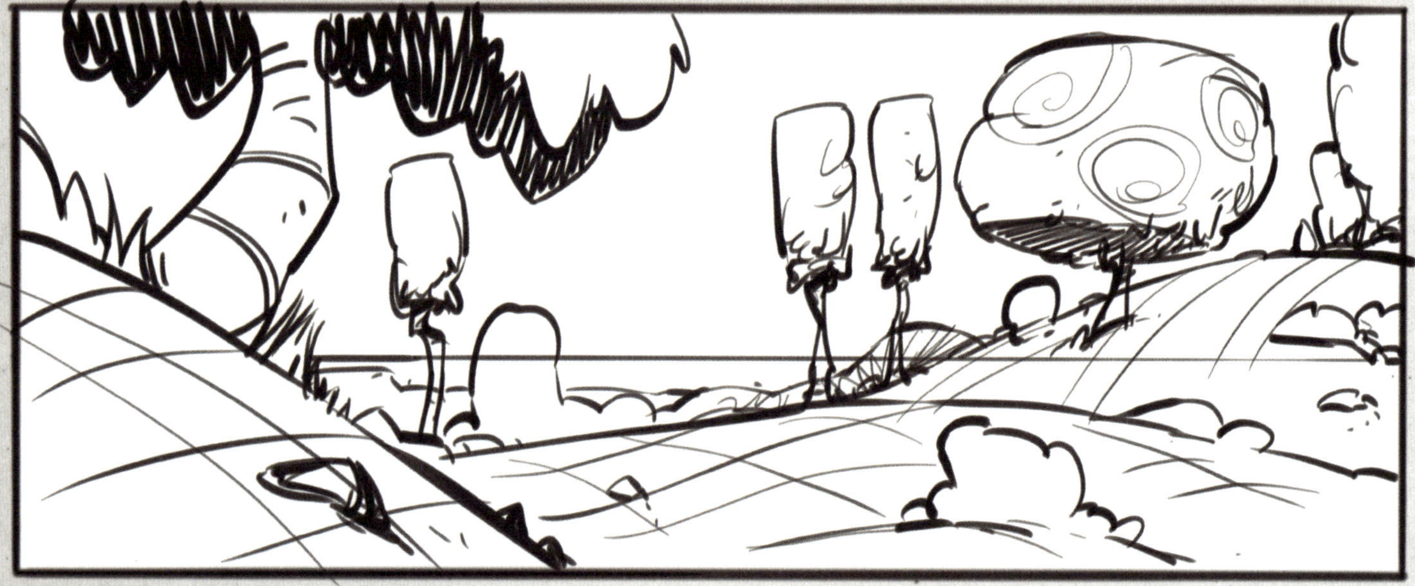

You may find it helpful to draw thumbnails and rough layouts when planning scenes in perspective.

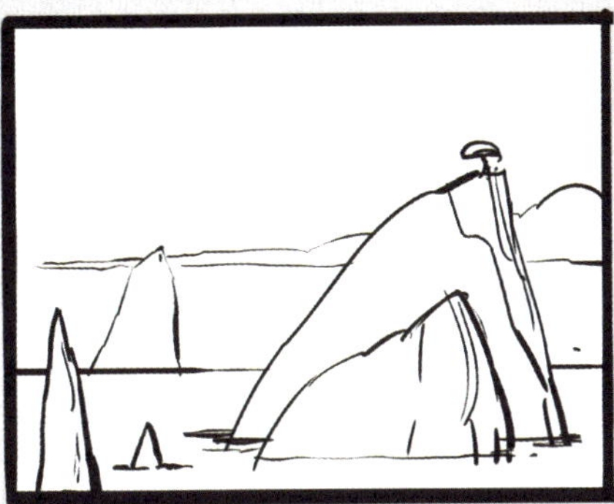
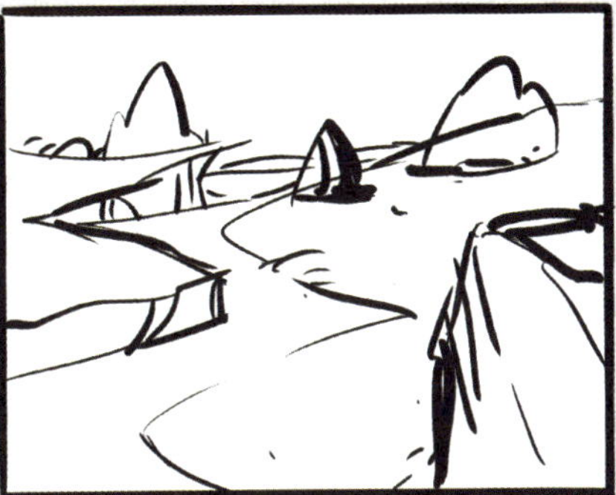
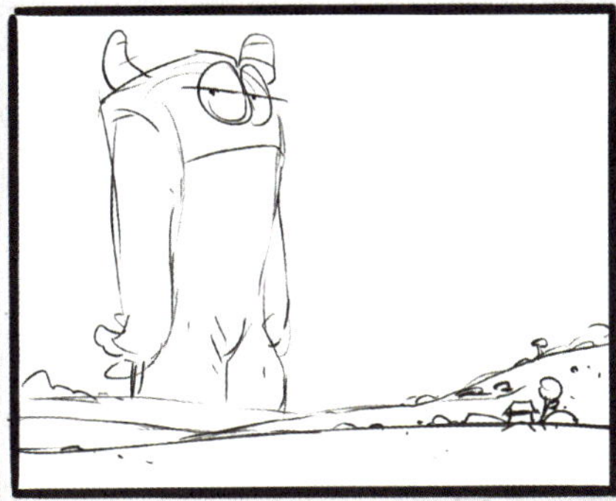

Remember that overlap creates perspective.
It can also be used to lead the viewer's eye.

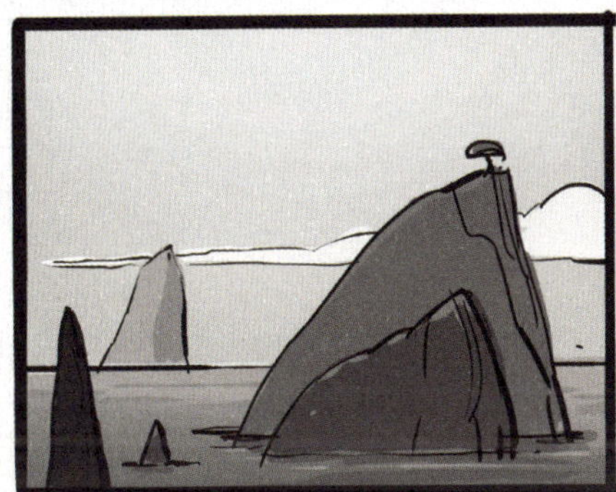
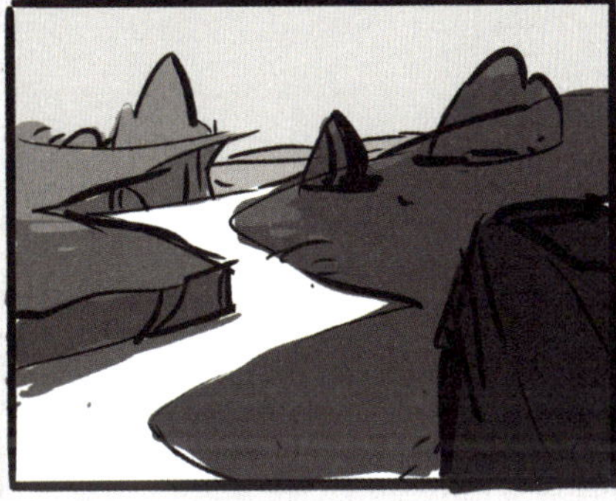
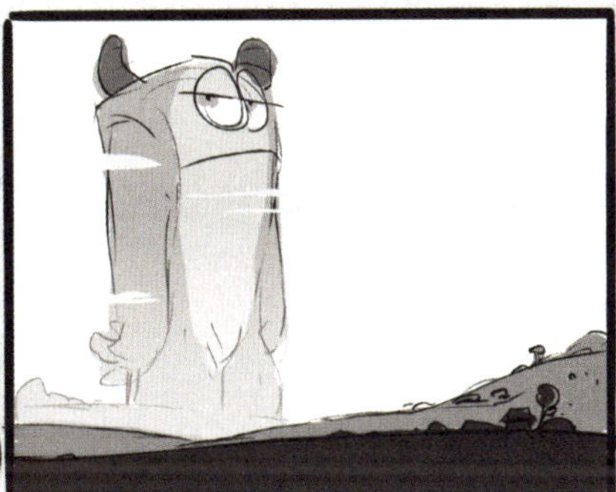

Adding tone will create depth and atmosphere, which is perceptive perspective.*
Distant objects usually appear cooler, greyer, and less detailed. As you get closer to the picture plane, you will notice stronger contrasts and more detail.

FINDING YOUR CENTRE

Drawing diagonal lines from the corners of a square will reveal its centre lines. You can do this the same way in perspective.

And since a circle fits into a square, this works too.

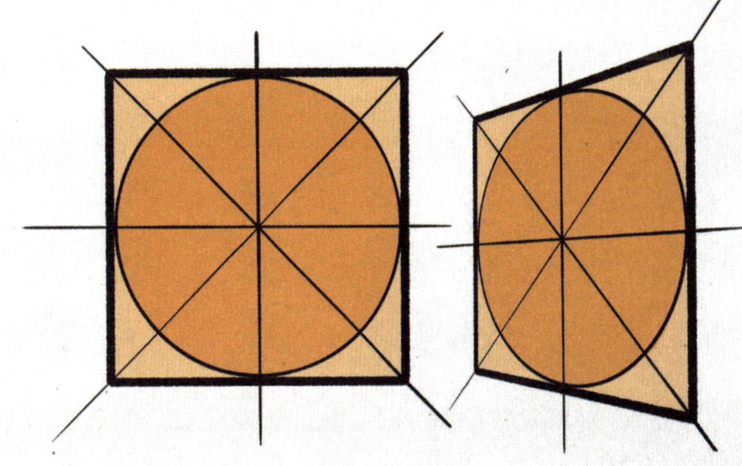

*Try saying that three times fast!

LIGHT & SHADOW

We need light to see!

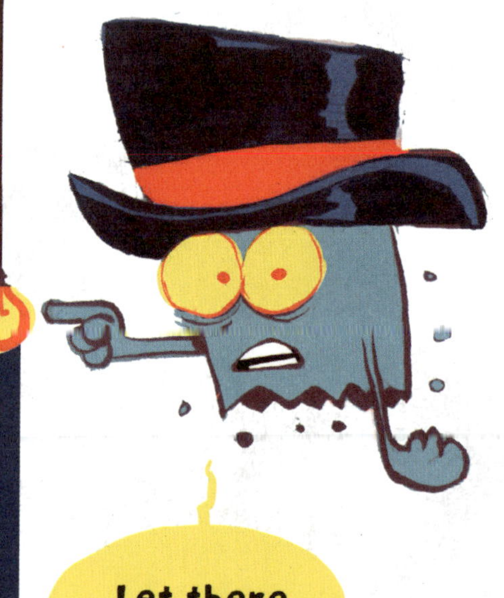

Being able to explain how light moves from light to shadow on an object allows us to see the form of the shape. Learning to see how light and shadow work together is a great way to make anything on a 2D plane of existence feel three-dimensional.

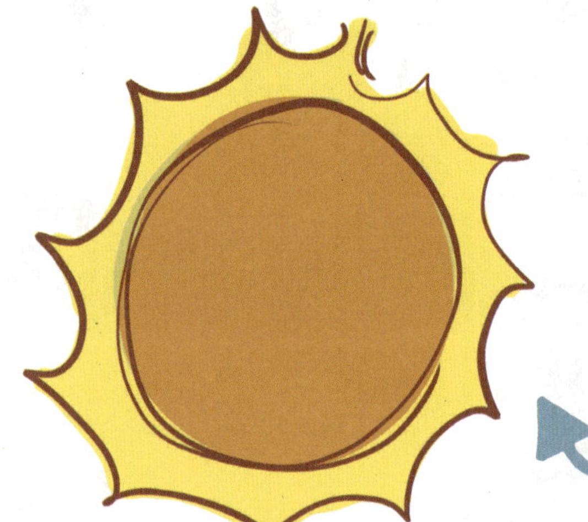

Rays from a light source radiate out in all directions. The sun is our biggest light source, but because it's so far away, its rays are less dramatic until the sun appears inside or near the picture plane (such as sunrises and sunsets).

Artificial light sources, such as lightbulbs, candles, or even mobile phones, are closer and radiate light rays that can set the tone for a scene or design.

Shadows made by the light always form in direct response to the objects the light hits, the angle the light is coming from, and the intensity of the light source. 'Light logic' is the idea that when a single light source shines against a cube, it will make a square shape. On a sphere, it will create an ellipse shape. Sounds logical, right?

HIGHLIGHT: Depending on the surface and what the object is made from, this is the brightest hot spot and moves with the viewer.

DIRECT LIGHT: Where the light hits.

HALFTONE: Where the values darken to the neutral, or local, base colour.

REFLECTED LIGHT: Known as bounce light, this is when the light surrounding an area reflects onto the object. Use this to show forms or remove it to add mood.

SHADOW: A tone between the lightest and darkest parts of the shadow.

CAST SHADOW: The silhouette that the object projects onto a surface. This will change based off the distance and angle of the light source.

CORE SHADOW: The contour of the shadow. This is usually darker because no direct light or reflected light is bouncing onto this part.

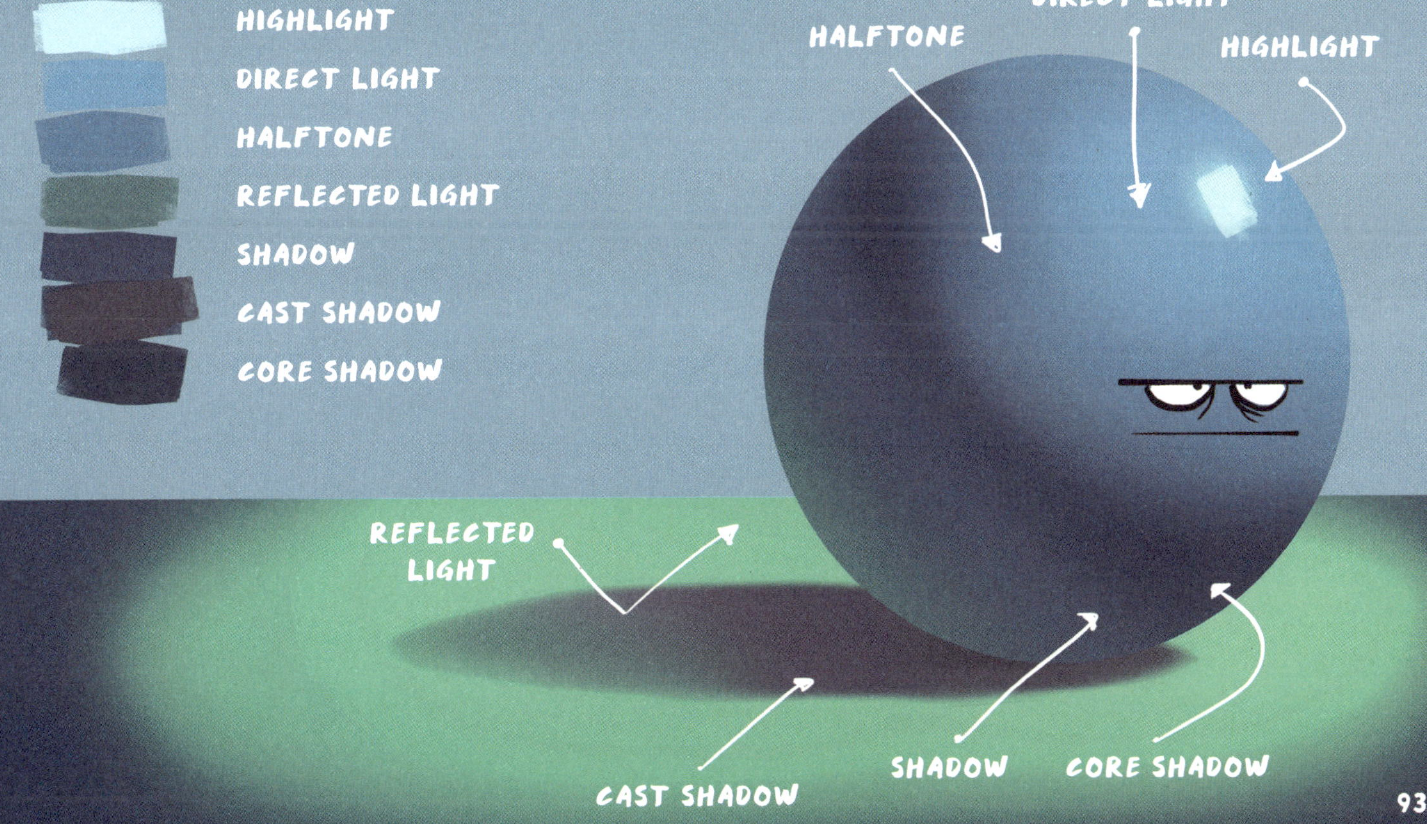

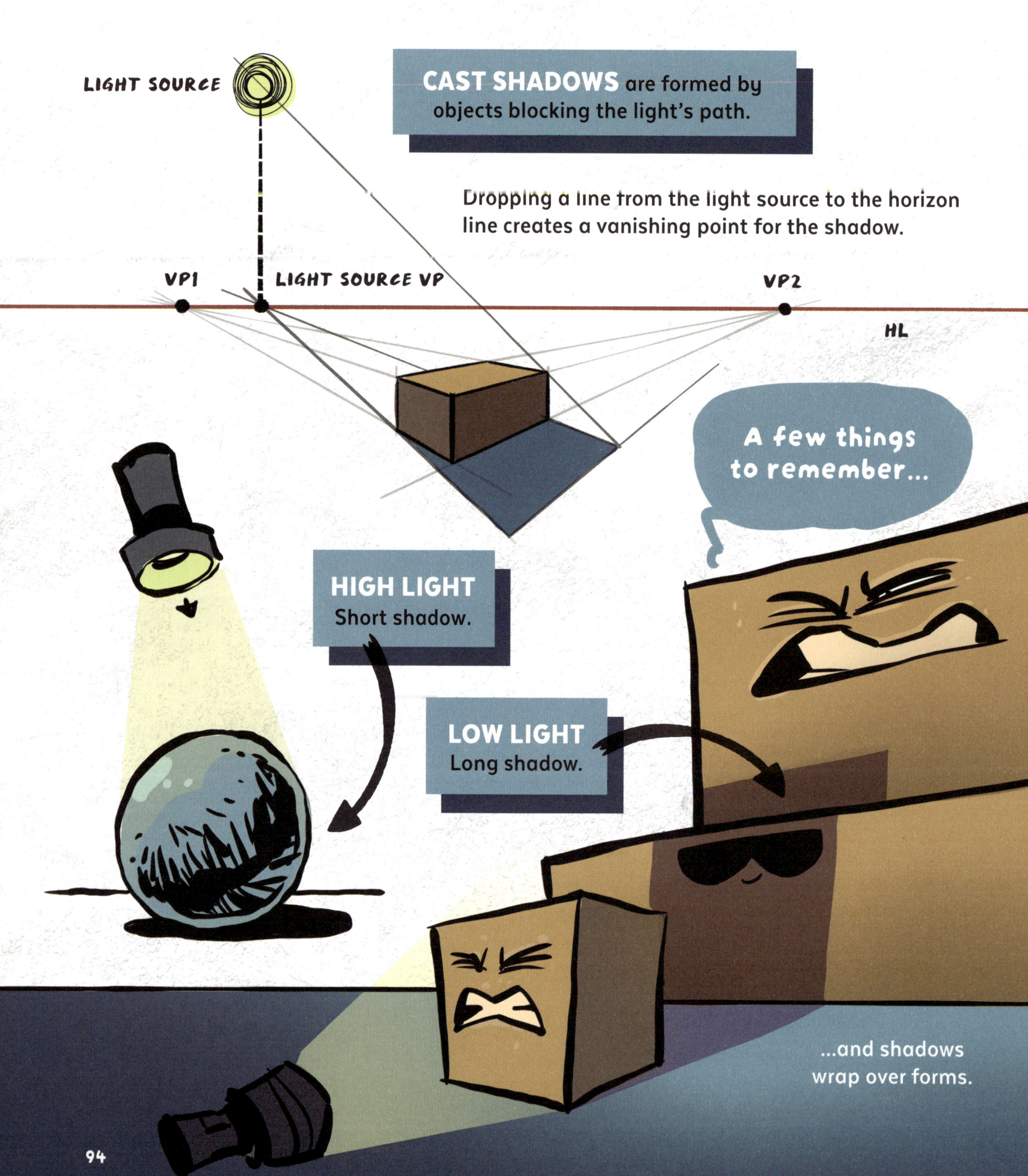

LIGHT SOURCE
CAST SHADOWS are formed by objects blocking the light's path.
Dropping a line from the light source to the horizon line creates a vanishing point for the shadow.
VP1
LIGHT SOURCE VP
VP2
HL
A few things to remember...
HIGH LIGHT
Short shadow.
LOW LIGHT
Long shadow.
...and shadows wrap over forms.
94

THREE-POINT LIGHTING is the traditional method for illuminating a subject in a scene. It includes light sources from three distinct positions called the key light, fill light, and rim light.

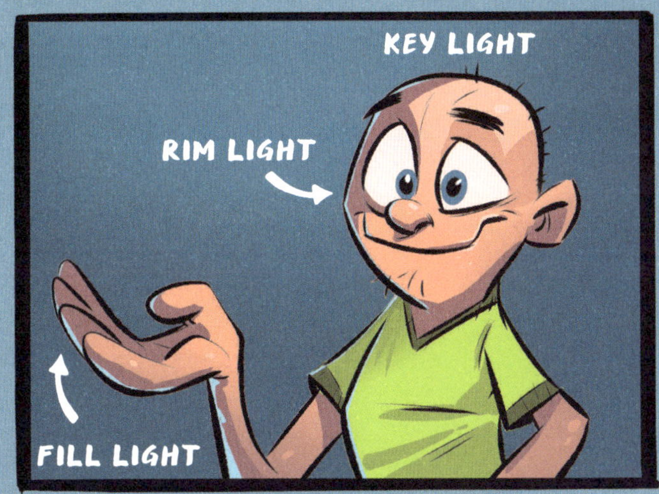

Experimenting with the size, distance, intensity, and position of these light sources will control how light and shadow fall on a subject, creating different moods.

KEY LIGHT: The primary light source gives a scene its overall colour and source of light, which allows you to understand forms. It's usually positioned in front of the subject to create shadows on the opposite side, giving it dimension and depth.

FILL LIGHT: Mirrors the key light on the opposite side of the picture plane. It fills in the shadows that the key light creates to bounce some light back. Together with the key light, the fill light determines the mood of a scene or design.

RIM LIGHT: The third source shines from behind to create a rim of light, or outline, around the subject to convey depth. It's typically positioned behind the subject or opposite the key light, pointing at the back of the subject.

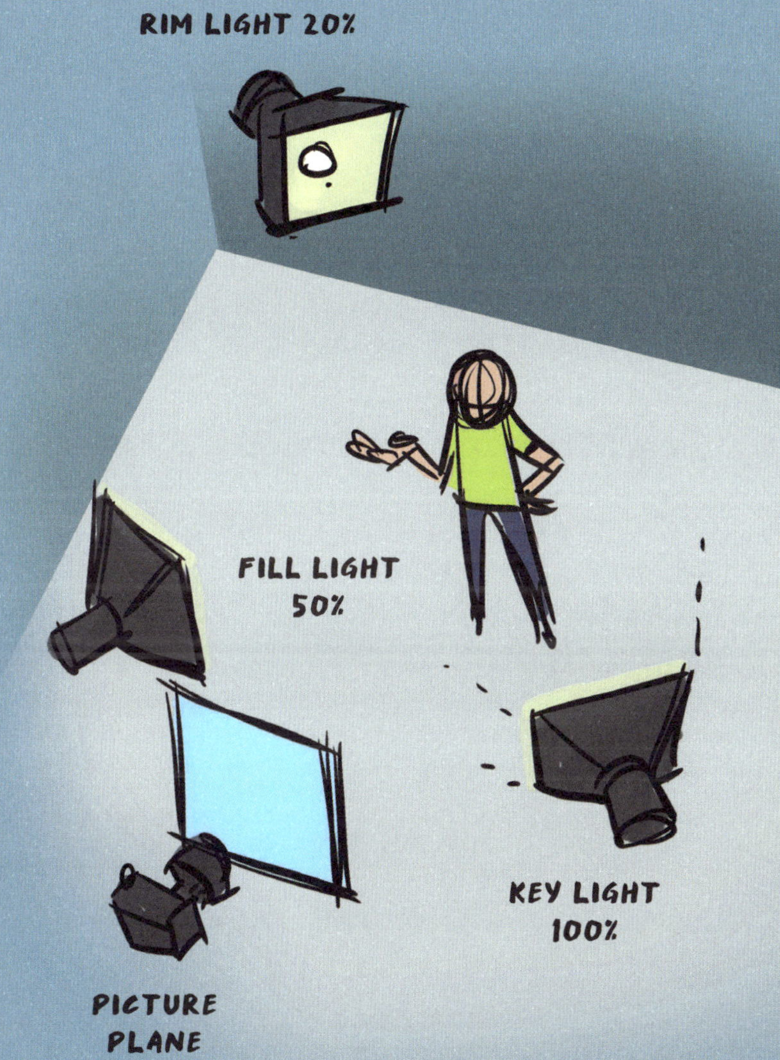

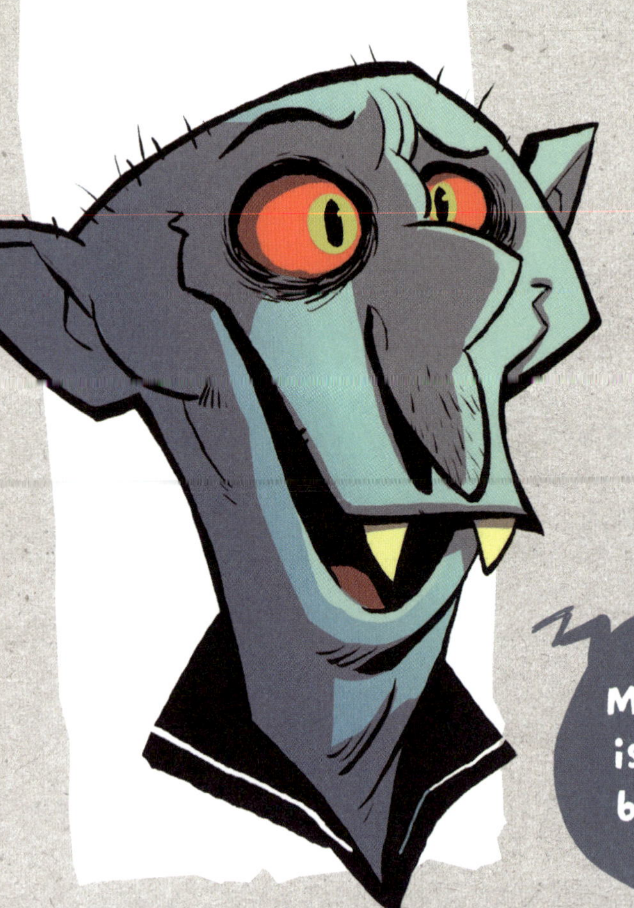

There are lots of light and shadow scenarios to experiment with. Not all of them need to be based in reality to work!

The more graphic you make your artwork, the more freedom you have to approach light and shadows differently.

Think of them as shapes within shapes and be **BOLD!** *

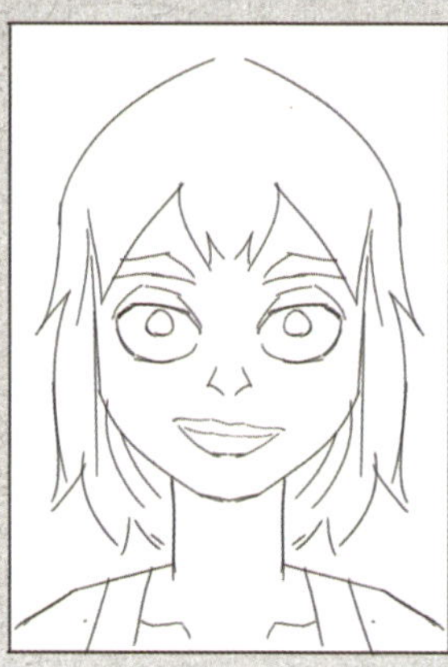

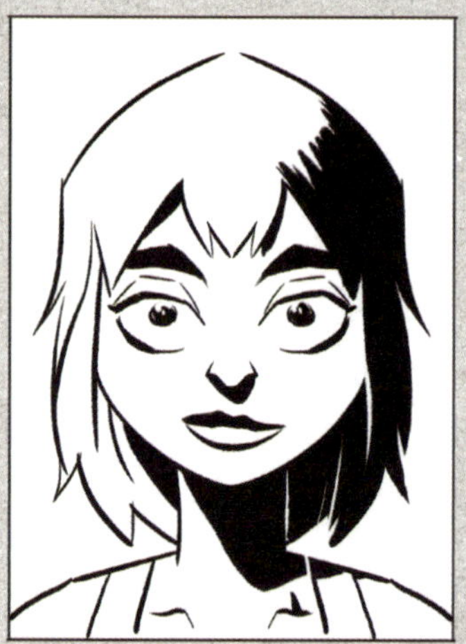

When inking, use shadow to tell the viewer where the light source is. Inking can inform the colours later, act as a basis for greyscale, or remain in stark black and white.

On the left is a drawing with one consistent line weight, beside the inked version on the right. The shadows show that the light source is above and to the left. They also communicate weight and volume.

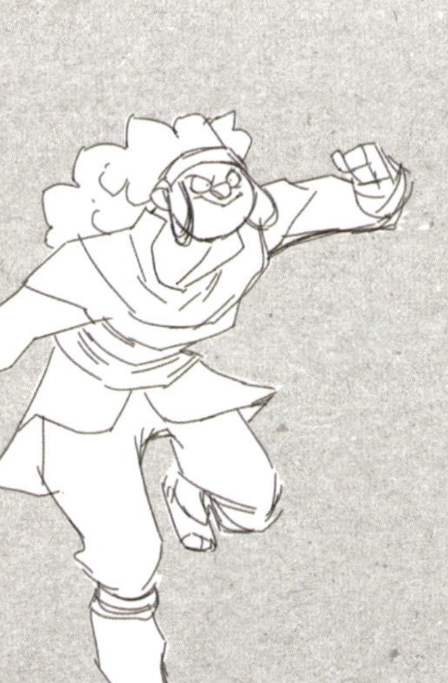

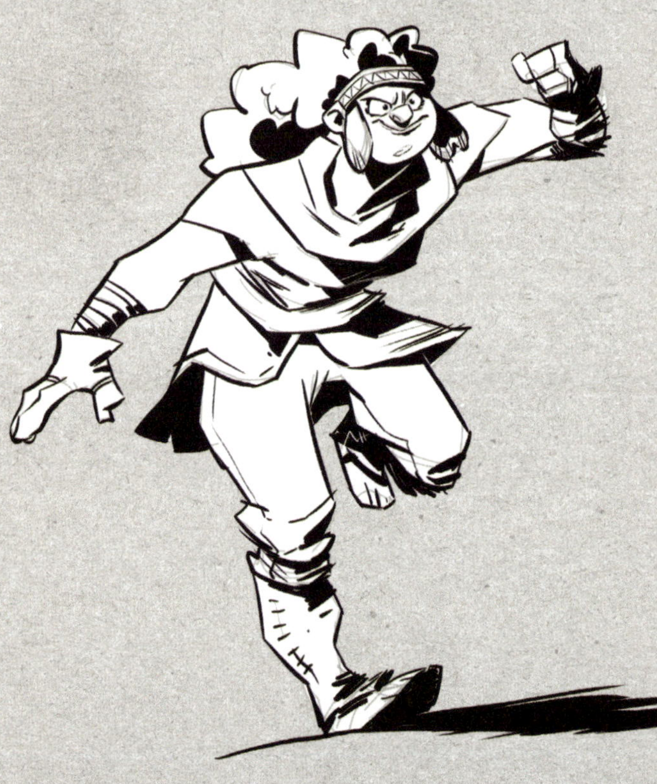

*Don't let a messy thing like reality get in your way!

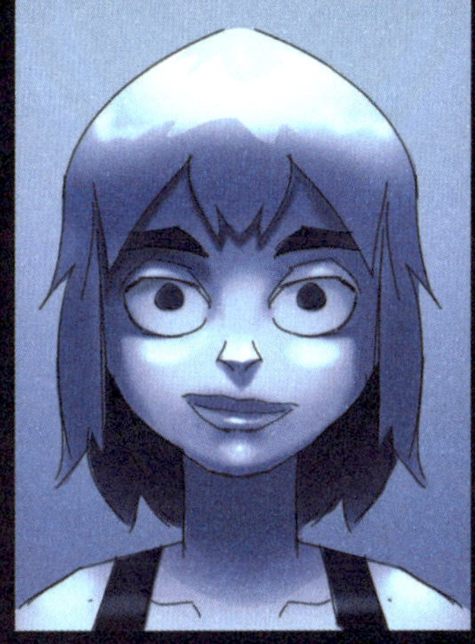

TOP LIGHTING

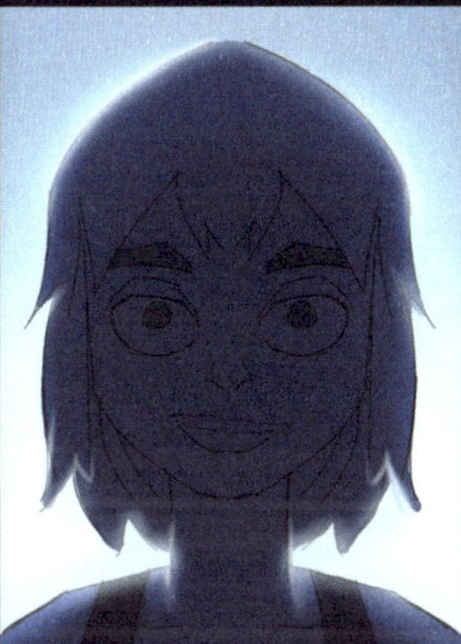

BACK LIGHTING

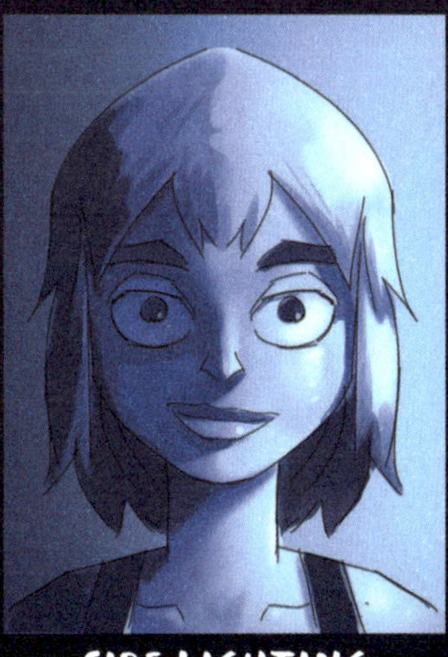

SIDE LIGHTING

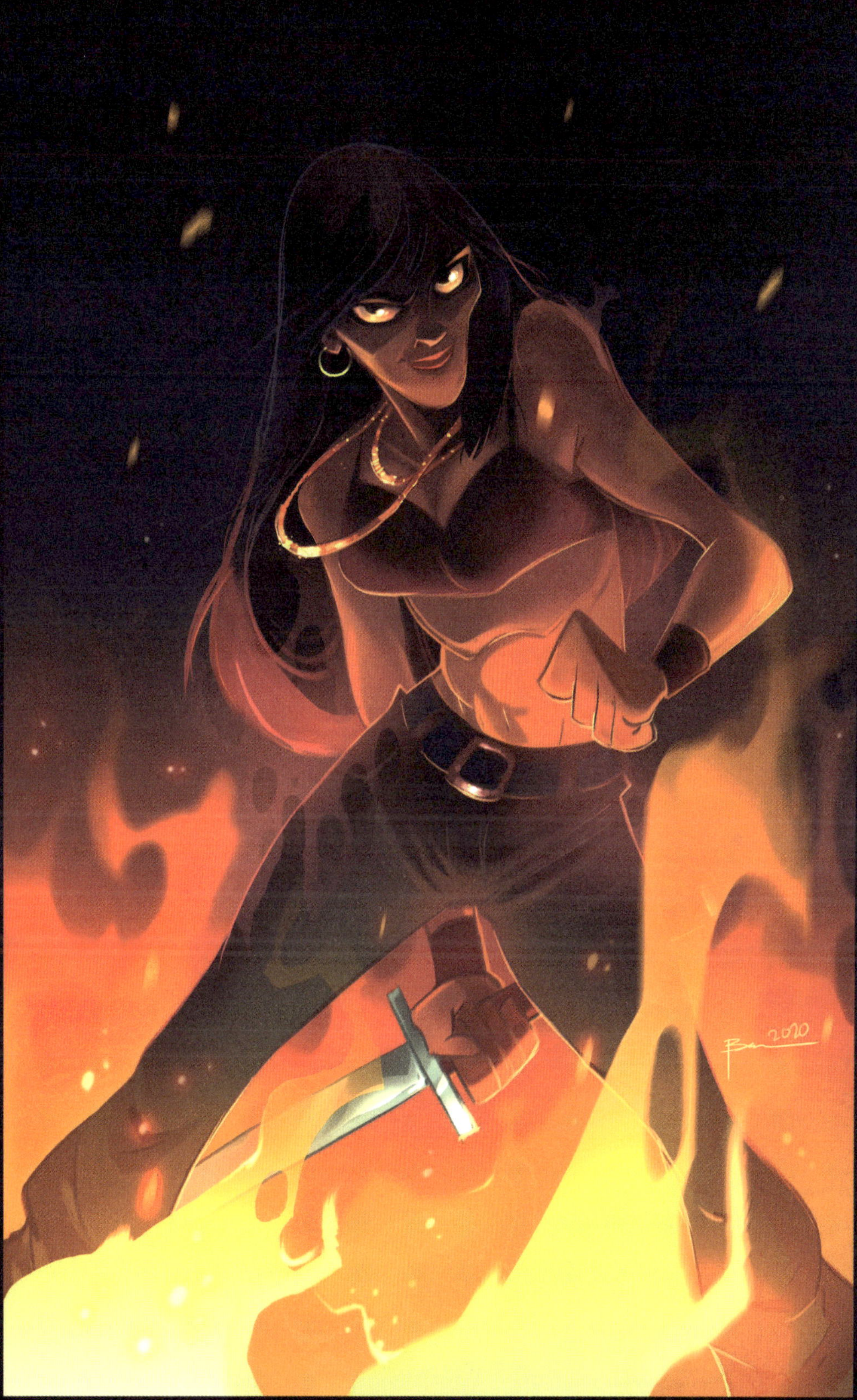

LIGHTING FROM BELOW

TOOL EXERCISES

Use tracing paper to draw over these pages, or take a photo/ scan them in to complete digitally. Alternatively, you can download all the exercise pages as PDFs to print out and draw on as many times as you like (see page 7 for the URL).

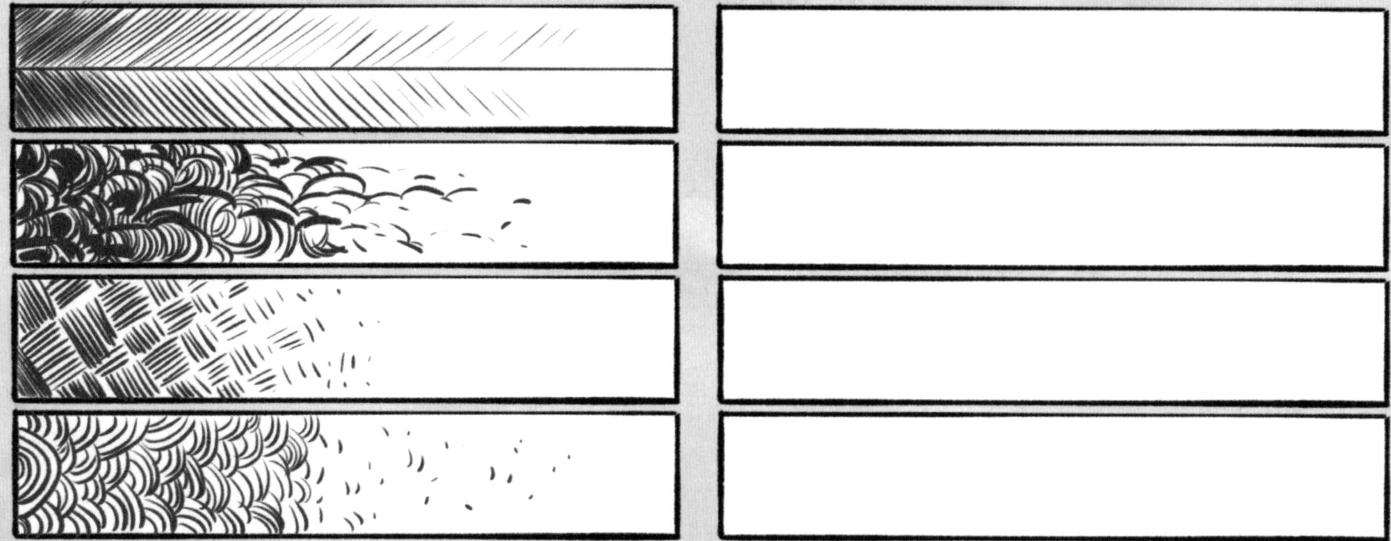

SKETCH 'FROM BUSY TO SIMPLE' USING ONLY LINES
Cross-hatch, texture, or pattern.

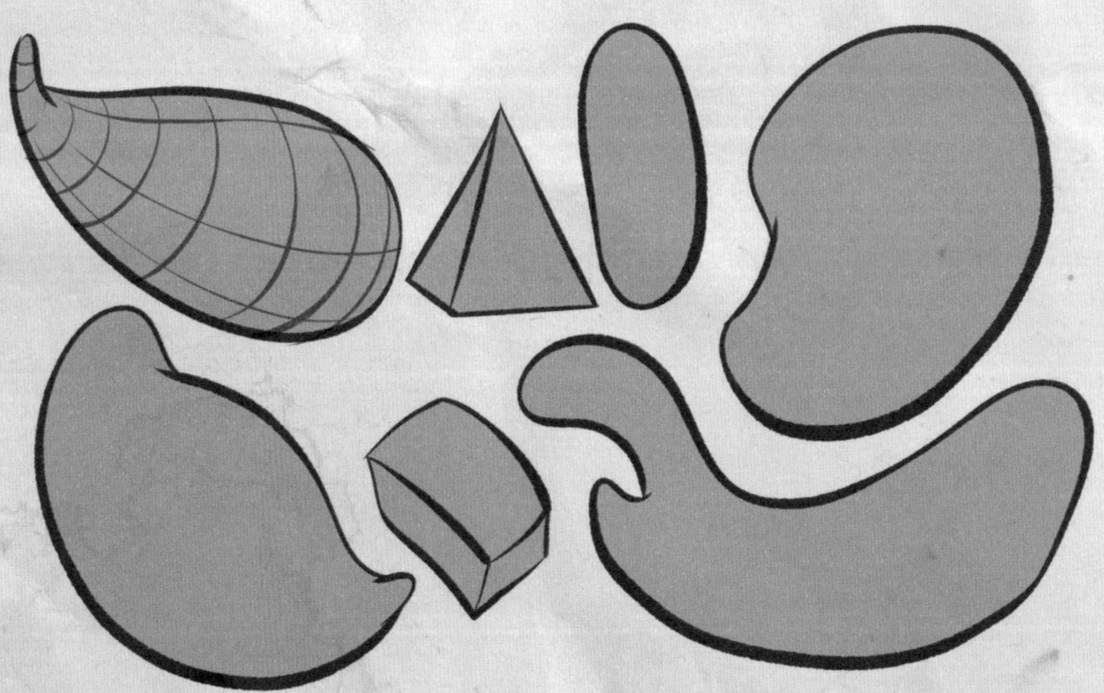

FIND THE FORM USING CONTOURS AND A CENTRE LINE
The centre line runs through the shape.

Draw a horizon line on a piece of paper, then draw
a box above it, below it, and in the middle of it.

Add value to the boxes.

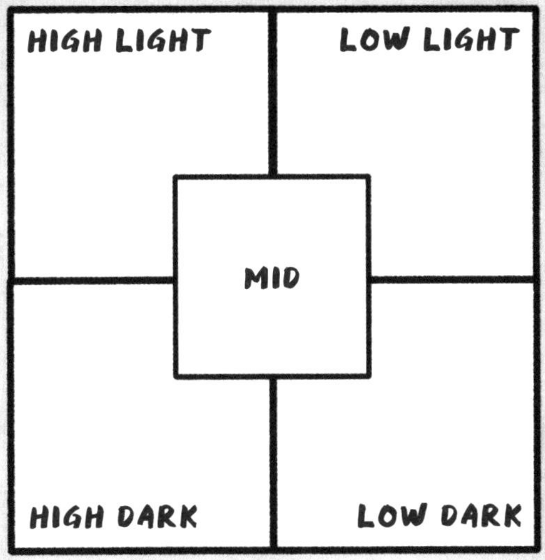

Draw a piece of fruit, but
only use negative space.

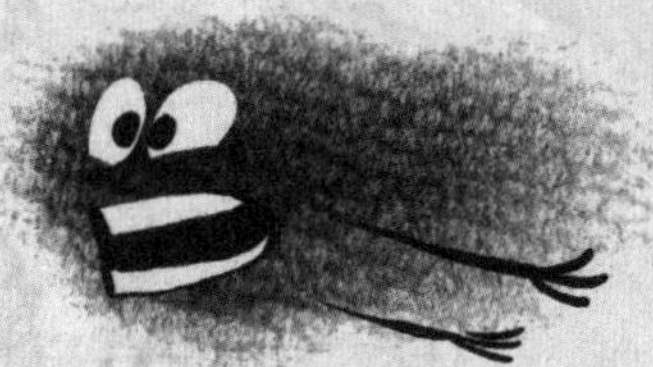

Draw trees based on the key words below.

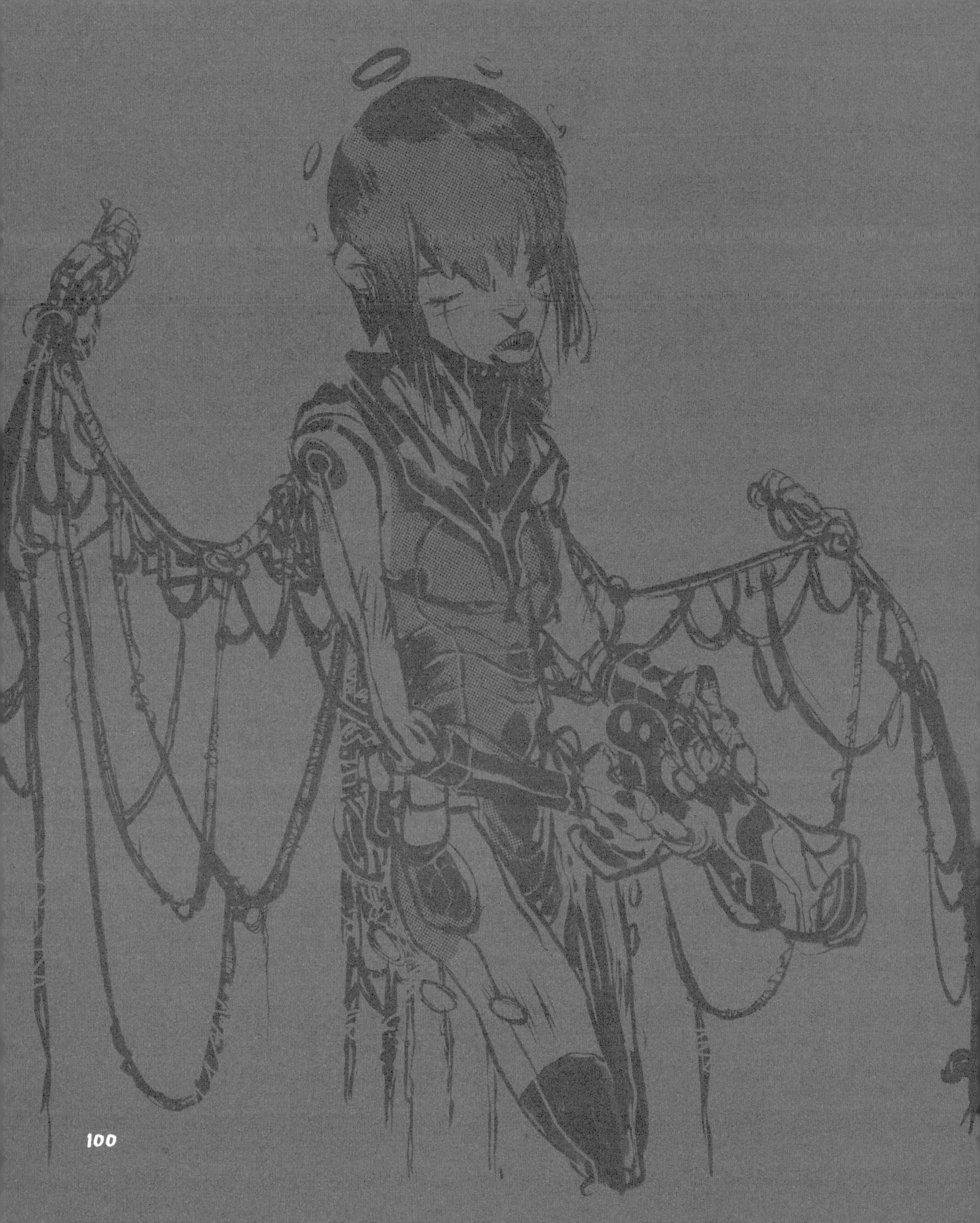

CHAPTER 04

BODY BREAKDOWN

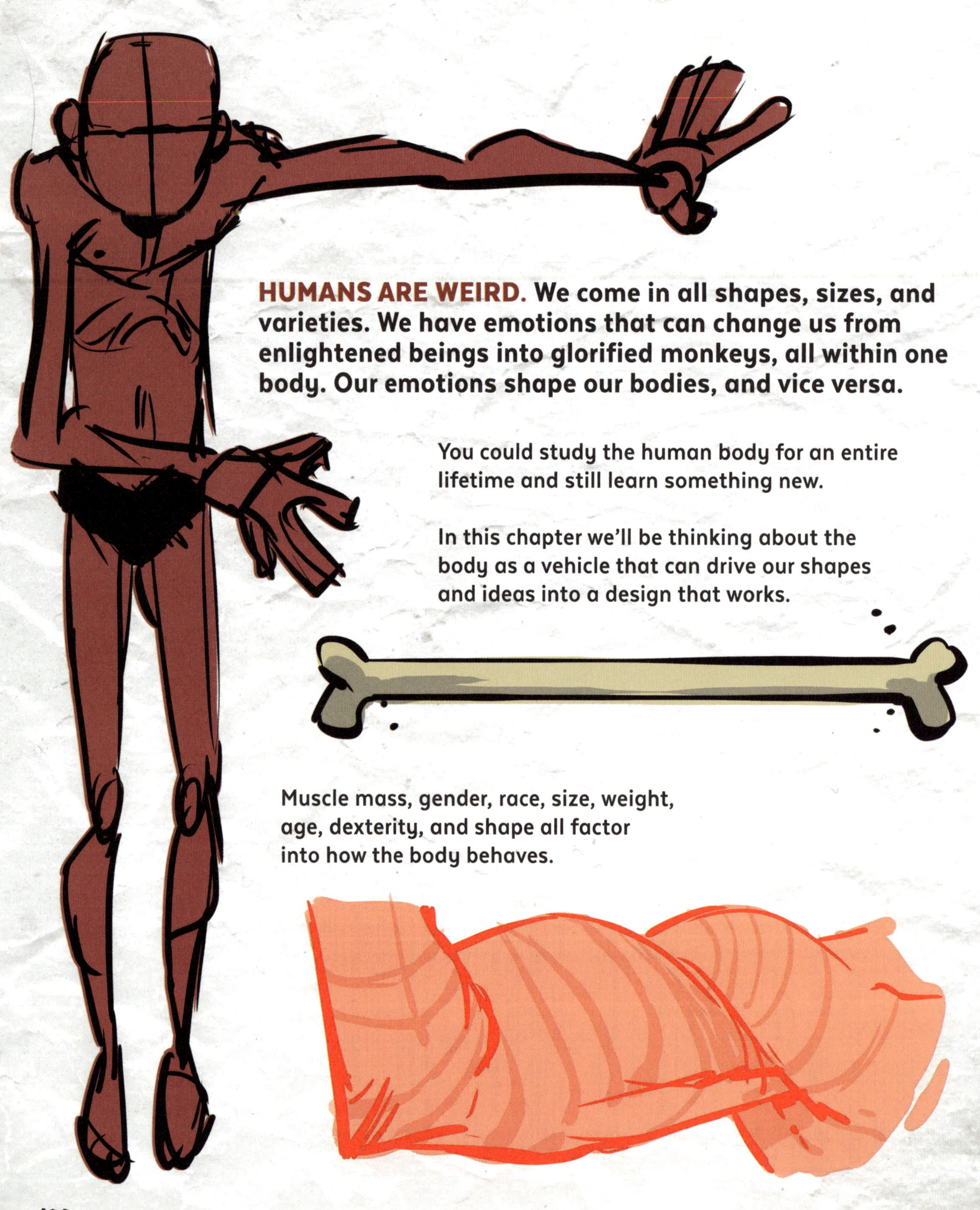

HUMANS ARE WEIRD. We come in all shapes, sizes, and varieties. We have emotions that can change us from enlightened beings into glorified monkeys, all within one body. Our emotions shape our bodies, and vice versa.

You could study the human body for an entire lifetime and still learn something new.

In this chapter we'll be thinking about the body as a vehicle that can drive our shapes and ideas into a design that works.

Muscle mass, gender, race, size, weight, age, dexterity, and shape all factor into how the body behaves.

STUDY & OBSERVE

Observe your fellow humans at coffee shops, parks, and parties. You will be surprised at how much you can see from physical interactions. Try to create your own stories from what you observe.

Draw over images from reference, but remember you're looking at something from a flat plane.

Never be afraid to get into a pose to feel the weight and how it's distributed. Feel where it pushes and pulls in your body.

Find a mirror and act out the emotions you want to convey.

Actions always speak louder than words. We use our bodies all the time to speak volumes.

Take a figure-drawing class at the weekends.

Study the body in an anatomy book.

Take turns posing with your peers.

Watch a sport and sketch quick gesture drawings based off the various poses.

Try to understand the world through someone else's body and literal point of view (for example, size, age, shape, and so on.)

...and you might learn something about art **AND** life.

THE BODY

The human body is fascinating and very complex. This section will explore the different stages you need to work through when drawing it, starting with the skeleton.

These parts help us to understand the body's structure, its direction, and how it moves within us.

The **SPINE** is vital, as everything else extends from it. It creates movement and flow in the body.

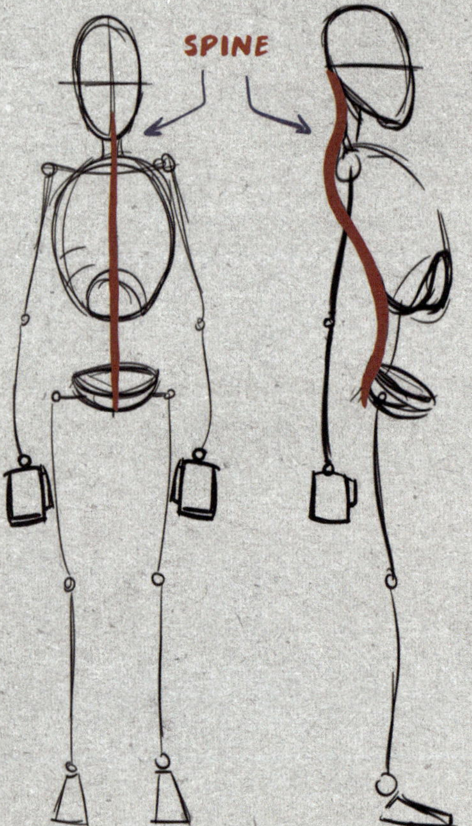

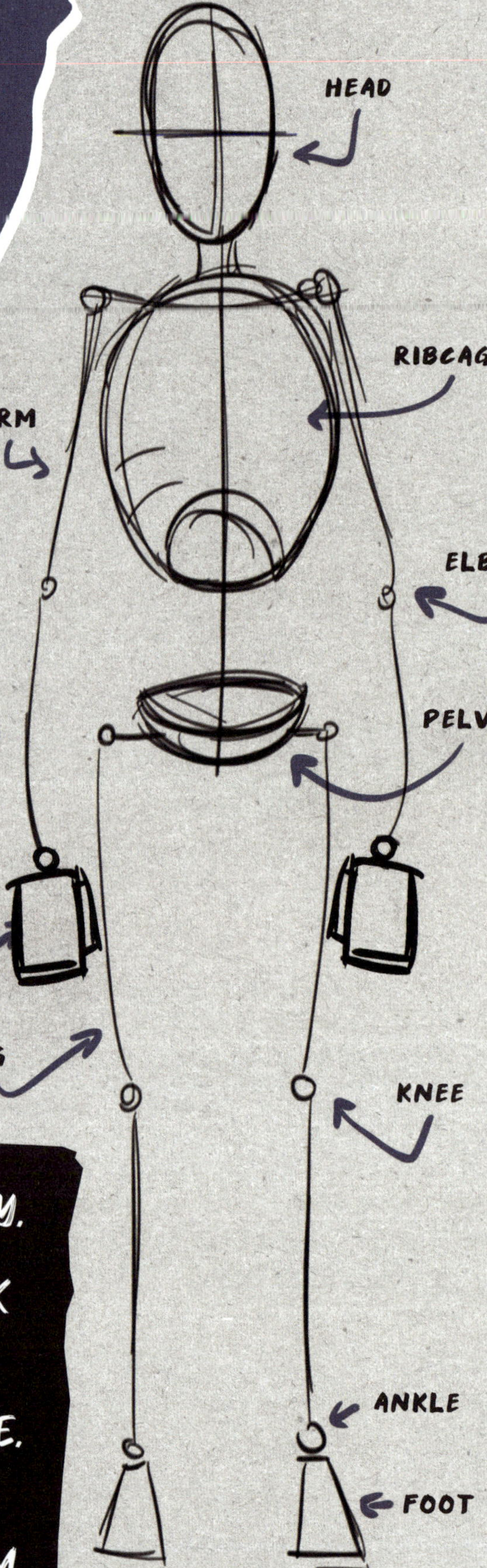

STUDYING ANATOMY, MUSCLES, AND HOW BODIES WORK WILL ALWAYS BENEFIT YOUR ARTISTIC PRACTICE, ESPECIALLY IF YOU PLAN ON BRINGING REALISM INTO YOUR ART.

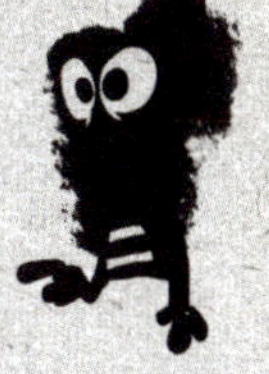

MASSES

The masses of the skeleton are the head, ribcage, pelvis, hands, and feet. Notice that the ribcage and pelvis show depth.

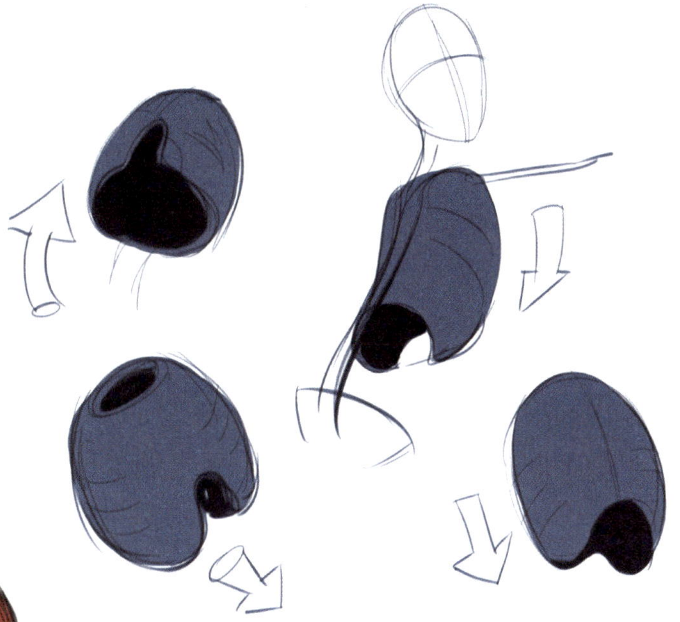

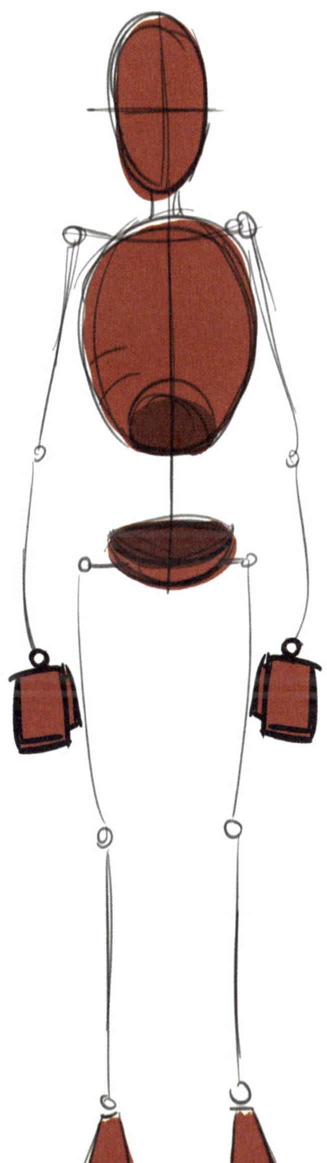

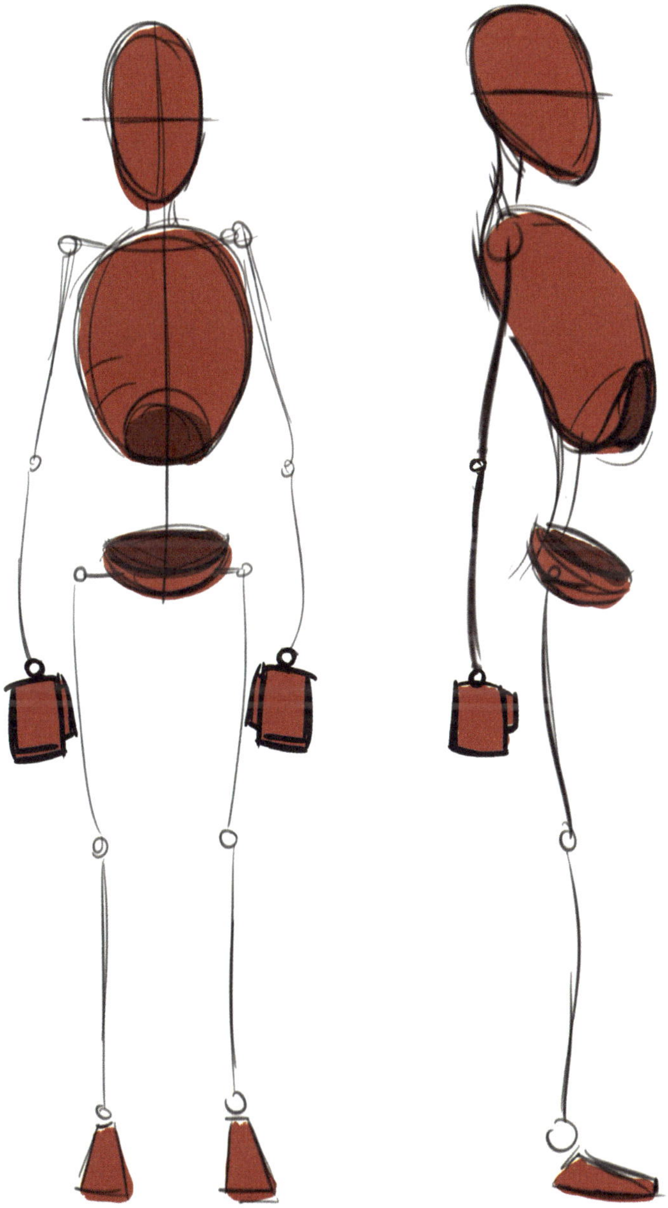

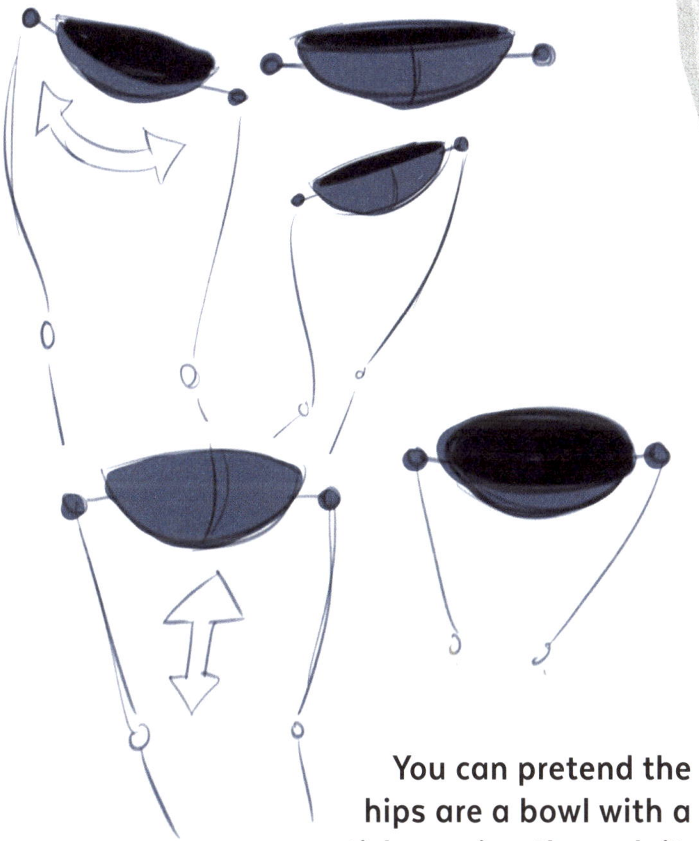

You can pretend the hips are a bowl with a stick running through it. As they tilt, you can look into them based on their direction.

PIVOT POINTS

These are the major pivot points that allow the body to move: the base of the head, upper arm, elbows, wrist, out of the pelvis, knees, and ankles.

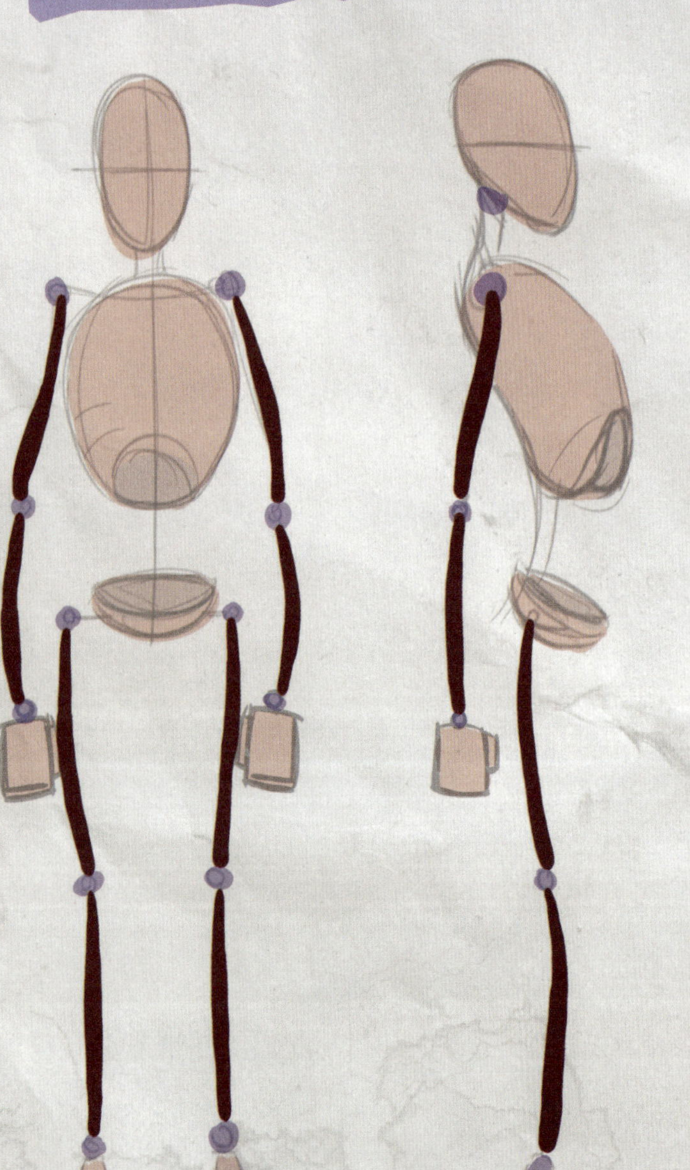

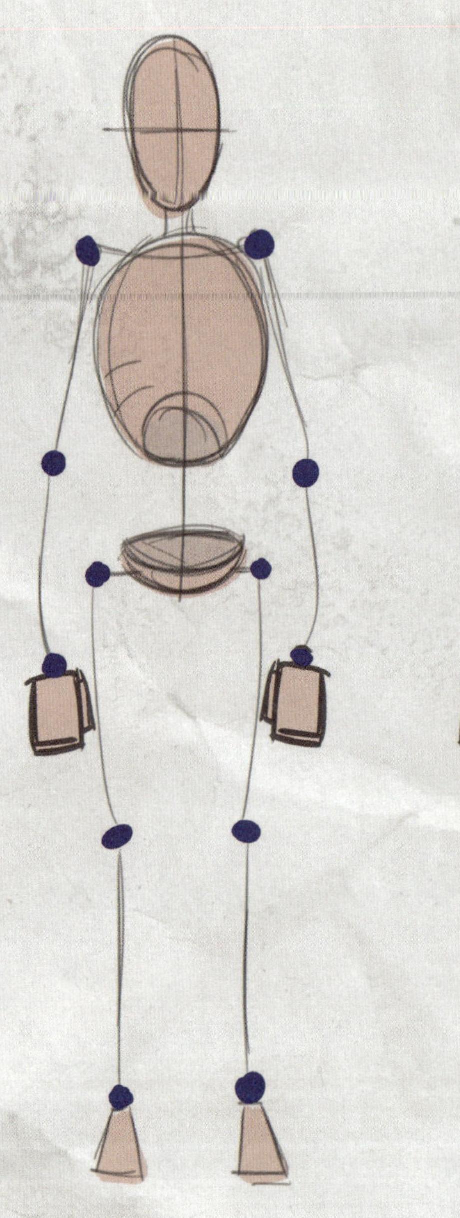

BONES

Clearly these aren't what bones really look like, but they represent the hard targets in between the pivot points and masses.

When drawing pivots and
bones, it's important to
remember what's rigid
(bones) and how far you can
pivot. If you want something
to feel real, don't let the
pivots go past a certain
point or they will 'break'.

Some people can hyper
extend and bend in very
peculiar ways, but the
average body can't do this!

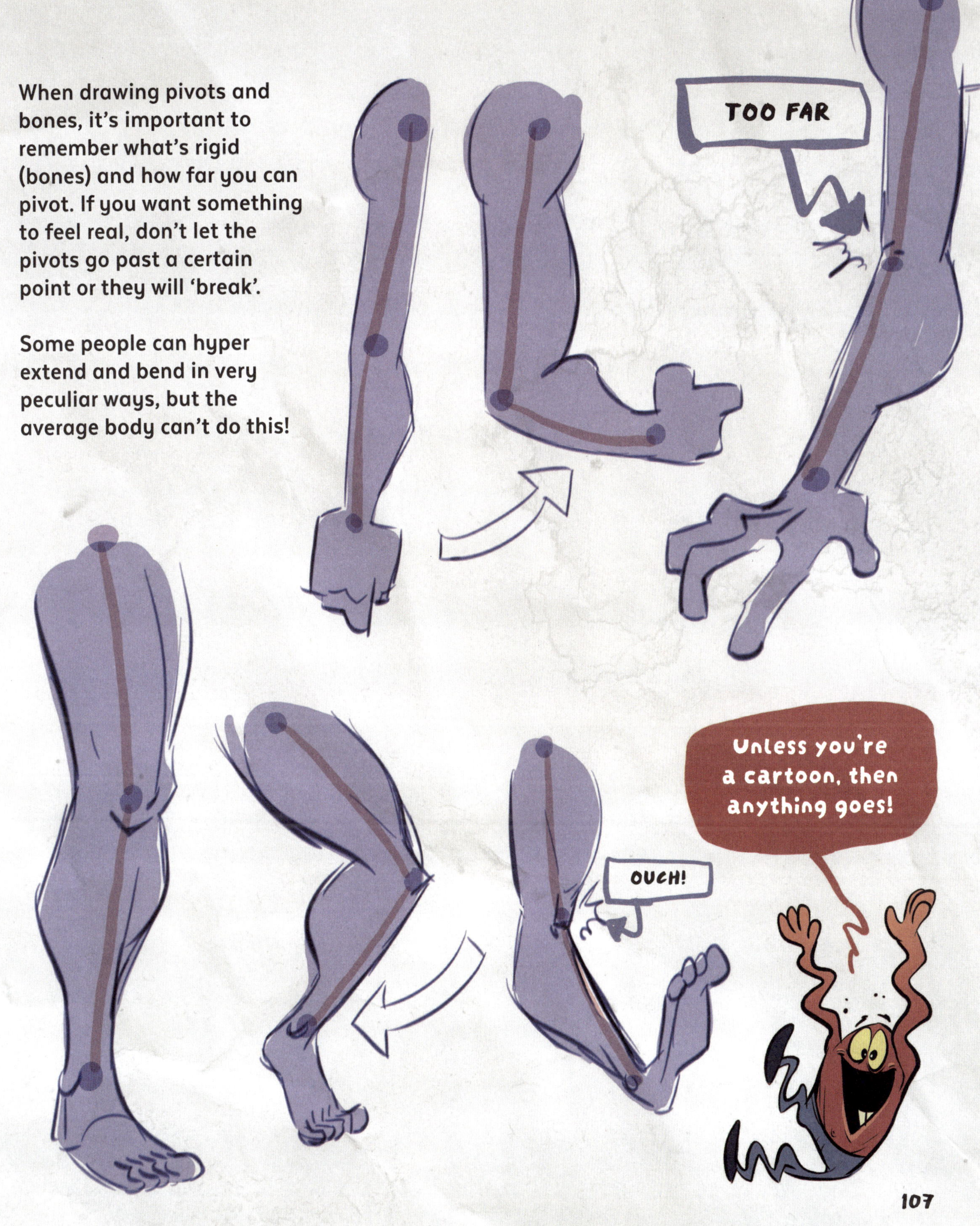

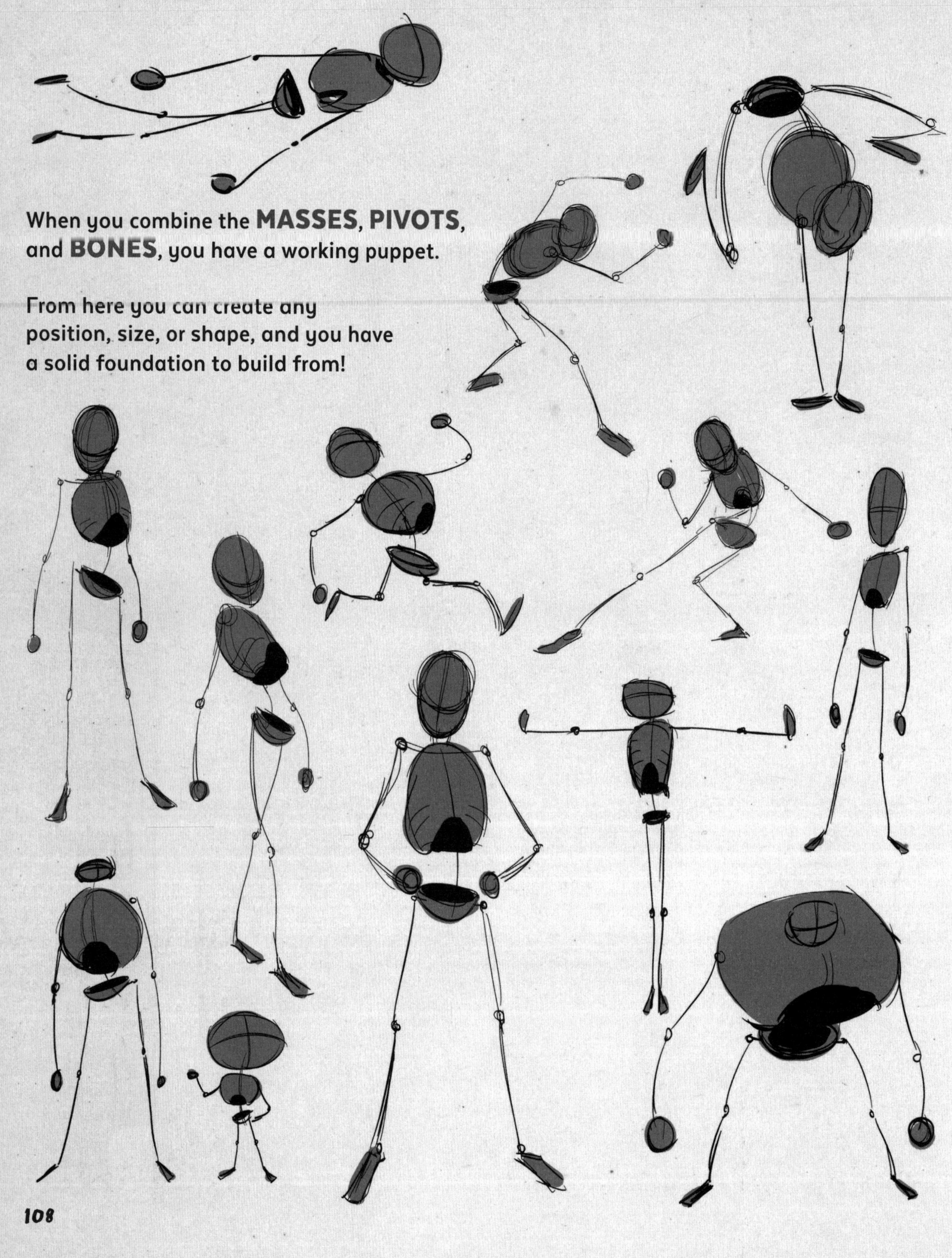

When you combine the **MASSES**, **PIVOTS**, and **BONES**, you have a working puppet.

From here you can create any position, size, or shape, and you have a solid foundation to build from!

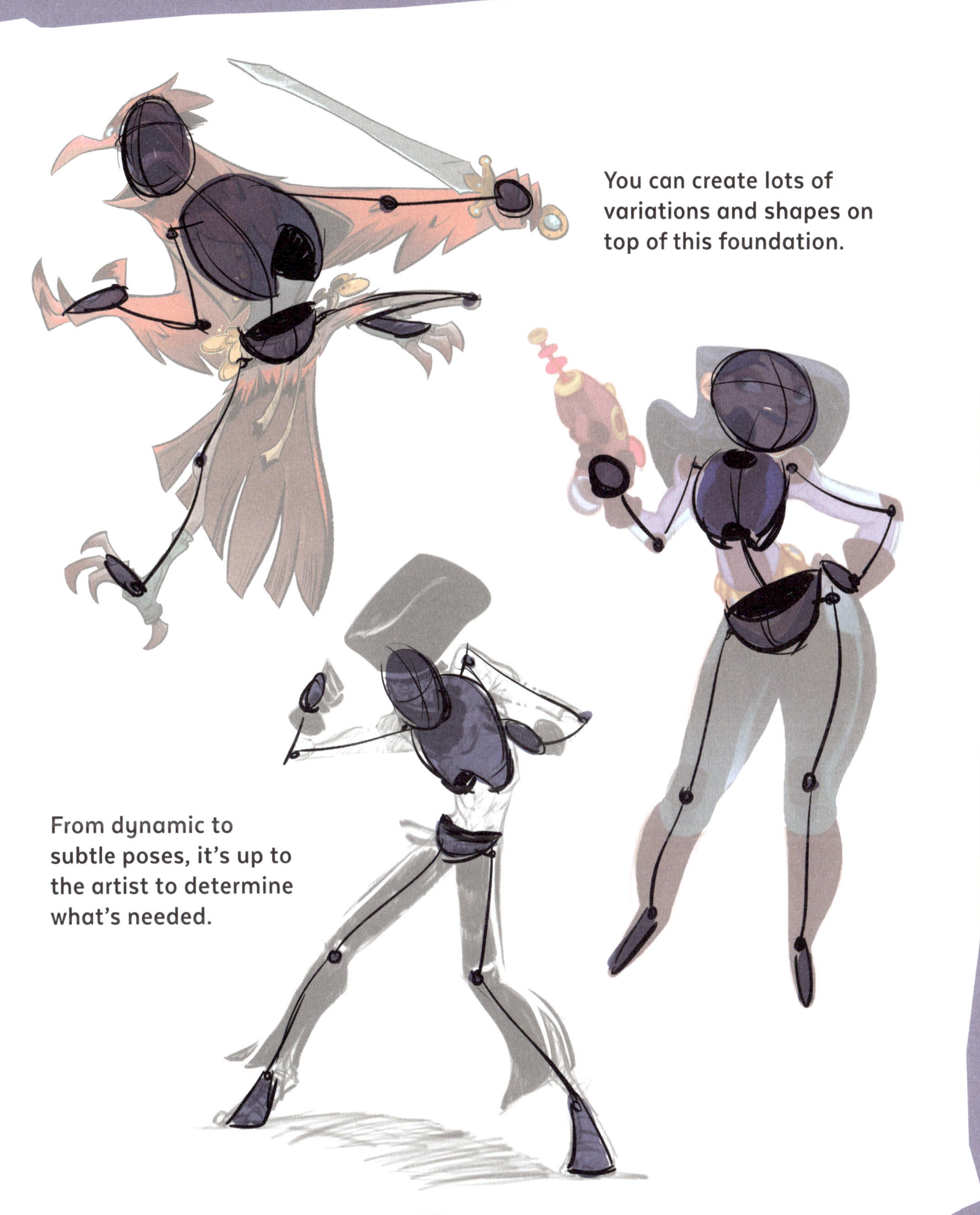

You can create lots of
variations and shapes on
top of this foundation.

From dynamic to
subtle poses, it's up to
the artist to determine
what's needed.

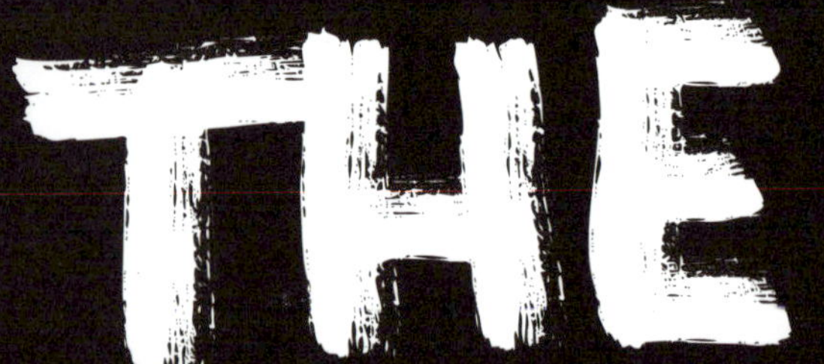
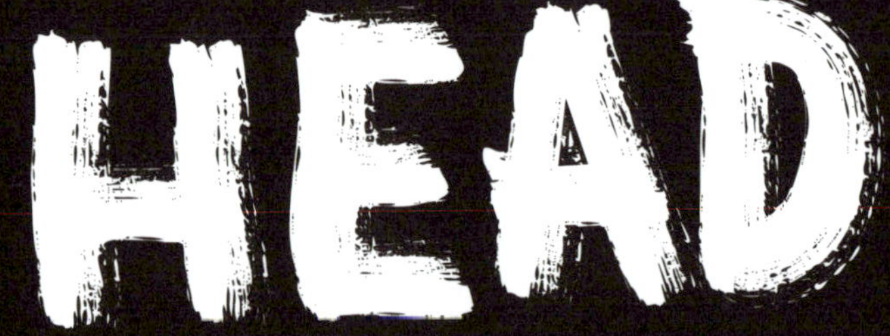

THE HEAD

FRONTAL
(As in lobotomy)

NASAL
(Hard part of your nose)

ORBITS
(Eye go where they go)

ZYGOMATIC
(Cheeky monkey)

MAXILLA
(Moustache to the max)

MANDIBLE
(Hum the *Jaws* theme tune)

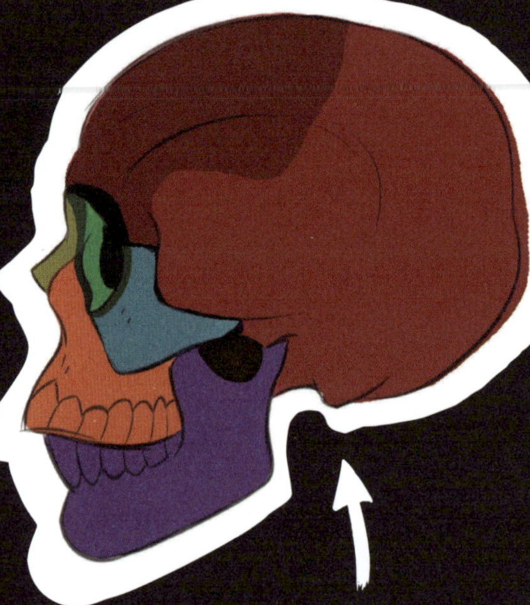

Heads up!
This is a cranium.

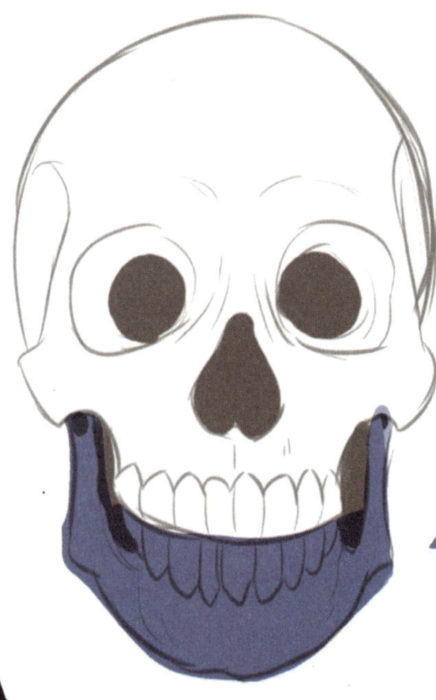

While skull is rigid bone, as artists we can play with the mandible because it's not attached!

The mandible isn't connected!

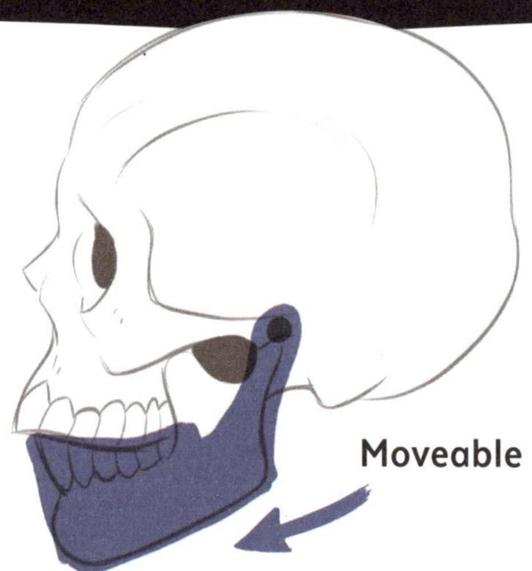

Moveable

The further you get from realism, the more playful you can be with a character's physical representation.

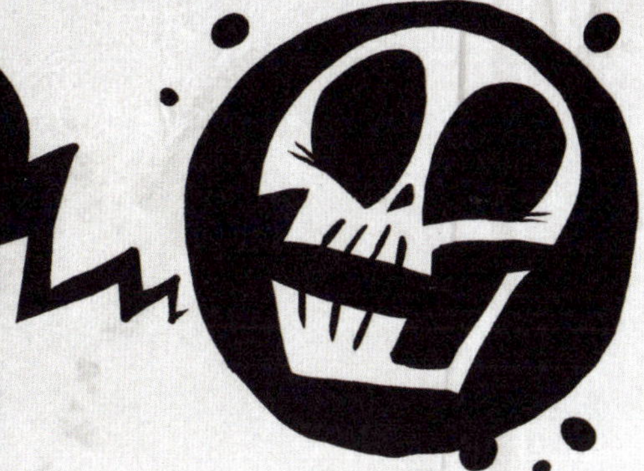

TRY THIS!

Practise sketching the skull, experimenting with the jaw.

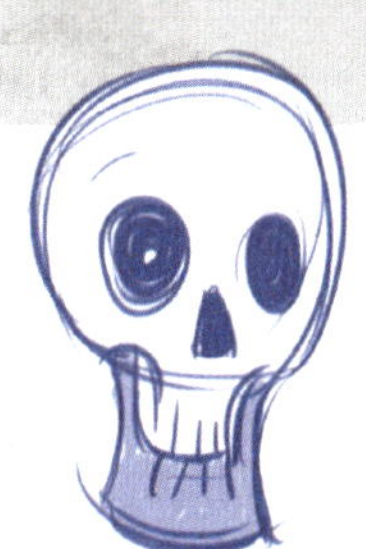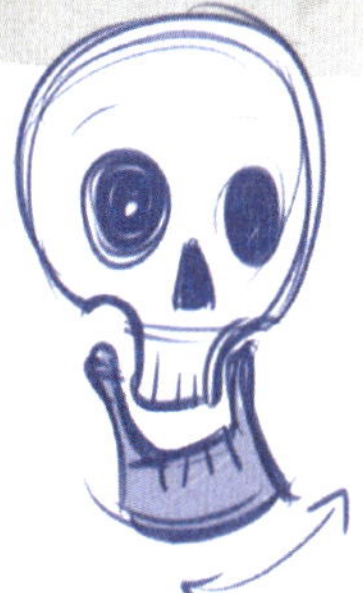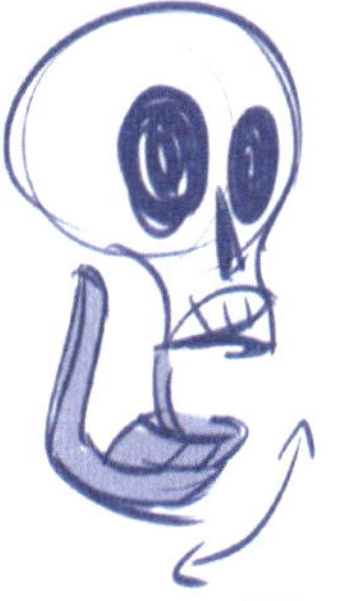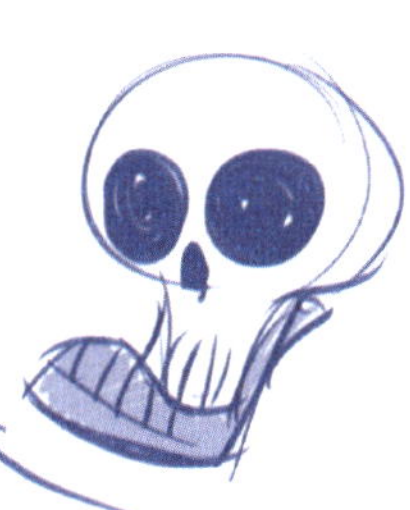

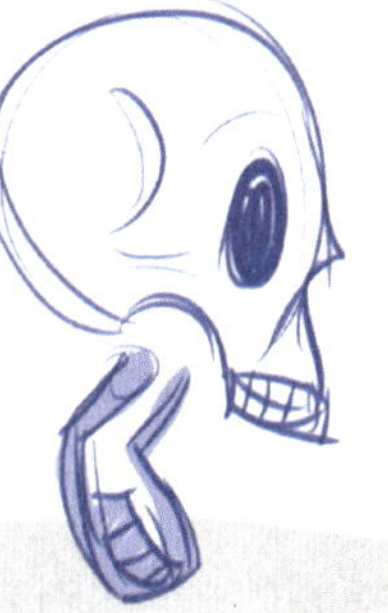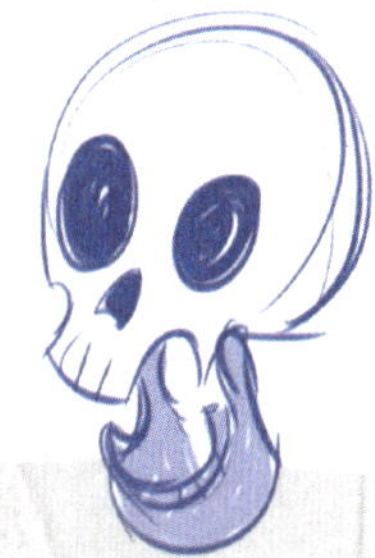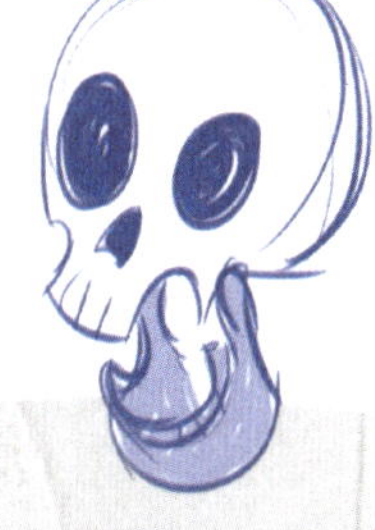

Move the jaw from side to side, and forwards and backwards, to achieve a full range.

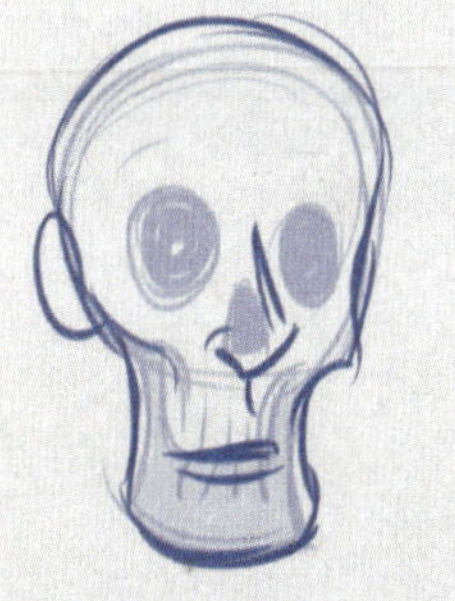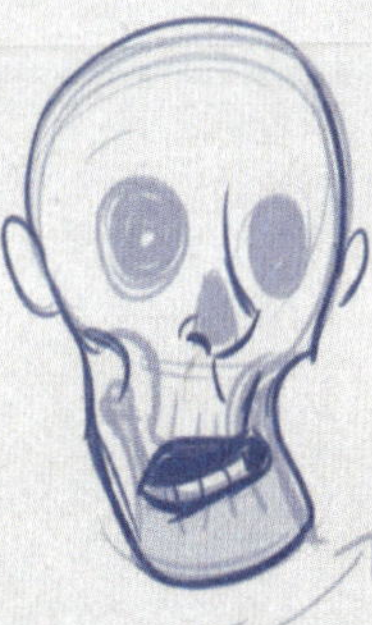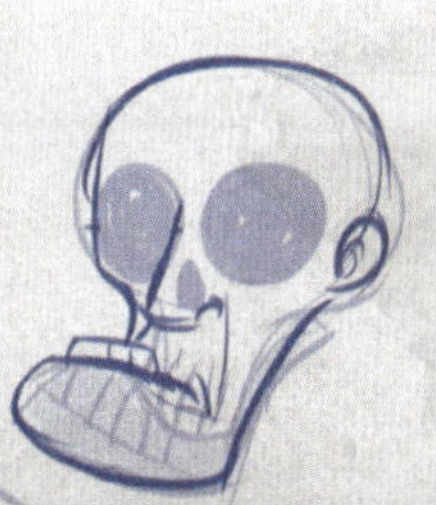

Next, squash and stretch to fit around the forms.

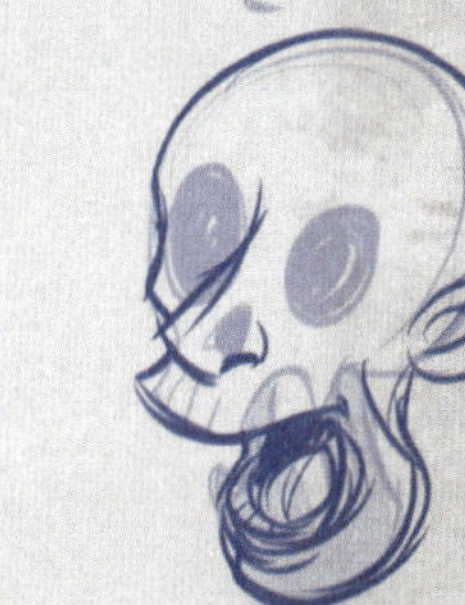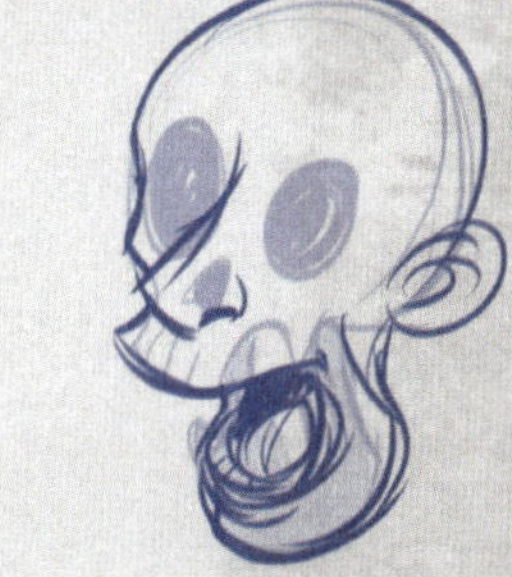

When adding skin, consistent volume is key. Like a sack of flour, the face will have the same weight, but it will move around.

NOSE & EARS

Noses and ears are complex shapes, but they can easily be broken down into simpler forms.

Once you have drawn the necessary elements, the variations are endless!

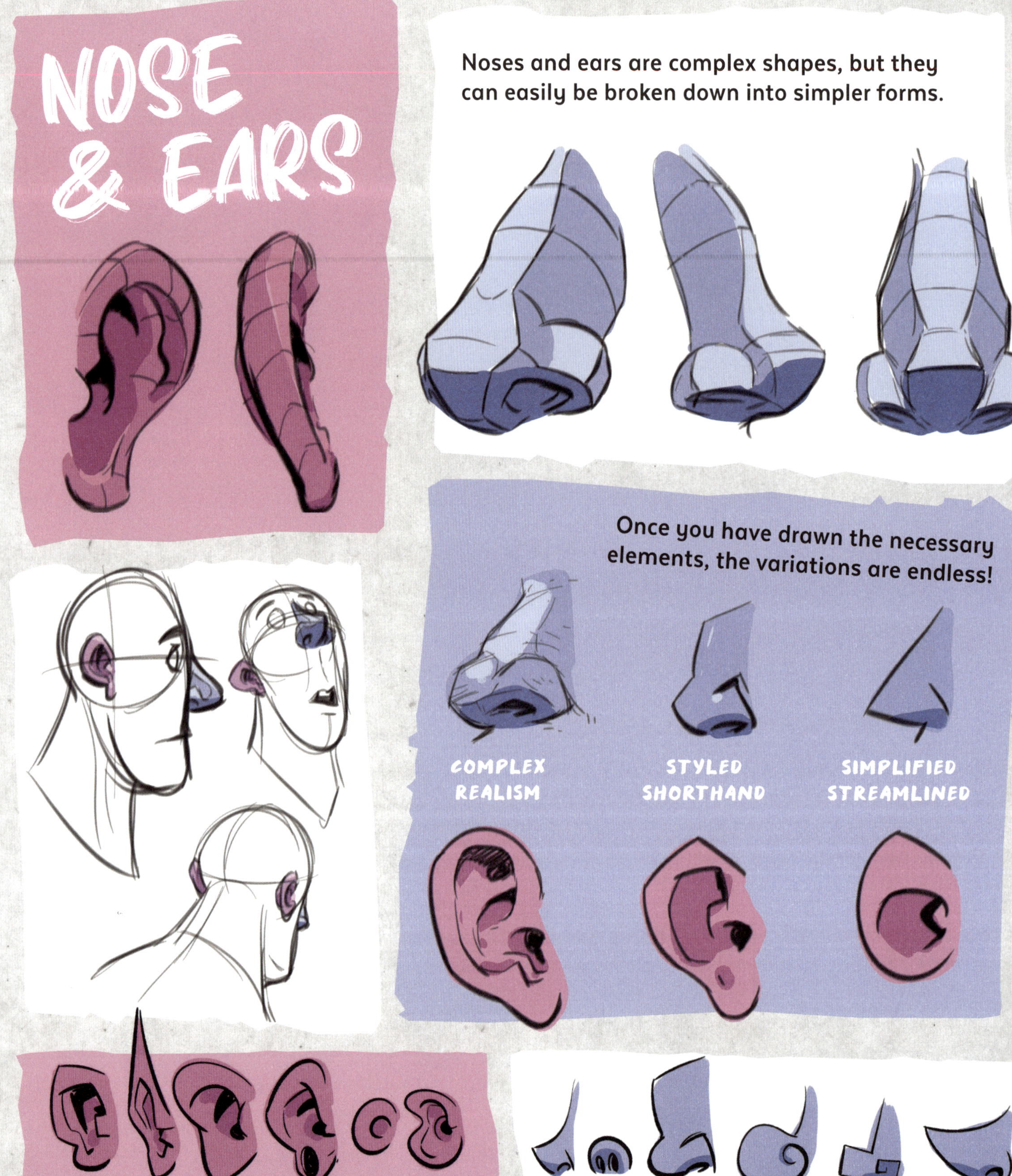

TEETH

You can draw teeth by starting with a cylinder, dividing it up, and adding rows.

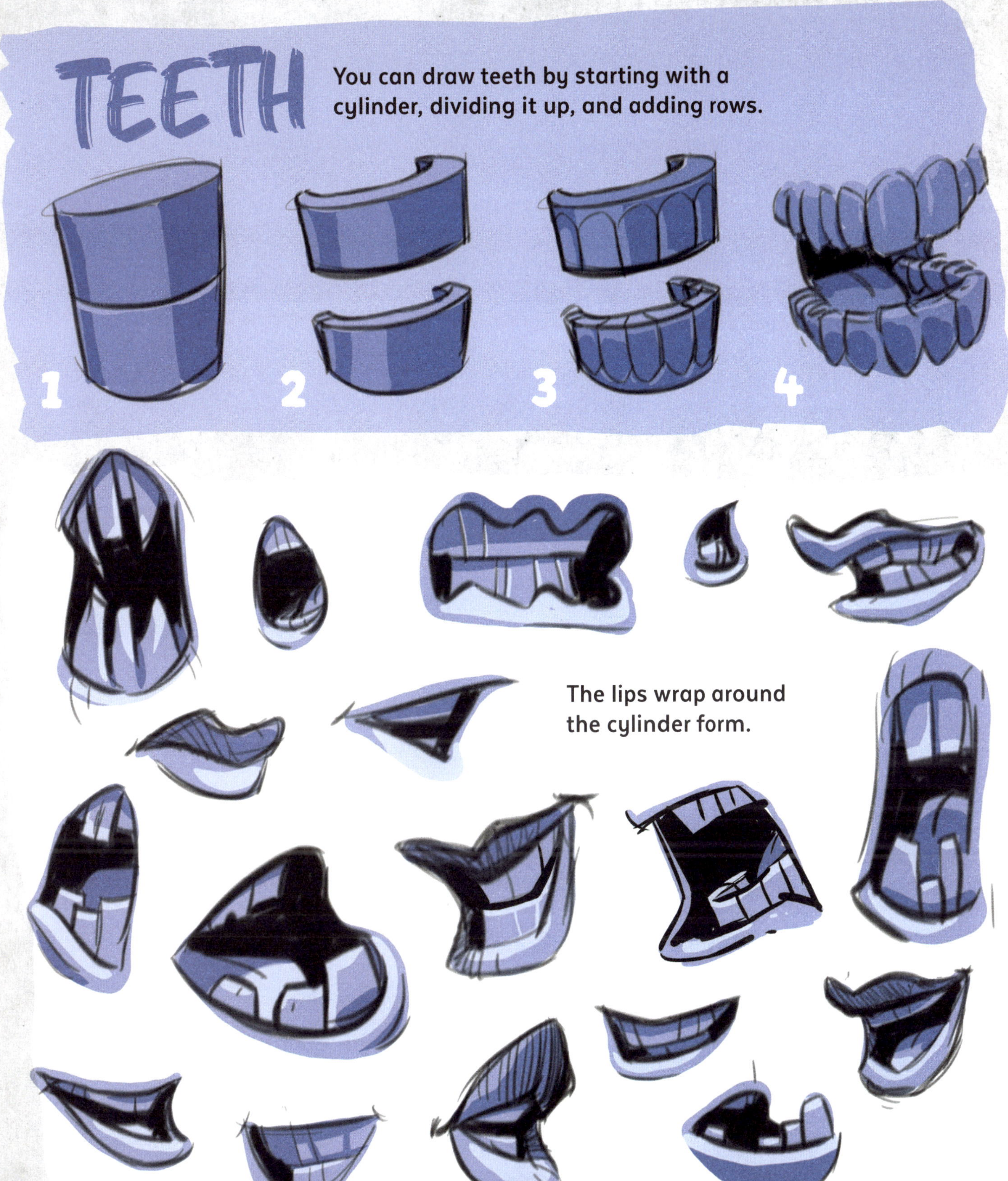

The lips wrap around the cylinder form.

EYES

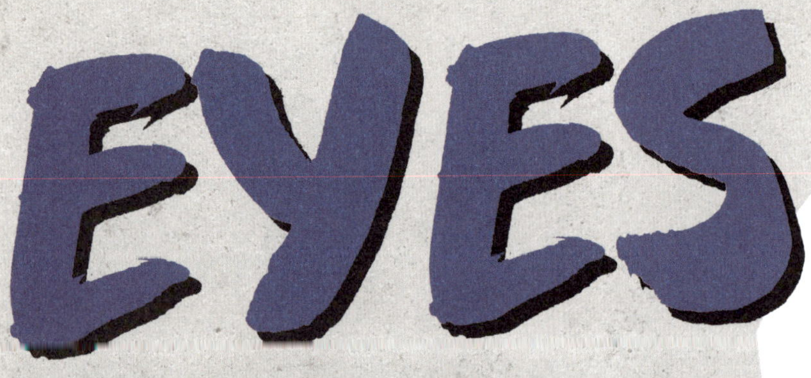

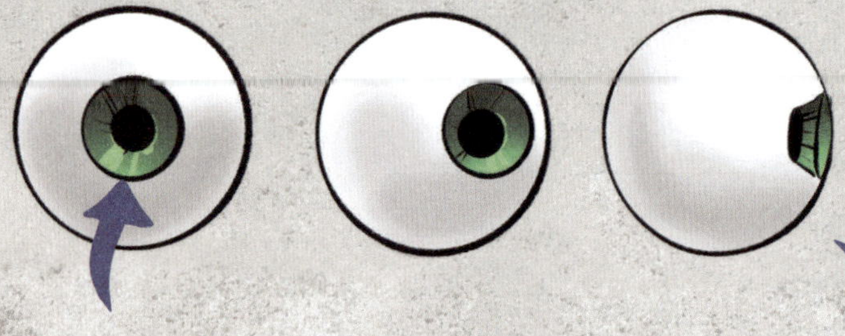

Picture the iris like a cone.
The black is the pupil at the centre.
Light bounces inside of the cone.

The eyelids wrap around the eye and can vary depending on gender and race.

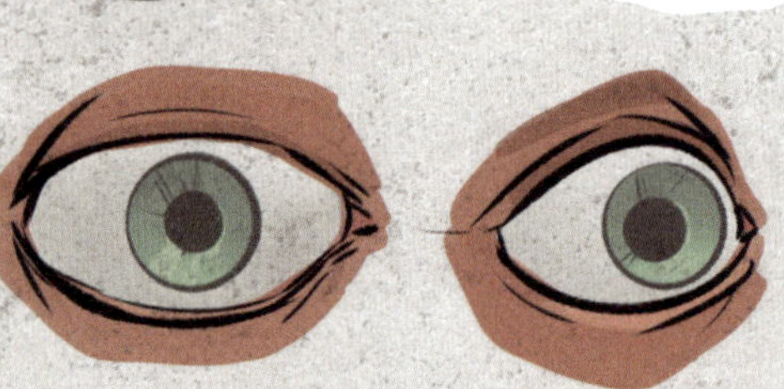

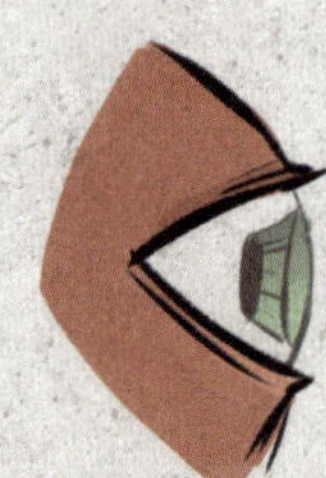

EYELIDS

1. The tear ducts.
2. The waterline.
3. The upper/lower eyelids.

When the eyelids close, they wrap around the sphere of the eye.

You will have already blinked while reading this. Did you notice that you mainly use your upper lid to blink with? This is because your bottom lids are primarily used by your cheeks. They can help to convey emotion.

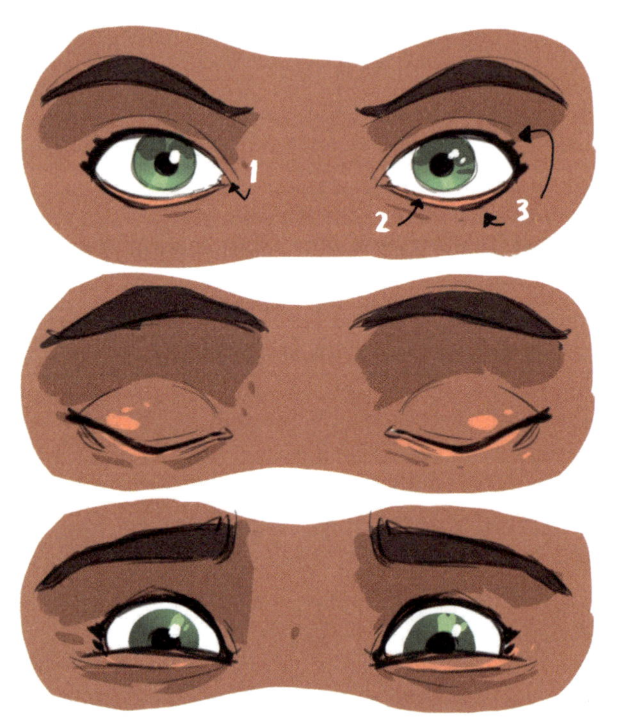

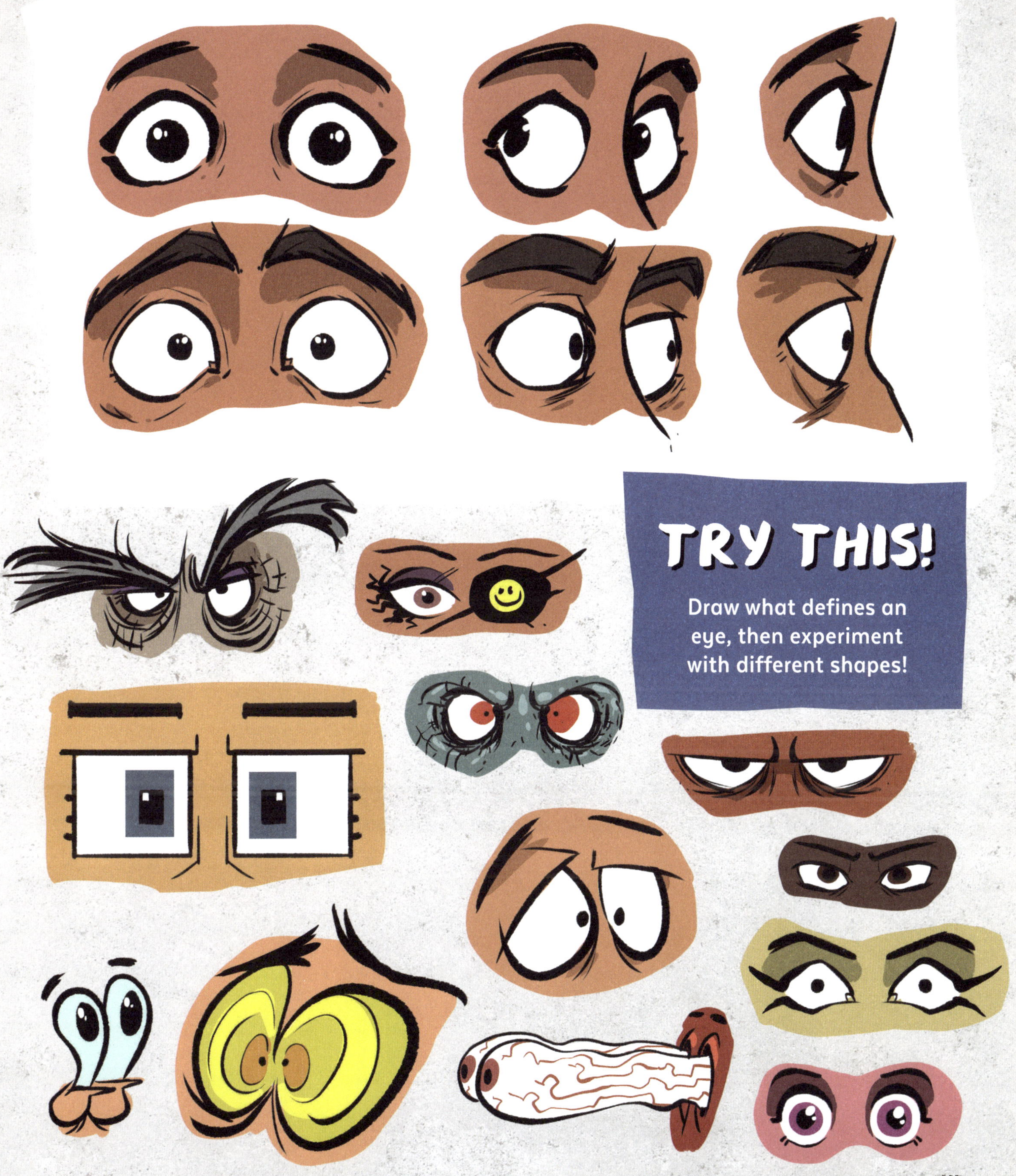
TRY THIS!
Draw what defines an eye, then experiment with different shapes!

Pretend the muscles around the eyes work like a bandit's mask. There are four points on the mask to push and pull to create expressions!

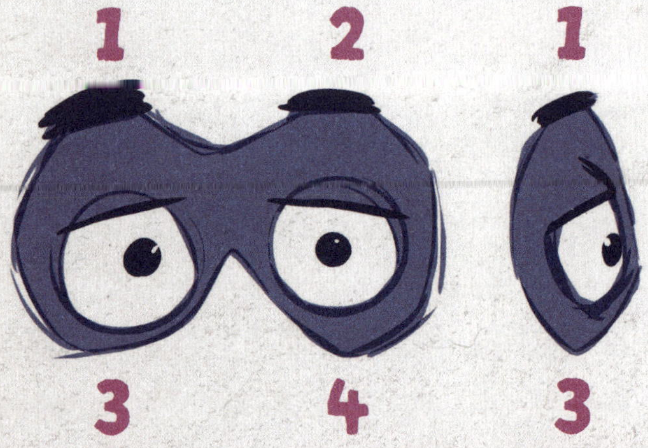

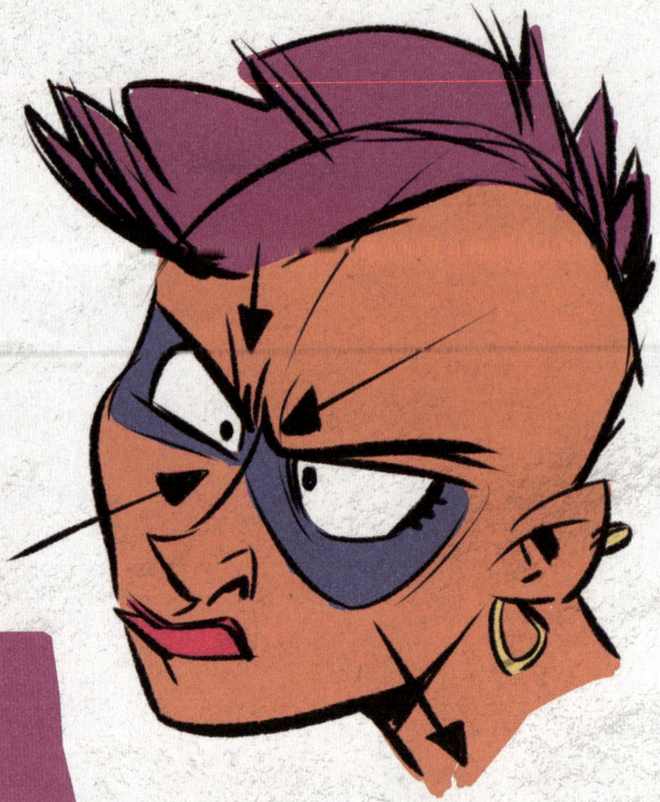

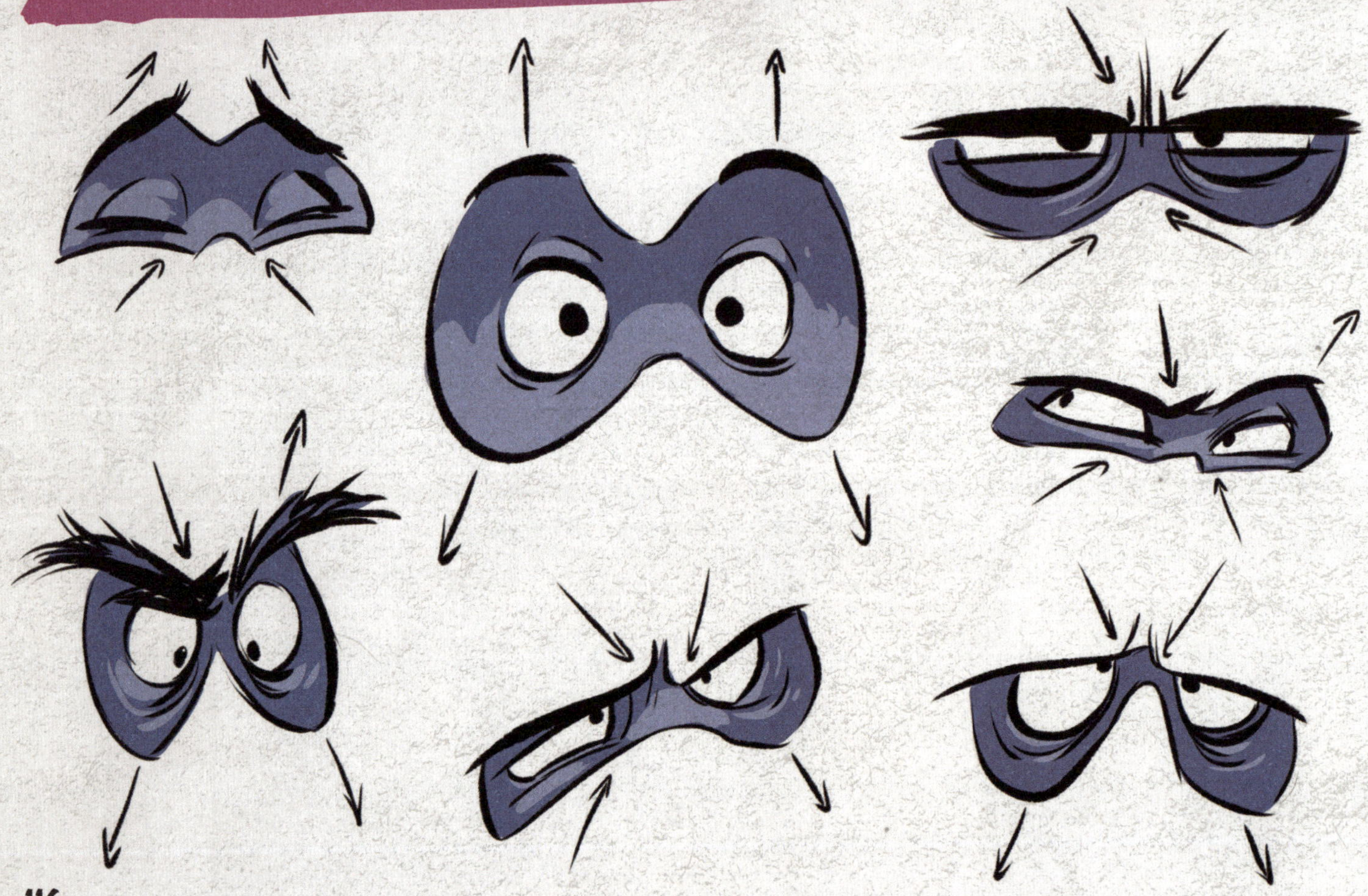

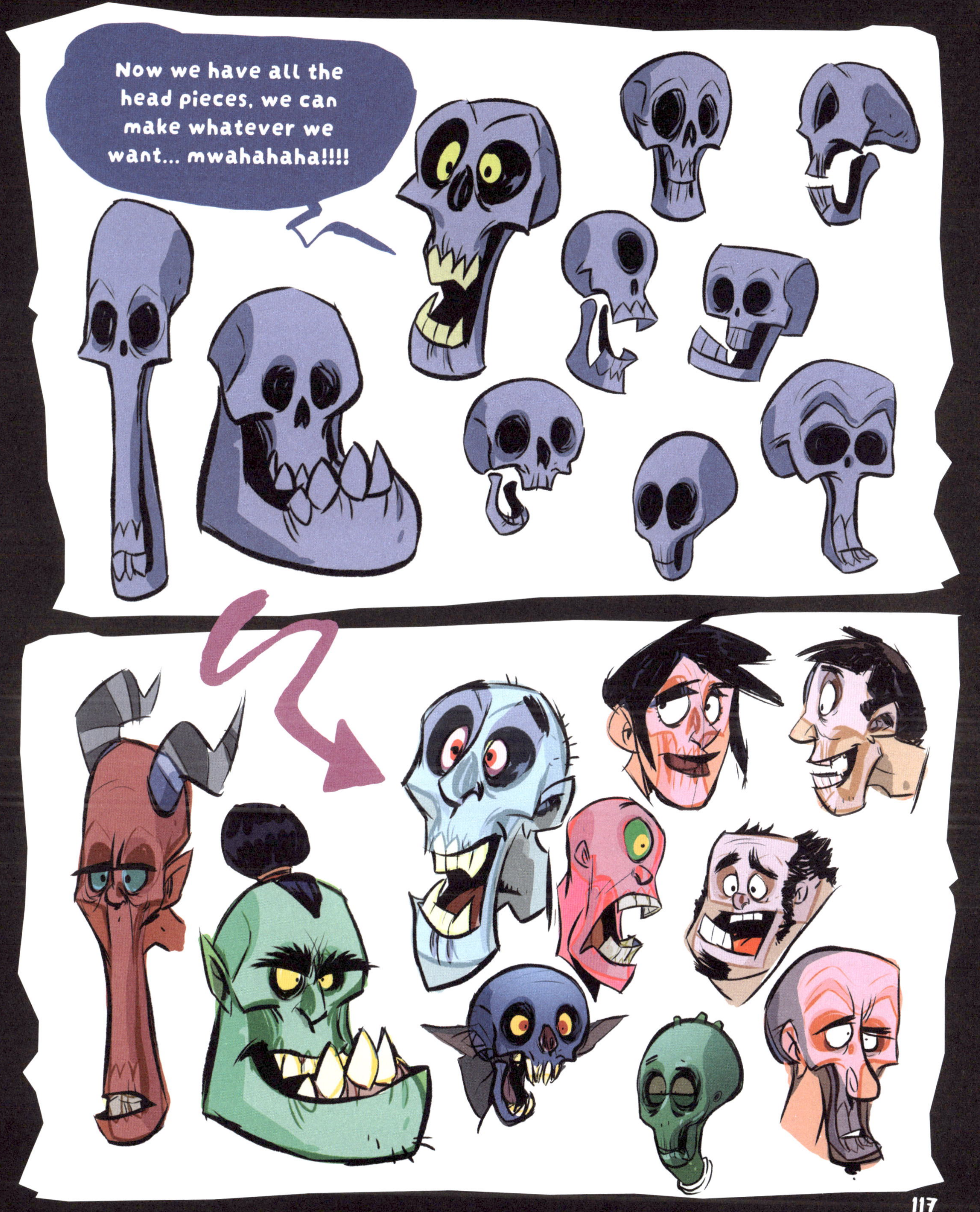

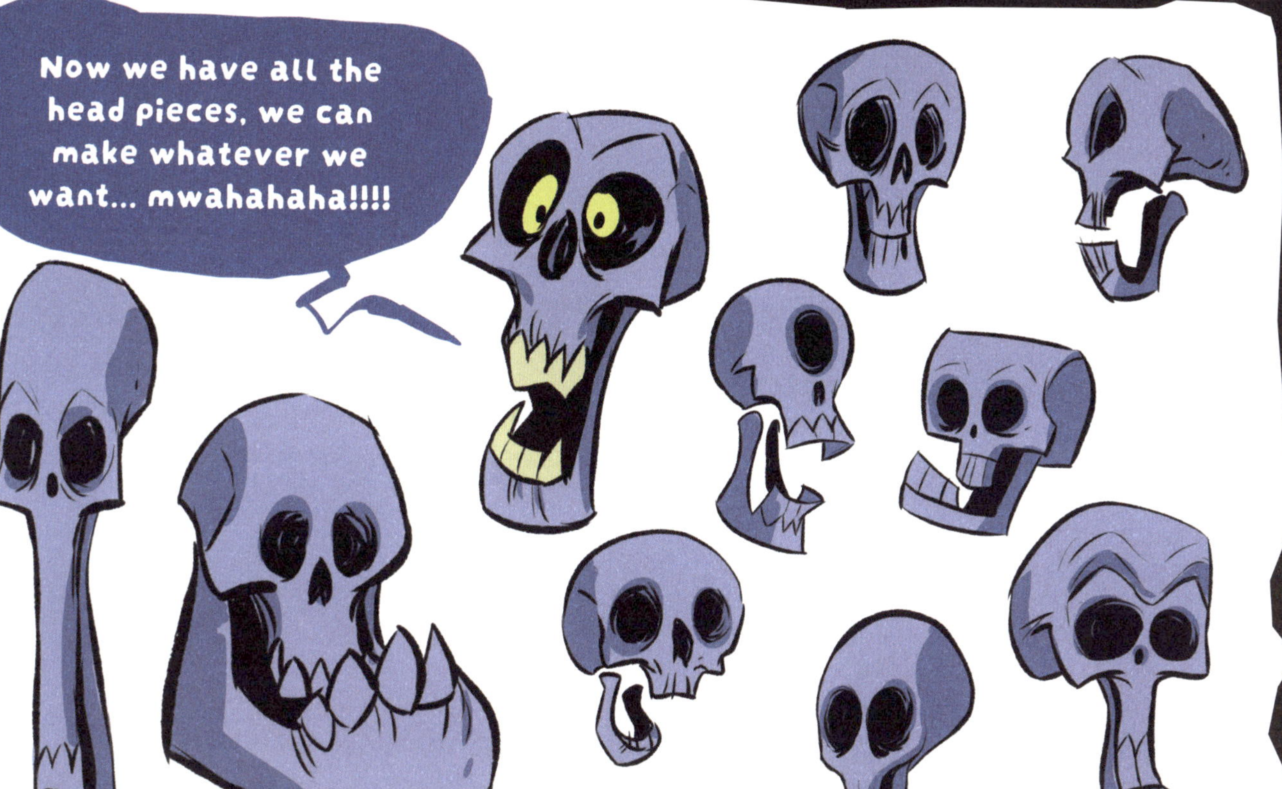

Now we have all the head pieces, we can make whatever we want... mwahahahaha!!!!

HANDS

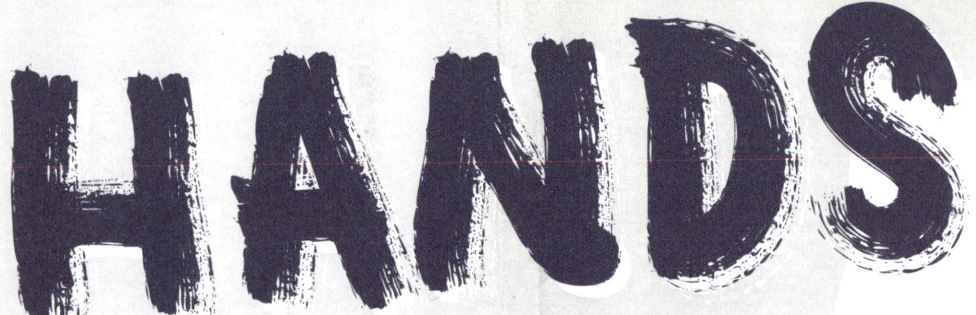

Hands are tricky to draw and it can take years to master their complexity.

Male hands are typically seen as larger and squarer, while female hands are usually slightly smaller and more streamlined.

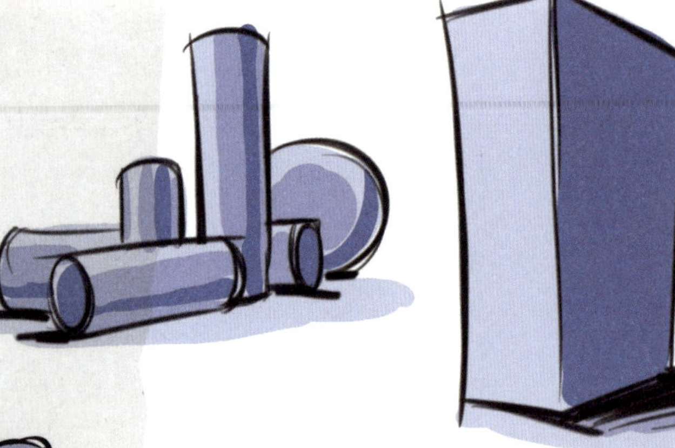

In geometric terms, hands are made up of rectangles, cylinders, and a ball for the thumb socket.

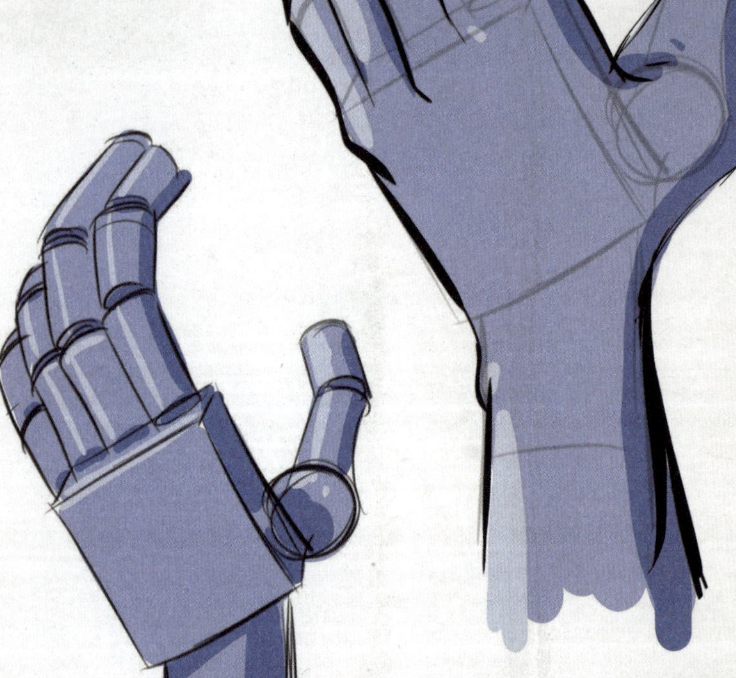

The middle finger should be the longest, the index and ring fingers should be similar lengths, and the pinkie finger should be the shortest.

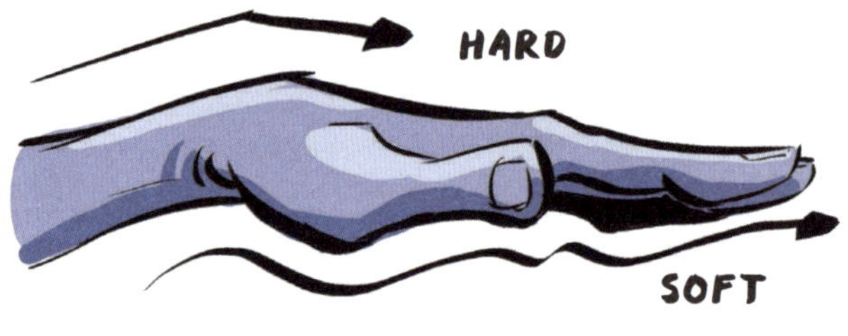

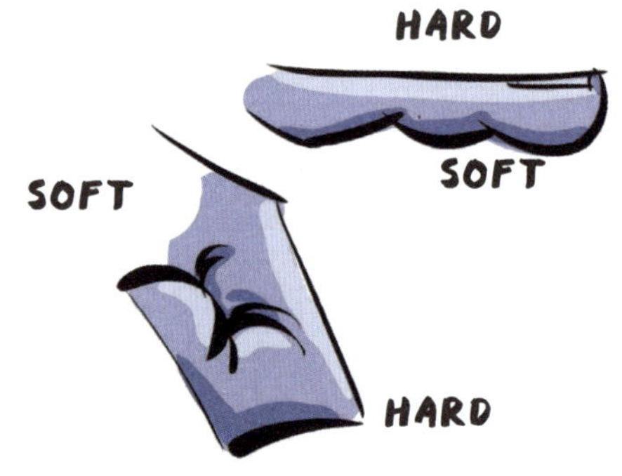

The back of the hand is harder than the softer underside (the palm).

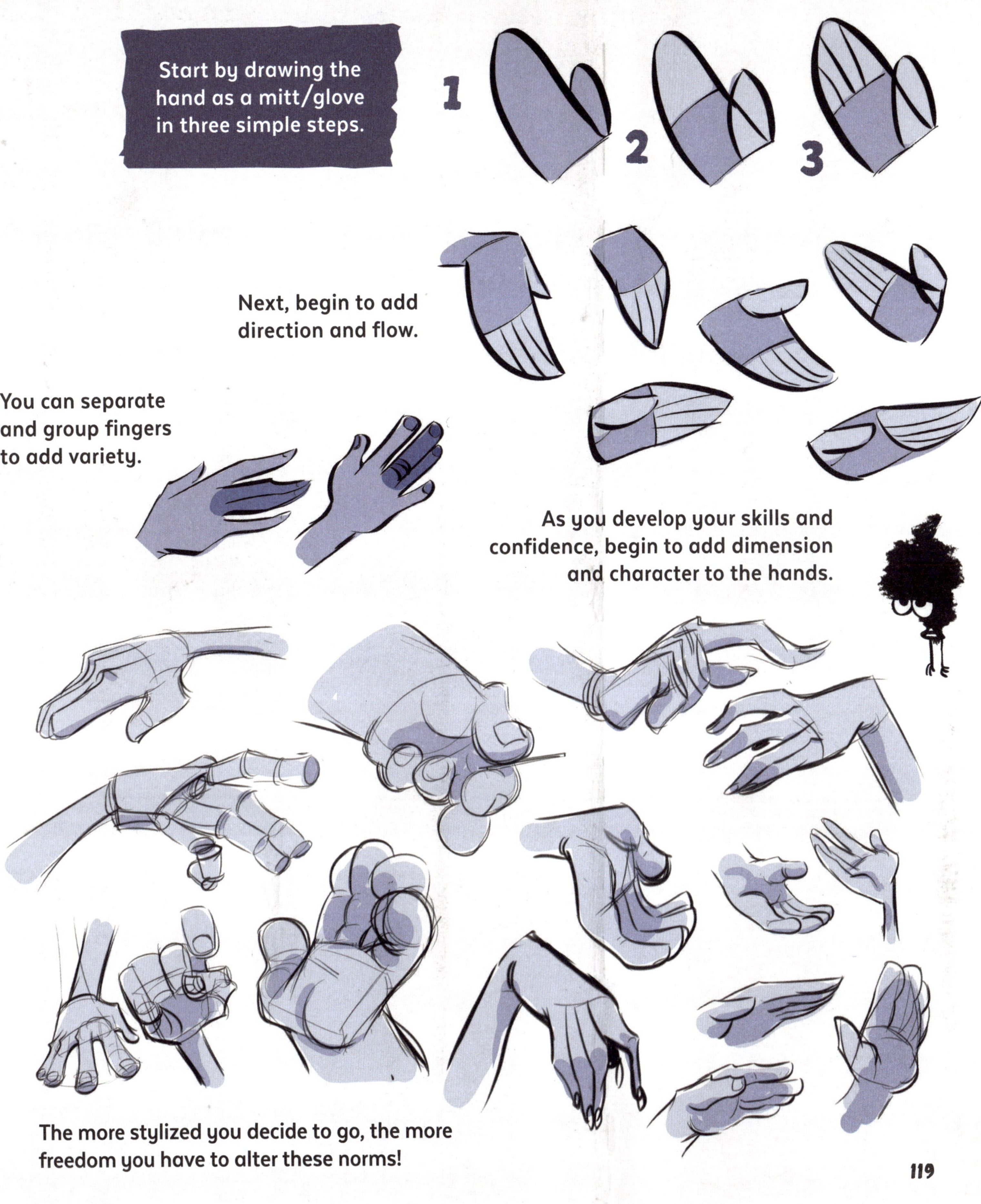

Start by drawing the hand as a mitt/glove in three simple steps.

1
2
3

Next, begin to add direction and flow.

You can separate and group fingers to add variety.

As you develop your skills and confidence, begin to add dimension and character to the hands.

The more stylized you decide to go, the more freedom you have to alter these norms!

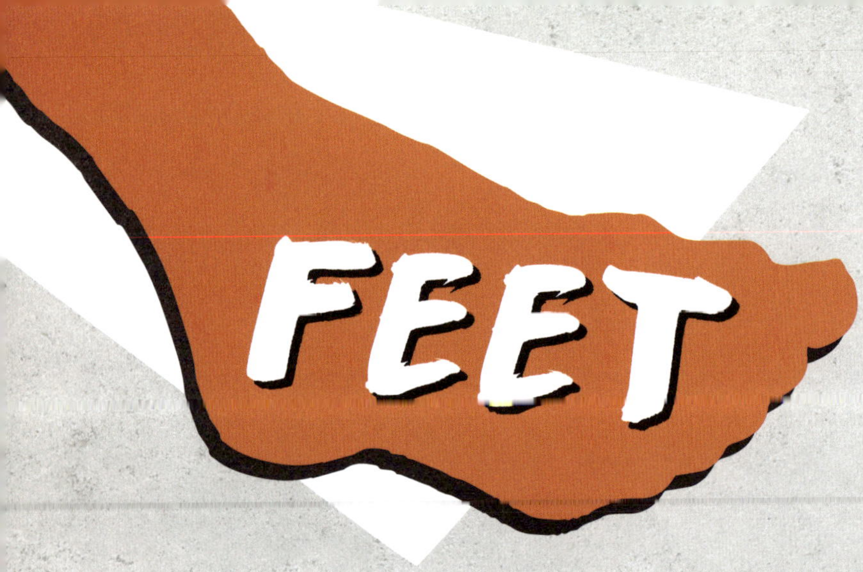

FEET

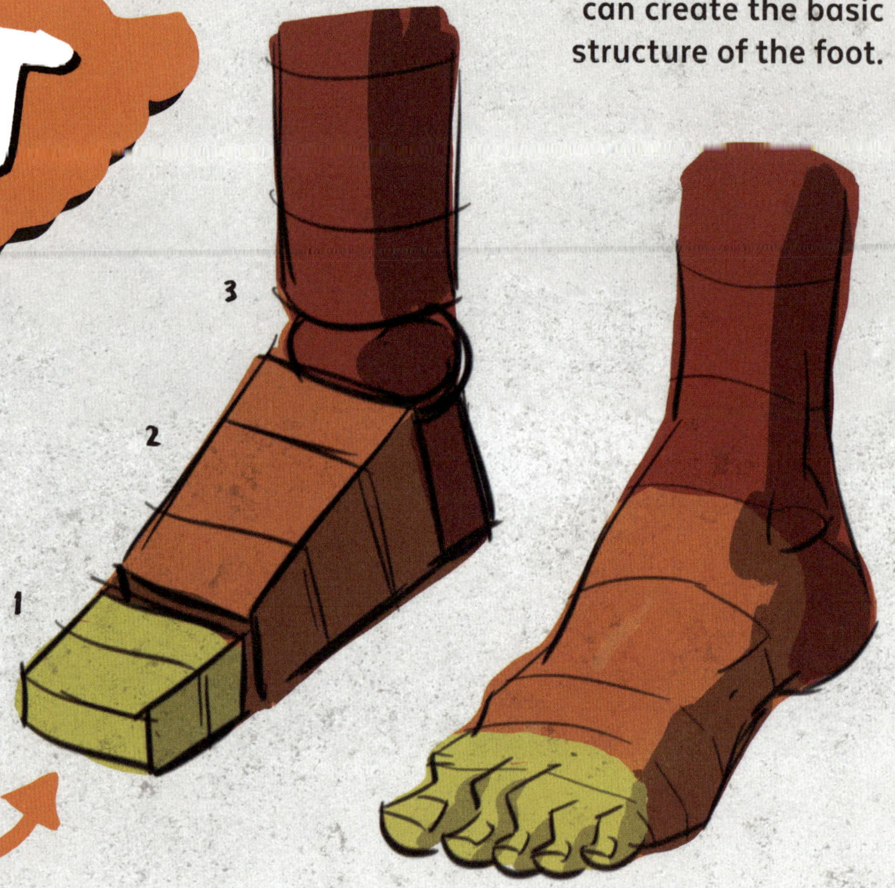

The shape of the foot is narrower at the heel and wider at the toes, but for our purposes let's stick to the basics.

Dividing the foot into three parts allows you to divide it into moveable sections.

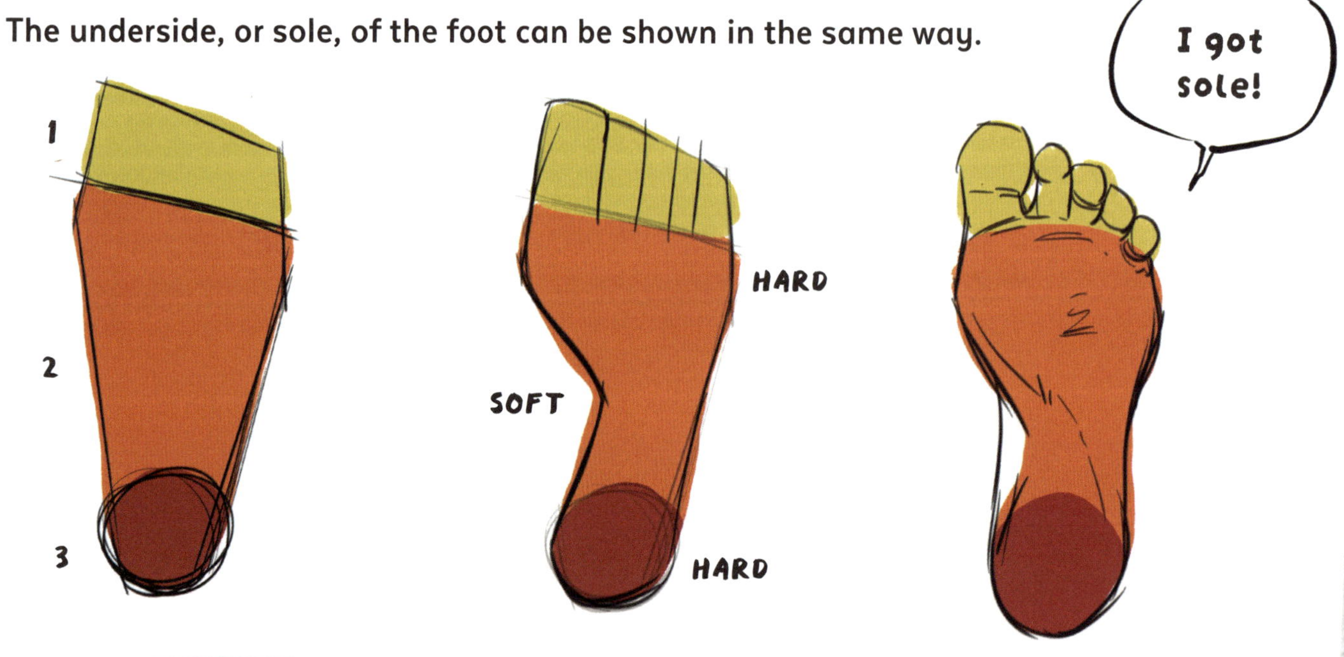

The underside, or sole, of the foot can be shown in the same way.

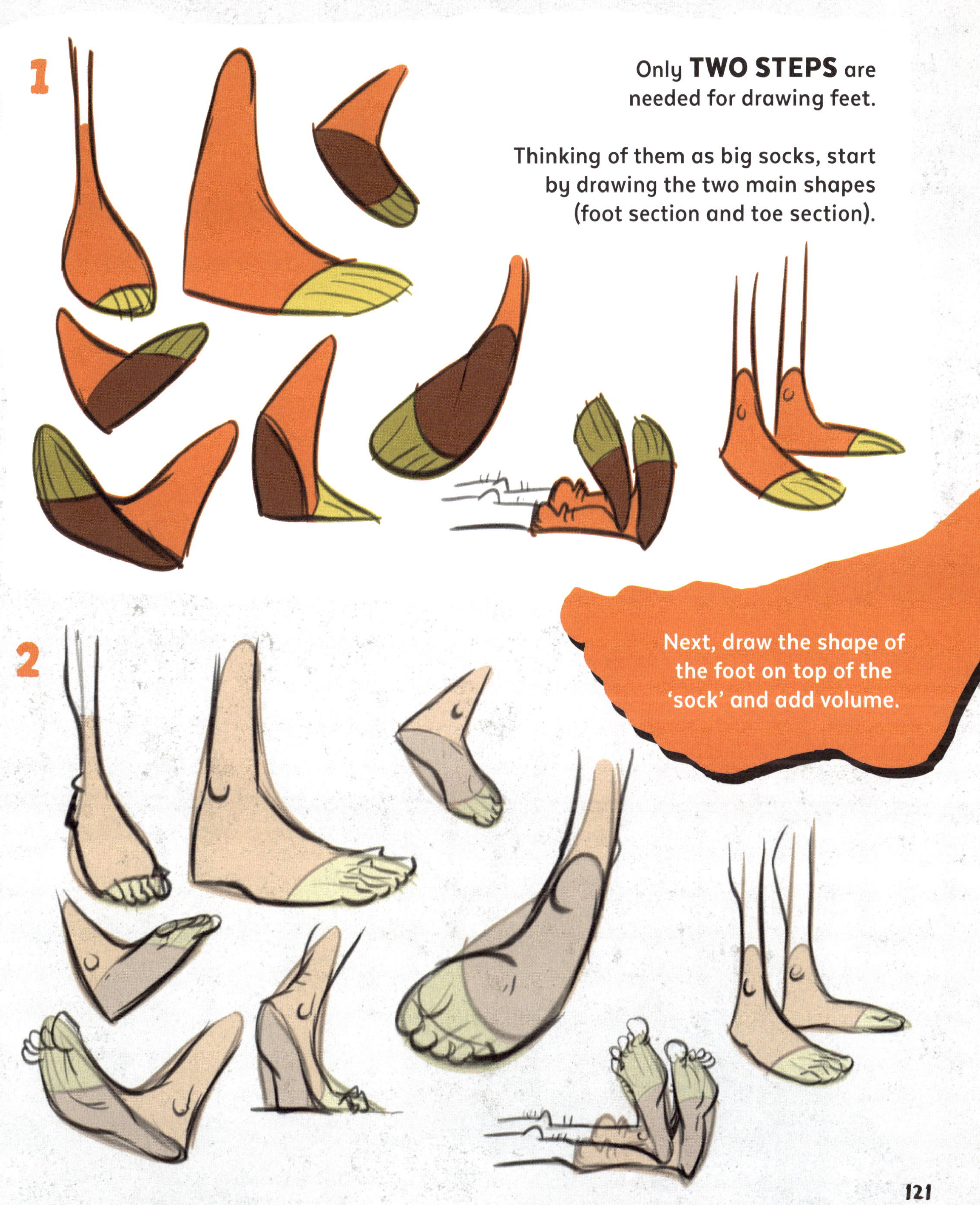

1
2
Only TWO STEPS are needed for drawing feet.

Thinking of them as big socks, start by drawing the two main shapes (foot section and toe section).

Next, draw the shape of the foot on top of the 'sock' and add volume.

PHYSICAL BALANCE

As earth-dwellers, we all live with gravity. The law of gravity is one of the few laws we can't break!

The **line of gravity** is an imaginary line that runs from the centre of gravity to the ground. When the line of gravity (**LOG**) falls outside of the base of support (**BOS**), a body reaction is needed to stay balanced.

The **base of support** is the area beneath a person that includes every point of contact they make with the supporting surface. These points of contact may be body parts, such as feet or hands, or objects like chairs or a walking stick.

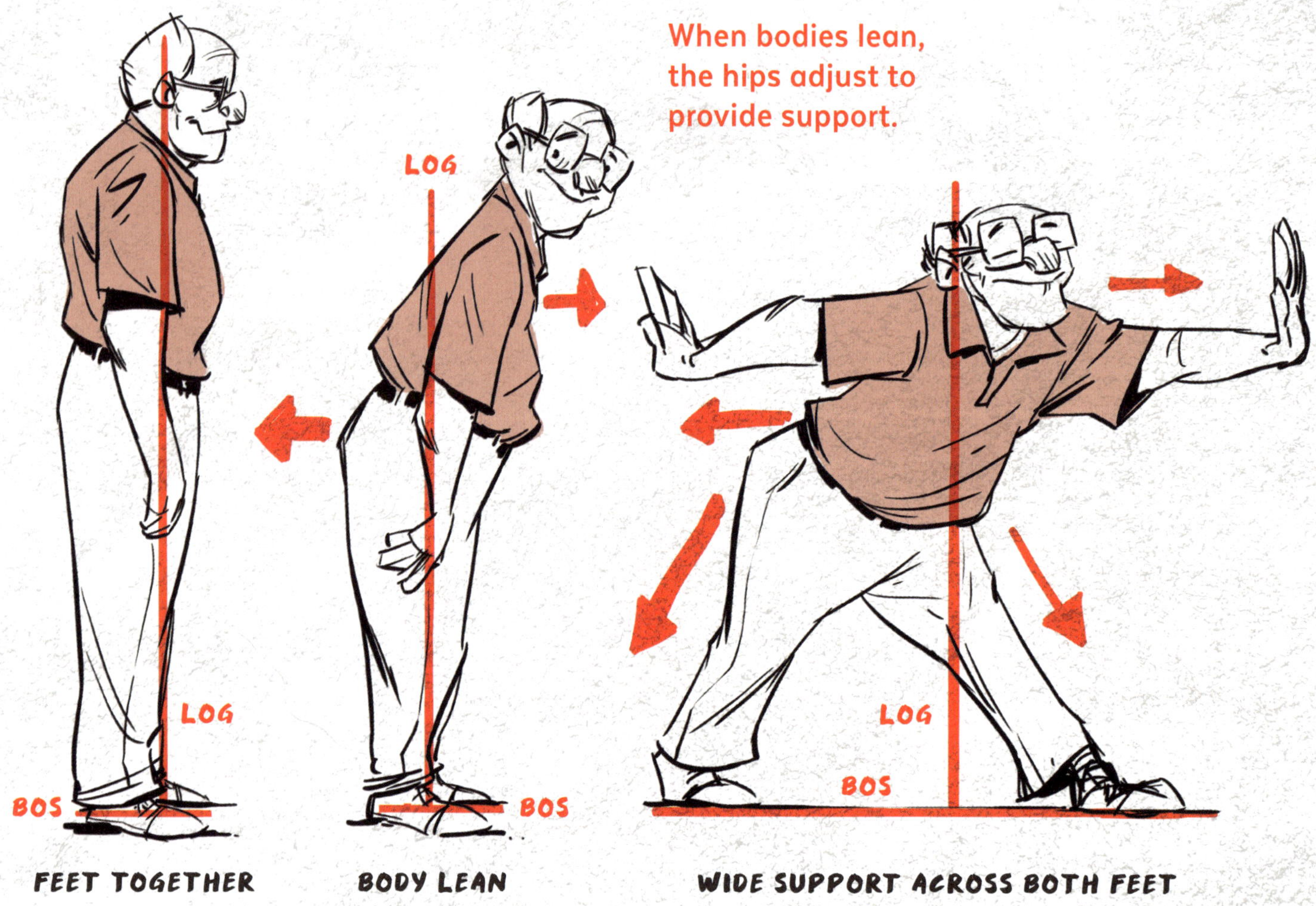

The body is always adjusting to maintain balance. Did you know we have to trip on purpose and catch ourselves just to walk?

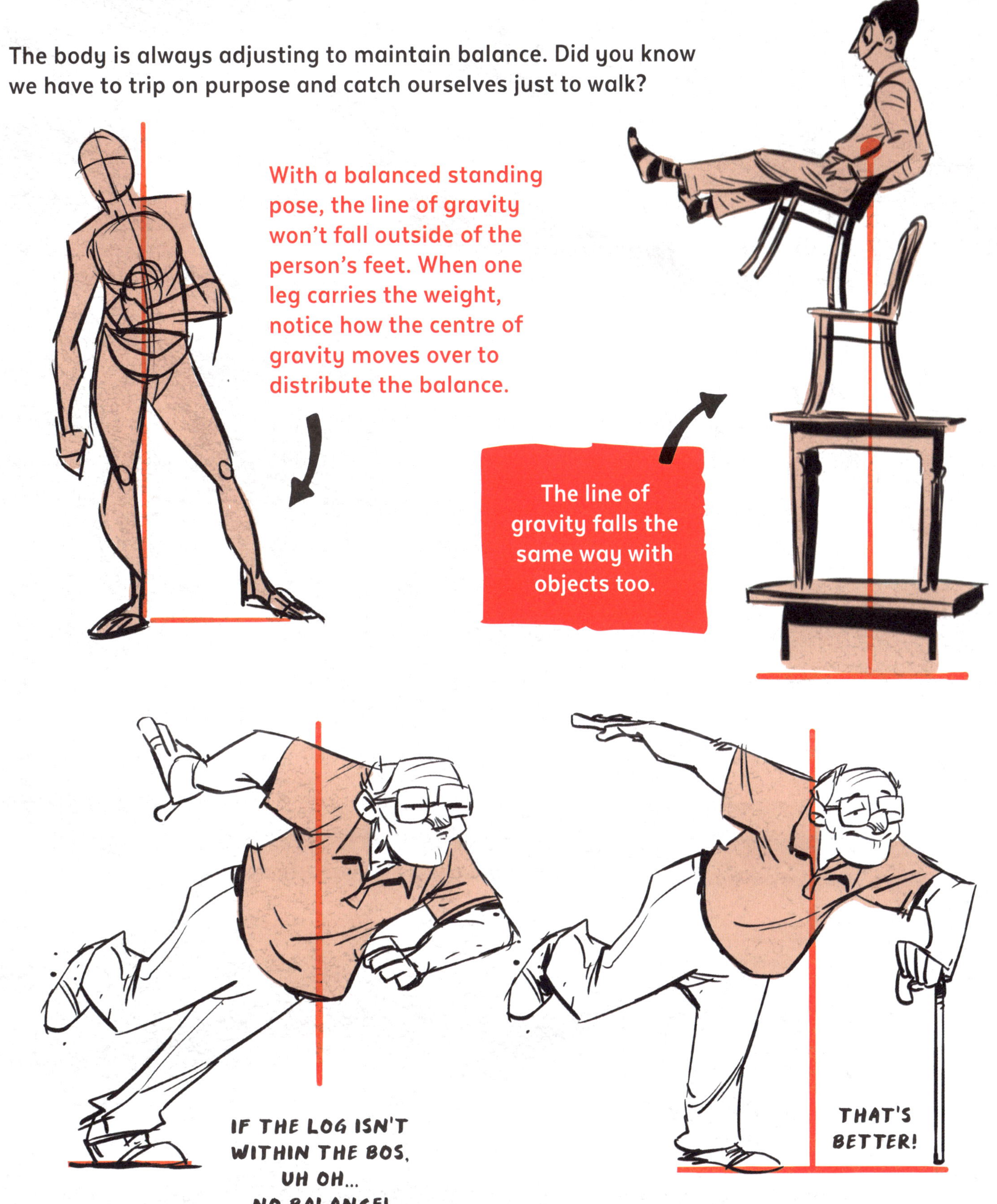

CLOTHING TIPS

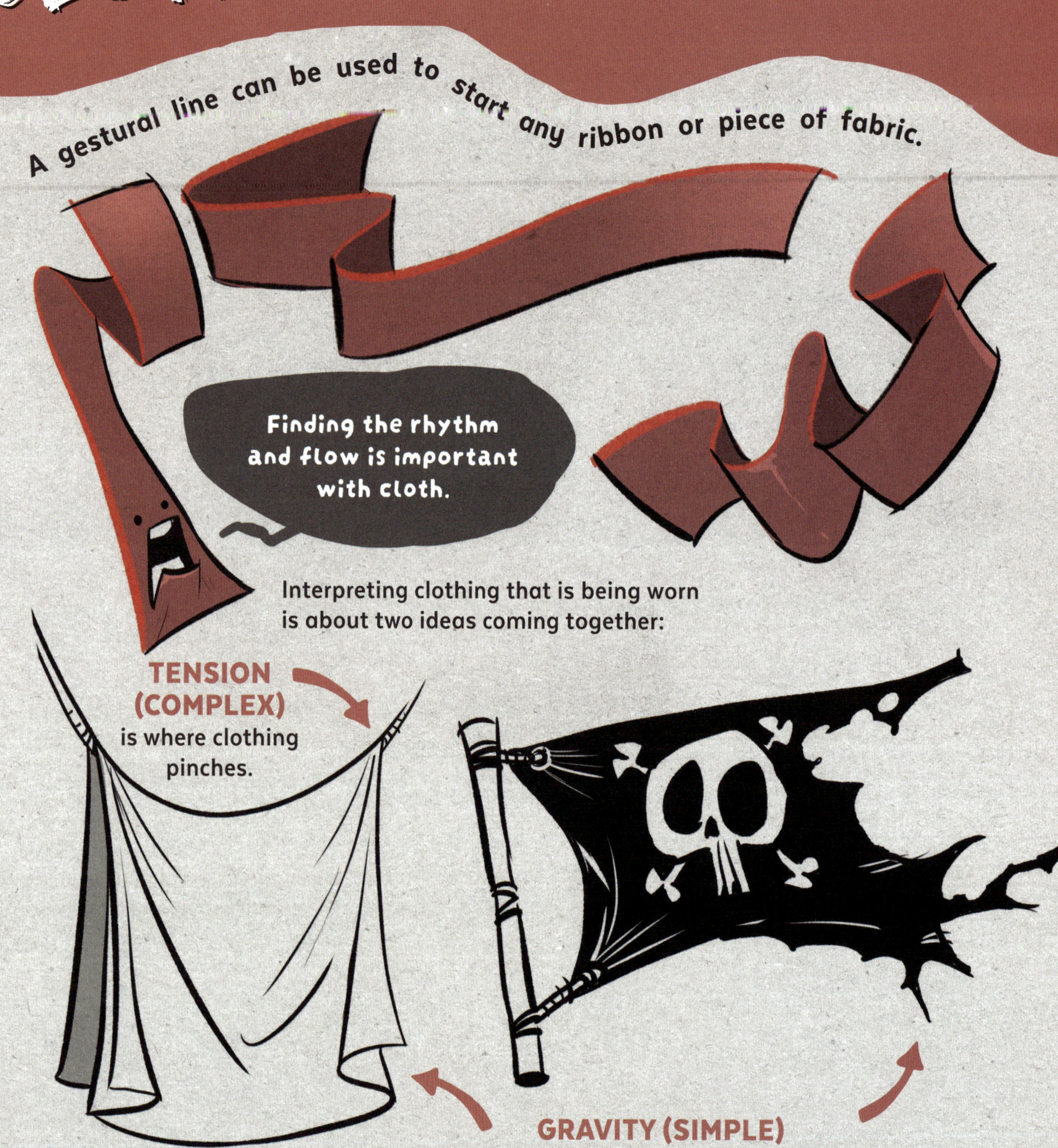

Think about what forms are underneath the clothes.

Gesture and motion create tension opportunities.

Planes and contours.

TENSION

GRAVITY

Pinches and contours will reveal the directions of the folds.

Drawing every fold would be pure madness!

Take it all in, but interpret what's important. Use this information to only draw what's necessary.

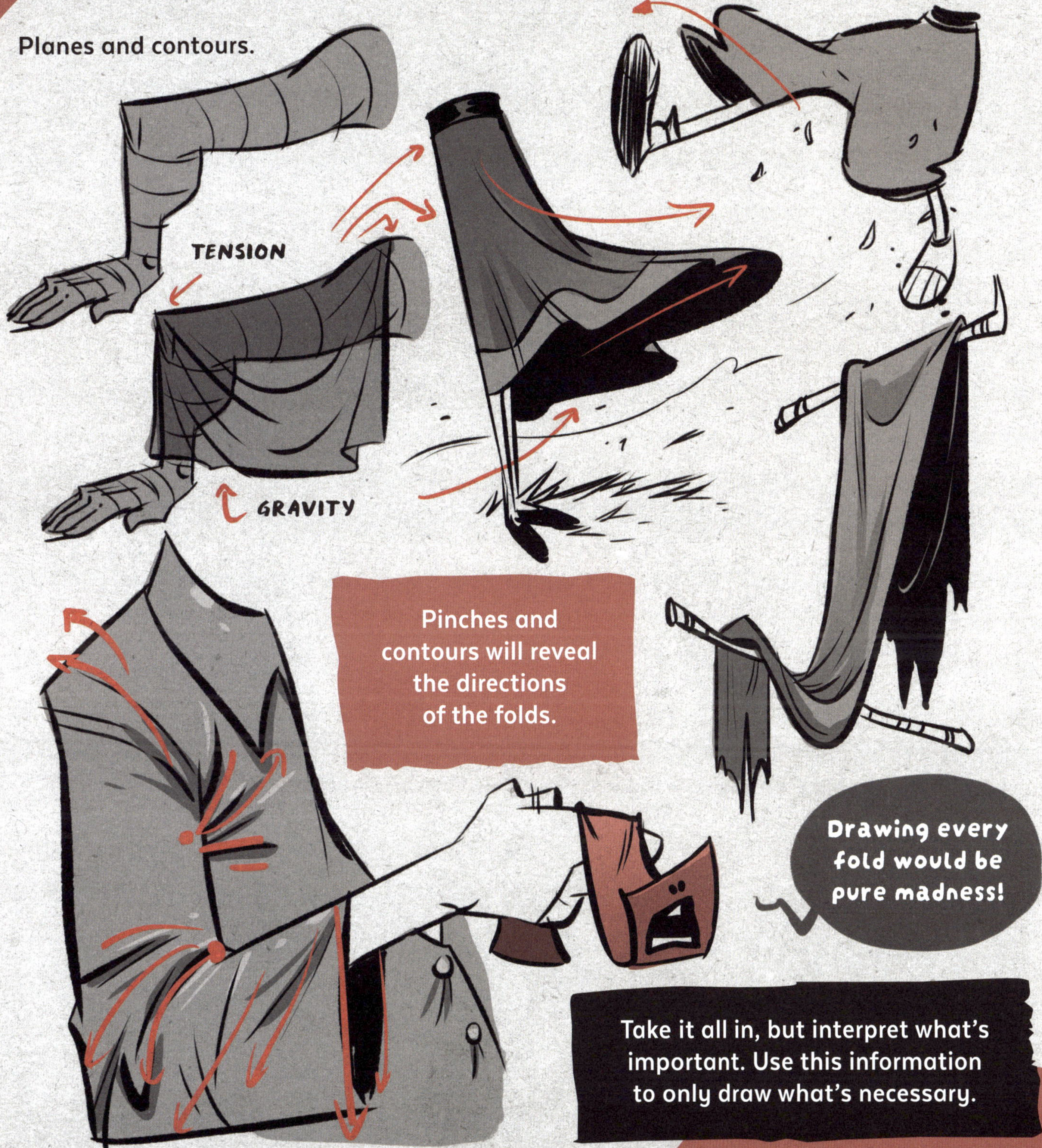

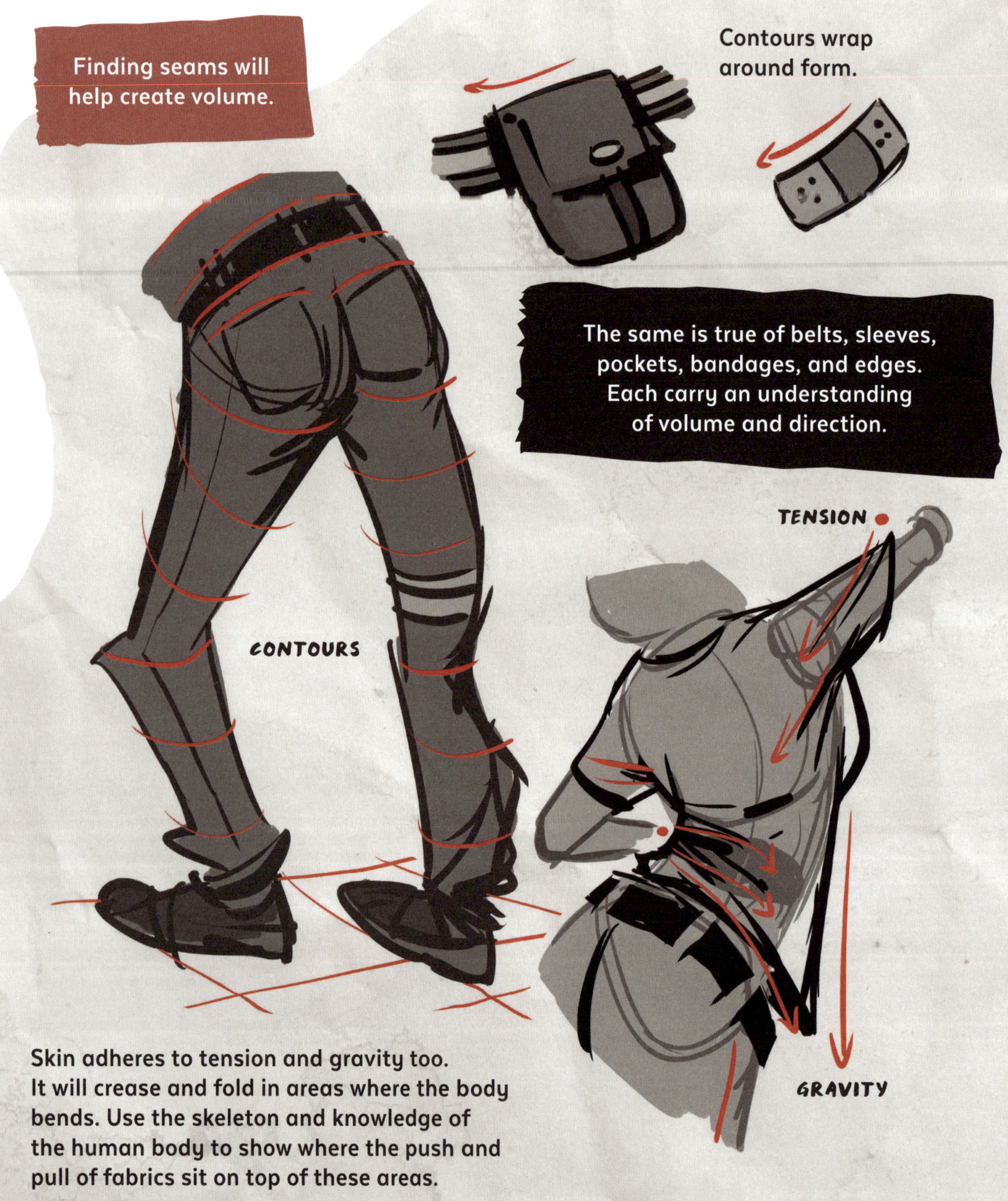

Skin adheres to tension and gravity too. It will crease and fold in areas where the body bends. Use the skeleton and knowledge of the human body to show where the push and pull of fabrics sit on top of these areas.

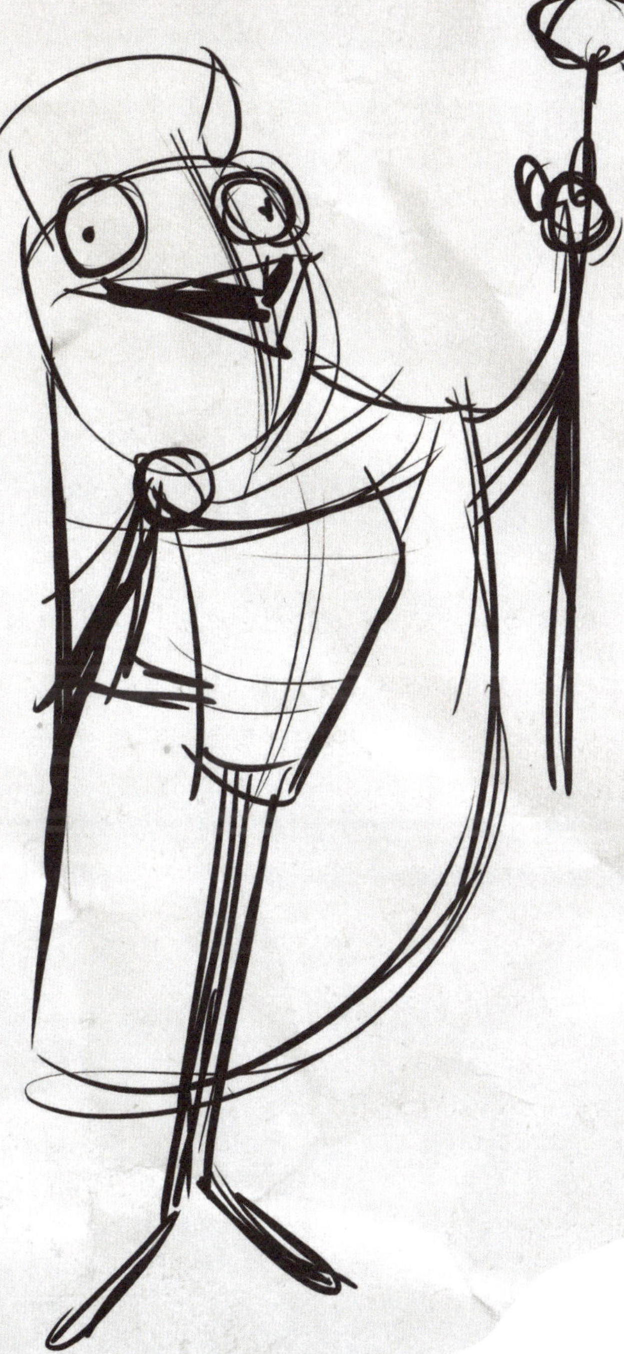

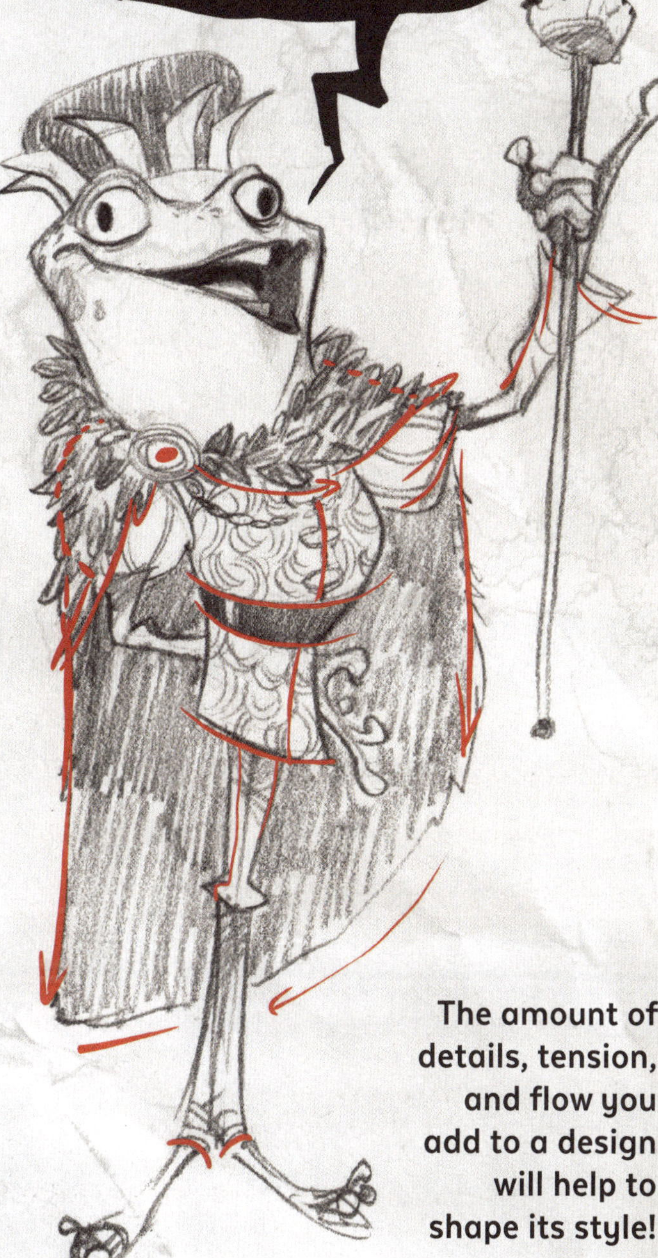

The amount of details, tension, and flow you add to a design will help to shape its style!

BODY EXERCISES

Trace over these, scan them, or take a photo to work digitally. Or download them (see URL on page 7).

Draw a head over these skulls.

Draw the line of gravity over the base of support on each figure.

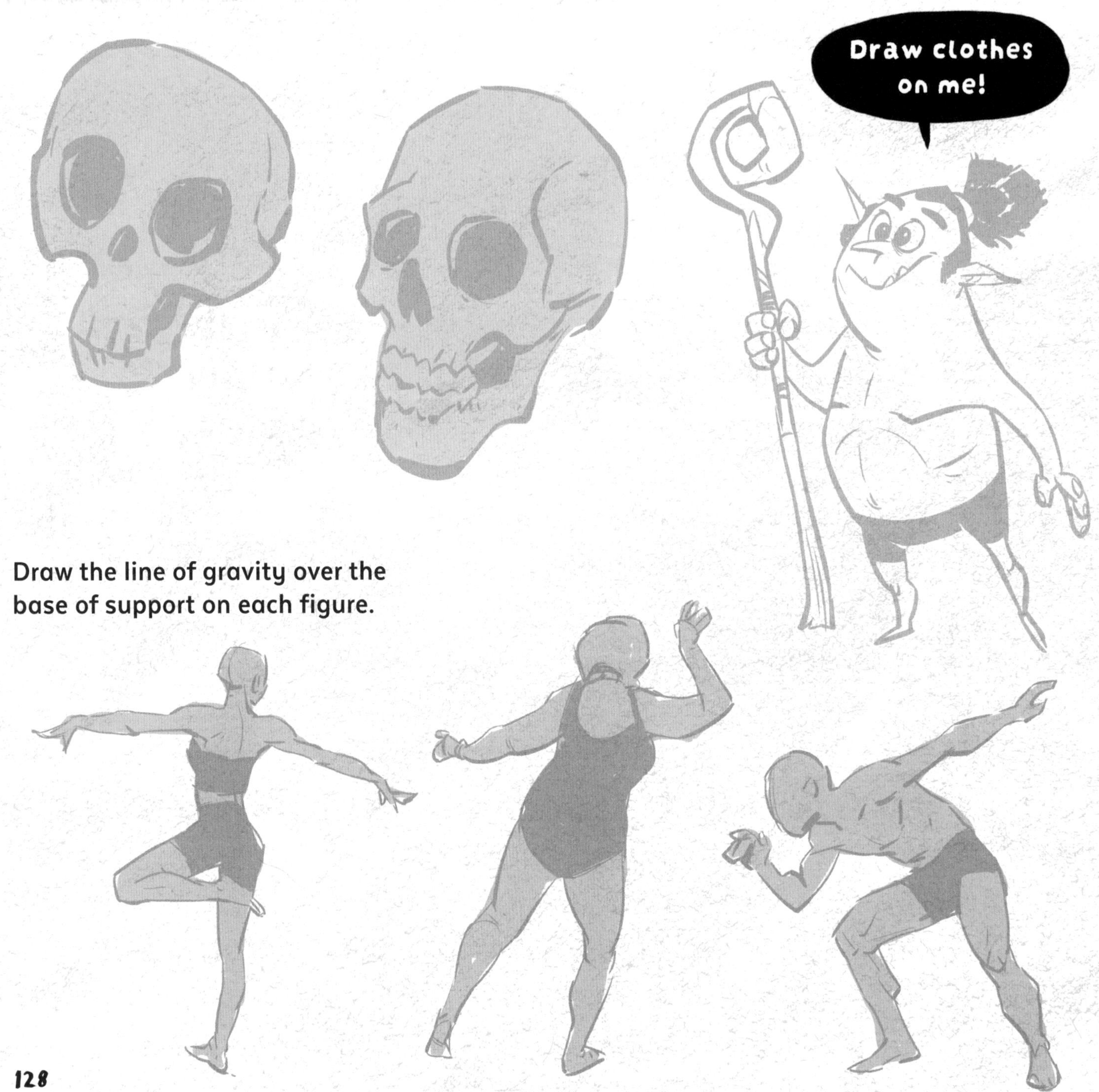

Draw the skeleton
inside each body.

The contours of
the shadows and
clothing will help
to communicate
direction.

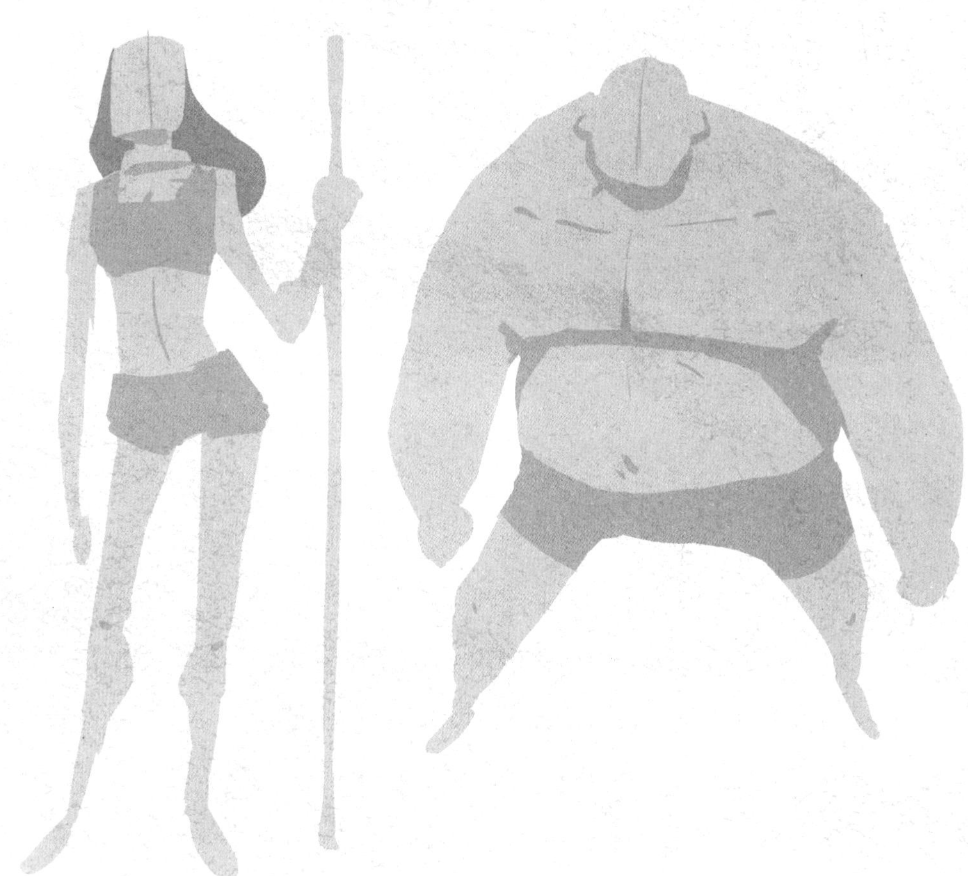

Draw a bandit-style facial mask over each design.

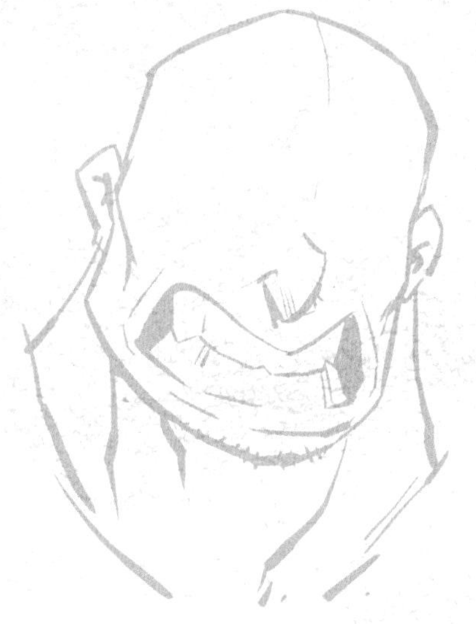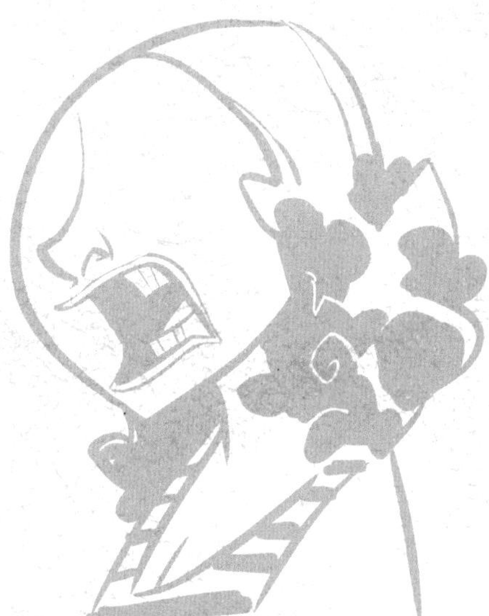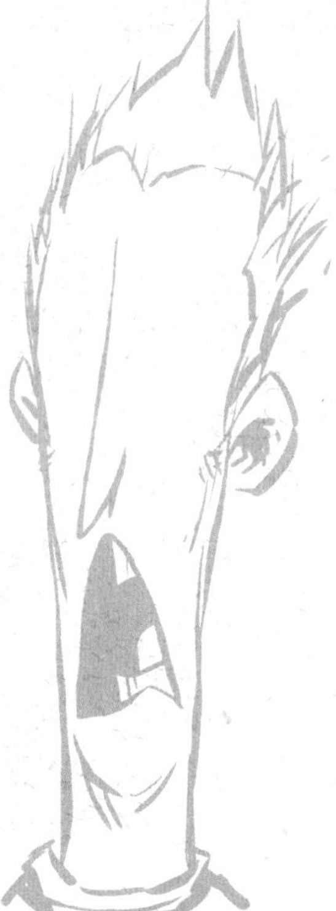

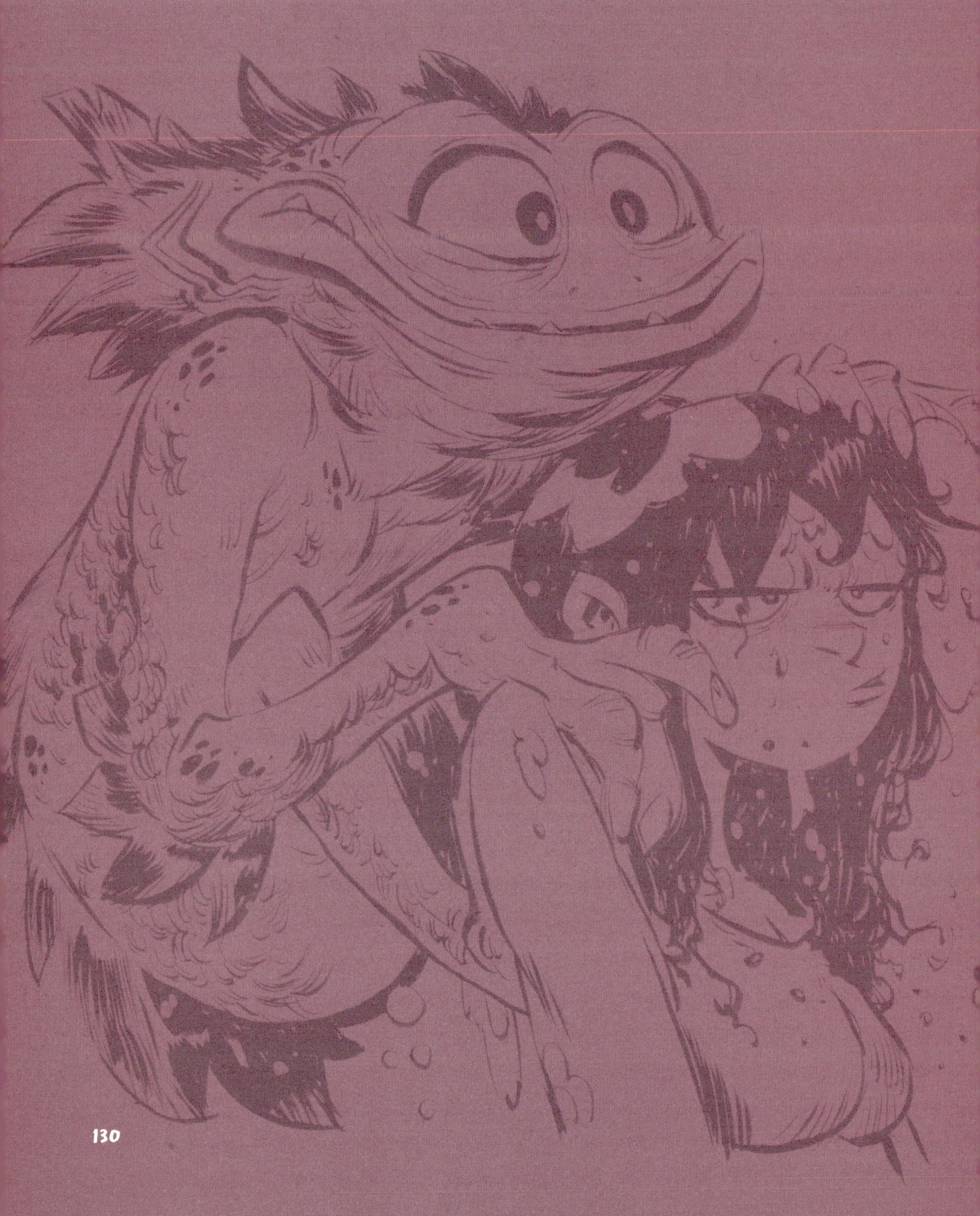

CHAPTER 05

BUILDING CHARACTER

Character design is broken up into two words for a reason.

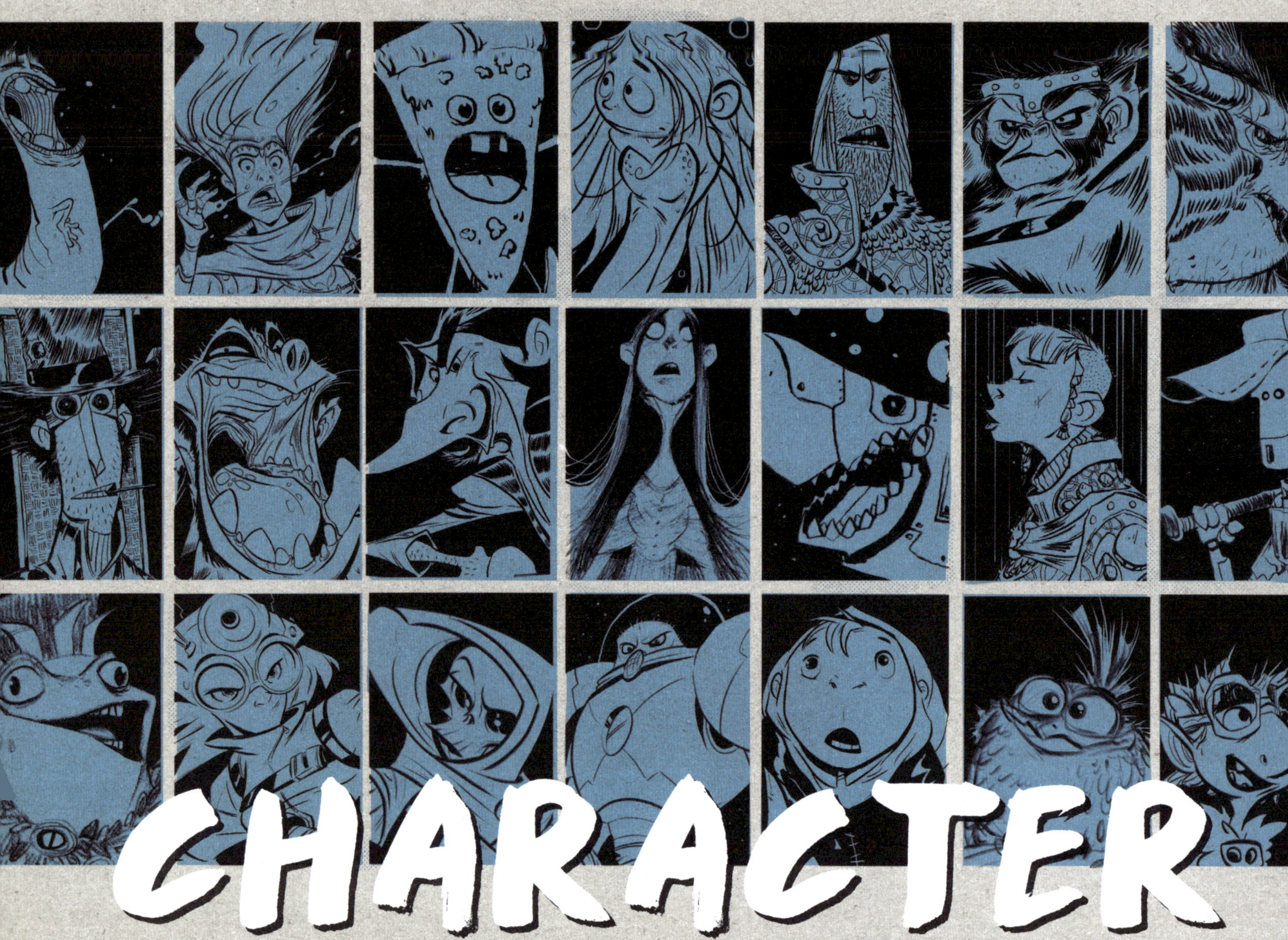

CHARACTER

Character is the mental and moral qualities distinctive to a person, animal, or other life form. Take yourself, for instance. Really think about yourself. Moods fluctuate, but your convictions do not. How you handle yourself, talk, speak, laugh, and get mad...

That's all **THE INNER YOU**: your character. As artists, we help to show this through posing and gesture. When we draw how a character feels and reacts, we accept that character as more real.

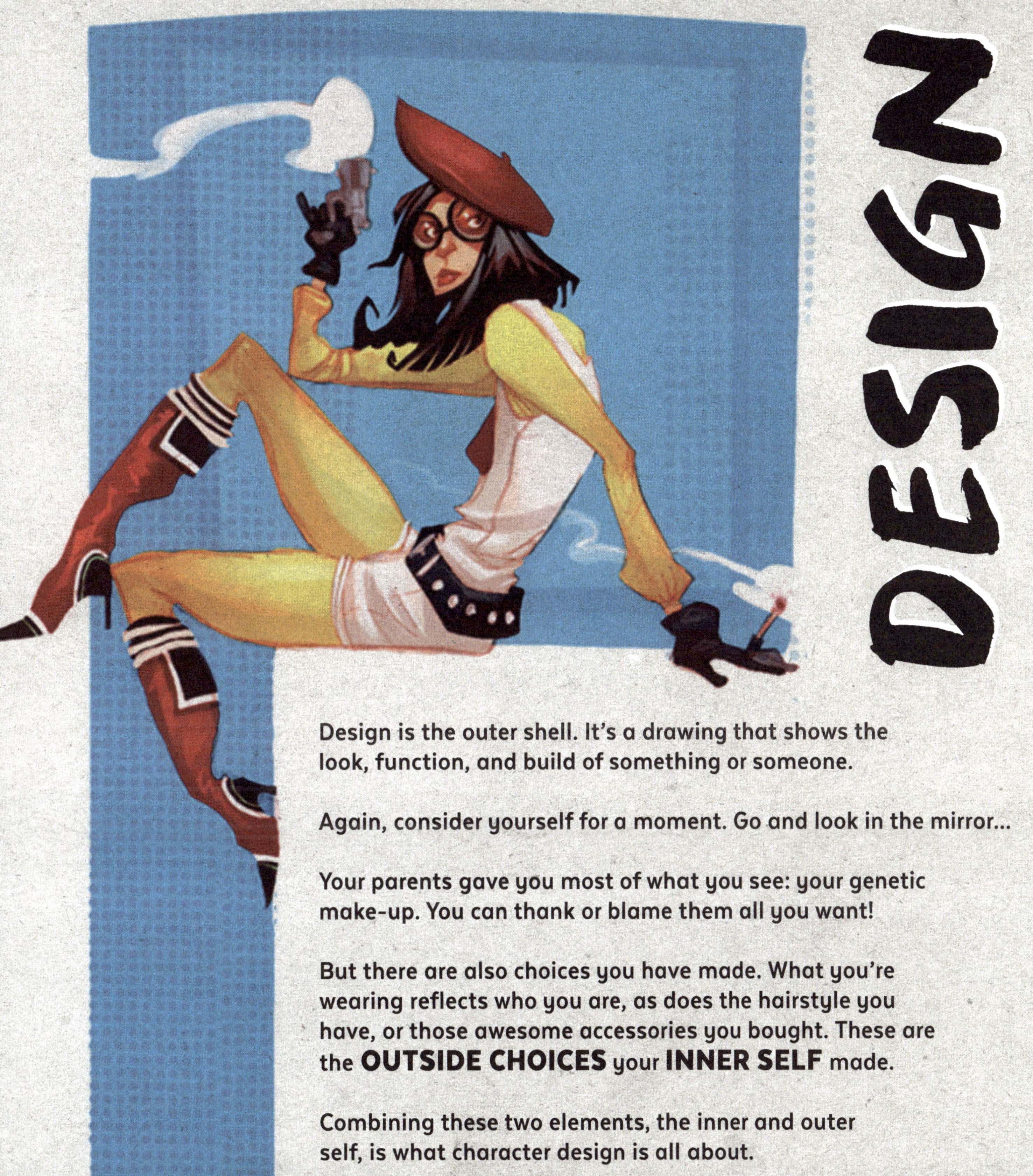

Design is the outer shell. It's a drawing that shows the look, function, and build of something or someone.

Again, consider yourself for a moment. Go and look in the mirror...

Your parents gave you most of what you see: your genetic make-up. You can thank or blame them all you want!

But there are also choices you have made. What you're wearing reflects who you are, as does the hairstyle you have, or those awesome accessories you bought. These are the **OUTSIDE CHOICES** your **INNER SELF** made.

Combining these two elements, the inner and outer self, is what character design is all about.

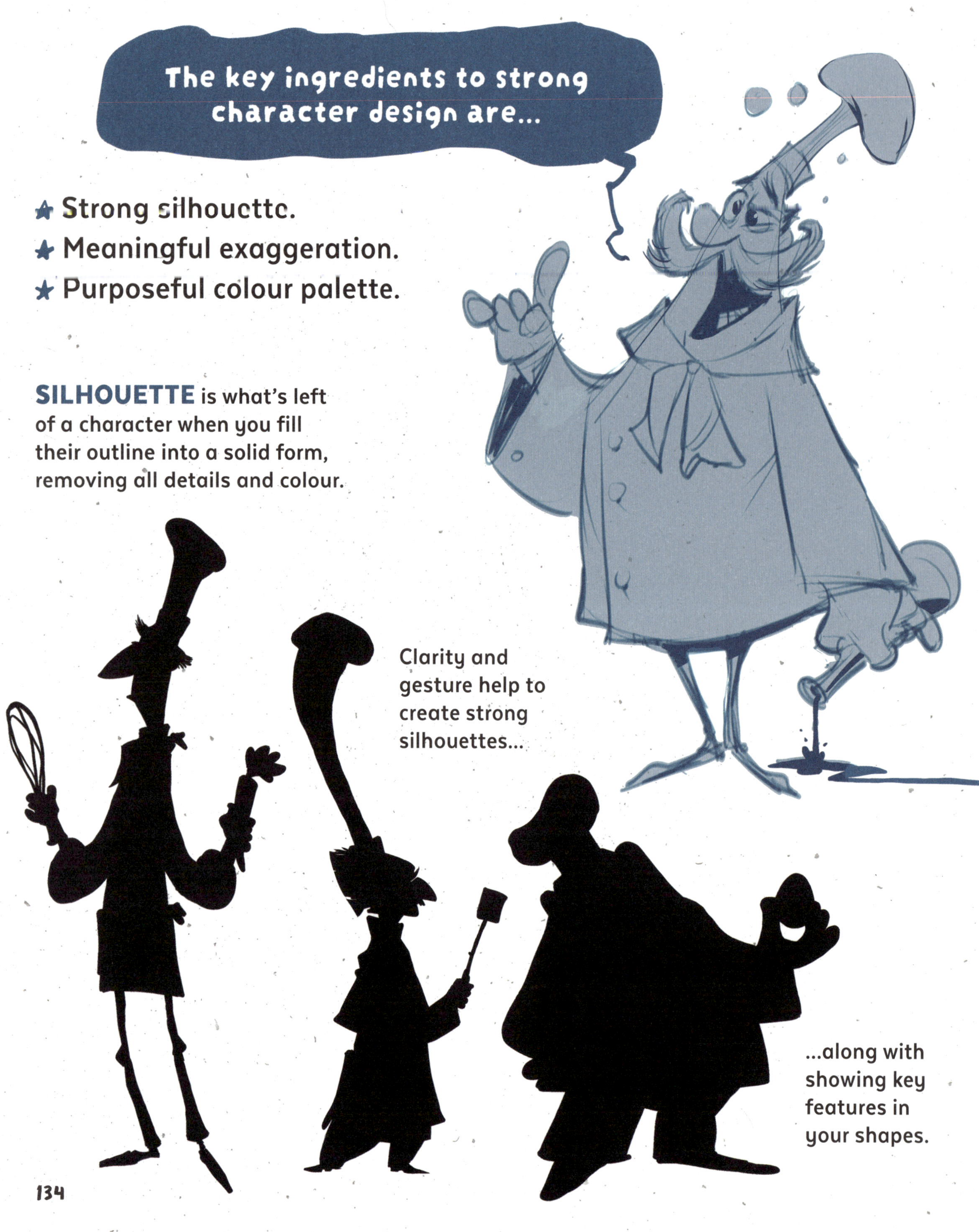

★ Strong silhouette.
★ Meaningful exaggeration.
★ Purposeful colour palette.

SILHOUETTE is what's left of a character when you fill their outline into a solid form, removing all details and colour.

Clarity and gesture help to create strong silhouettes...

...along with showing key features in your shapes.

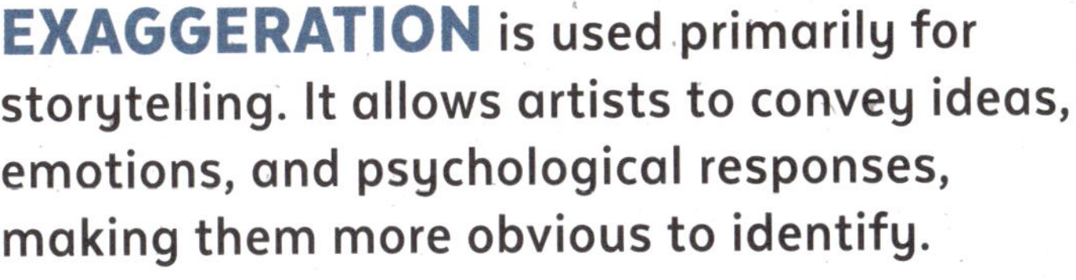

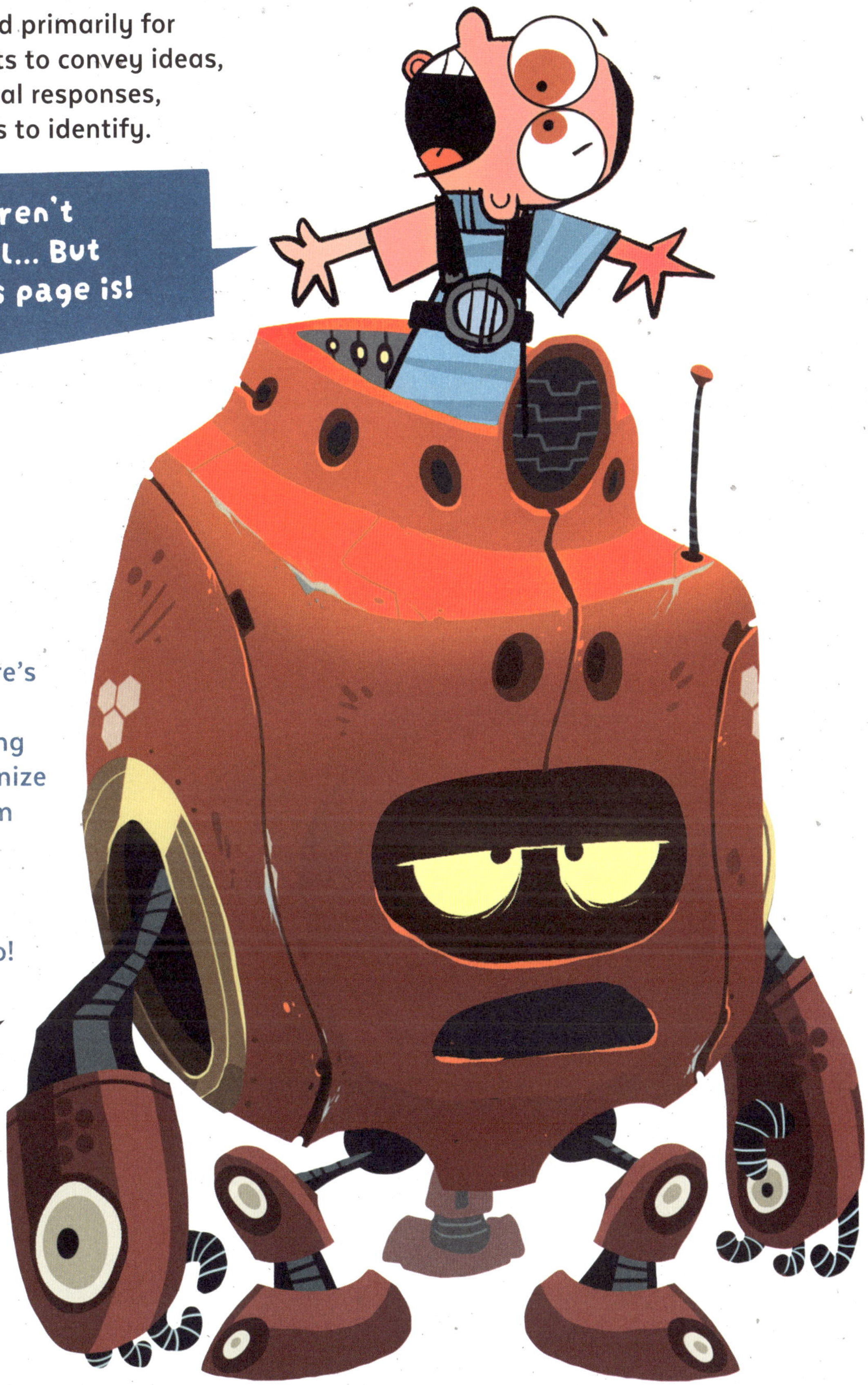

Whether drawing a static image, movie, TV show, book, or game, artists only have so much time to visually communicate who a character is.

Within your character, there's a story containing details and emotions. Exaggerating them lets the viewer recognize good from evil, heroes from villains, or somewhere in between. This can also be used to flip the archetype and surprise the viewer too!

A **COLOUR PALETTE** is made up of the specific colours used for a character design.

Choosing colours can help to determine who the character is, both inside and out.

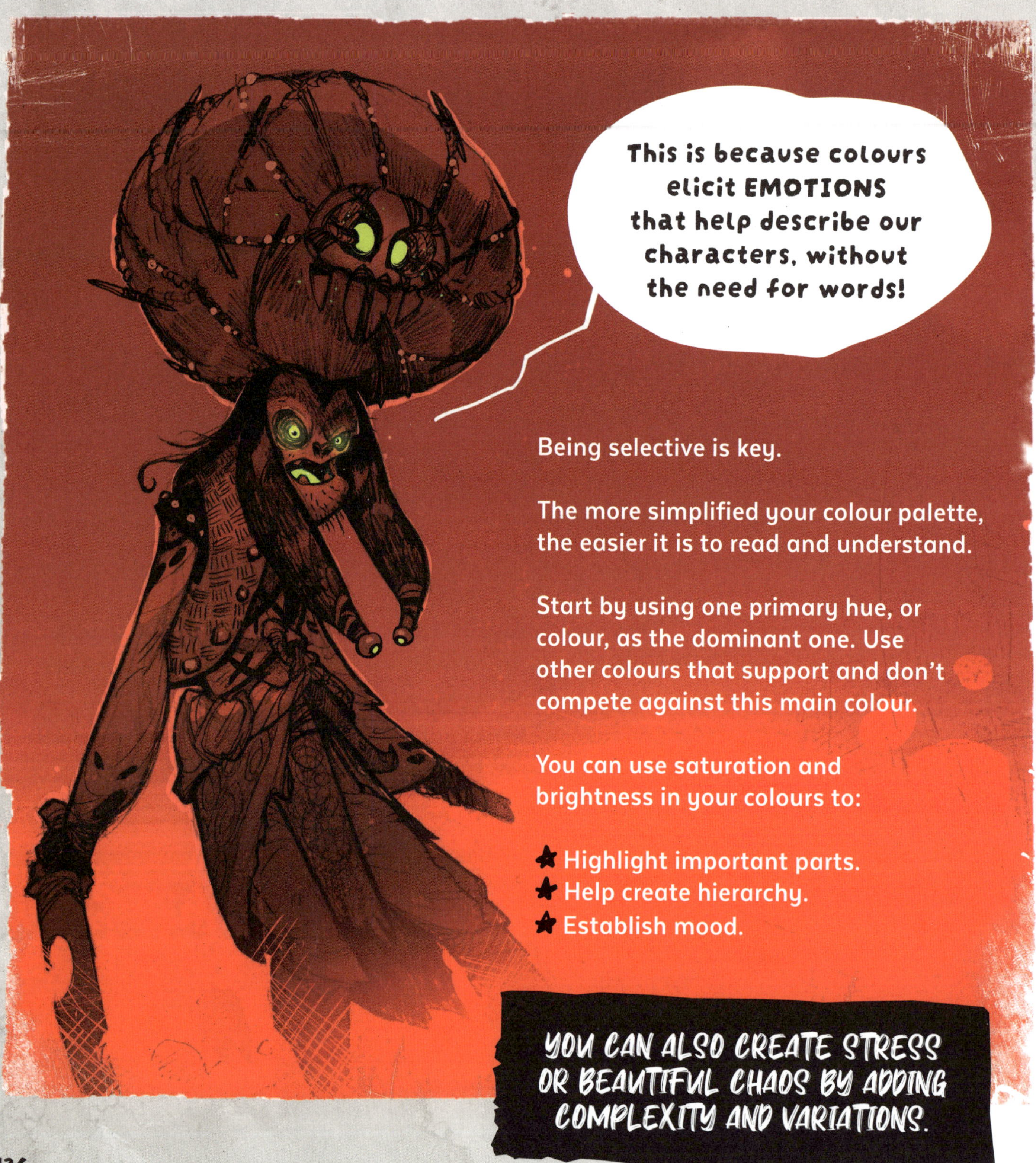

Being selective is key.

The more simplified your colour palette, the easier it is to read and understand.

Start by using one primary hue, or colour, as the dominant one. Use other colours that support and don't compete against this main colour.

You can use saturation and brightness in your colours to:

★ Highlight important parts.
★ Help create hierarchy.
★ Establish mood.

YOU CAN ALSO CREATE STRESS OR BEAUTIFUL CHAOS BY ADDING COMPLEXITY AND VARIATIONS.

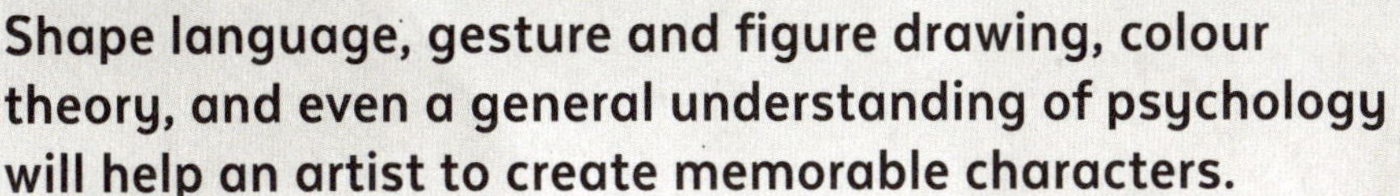

Shape language, gesture and figure drawing, colour theory, and even a general understanding of psychology will help an artist to create memorable characters.

This is why artists observe life! Not just in anatomy class, but in everyday life too.

Put down your phone and observe the colours in nature, the bustle of streets, and people waiting in queues.

To understand life, you must live one.

Smell the ocean, watch a puppy, listen to the forest...

It's important to look up from your sketchbook and live a little!

The most important things for me when observing are:

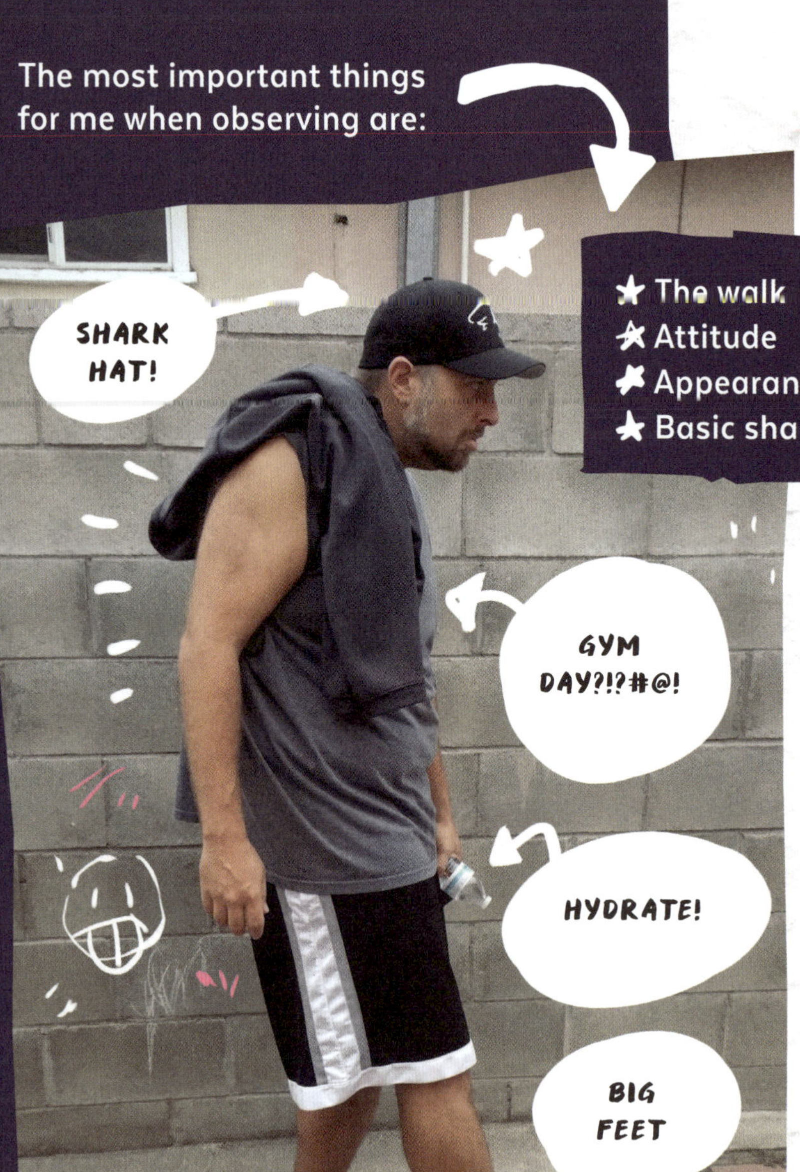

You aren't drawing this person, but what you've decided is the **IDEA** of this person:

'A tired grump from the gym.'

HERE'S A STUDY OF HOW TO THINK WHEN DOING OBSERVATION DRAWING

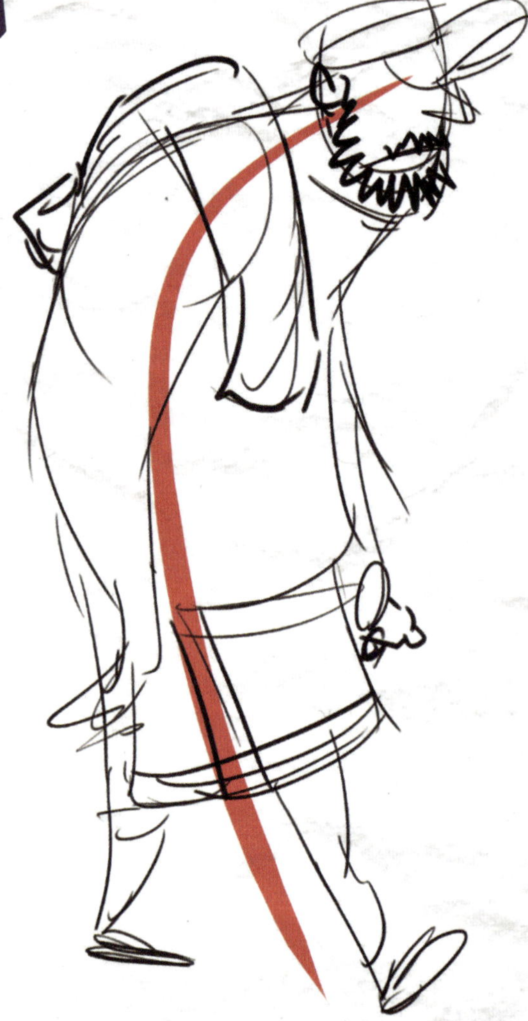

TAKE THIRTY SECONDS TO QUICKLY SKETCH OUT YOUR LINE OF ACTION AND STORY/IDEA.

What you decide to keep, remove, remember, change, enhance, or detract should be conscious decisions. Remember that shapes, colours, gesture, and details should add and reflect the main story/idea.

I push his neck and head forward, draw more beard, give him droopy arms and face, and add colour.

Try these exercises in your sketchbook.

LOOK, DRAW, LOOK, DRAW

Go back and forth between subject and art until you're finished. This helps with capturing the anatomy correctly.

LOOOOOOOOOK DRAW

Observe the subject for a while, without being creepy, and then draw what you remember. This helps to build up your mental ability to remember key features and forget the elements your designer brain doesn't need.

LOOK, DRAW TOMORROW

Take in what you can and then go about your day. Draw the subject the next day. This will fine-tune your designer brain, challenge your memory, and channel your inner designer to make big decisions.

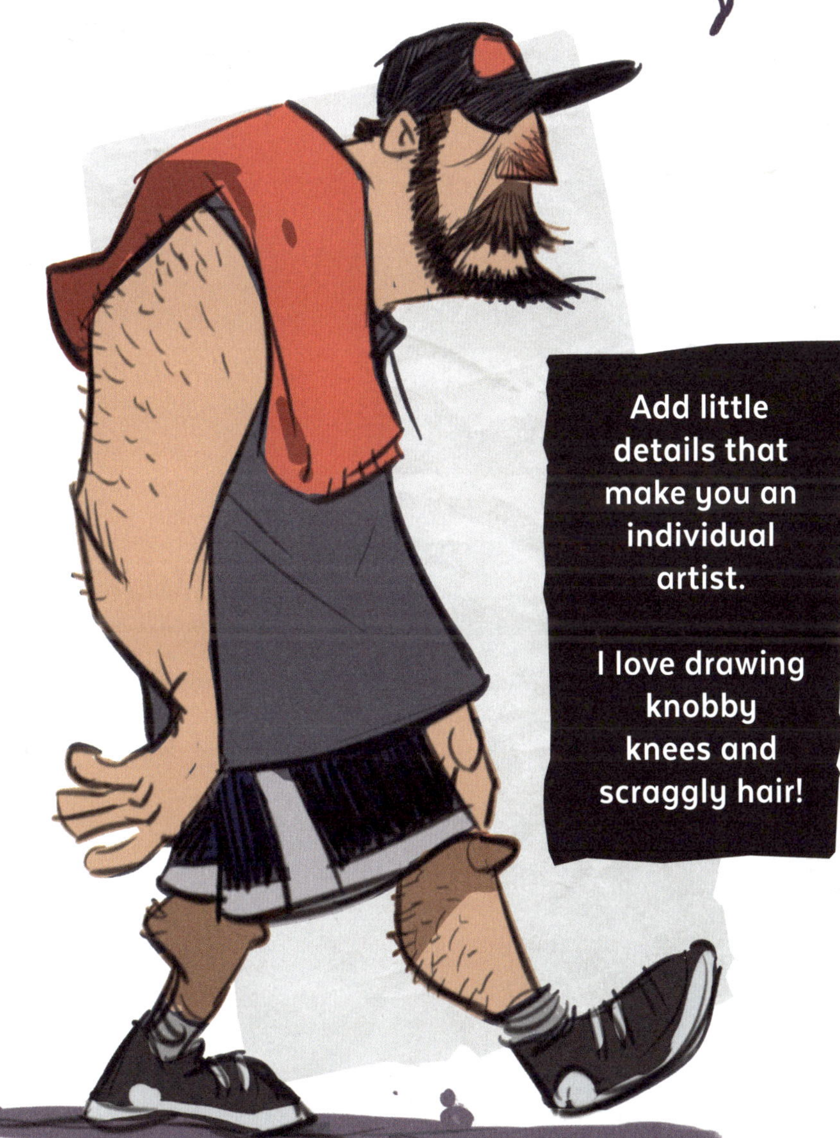

GESTURE DRAWING

Gesture and posing play a very important part in character design.

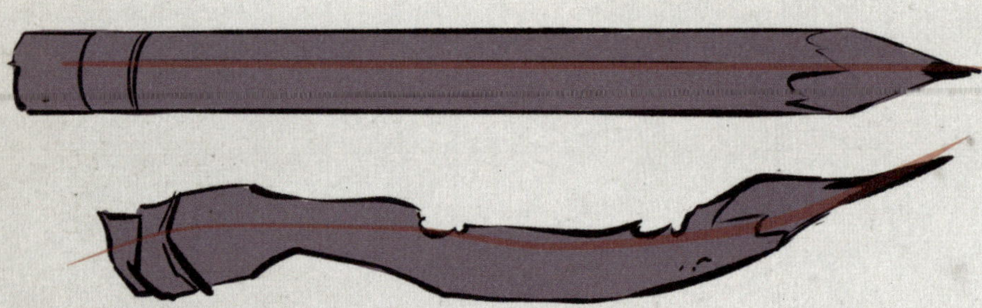

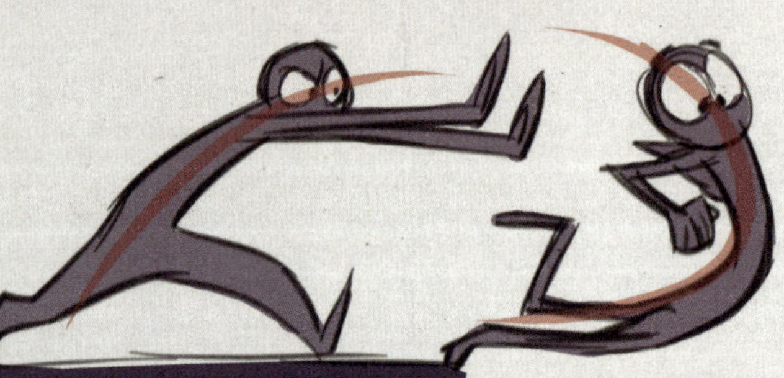

The line of action (LOA) is an imaginary line that flows through the strongest action that your object, person, or composition takes.

Creating a strong line of action will have an immediate dramatic effect on the character.

Don't forget that in groups, the line of action of the characters and props can flow into one another and create an even bigger line of action together!

This is how artists control the journey the eye takes through a scene.

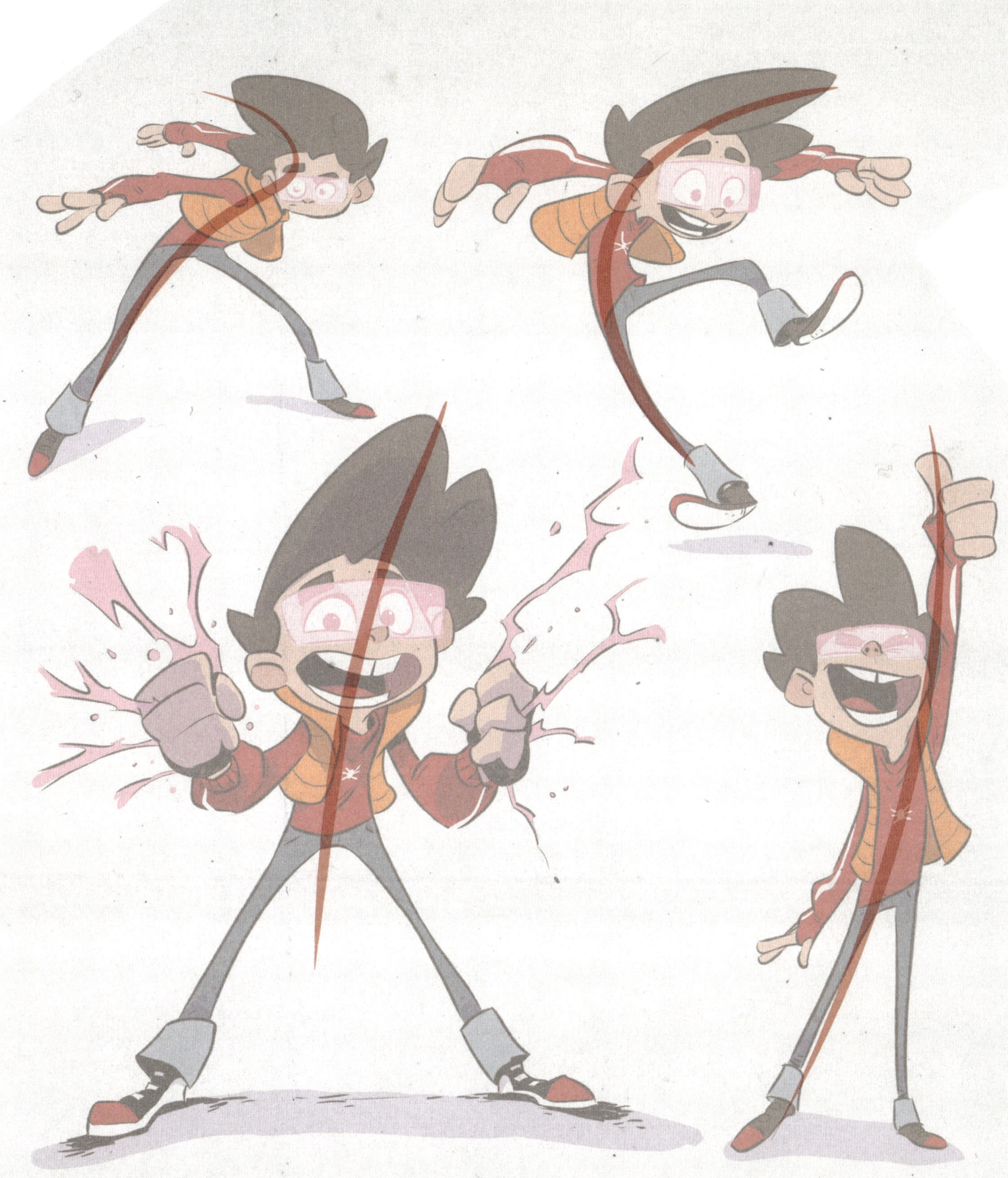

When it comes to characters, gestures are their emotional state in physical form.
They can also include extensions of the body, such as props, tails, and effects.

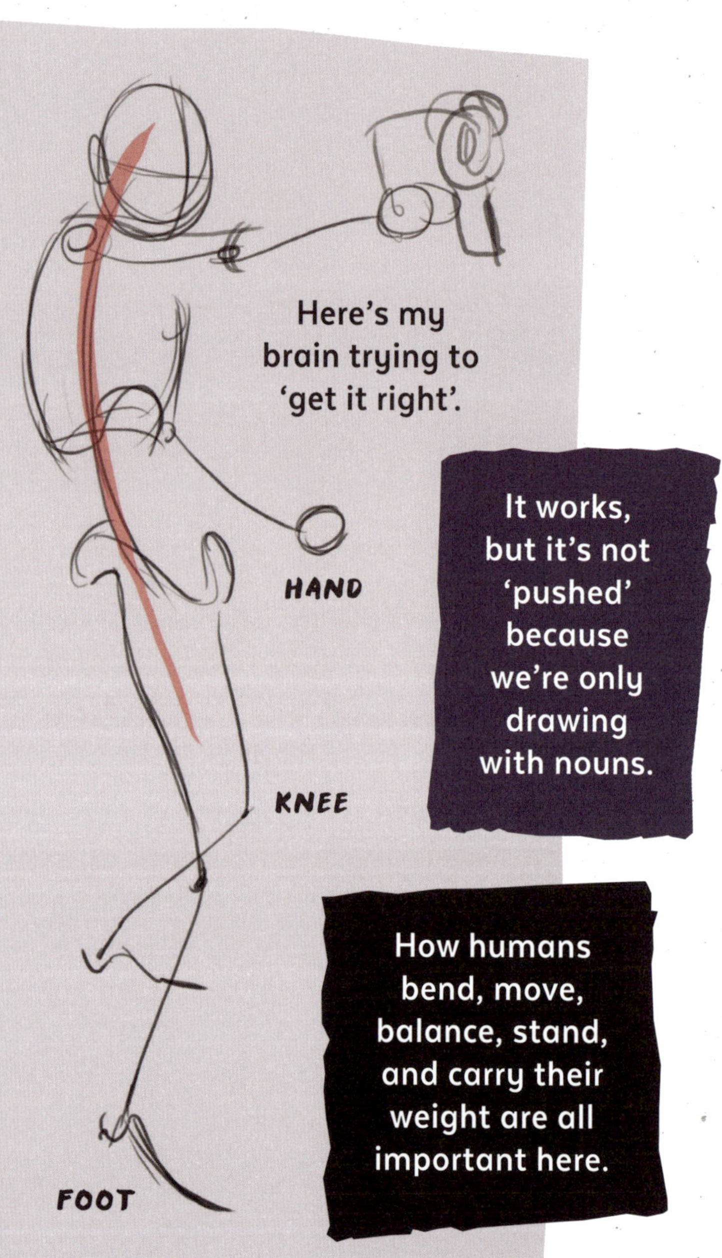

GESTURE DRAWING EXERCISE

Start with observation and anatomy. These are the nouns that make up a gesture and are important to understand.

Now let's introduce gesture to the pose.

When capturing the gesture, aim for the 'feel' of the pose. Stand up and get into the same stance. **FEEL** your body and where it's pushed and pulled.

Use more descriptive words, such as adjectives, verbs, and participles.

You can then build upon this to create a more 'extreme' version of the pose, pushing the energy and character.

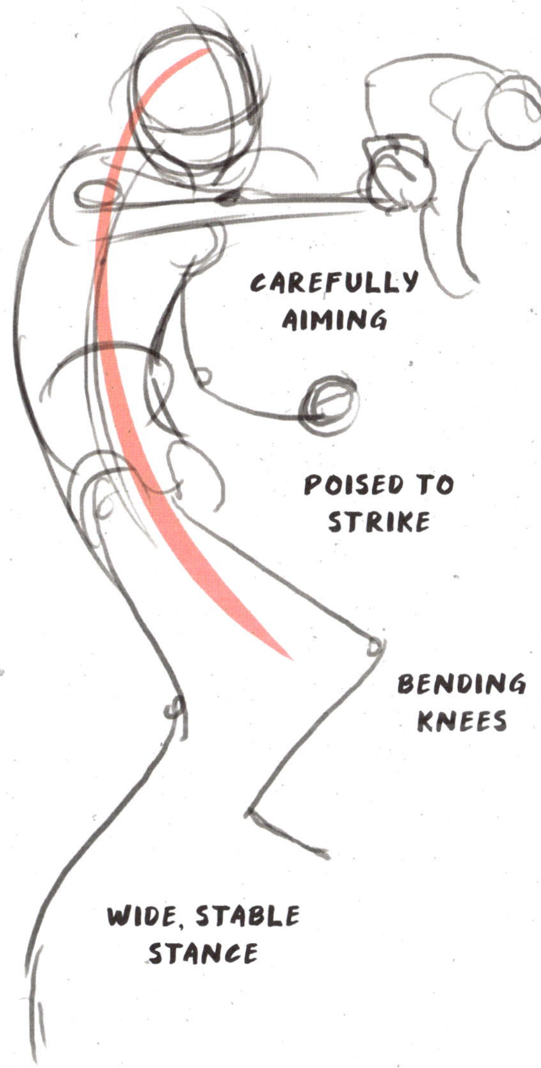

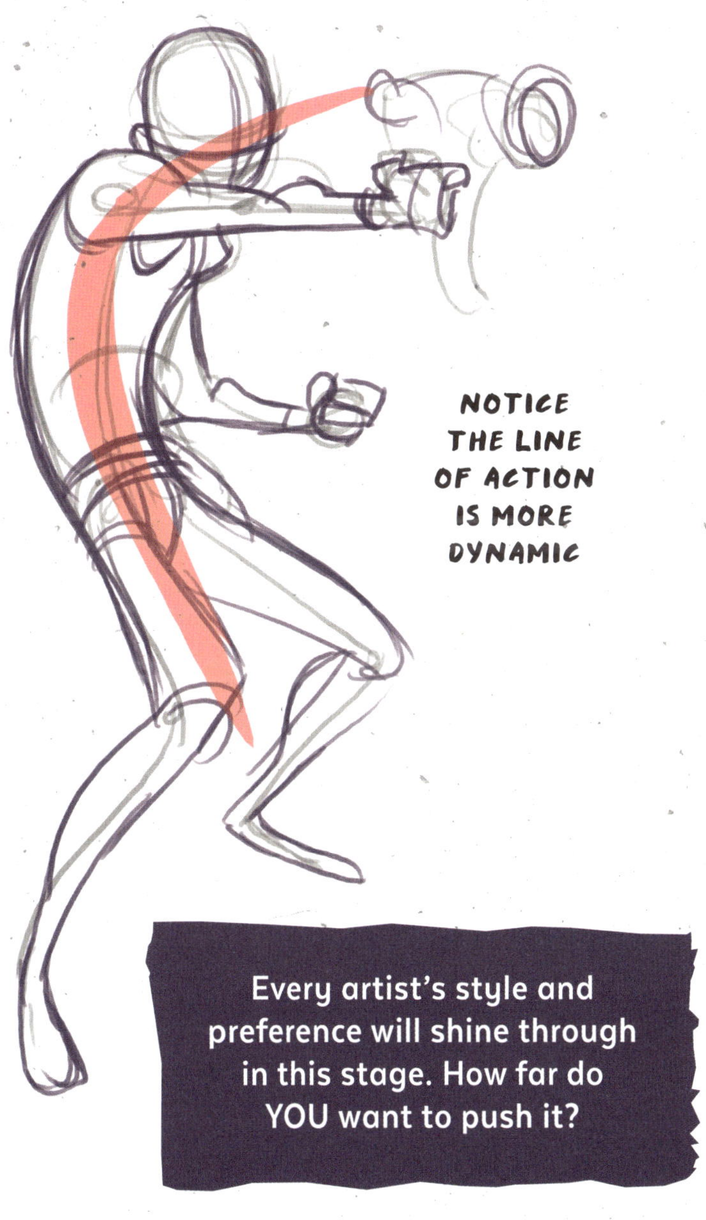

Every artist's style and preference will shine through in this stage. How far do YOU want to push it?

THIS WILL CREATE:
- A clearer silhouette.
- Better flow.
- More personality.

MEET DASH KICKERS

AND HIS SPACE BURRITO

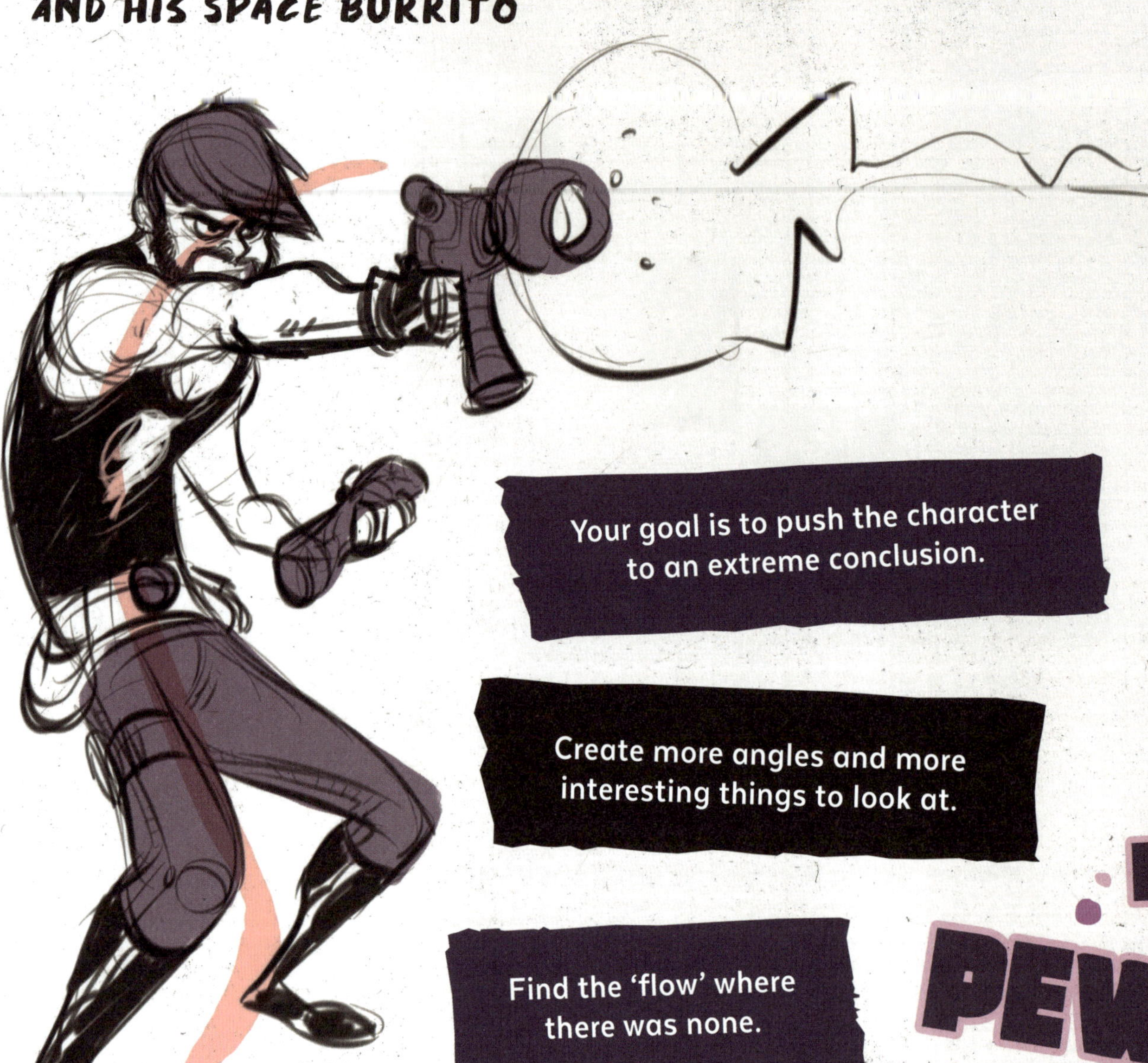

Try to tighten up the design as you go, while still keeping it loose. It's a balancing act to maintain detail while preventing the character from appearing too stiff!

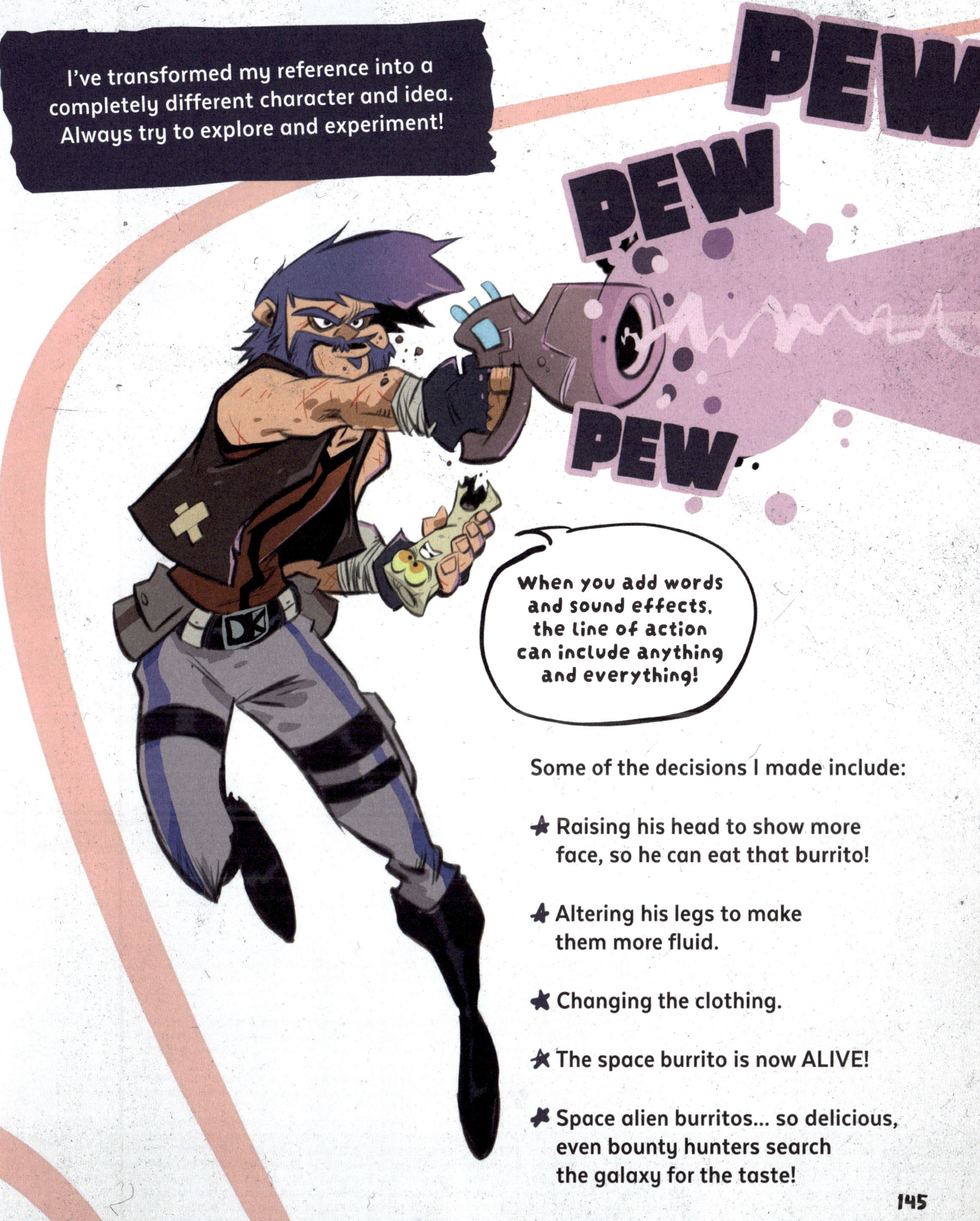

I've transformed my reference into a completely different character and idea. Always try to explore and experiment!

Some of the decisions I made include:

* Raising his head to show more face, so he can eat that burrito!

* Altering his legs to make them more fluid.

* Changing the clothing.

* The space burrito is now ALIVE!

* Space alien burritos... so delicious, even bounty hunters search the galaxy for the taste!

SHAPE EXPLORATION

Using shapes to find your character can lead to unique silhouettes.

Start by creating a series of shapes on a page. These can be drawn digitally, with markers, or any wide tool that will create big shapes. Have fun and get creative, free of constraints. You can always add to a shape later.

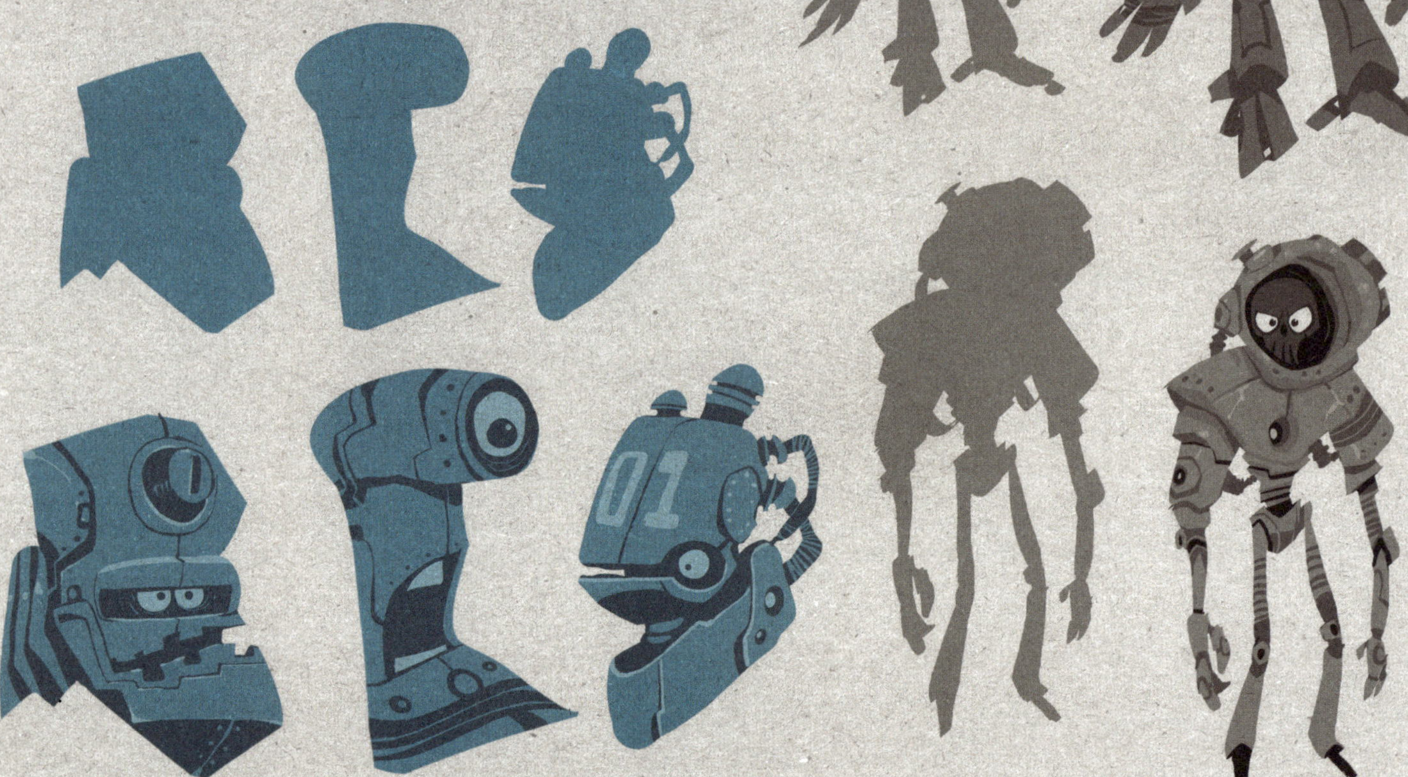

Next, draw within those shapes to find a face, body, and design.

If working digitally, you can lock the layer to draw without worrying about going outside of the shape.

Another method for finding characters is by pairing specific shapes.

Try combining shapes, whether the same or different, to see where they lead you. The more shapes combined, the more complex your design will be!

There is an endless variety of shapes and each communicates a different idea and message.

Shape language can range from abstract to realism, and your choices help establish the style.

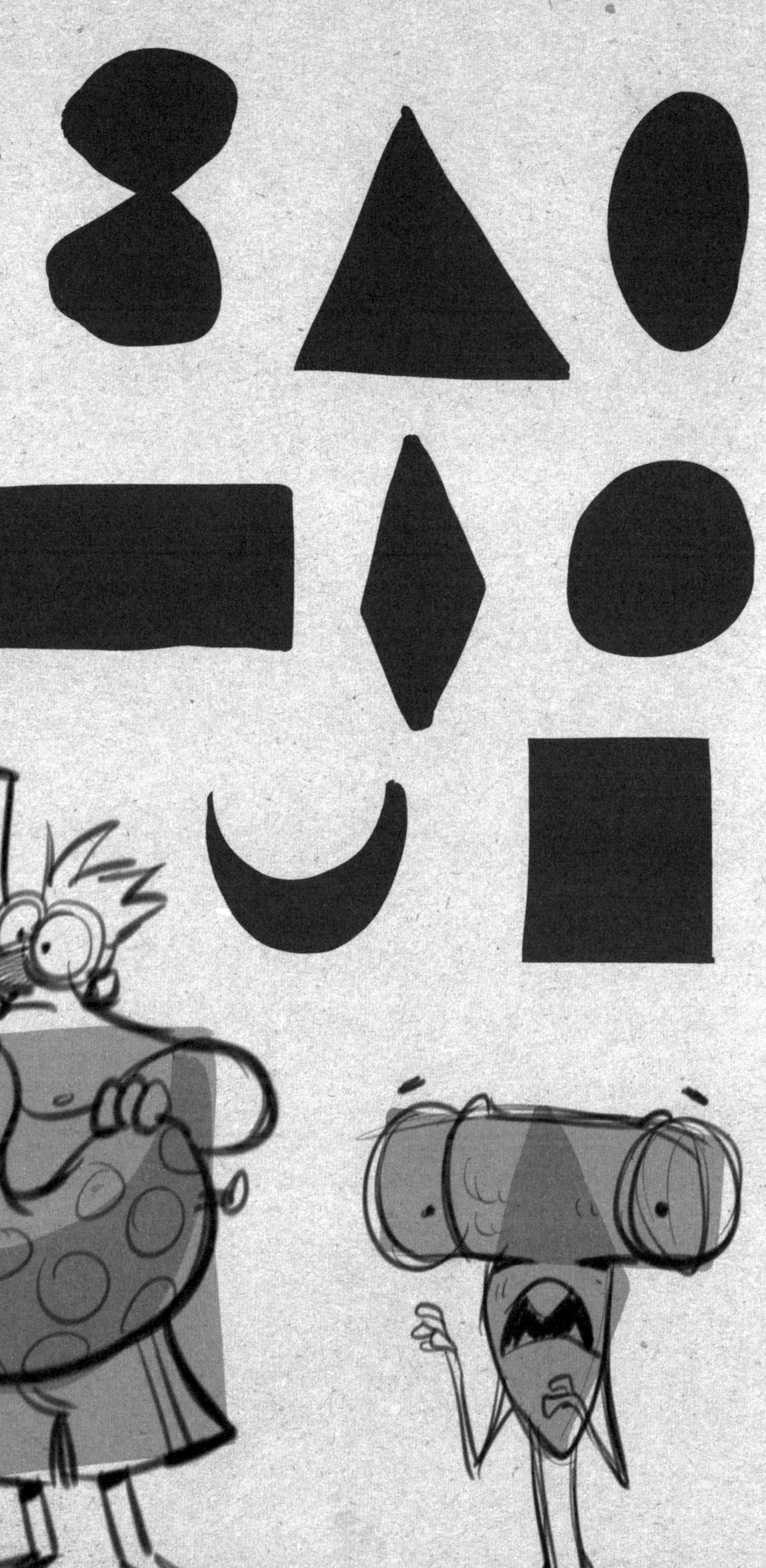

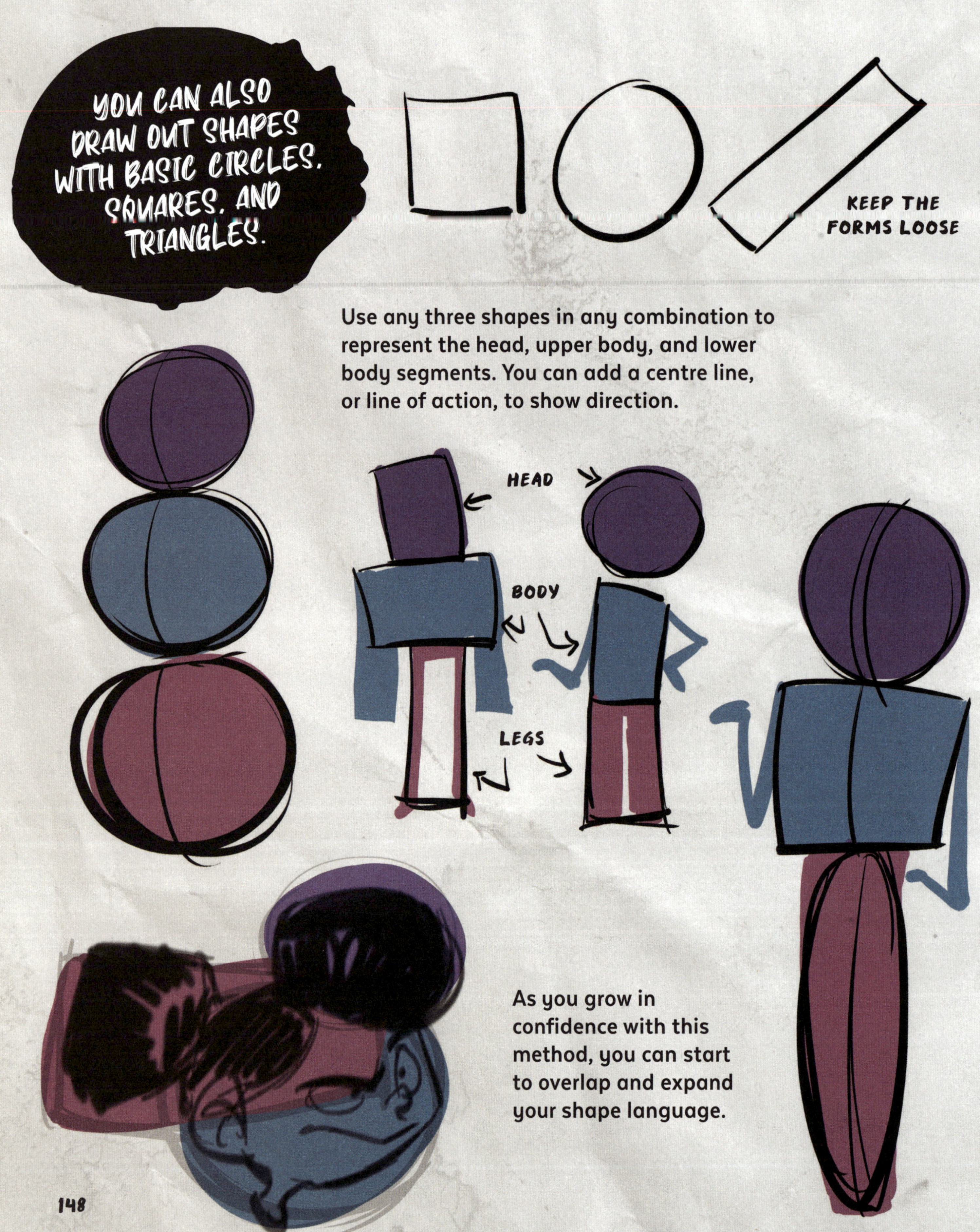

Use any three shapes in any combination to represent the head, upper body, and lower body segments. You can add a centre line, or line of action, to show direction.

As you grow in confidence with this method, you can start to overlap and expand your shape language.

As you add complexity, start using combinations of hard and soft shapes, straights, and curves. These choices will help to define who you are as a designer. There is no 'right' or 'wrong' choice, but it's important to search for how **YOU** want to see the world.

Realize that for every action there is an opposite design reaction. Every shape decision should lead you to new shapes to add or remove.

Even the closeness of your shapes can tell a story.

Because shapes make relationships!

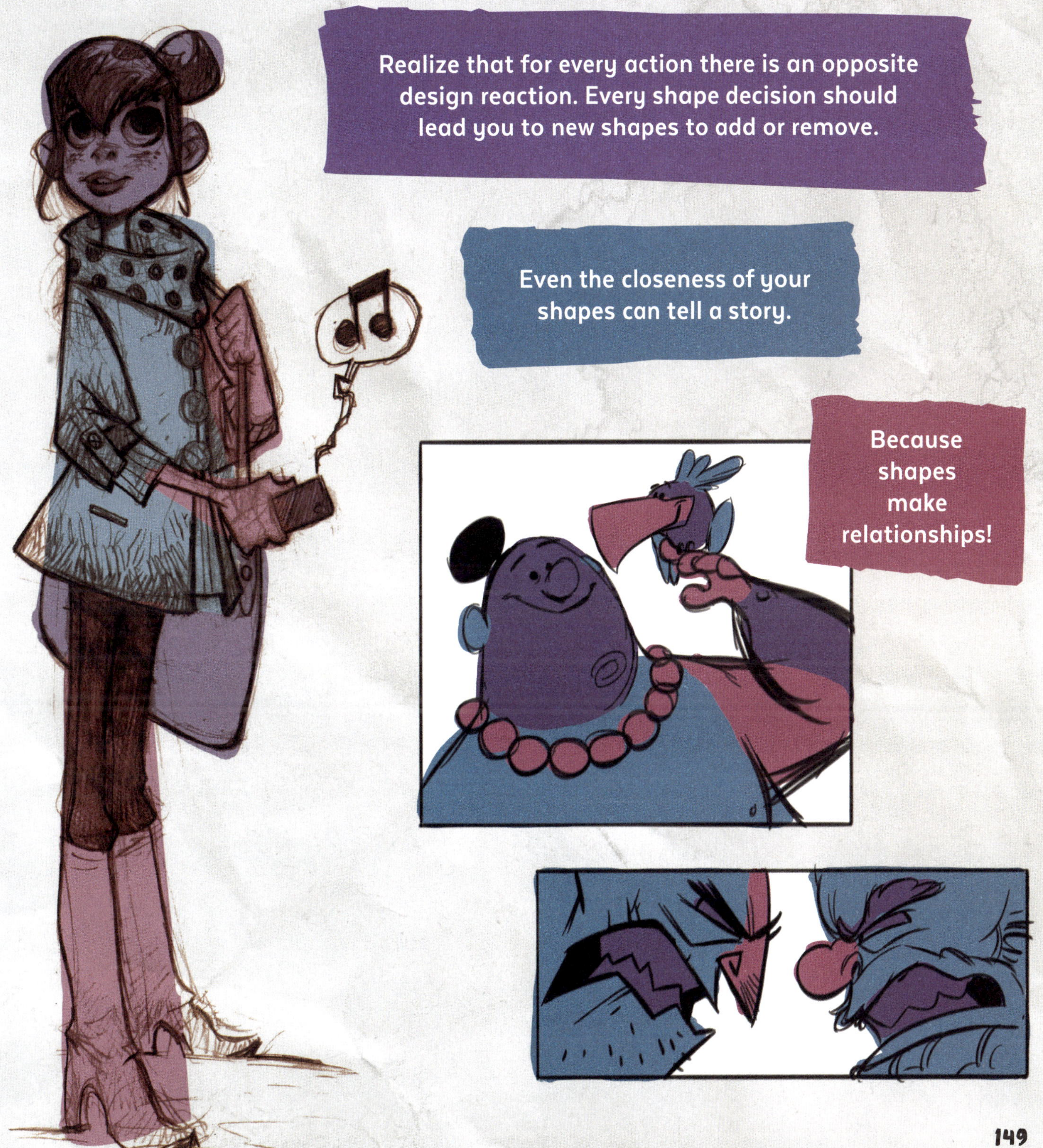

THE SCRIBBLES METHOD

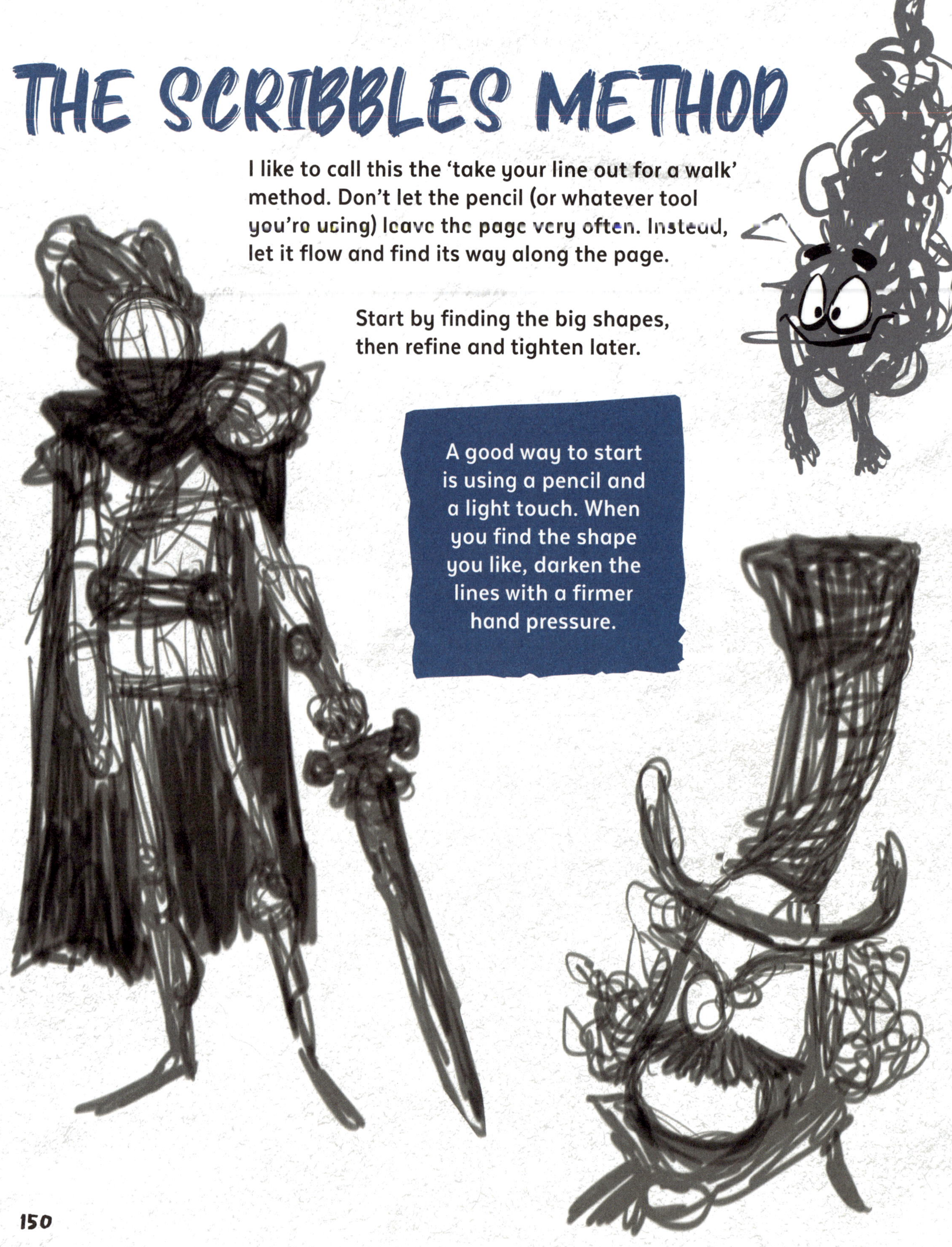

I like to call this the 'take your line out for a walk' method. Don't let the pencil (or whatever tool you're using) leave the page very often. Instead, let it flow and find its way along the page.

Start by finding the big shapes, then refine and tighten later.

A good way to start is using a pencil and a light touch. When you find the shape you like, darken the lines with a firmer hand pressure.

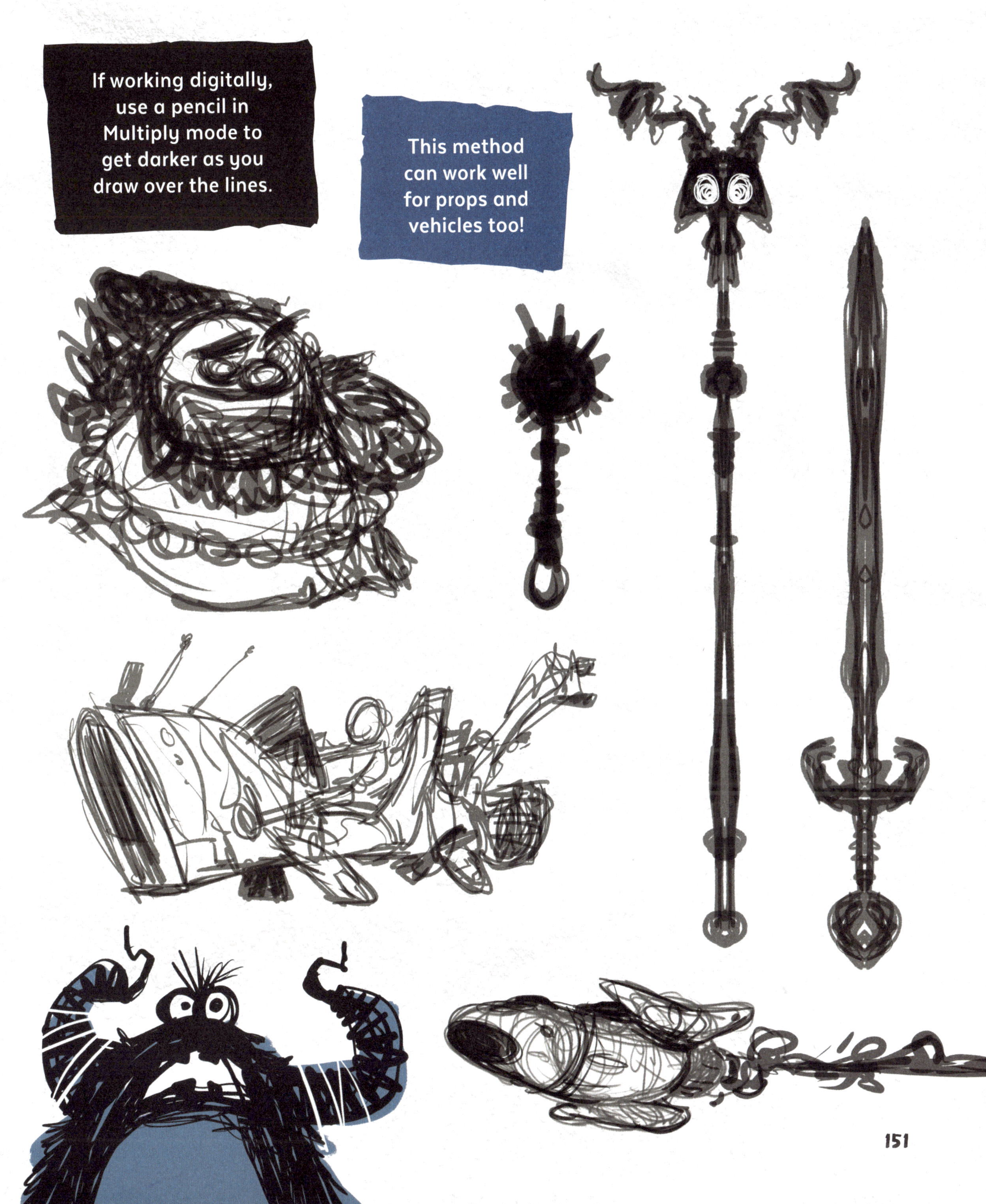
If working digitally, use a pencil in Multiply mode to get darker as you draw over the lines.
This method can work well for props and vehicles too!

BUILDING UP A CHARACTER WITH BASIC SHAPES

In this exercise we will be creating a character from basic shapes. Remember to work big to small. Designing a character is hard work. There are lots of decisions, problems, and issues that will come up. For this first stage, let's concentrate on a few key aims:

★ Effective visual communication.
★ Simple designs.
★ Finding a nice line of action.
★ A clear silhouette.

If you solve your character designs in stages, working from big to small, it makes it easier to problem-solve the entire solution. We'll think about tightening up later. For now, stay loose, mentally and figuratively!

Come up with your own basic shapes or use these as examples. The main objective is creating!

You'll see that I have added three colours:

PURPLE = main shape
BLUE = secondary shapes
PINK = third shapes

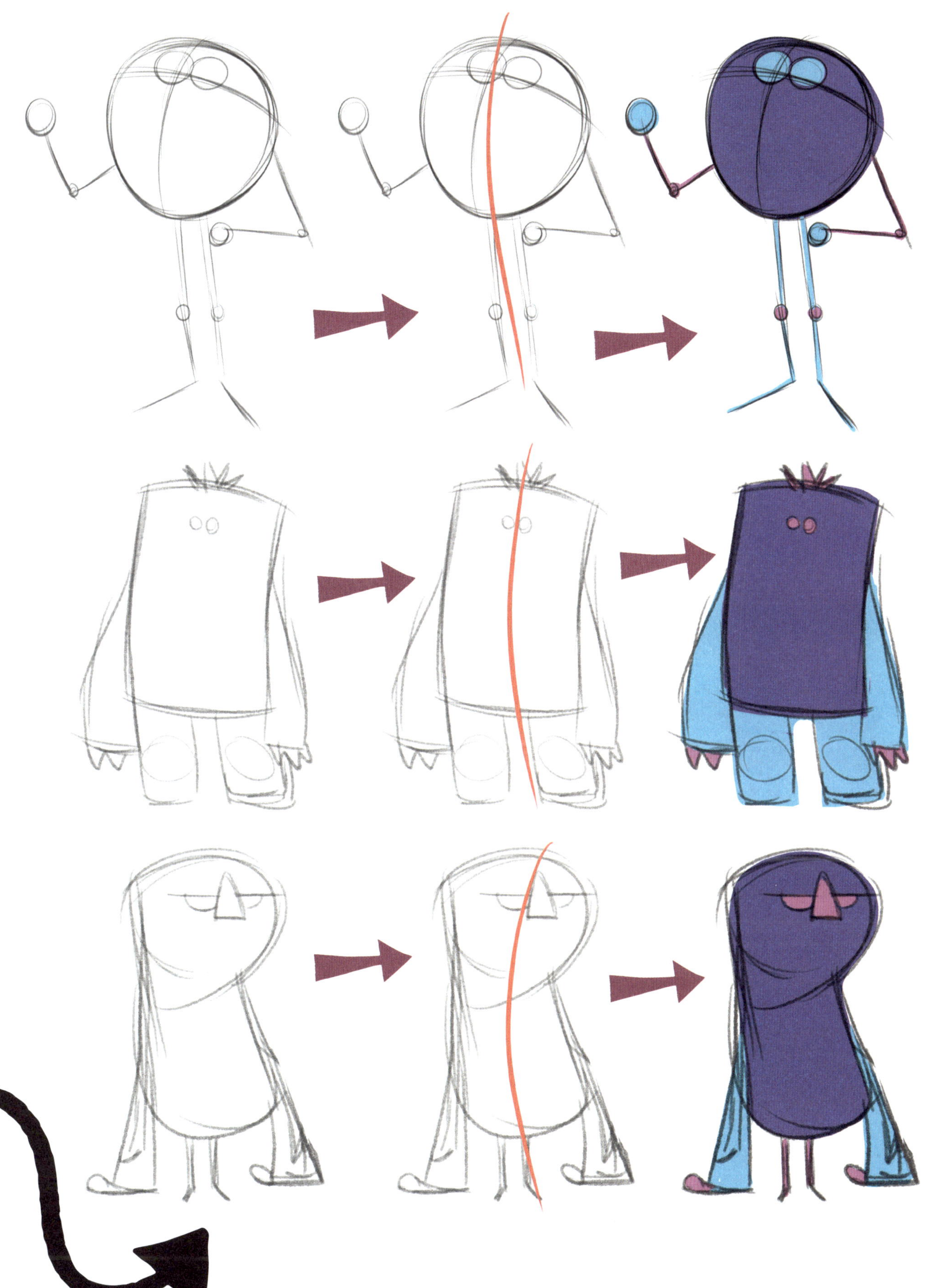

BUILDING ON THE DESIGN

Now I've chosen one of the characters, it's time to build on the design...

Remember that contrast creates interest. After you've drawn your dominant shape, everything that follows will either echo the shape language or contrast with it.

Creating a three-tiered design can be used for great effect. As you add shapes and elements, you'll see the character become more complex as you work.

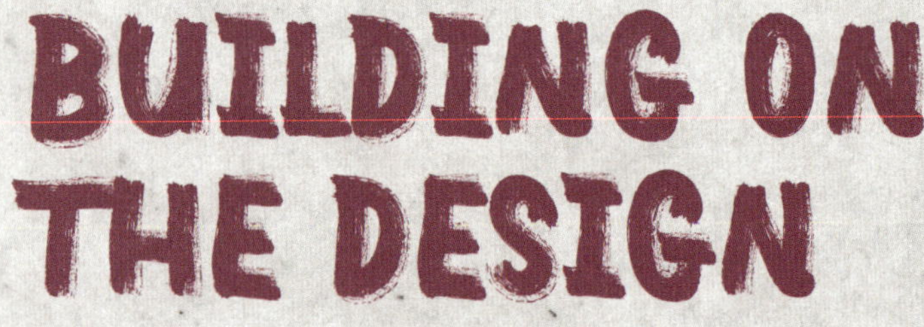

Still staying within my big shape, I add contrasting triangles to my circles in the form of:

★ Horns.

★ A tail and stronger feet.

★ A sense of happiness to the character's personality with a smiling mouth shape.

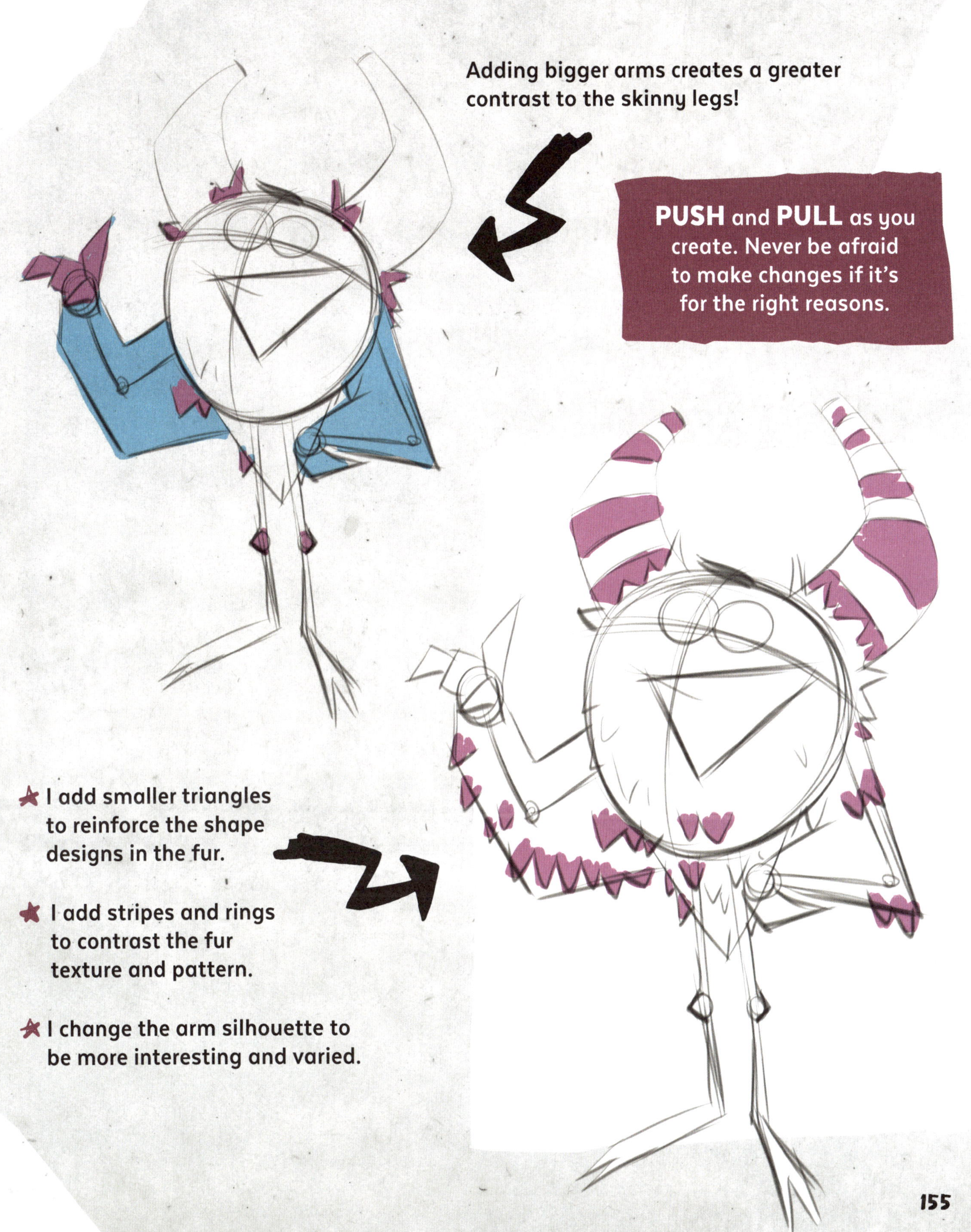

Adding bigger arms creates a greater contrast to the skinny legs!

PUSH and **PULL** as you create. Never be afraid to make changes if it's for the right reasons.

★ I add smaller triangles to reinforce the shape designs in the fur.

★ I add stripes and rings to contrast the fur texture and pattern.

★ I change the arm silhouette to be more interesting and varied.

You'll notice that we only need to work on the smaller issues now that we've solved the bigger, structural problems. From here, I'll be drawing shapes within shapes to further the design.

Changing small parts of the arm silhouette will provide interest and keep the overall triangle created in the arms. This includes:

* Adding stripes to provide texture and to change the direction of some of the design's energy.

If we keep it small and focused, it will enhance the design rather than taking away from it.

* Adding nails and finishing the feet.

TO FINISH OFF THIS BEAST:

★ Add lines and texture to the fur to visually communicate the surfaces.

★ Add shading while being mindful of the 'busy to simple' tool. Here you'll notice that the space around the face is clear of detail, giving our eyes room to see and focus on the face.

★ Varying the line widths of the stripes will ensure a playful and lively drawing. If you drew them straight and all the same size, the character would feel less natural and organic.

★ Draw little hairs that stick out in random places to create a sense of realism. Though this character isn't real, the way hair and fur behave is. Even when drawing a fantastical character, you can find ways to make them feel believable.

OTHER THINGS TO TRY WHEN CREATING CHARACTERS:

★ Come up with a voice for them.

★ Ask yourself, what's their favourite thing to do?

★ And how would they react if they saw a mouse?

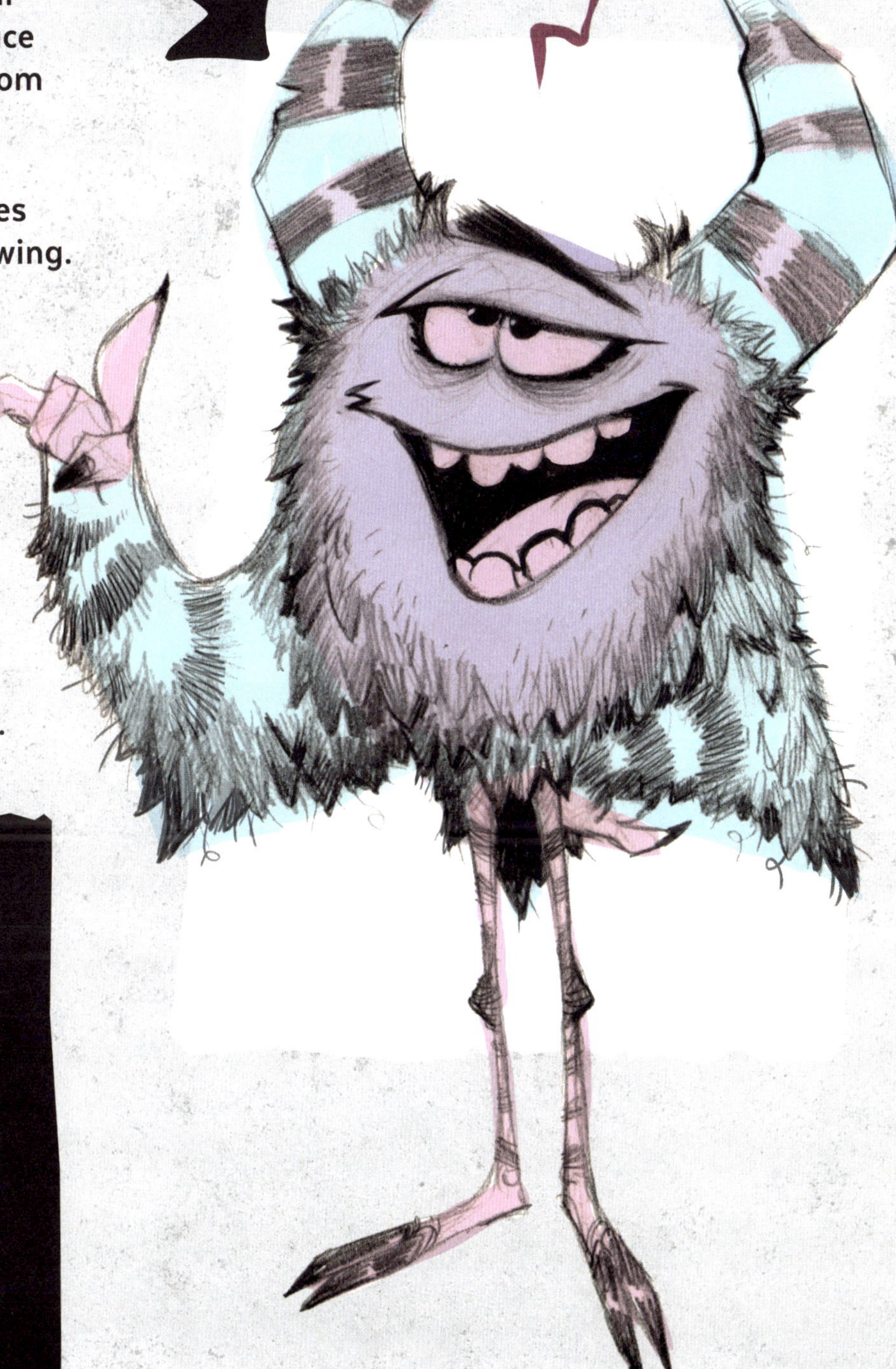

BUILDING UP A HUMAN CHARACTER

Character design is one area of illustration in concept art.

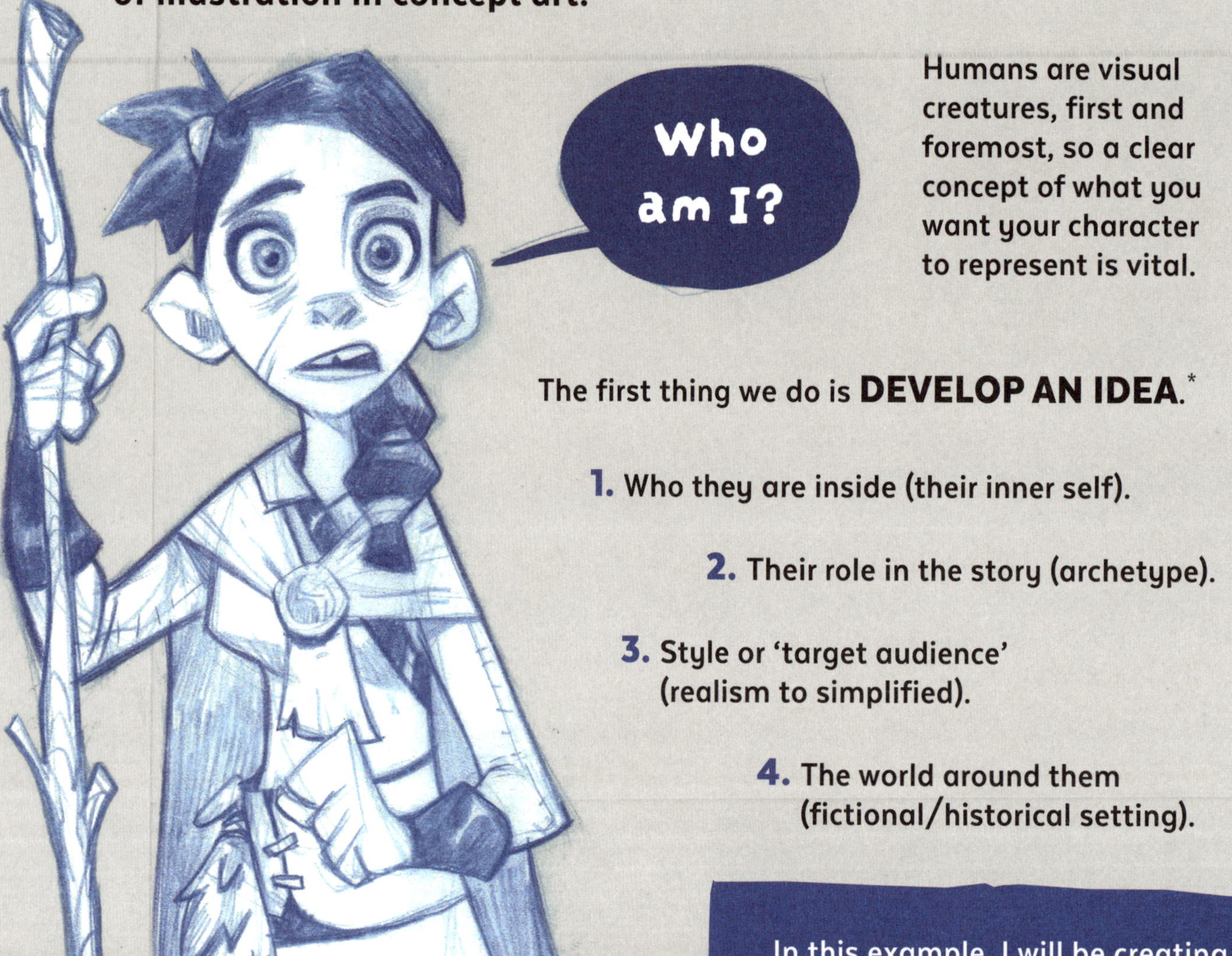

Humans are visual creatures, first and foremost, so a clear concept of what you want your character to represent is vital.

The first thing we do is **DEVELOP AN IDEA.**[*]

1. Who they are inside (their inner self).

2. Their role in the story (archetype).

3. Style or 'target audience' (realism to simplified).

4. The world around them (fictional/historical setting).

In this example, I will be creating a confident anti-hero bounty hunter in a science-fiction setting.

You can do the same, or create your own design - the steps will be the same.

[*] If the work is for a client, this will most likely be given to you in what's called a 'brief'.

THE THUMBNAIL

Start to create thumbnail
ideas for the character.

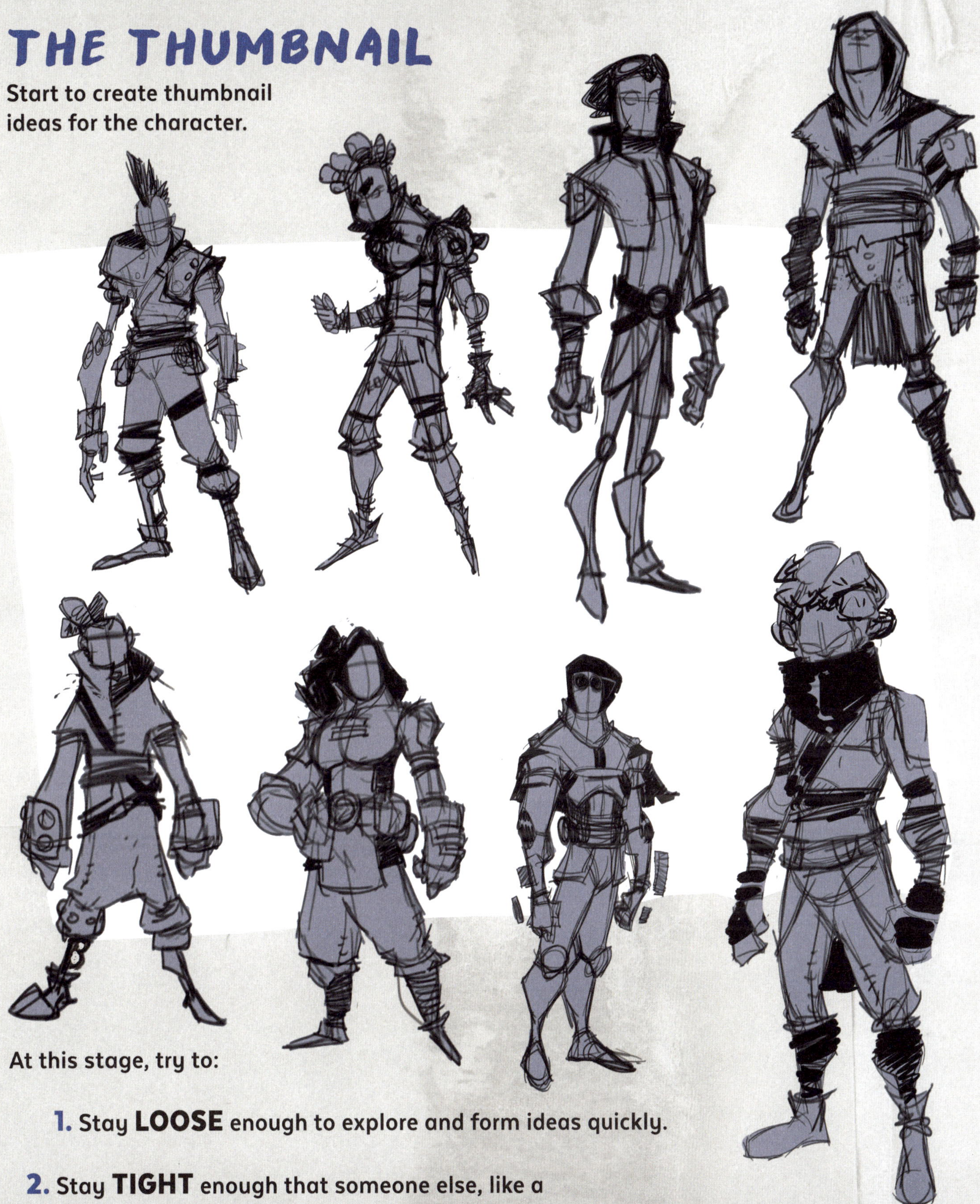

At this stage, try to:

1. Stay **LOOSE** enough to explore and form ideas quickly.

2. Stay **TIGHT** enough that someone else, like a
client, can understand your visual language.

DESIGN REFINE

Highlight any 'right' ideas from the other sketches,
We will consolidate all of them as we draw.

You may not like the choices I've made. That's the wild thing about art – this is all subjective!

It's not like maths: 2 + 2 = 4. Art is so random! It's more like: Fuzzy + Pickle = Poodle-Doodle.

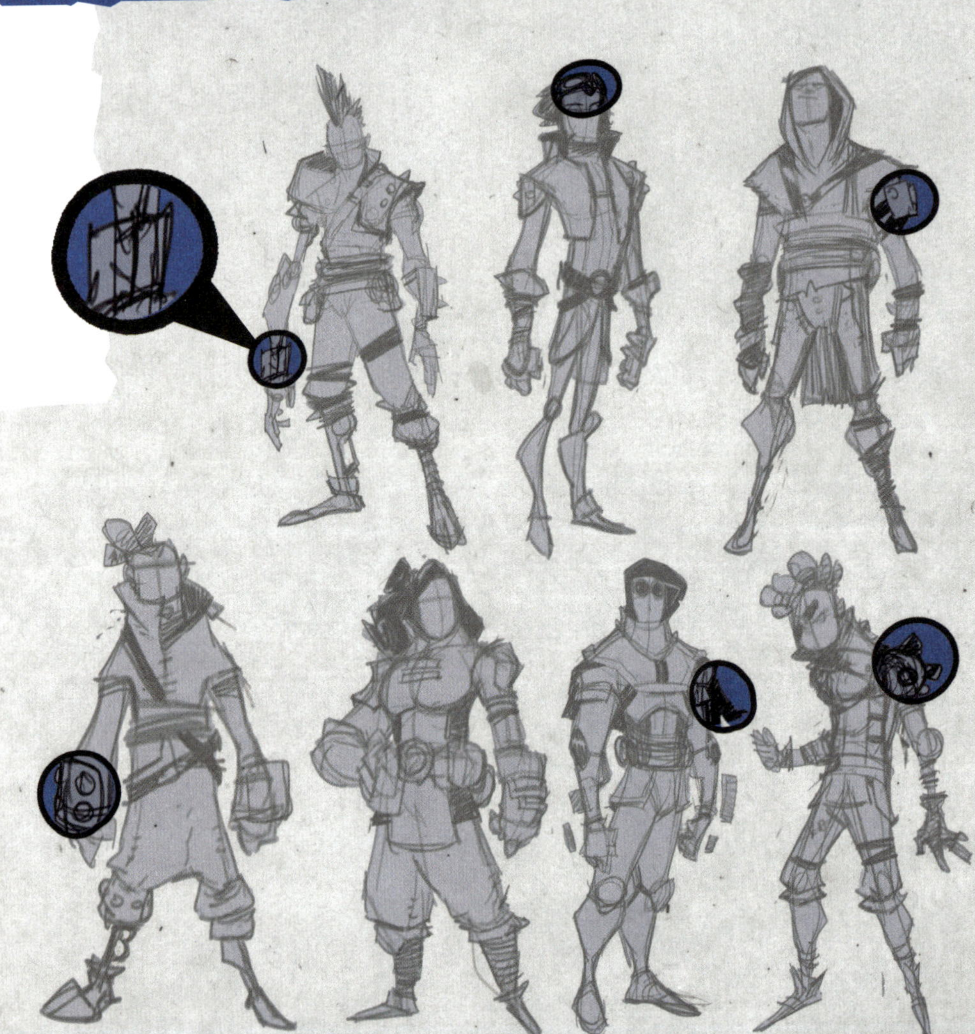

* If you're working for a client, they will be the ones telling you which design elements suit their needs. News flash... it's NEVER the one you want!

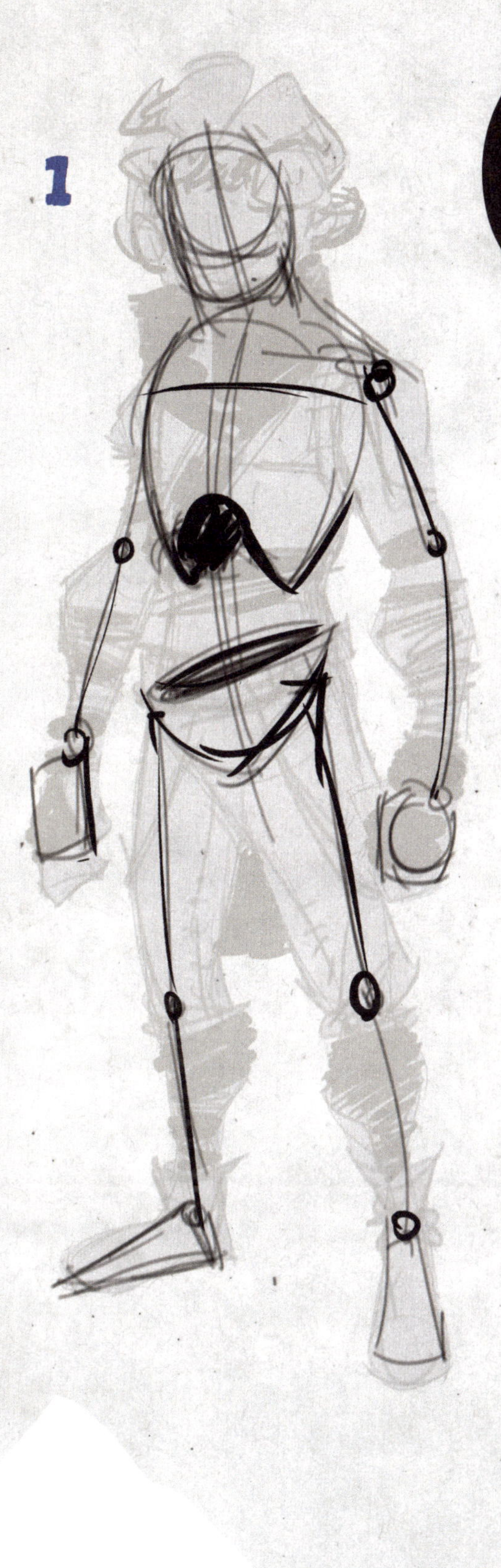

1. You can find the character's basic structure from the thumbnail.

2. Working big to small, design the various muscles into the shapes and sizes needed for the character.

3. Refrain from adding too much detail at this stage. You will then have a cohesive and strong design to build on top of.

4. Draw on basic information, such as contours for belts, clothing lines, and so on.

DESIGN DETAIL

Now you can begin to use all of your tools to start defining the character.

You can see how I've started to change and push as I design. This feels more like sculpting from a base.

1. Make the hair weighted and streamlined.

2. Add goggles from a different thumbnail design.

3. Alter the cloak so it doesn't cover his face, and add length.

4. Make the hands and gloves bigger.

5. Refine the feet and make them larger.

6. As the character gets larger, adjust the leg to redistribute the overall stance to handle the weight.

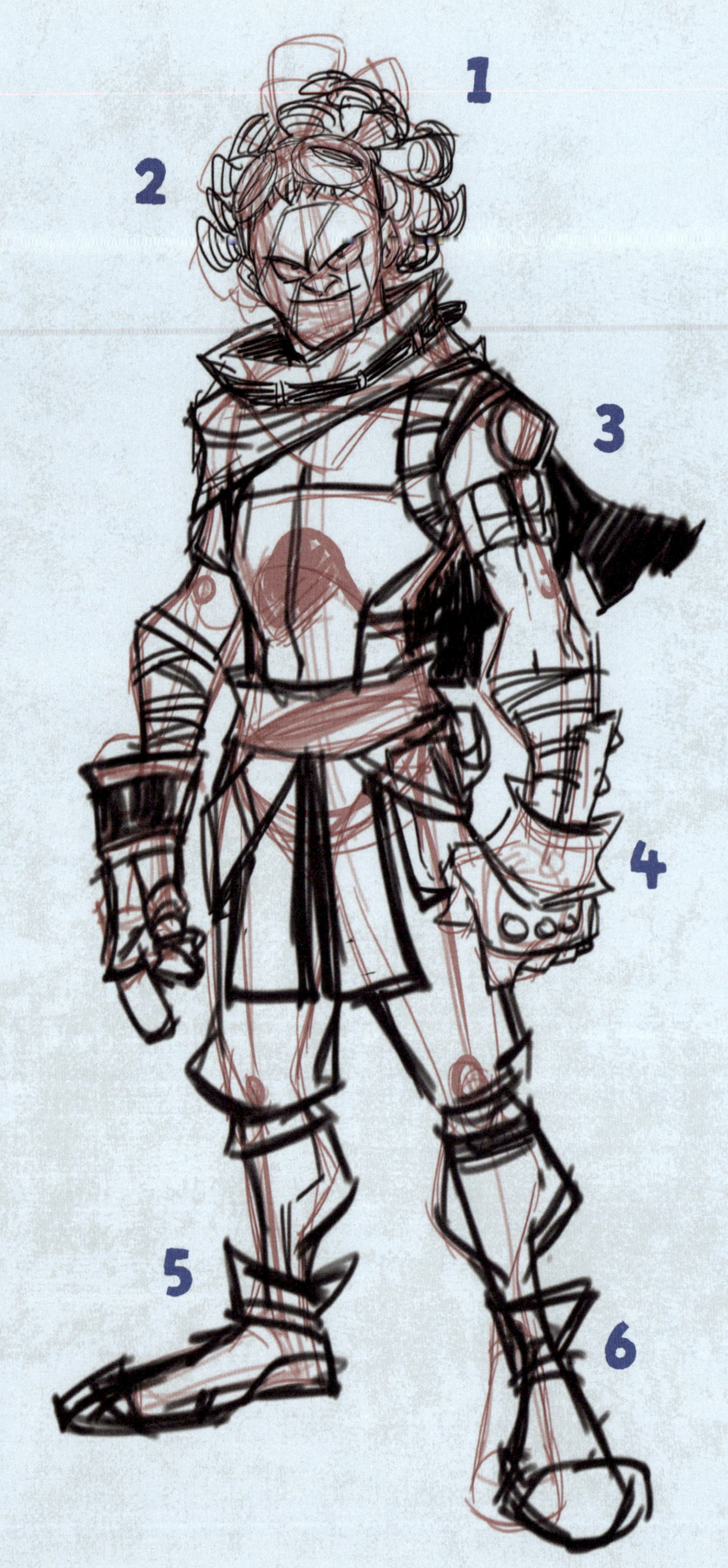

This is the stage for making final decisions.* Add details and little choices that only you as the designer can make. Ask yourself, what can you add that makes it especially 'yours'?

1. Design the goggles.

2. Strengthen the neck and add face paint.

3. Introduce details and streamline the cloak to add an implied line past the metal shoulder pad.

4. Add a metal shoulder pad to disrupt the shape and make him feel less orderly.

5. Paint on the body armour.

6. Add a darker glove and leg to balance out the design. If they were both on the same side, it would feel too lopsided.

7. Extend and push the gloves and metal.

8. Design and detail the shoes.

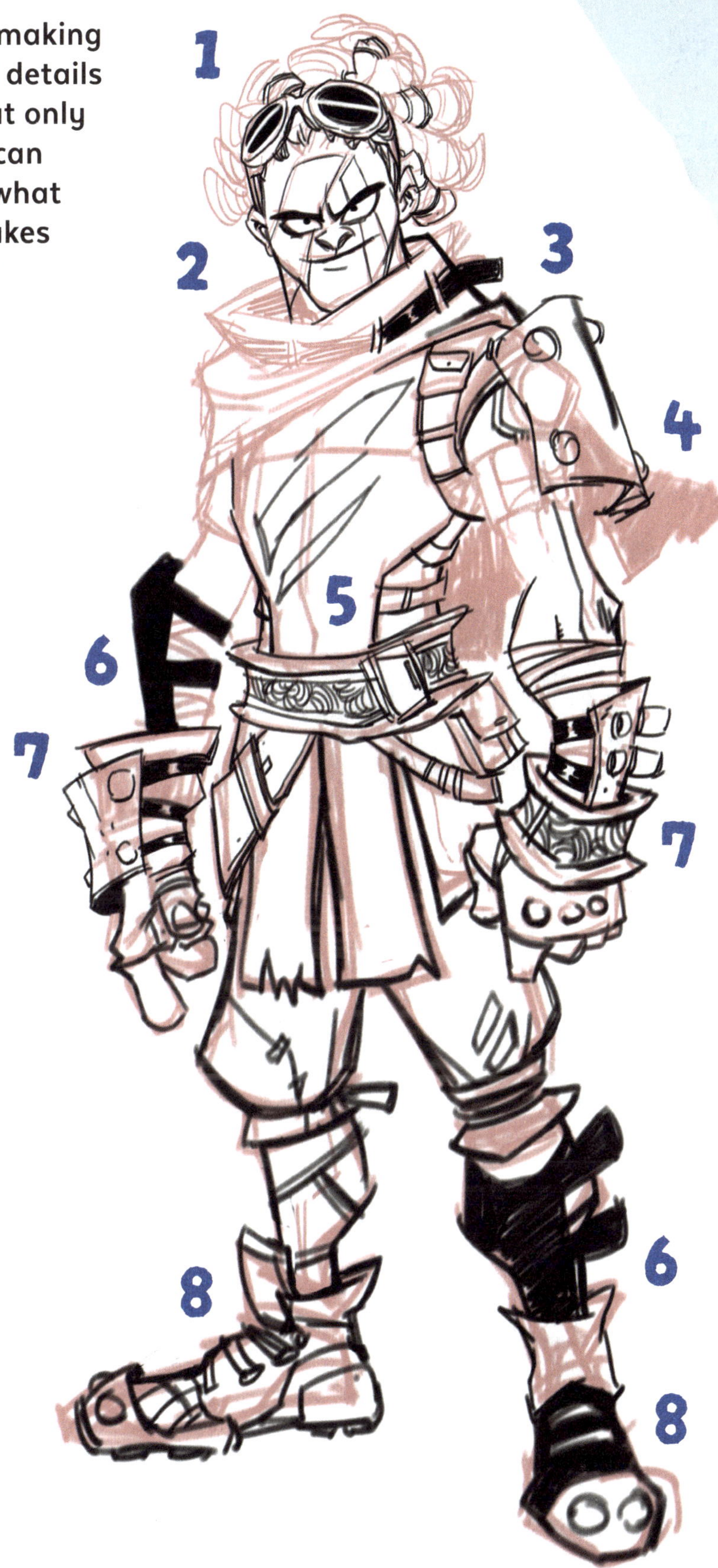

* As you progress as an artist, these stages may blend into one another. For example, I rarely draw the skeleton any more, but instead visualize it internally as I draw.

COLOUR THUMBNAILS

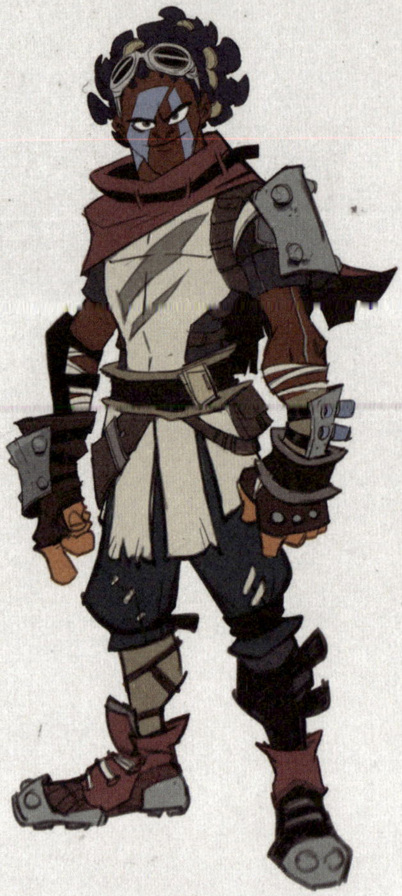

Making smaller versions of the character allows for quick experimentation with various colours and options.* Use local colour choices with no lighting to establish the range of your design. Creating multiple versions will help you to make wise decisions.

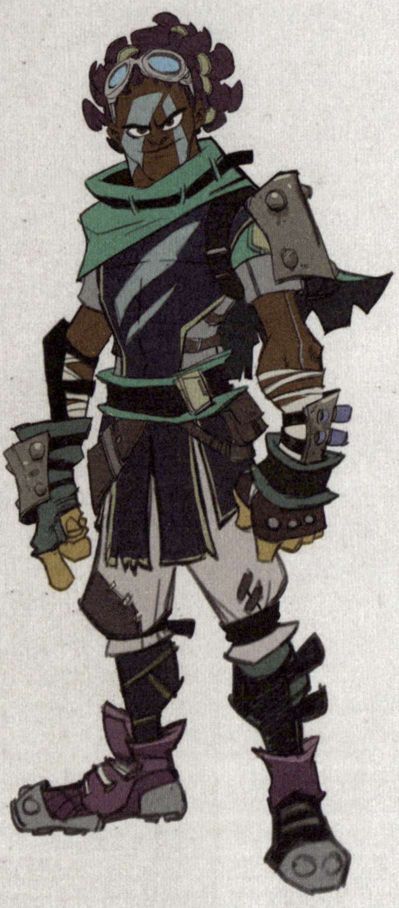

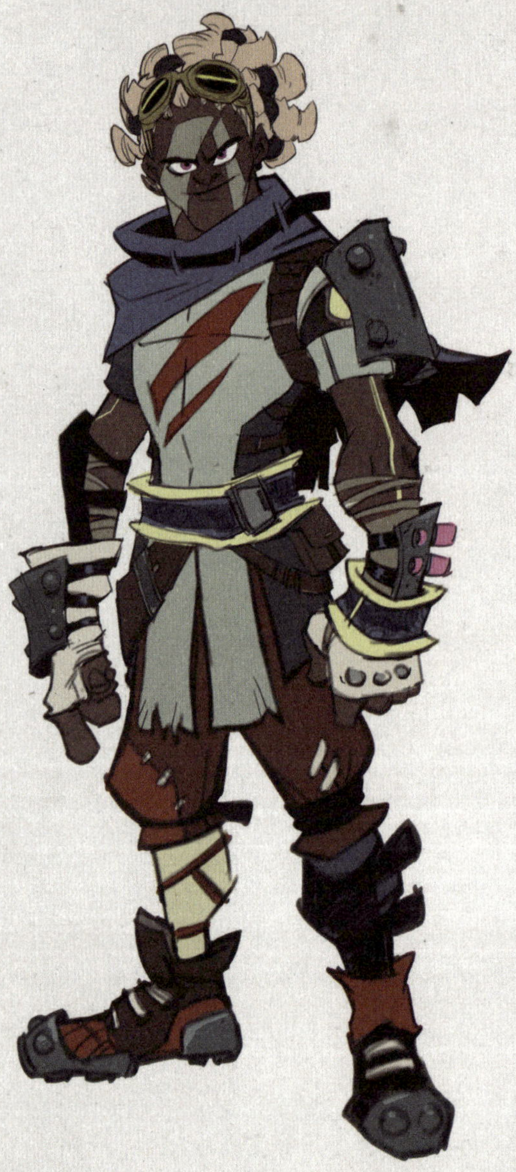

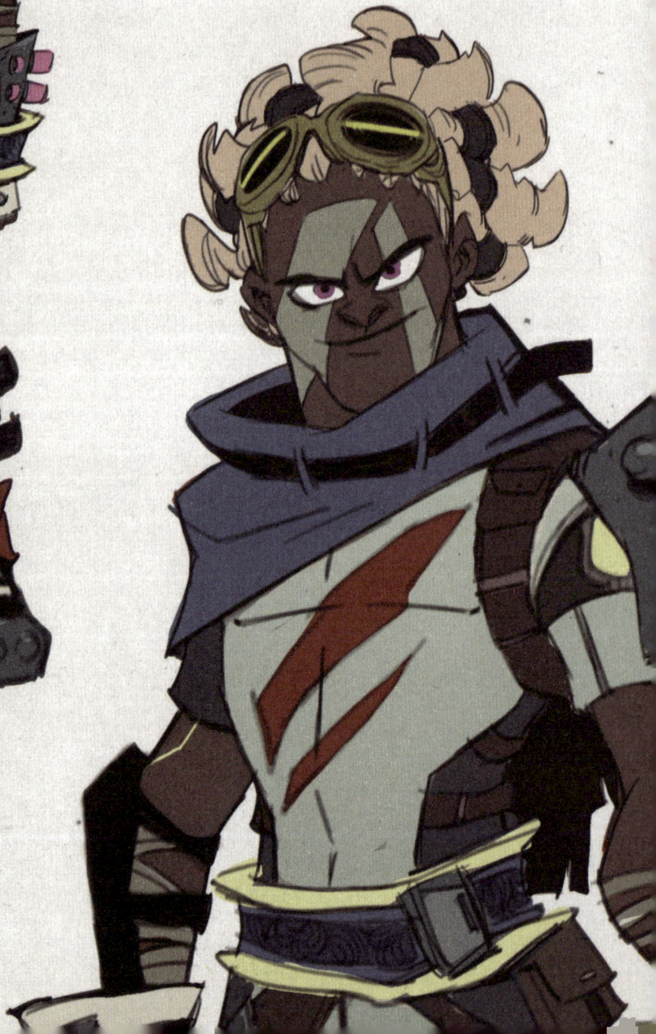

* For client work, this may include many more options and rounds of the 'Frankenstein method'. Remember, this is not about getting things right, but revealing the correct solutions for the problem at hand.

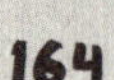

GREYSCALE

Convert your chosen colour
thumbnail to greyscale.

1. Modify any tones that don't
contrast enough. (This will be
subjective to the designer.)

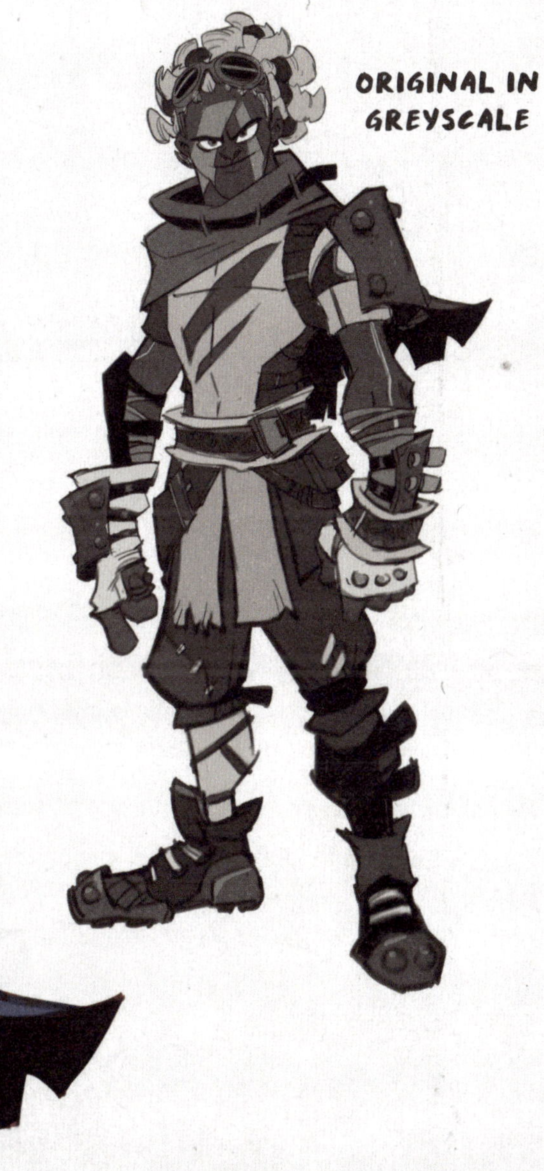

ORIGINAL IN
GREYSCALE

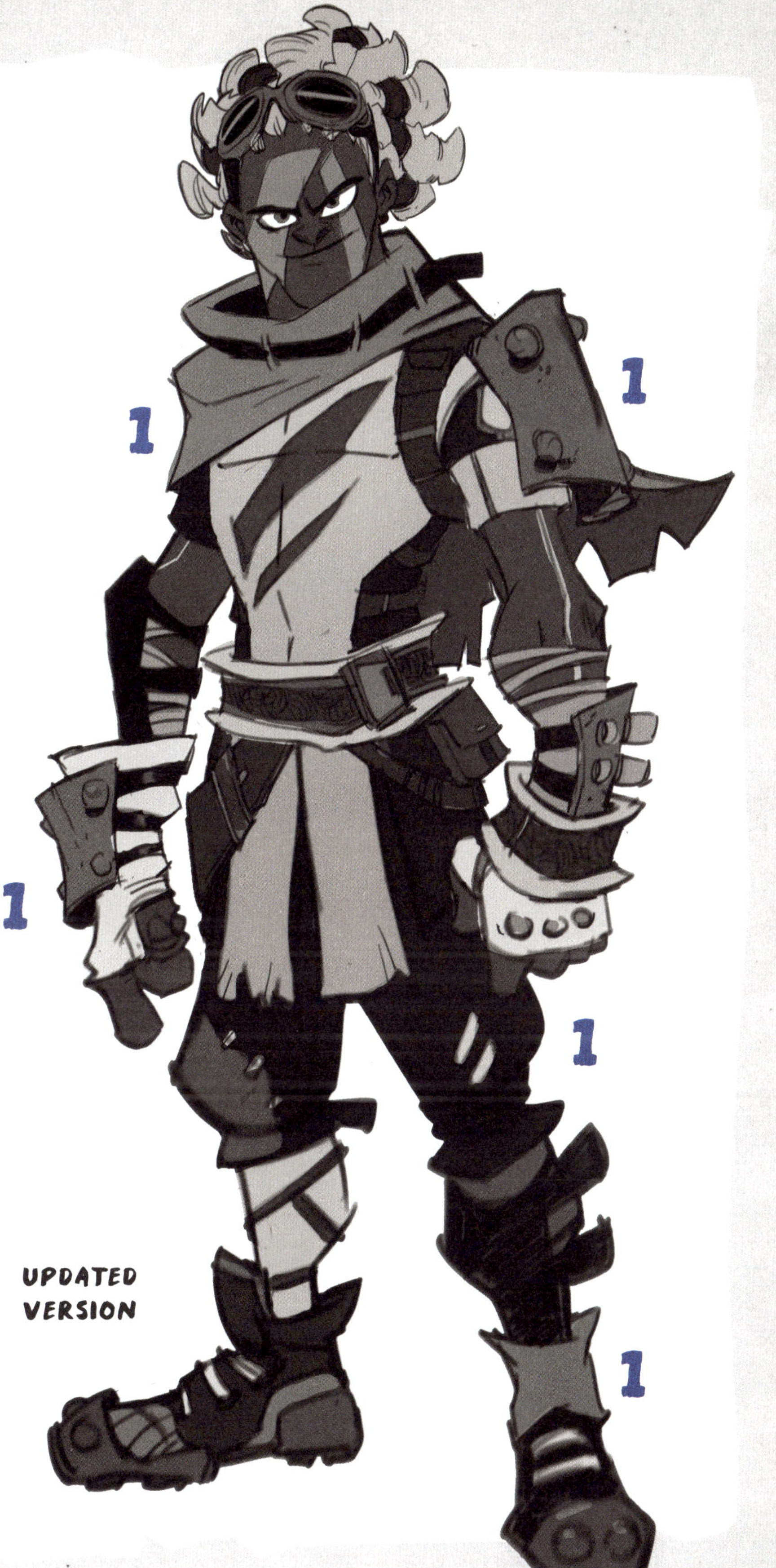

UPDATED
VERSION

FINAL DESIGN

After the tones are established, add them on top of the colours. If working digitally, a layer on Luminosity should do the trick.

From here you have a base character design with local colours established.

Designing and drawing is hard work. Sometimes it's best to solve one problem at a time, instead of all at once.

Creating a character design in stages provides you with a foundation to keep making smart decisions as you go.

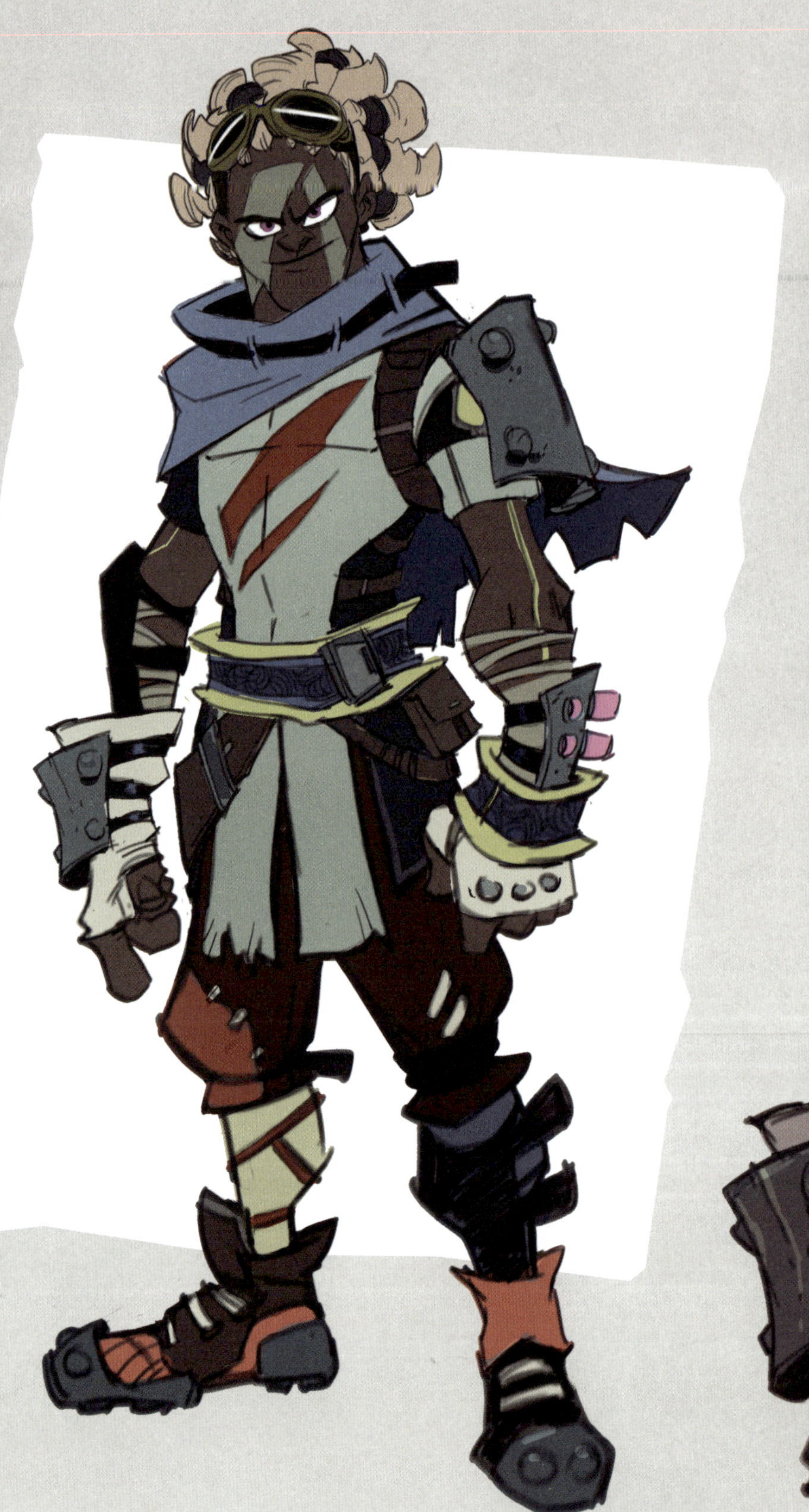

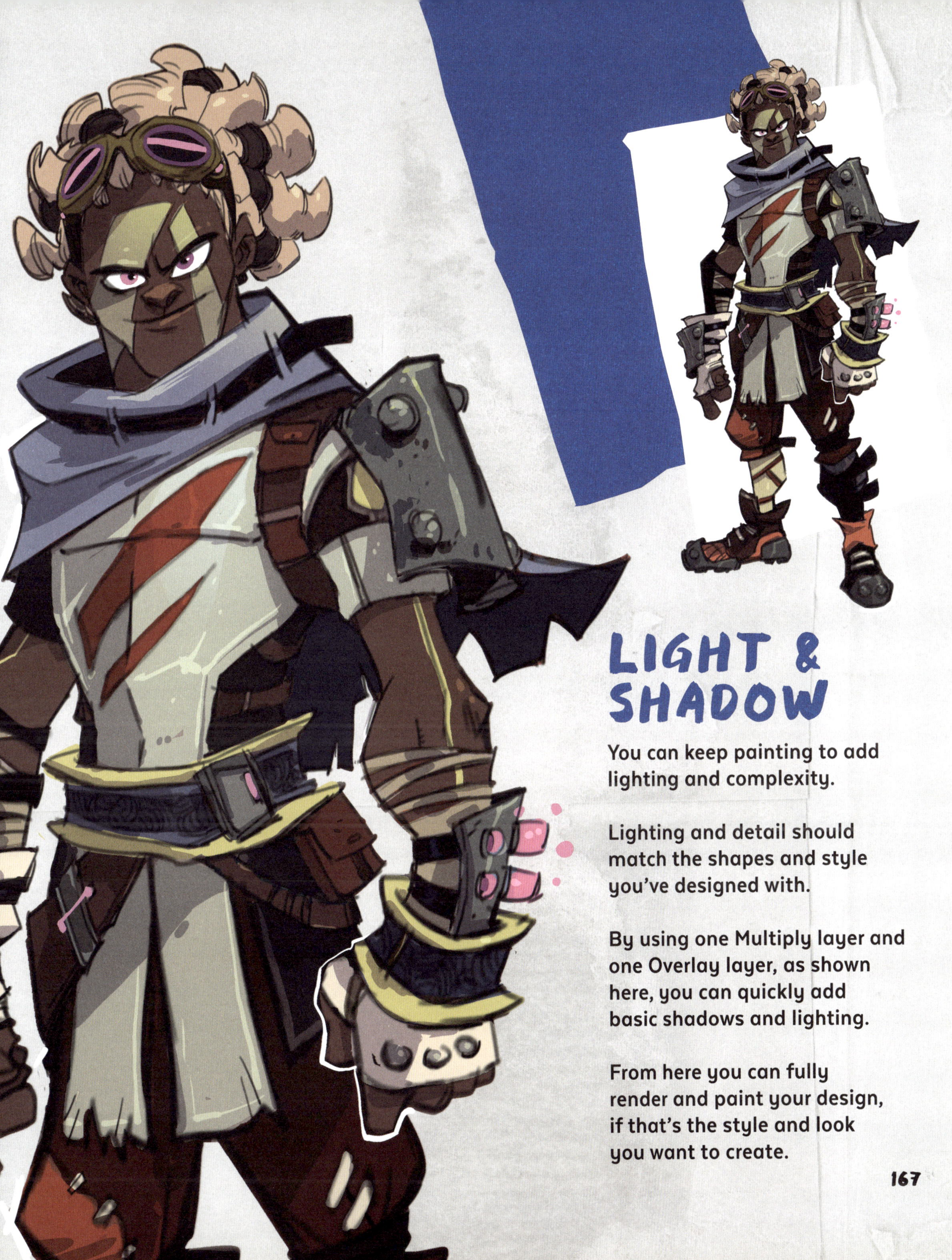

LIGHT & SHADOW

You can keep painting to add lighting and complexity.

Lighting and detail should match the shapes and style you've designed with.

By using one Multiply layer and one Overlay layer, as shown here, you can quickly add basic shadows and lighting.

From here you can fully render and paint your design, if that's the style and look you want to create.

CHARACTER DESIGN EXERCISES

Trace over these, scan them, or take a photo to work digitally. Or download them (see URL on page 7).

Draw a monster with an attitude.

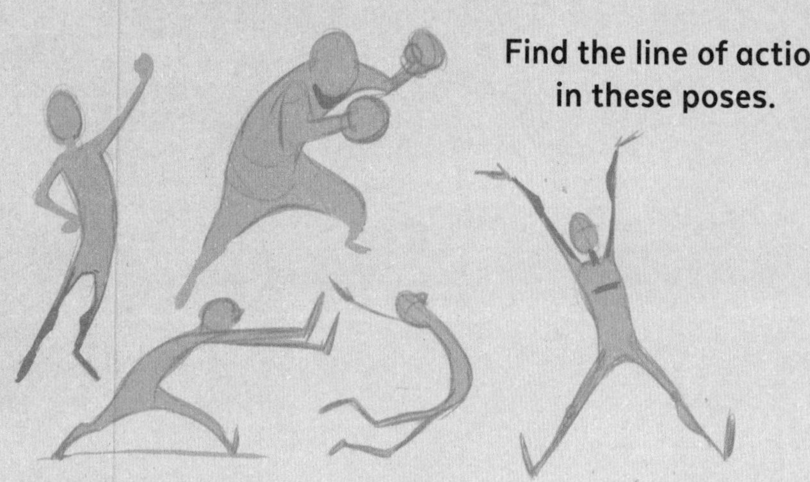

Find the line of action in these poses.

Design three human heads and one robotic head.

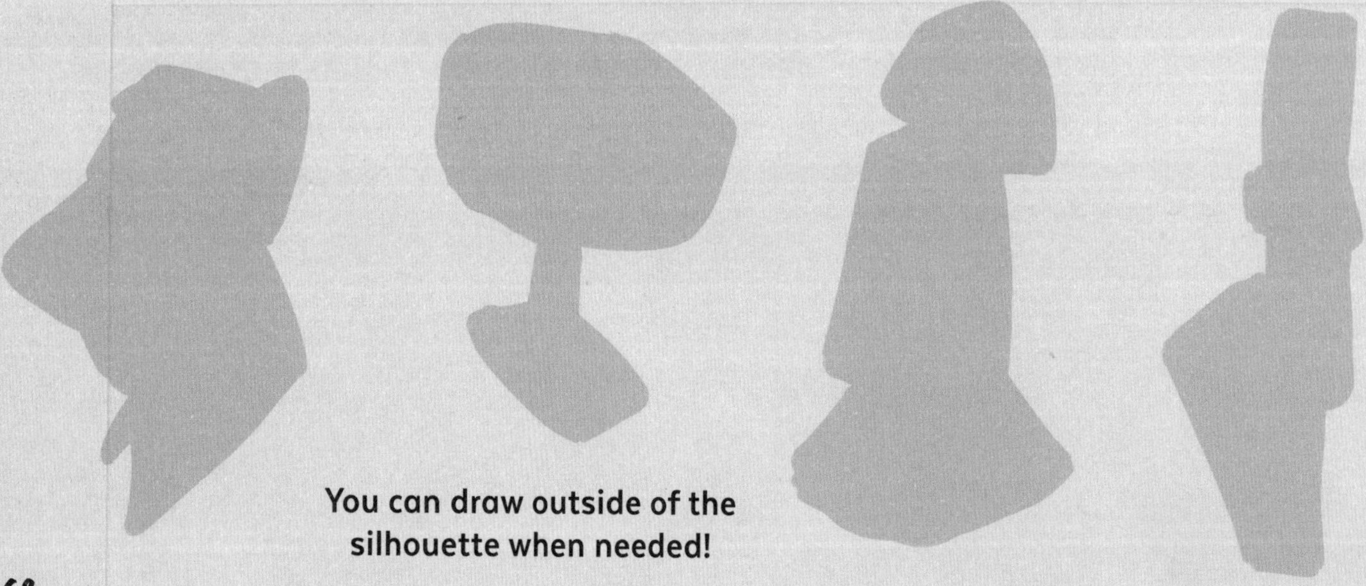

You can draw outside of the silhouette when needed!

Design bodies based off these shapes, treating
each shape as the character's torso.

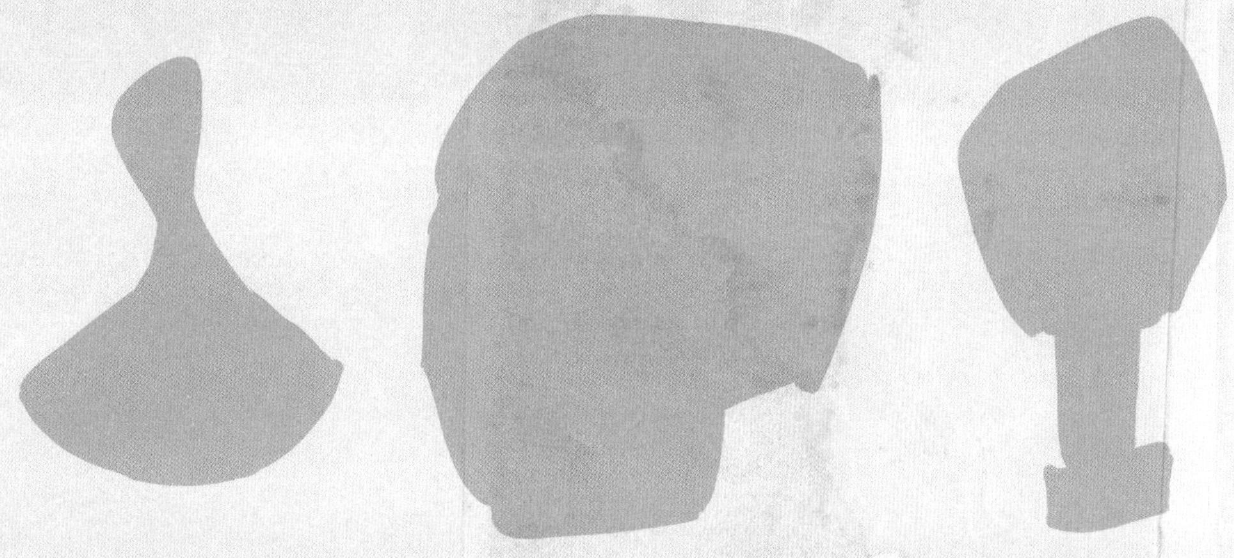

Draw one of each:

★ Ten-second gesture drawing.
★ Thirty-second gesture drawing.
★ One-minute gesture drawing.

Get into each pose so you
can feel it out first!

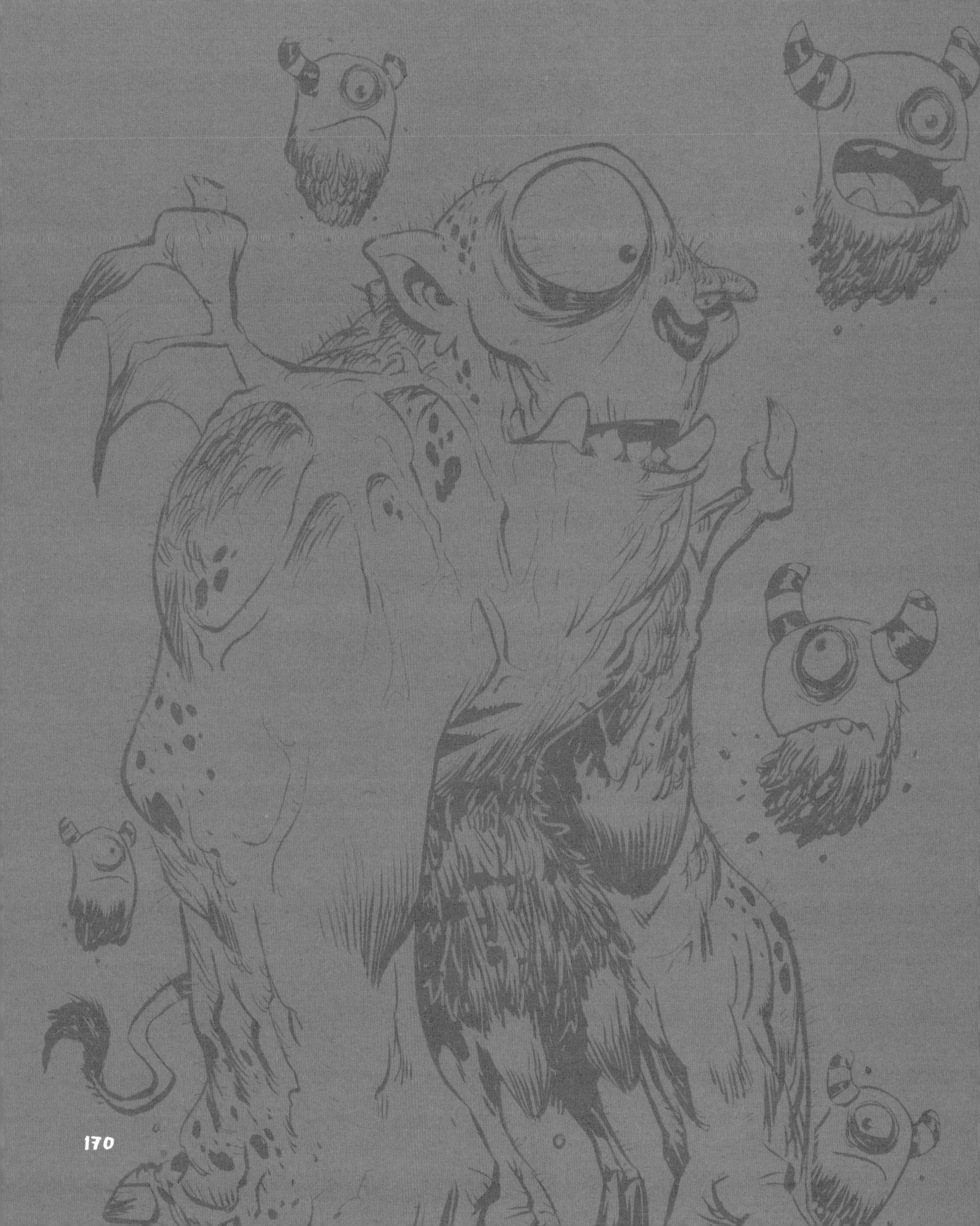

CREATURES

CREATURE DESIGN

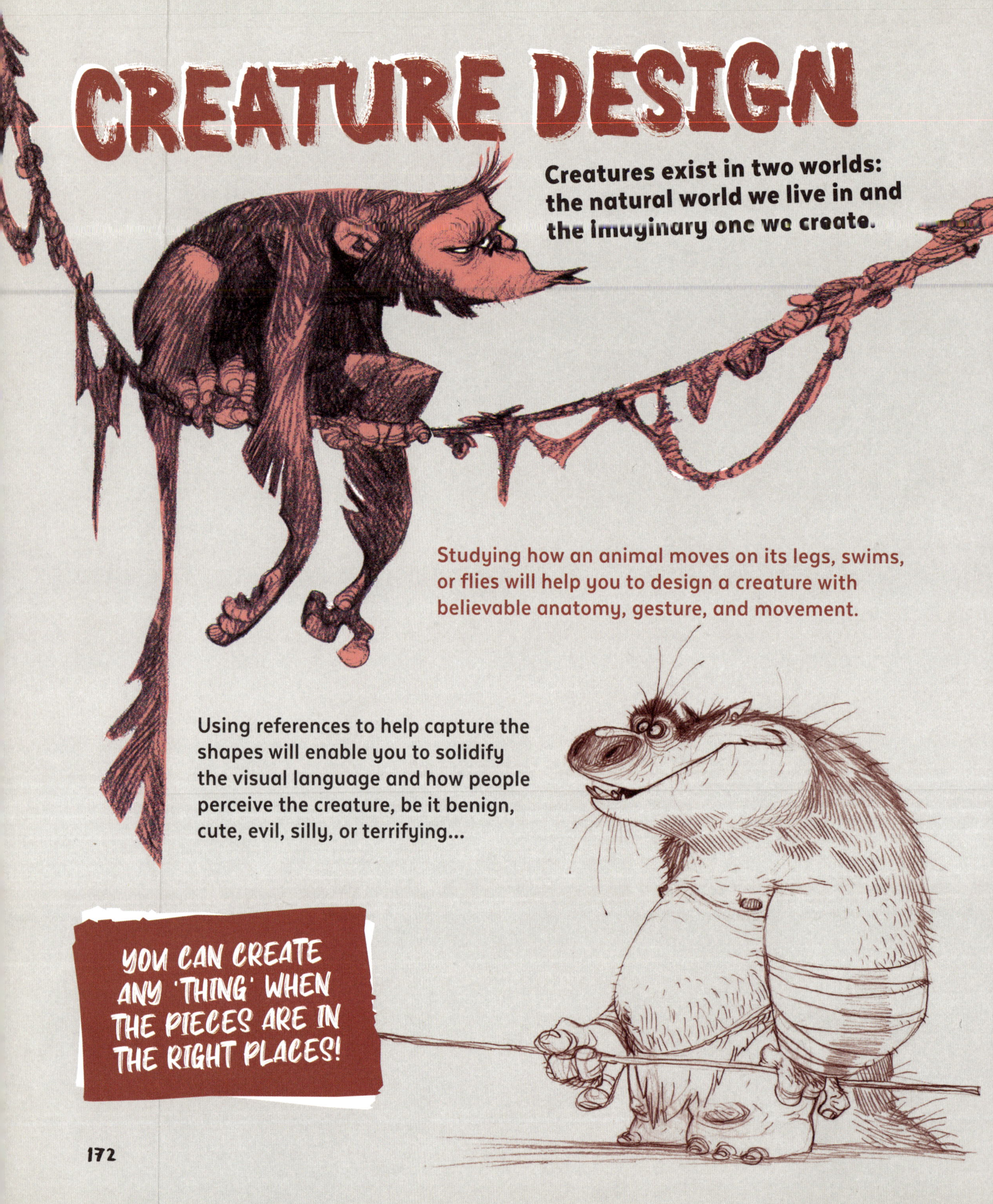

Creatures exist in two worlds: the natural world we live in and the imaginary one we create.

Studying how an animal moves on its legs, swims, or flies will help you to design a creature with believable anatomy, gesture, and movement.

Using references to help capture the shapes will enable you to solidify the visual language and how people perceive the creature, be it benign, cute, evil, silly, or terrifying...

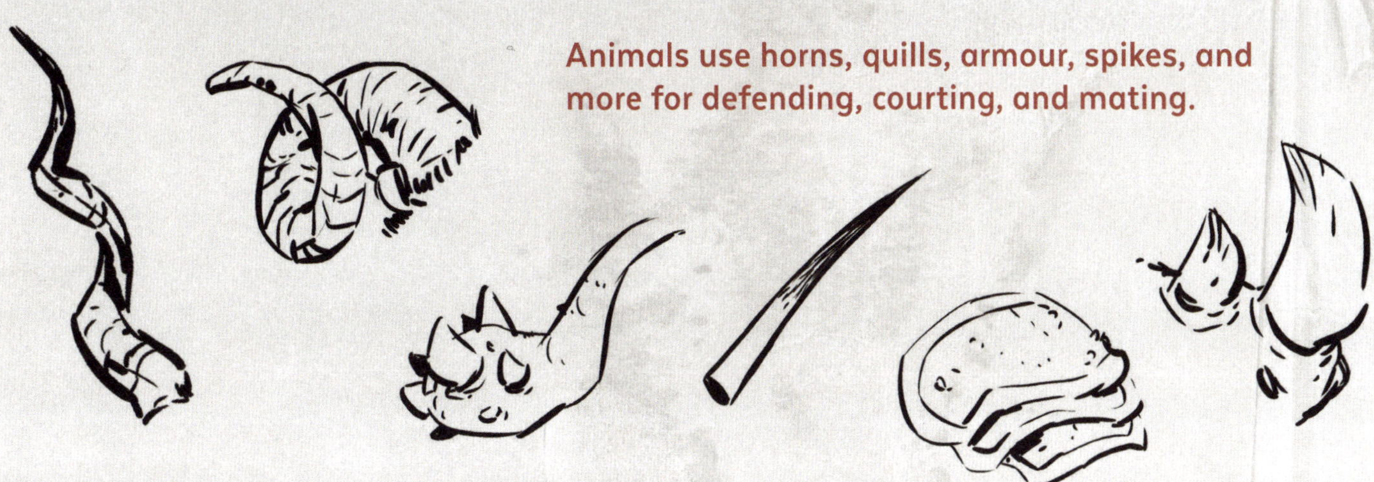

Spots, stripes, scales, feathers, and fur can hint at the creature's environment, provide design interest, and remind us of a species we can relate to from the real world.

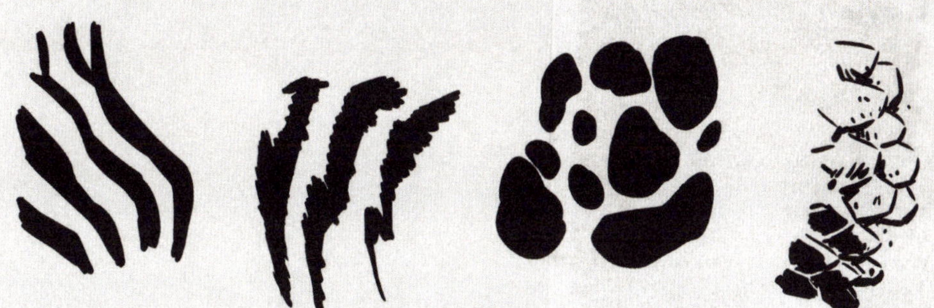

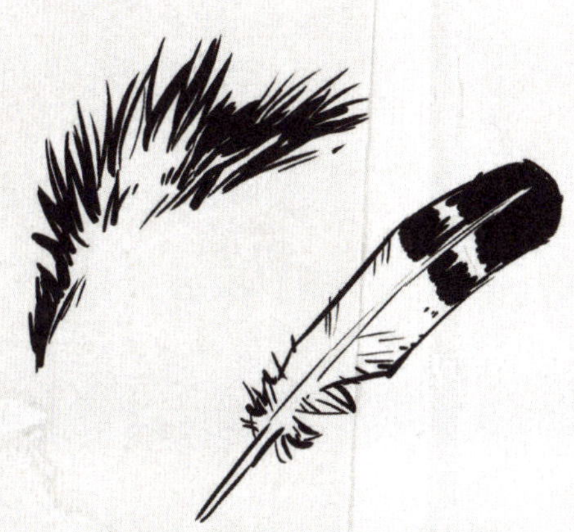

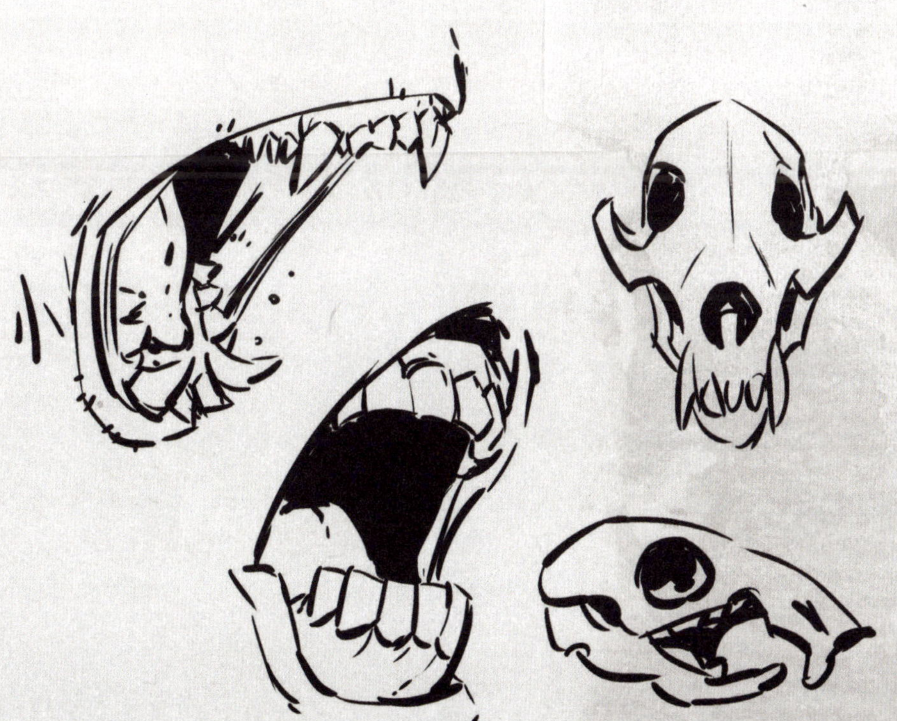

Teeth and eye placement are also useful to study.

★ Carnivores typically have aggressive, sharp teeth, whereas herbivores have shorter, less pointy teeth.

★ Predators often have sharp, focused eyes on the front of their heads to lock onto prey.

★ Prey tend to have big eyes on the sides of their heads to allow them the most vision for quick escapes!

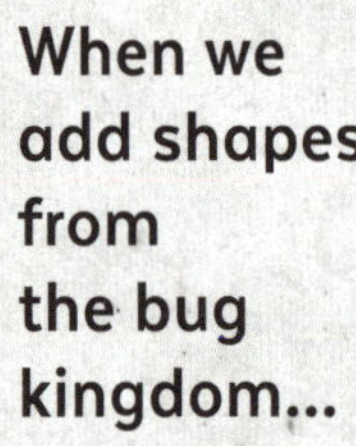

When we
add shapes
from
the bug
kingdom...

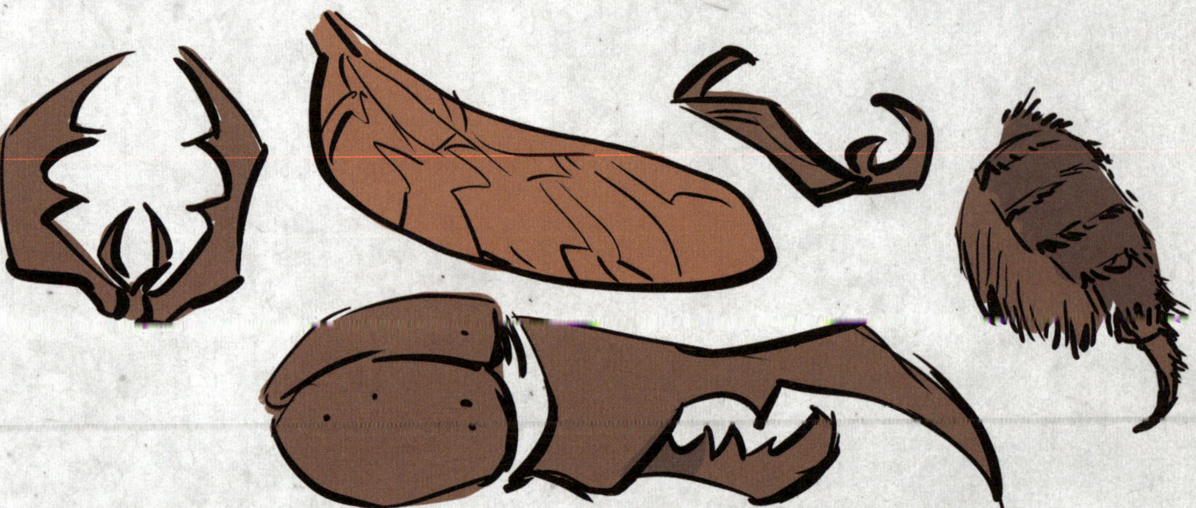

...under the sea...

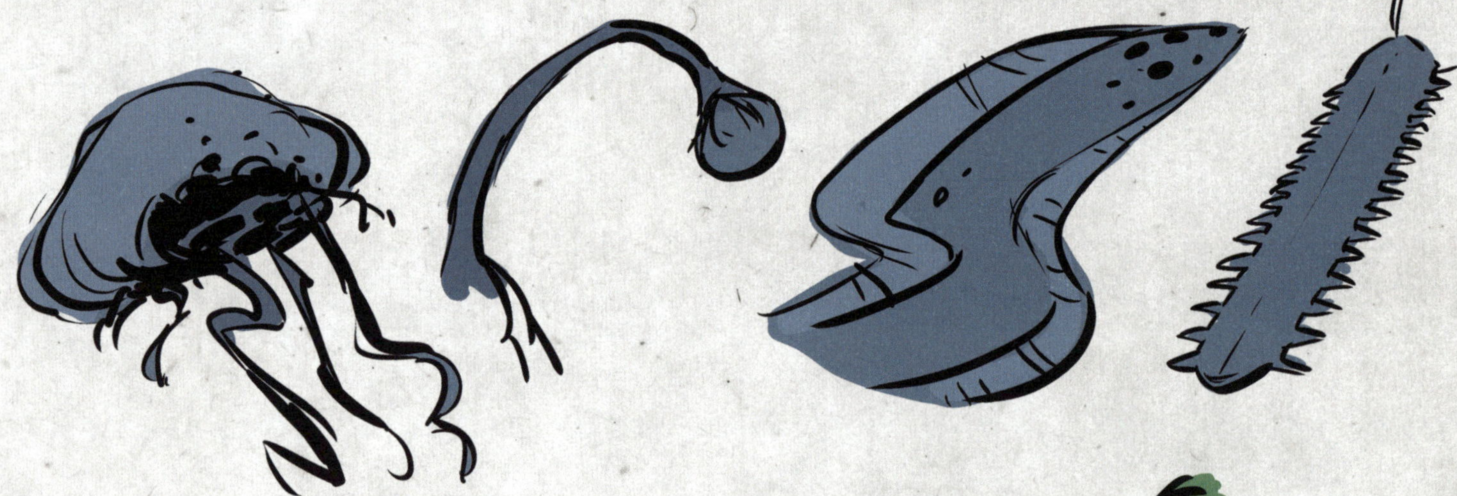

...and up in the air...

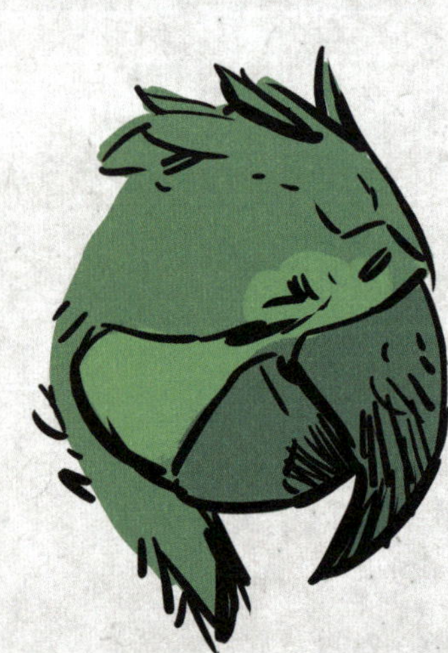

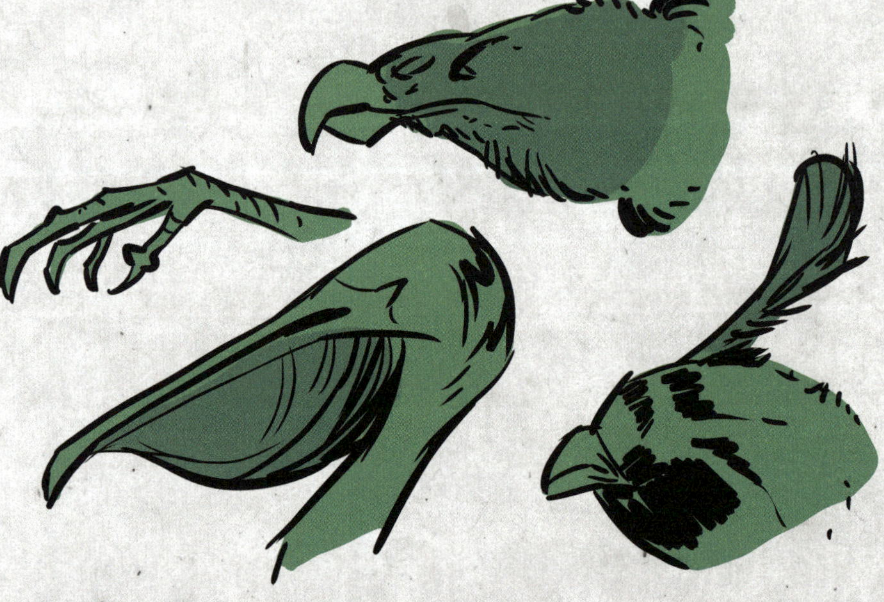

...the design elements are endless! There are too many to draw in one book, and that's just the obvious **PHYSICAL** shapes.

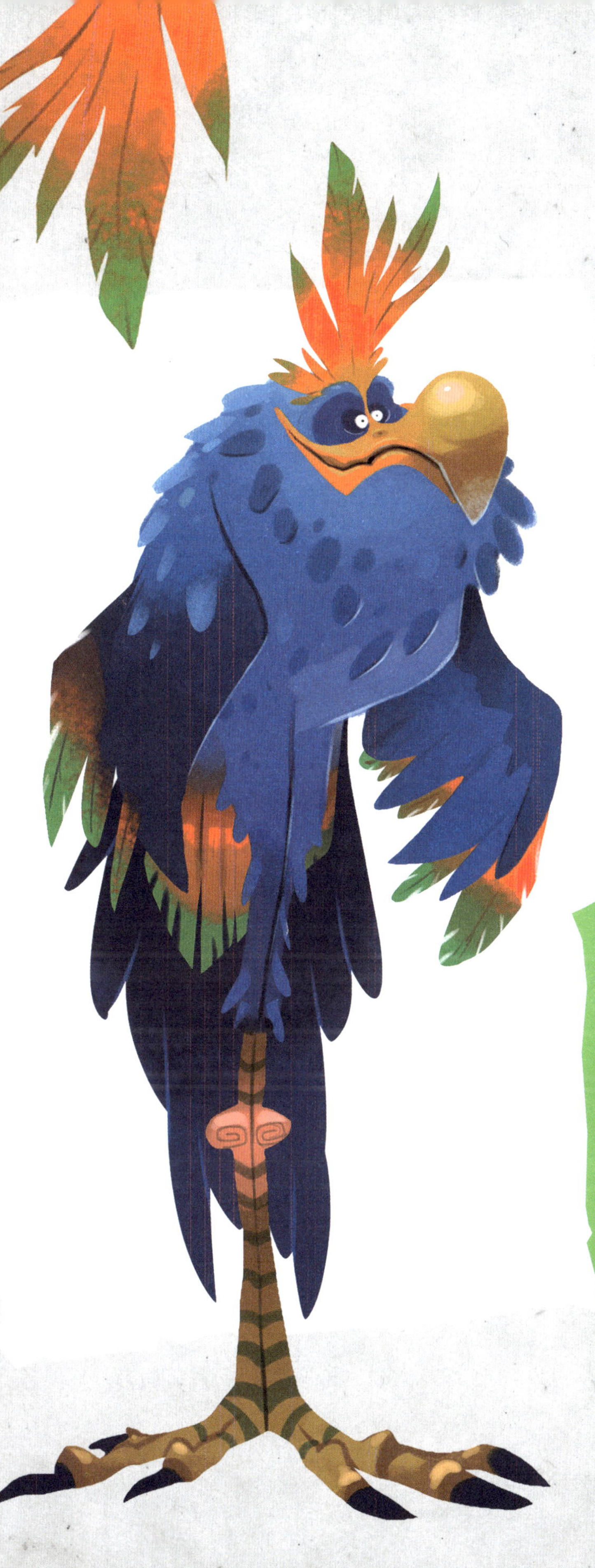

Don't forget that animals spit, ooze, drip, camouflage, group up, blow up, intimidate, bluster, vomit, rattle, shake, growl, and hiss.

They hop, jump, fly, run, glide, skid, slither, swim, slide, burrow, soar, climb, hover, wiggle, creep, and crawl.

And they come in **ALL** the colours!

Really, the list is exhausting...

As there are so many variations we can pull from the real world, it's important to understand the **INTENT** of the creature design you're creating. This is the place you should start drawing from.

CREATURES CAN BE:

- Trainable for riding or as a pet.

- From myth or legend.

- Background for an environment.

- Anything from humorous to horrific.

- A main character or a villain.

- For reference, practice, or study.

For practice and study, visit zoos, farms, or stables, as well as people you know with pets. Drawing from real life will give you knowledge and understanding that a stock photo or online search just won't provide. The sounds, smells, and immediate nature of live drawing is a unique opportunity to take in all the elements.

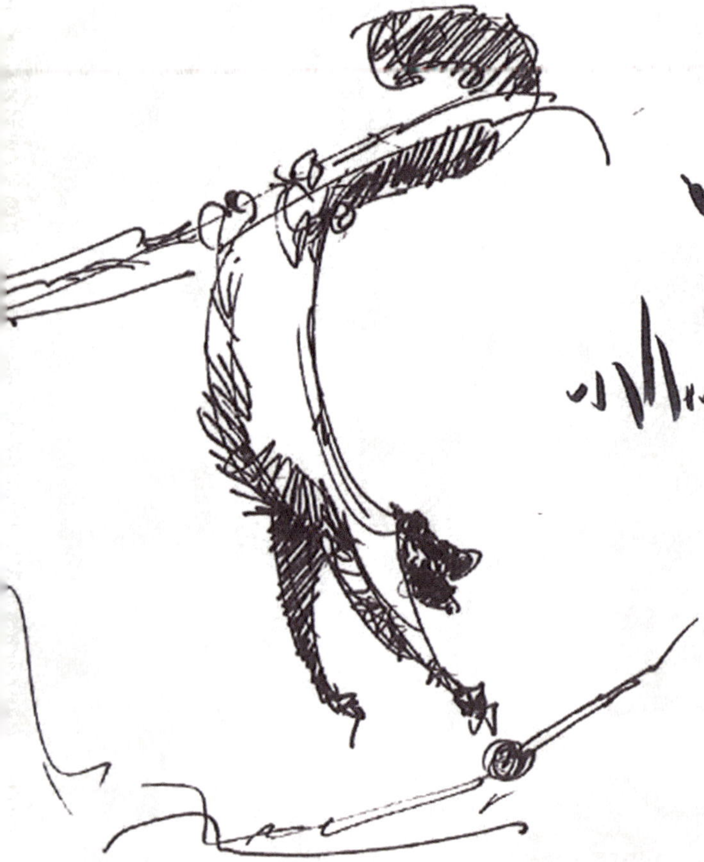

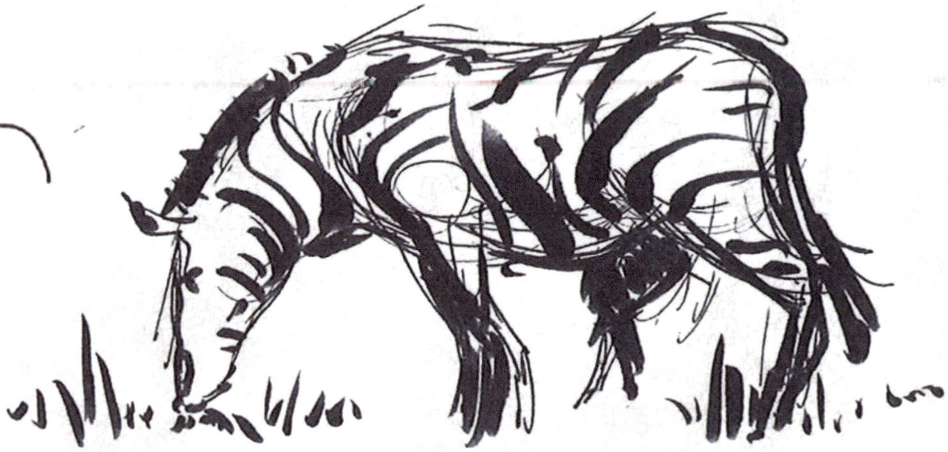

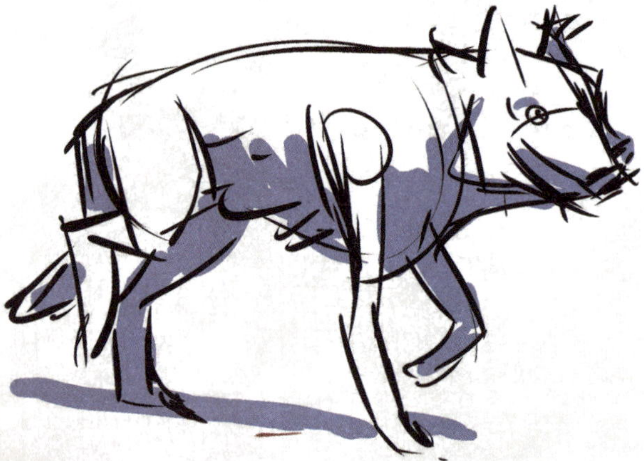

You may find it challenging to capture an animal on the move. Practise taking mental snapshots of what you see, then start by drawing the line action and gesture. You can then add the shapes and details when they are still.

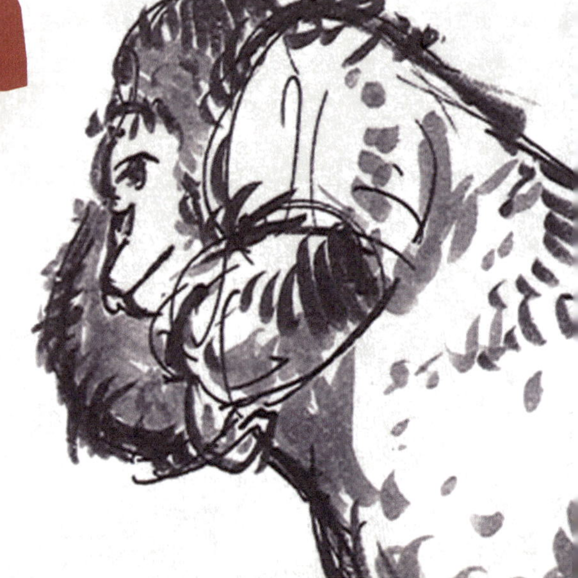

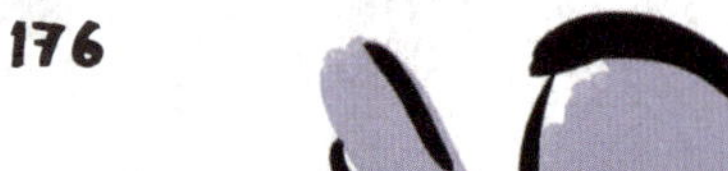
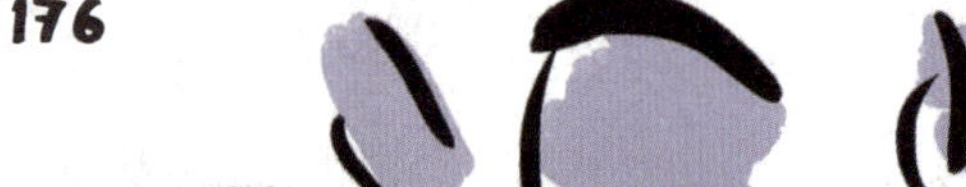

Earlier in the book we explored the process of breaking down shapes. Let's do that again here.

Capture a quick gesture sketch.

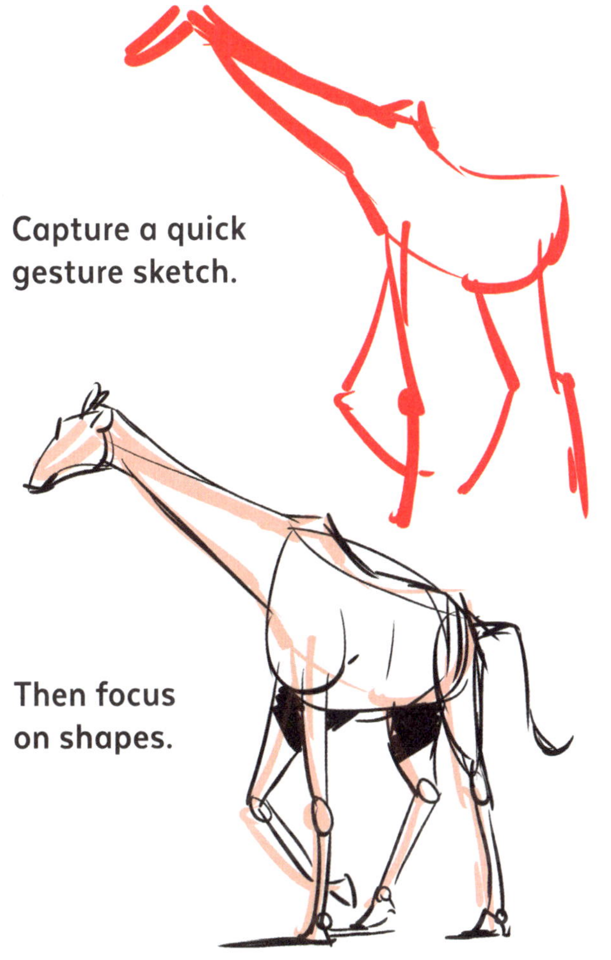

Then focus on shapes.

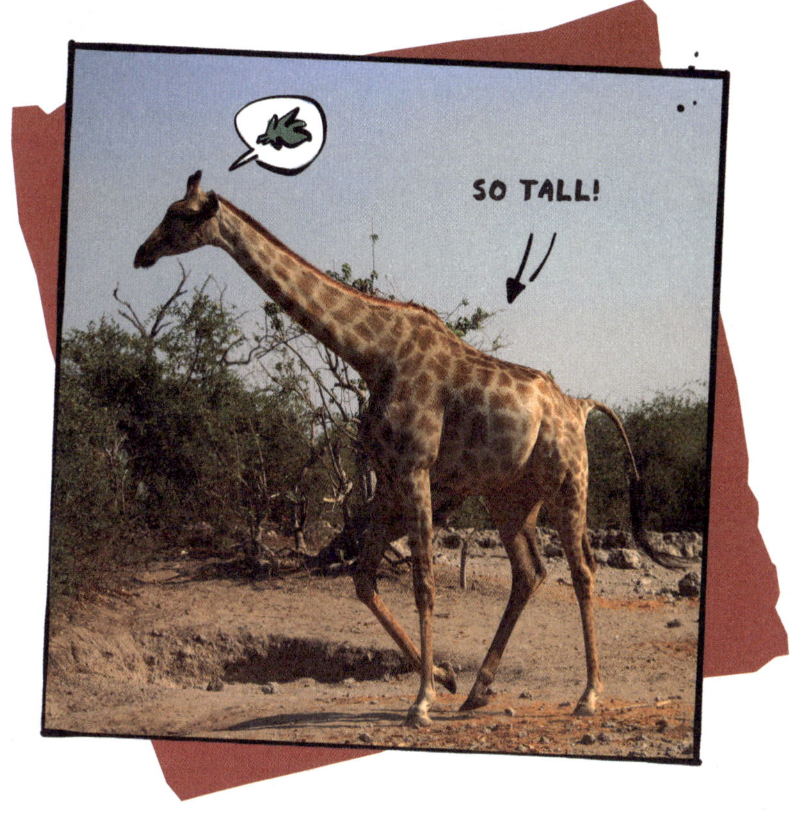

I'm no animal expert, but I **DO** need to know enough about muscles, limbs, directions, and details to provide the design with the necessary information.

The visual communication should tell the viewer that this is a giraffe, not an aardvark...

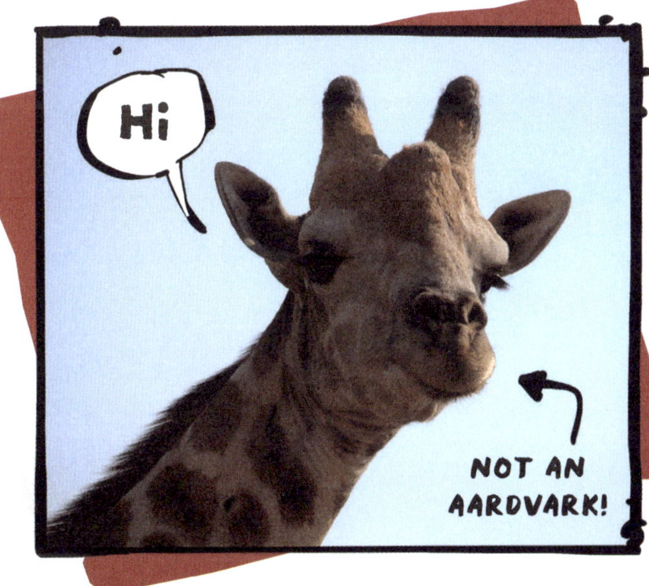

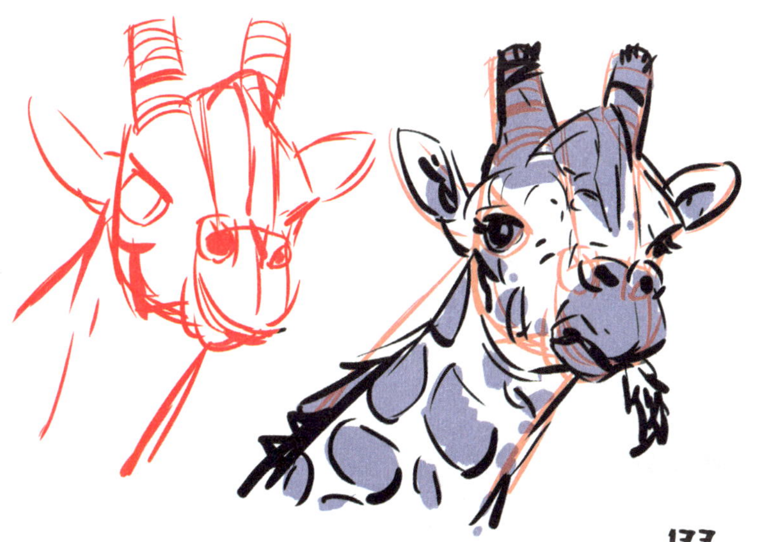

For now, let's identify a creature as any critter, monster, or animal that can't read, write, or have nuanced emotions. It's a fine line, but the choices you make with how a creature acts more animalistic over perceived human emotions will place the design one way or the other. I find that the intelligence level is the key difference. More on that later...

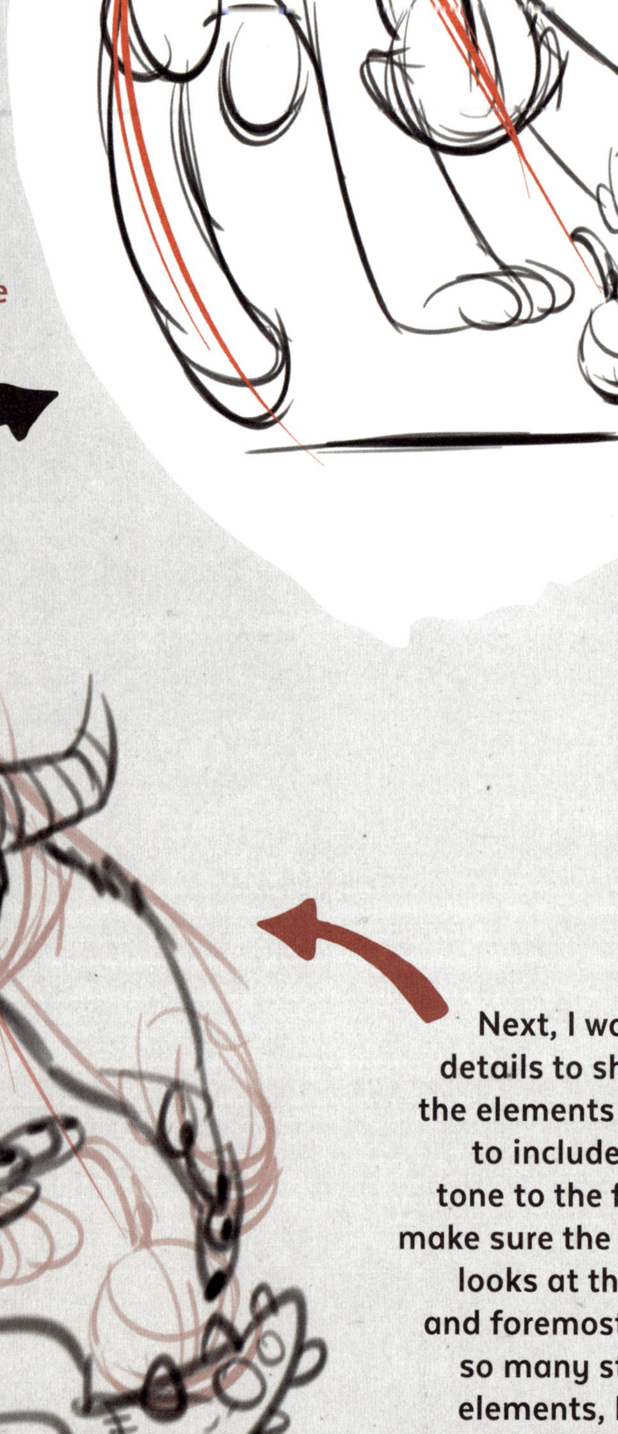

Next, I work out details to show all the elements I need to include. I add tone to the face to make sure the viewer looks at this first and foremost. With so many strange elements, I felt it was needed.

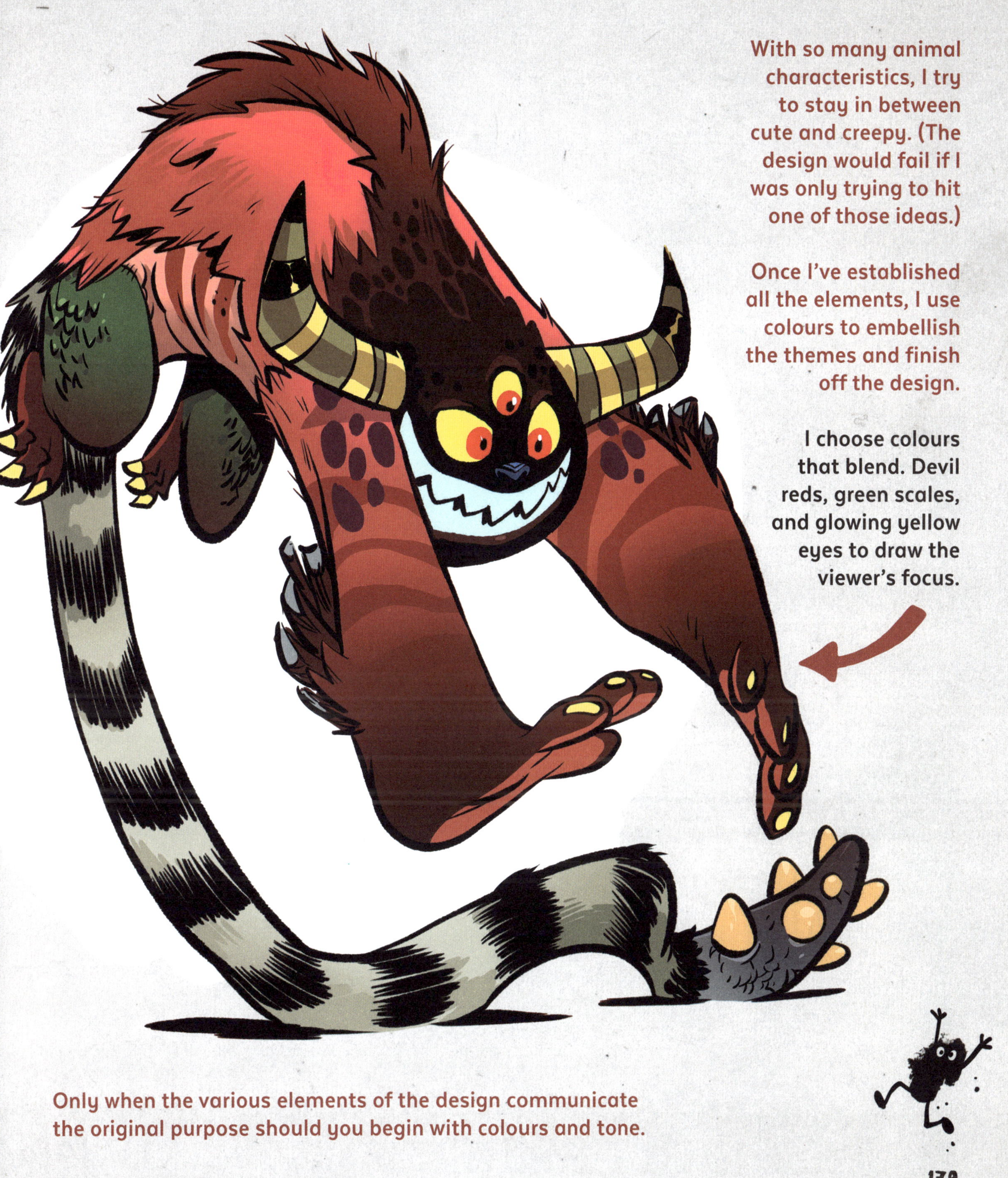

With so many animal characteristics, I try to stay in between cute and creepy. (The design would fail if I was only trying to hit one of those ideas.)

Once I've established all the elements, I use colours to embellish the themes and finish off the design.

I choose colours that blend. Devil reds, green scales, and glowing yellow eyes to draw the viewer's focus.

Only when the various elements of the design communicate the original purpose should you begin with colours and tone.

Now let's design a creature that thinks, acts, talks, or communicates in an intelligent way. A good exercise is to take a design and transform it from feral to sophisticated.

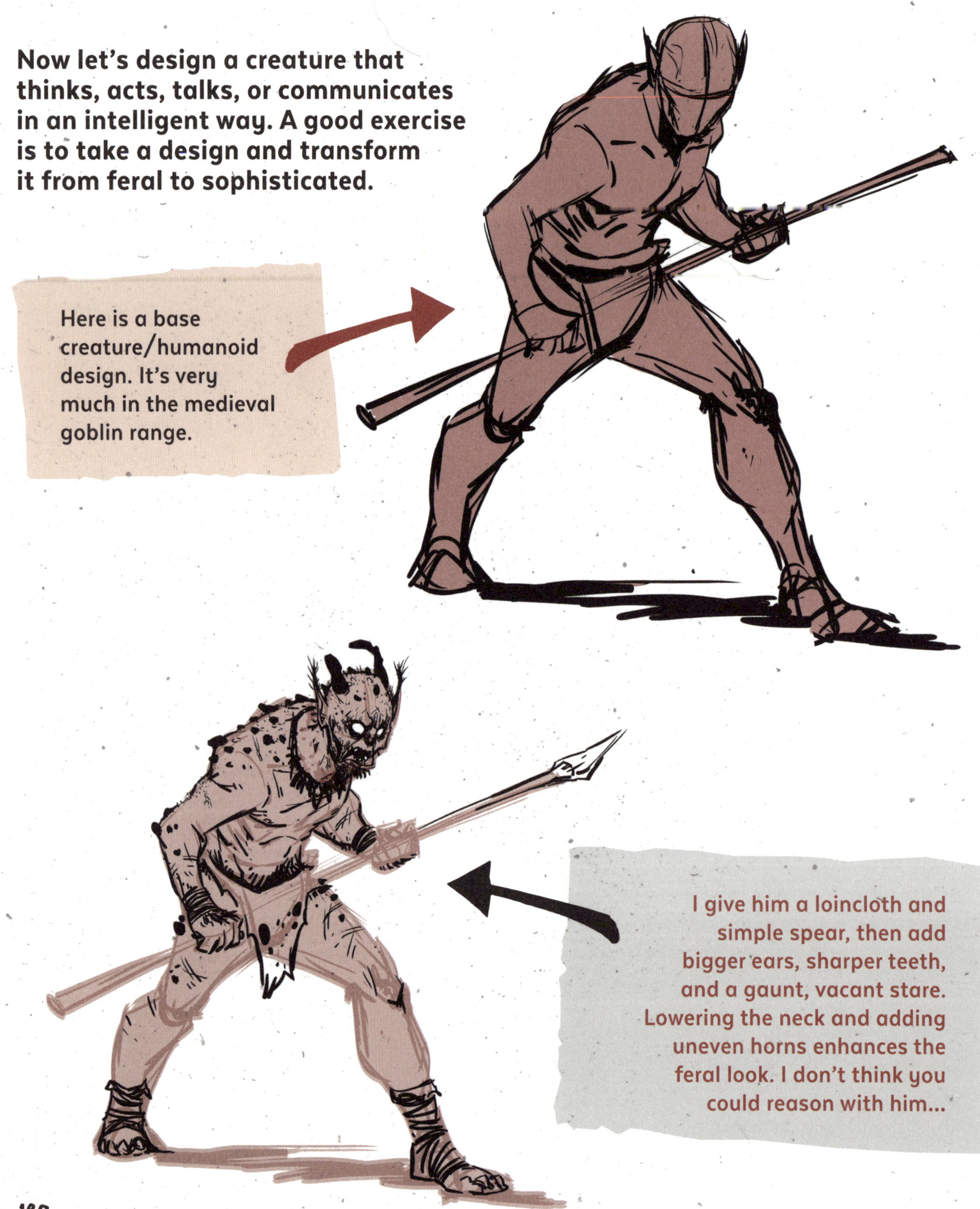

Here is a base creature/humanoid design. It's very much in the medieval goblin range.

I give him a loincloth and simple spear, then add bigger ears, sharper teeth, and a gaunt, vacant stare. Lowering the neck and adding uneven horns enhances the feral look. I don't think you could reason with him...

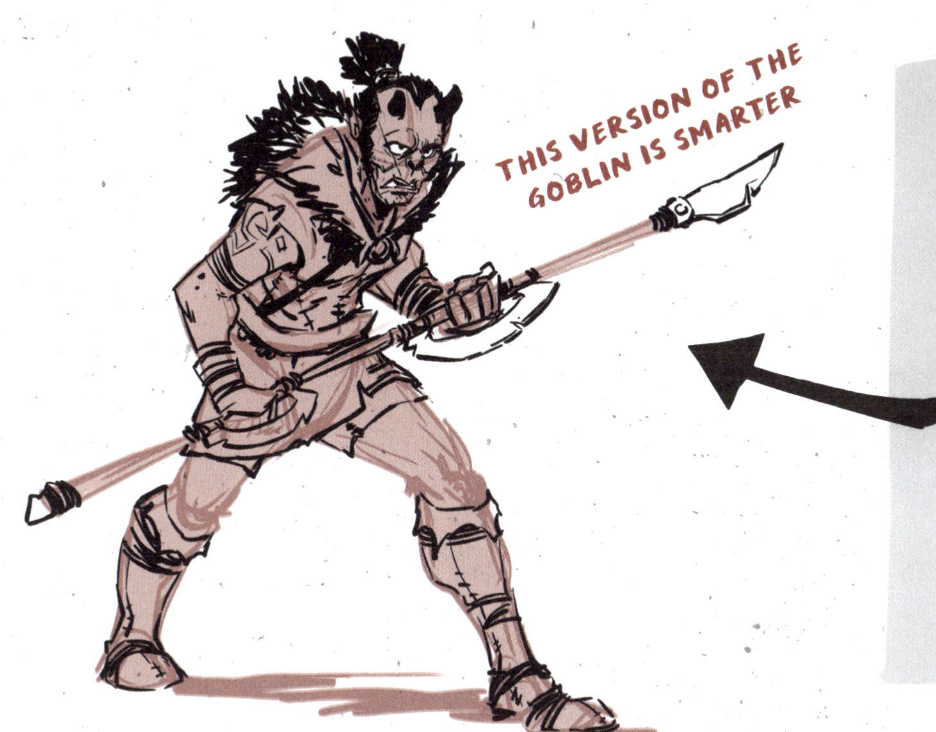

He's learned how to write, draw tattoos, stitch, and make clothing from animal fur. Adding pupils and a smaller mouth furthers the story of mental growth. He's dabbled in metals, making a stronger and more formidable weapon for hunting. He's even had a little time for a hairstyle. He may not understand our language, but I feel you could communicate with him.

The goblin has peaked! He has learned metallurgy and now has the knowledge and ability to not only make armour, but to style it too. This means he's had time to think, design, and create. Piercing eyes and a closed mouth help enhance his more intelligent look.

Be it creature, alien, or anthropomorphic animal, if we see complex emotions, wearables, or written language, we will project ourselves onto it. We see them as a branch of humanity, just different.

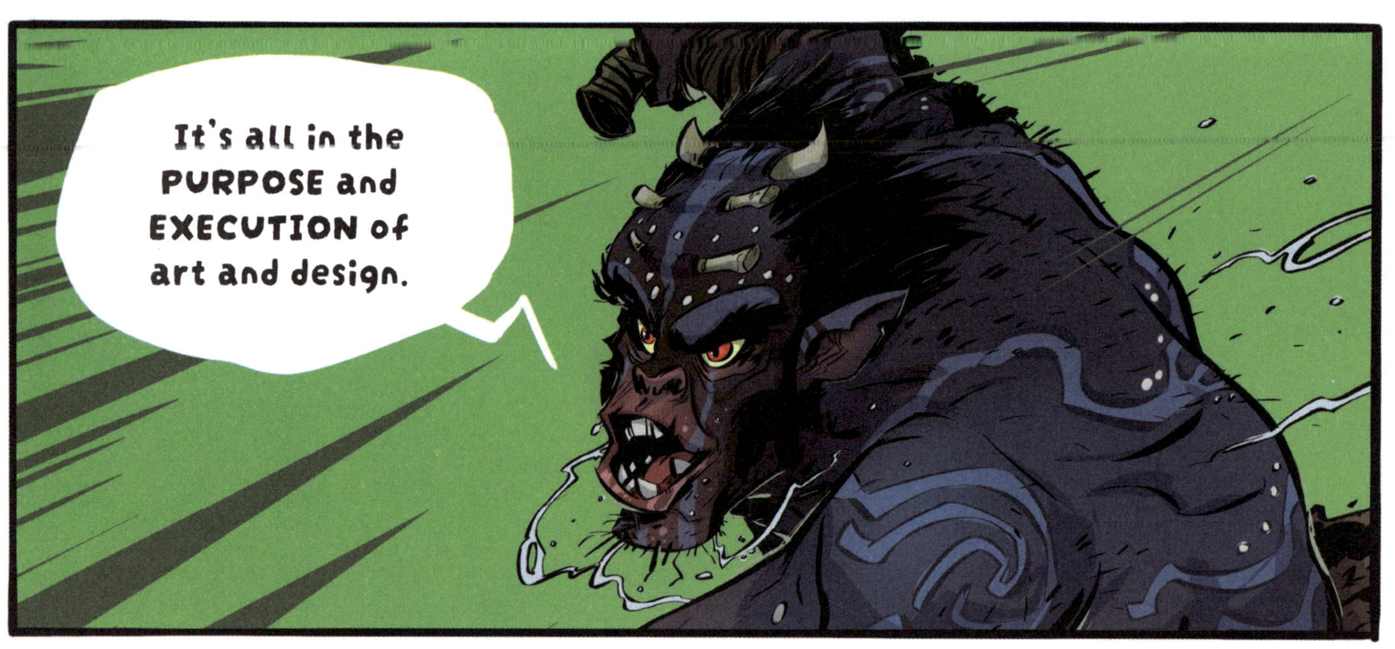

This can be used to great effect for endearing a creature to the audience.

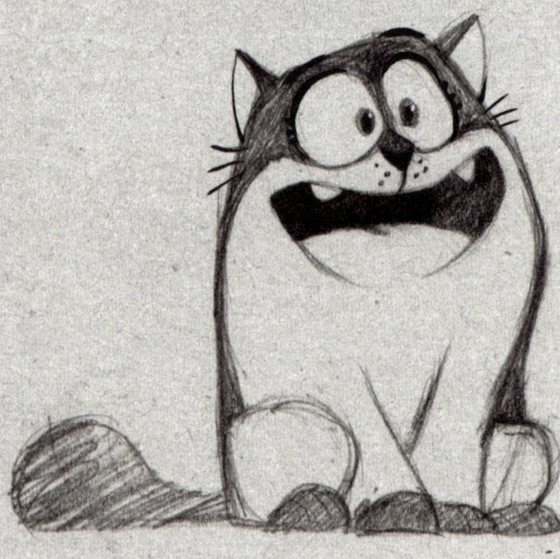

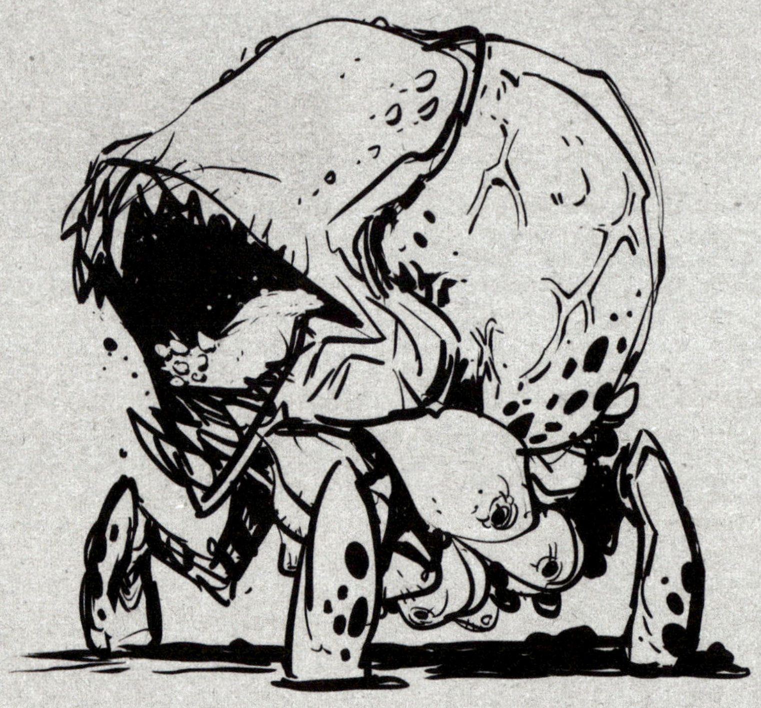

Or removing its humanity and recognizable features to make it feel creepy and unnerving.

REMEMBER:

★ Every being has basic needs, including food, water, sleep, procreation, and how it evolved in adapting to its environment. It will have defences (usually to prevent it from being eaten) or offences (usually for hunting and eating). You can create entire backstories for any species' evolution!

★ Think about your intent. Come up with **KEYWORDS**, for example: bug-like, alien, desert climate, winged, equestrian...

★ Gather shapes from reference material that reflect your main ideas and keywords. Create a few studies before skipping ahead to design.

★ Consider its intelligence level. From basic level to advanced thinking, or even beyond human understanding!

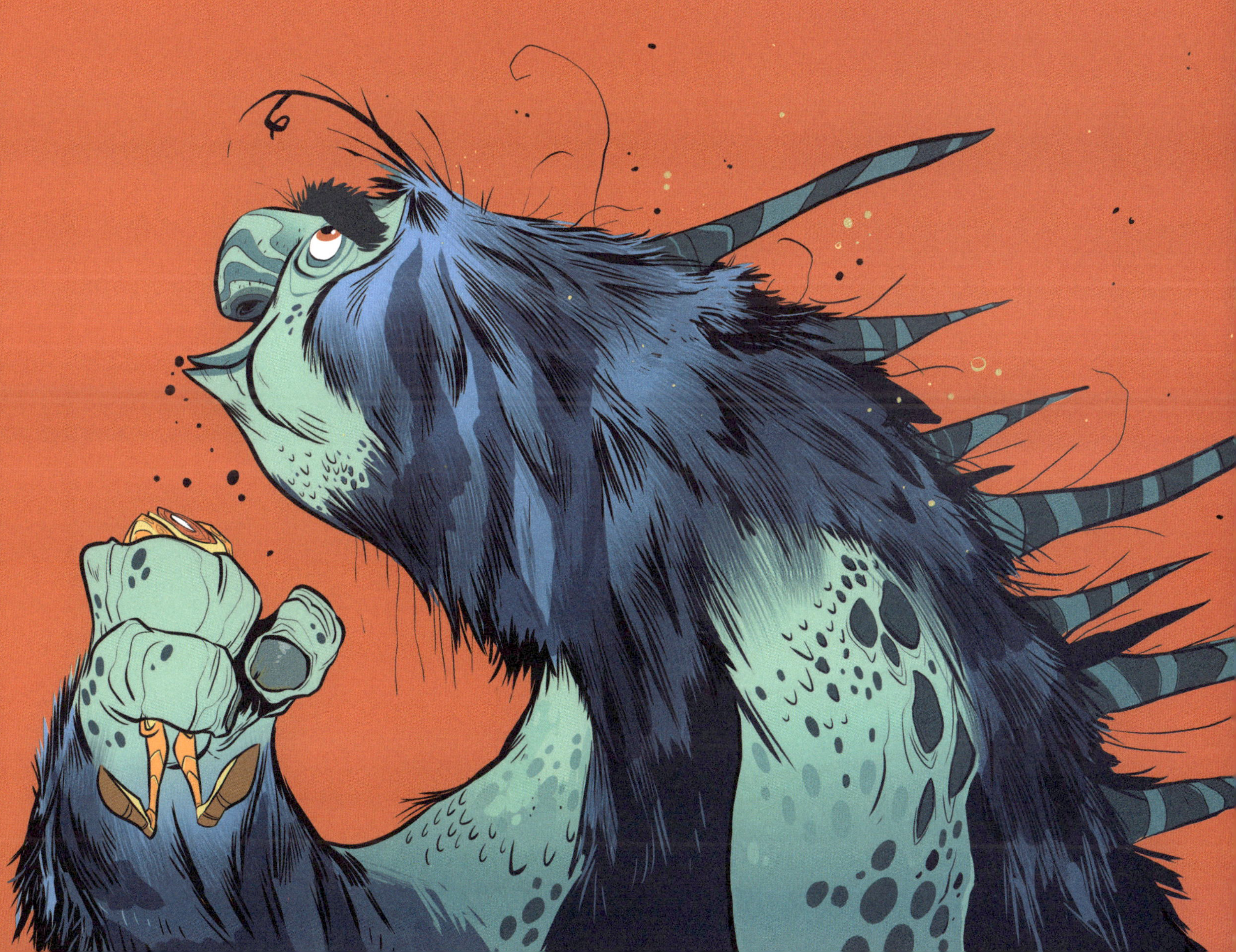

CREATURE DESIGN EXERCISES

Trace over these, scan them, or take a photo to work digitally. Or download them (see URL on page 7).

Find an animal (in real life!) and sketch it.

Draw an intelligent monster with a specific attitude.

Draw the same monster, but wild and feral!

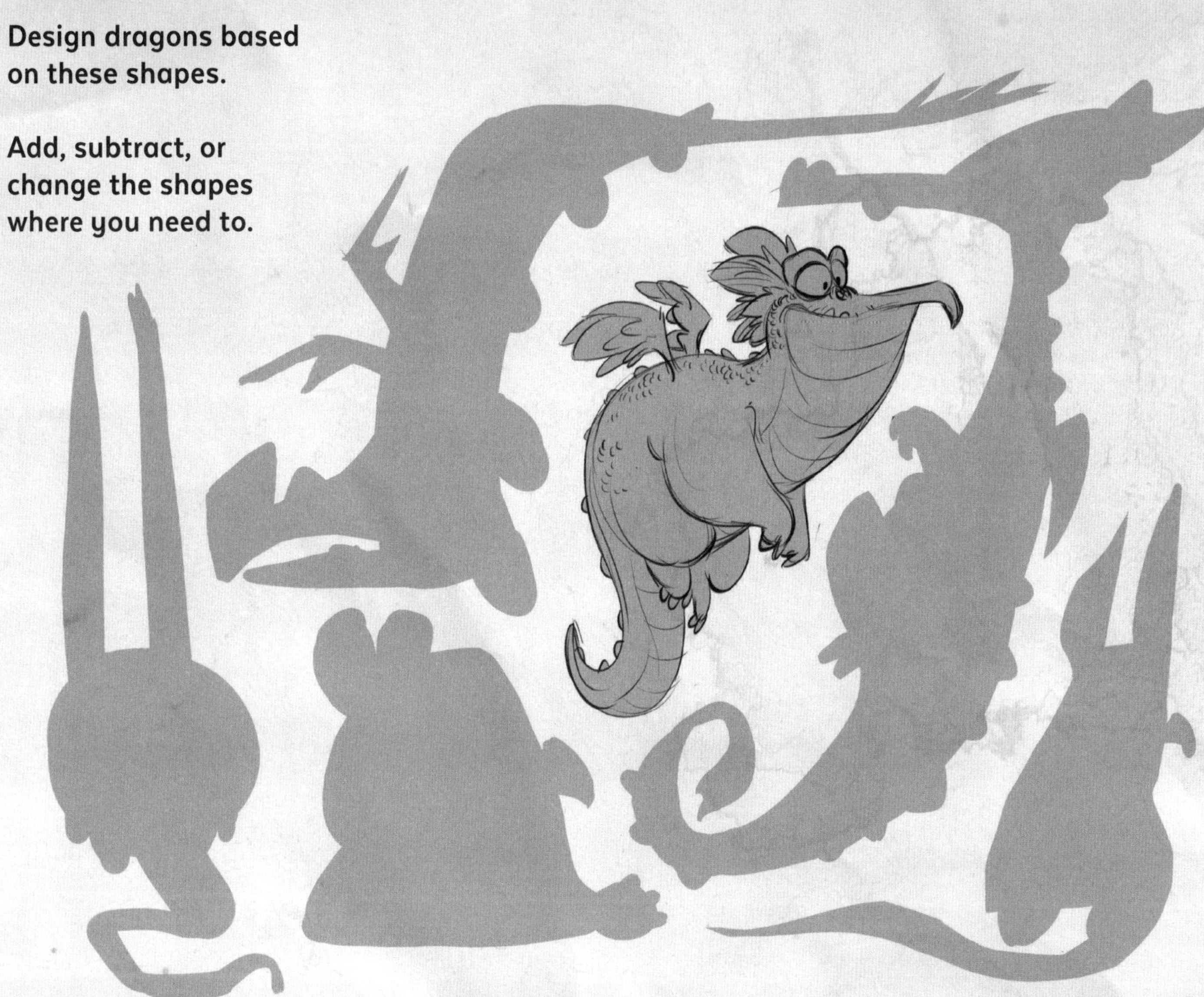

Draw stripes | **Draw spots** | **Draw scales** | **Draw fur**

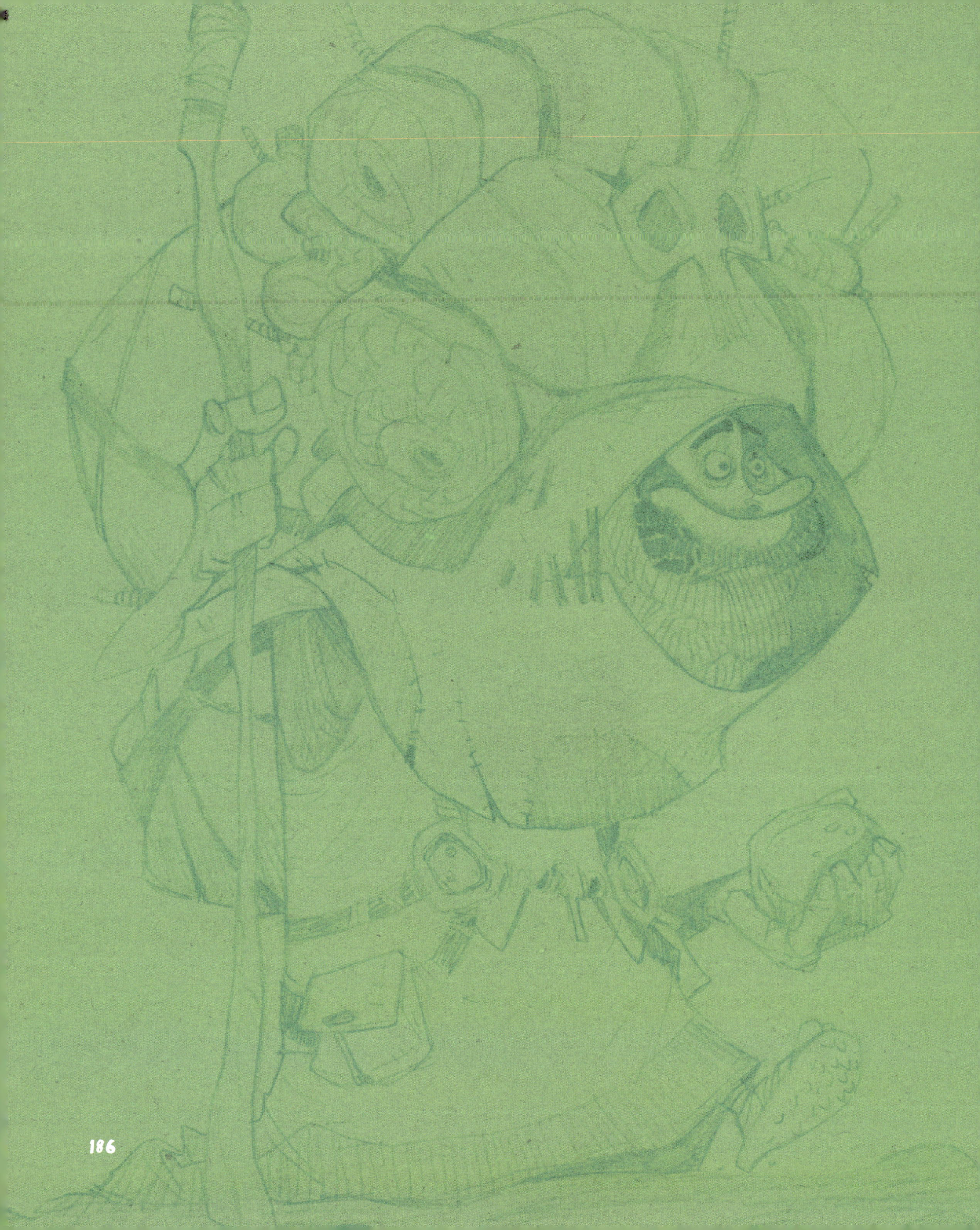

PROPS & VEHICLES

PROPS

Yeah, that's right... even vehicles are props!

It's all size related. Like this kid's toy...

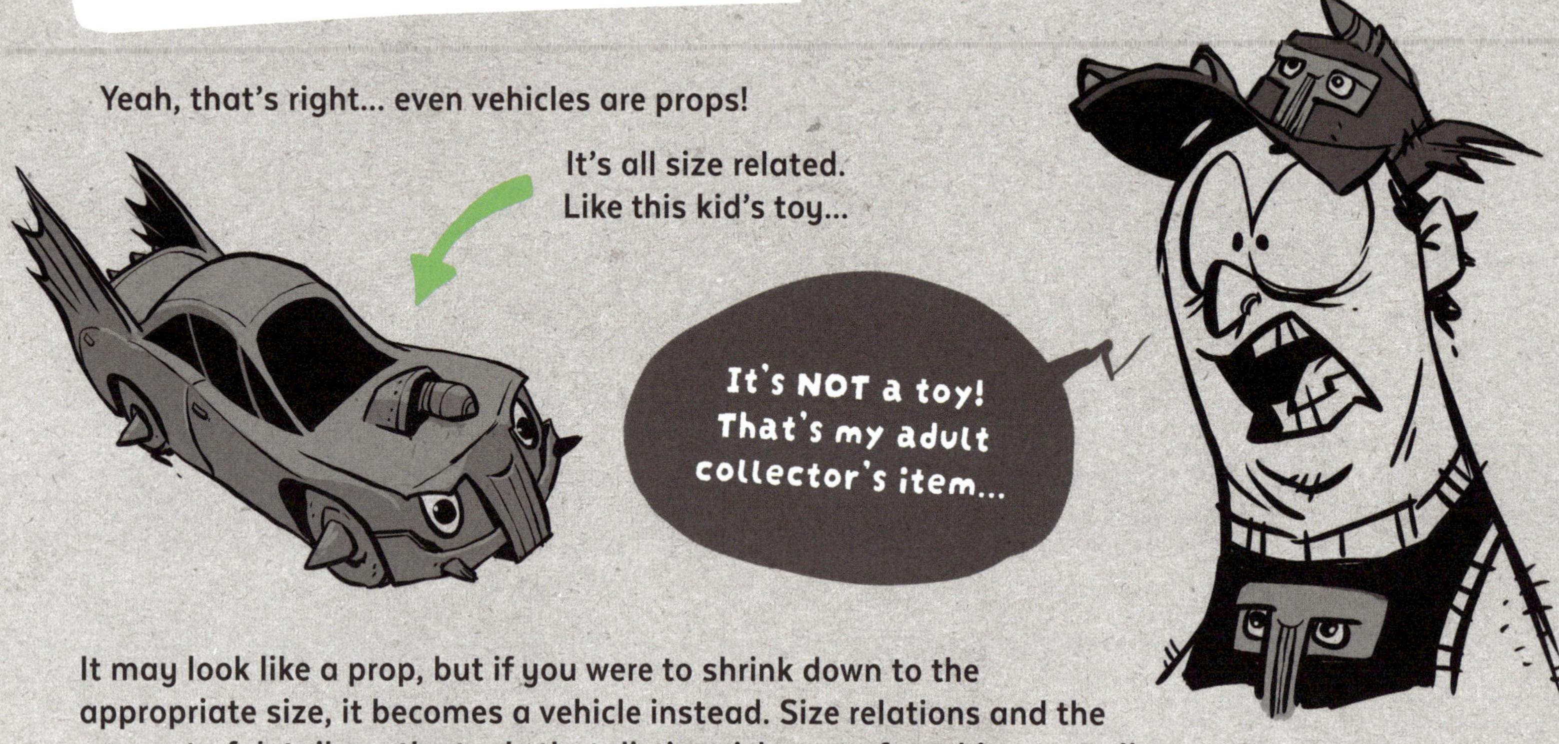

It may look like a prop, but if you were to shrink down to the appropriate size, it becomes a vehicle instead. Size relations and the amount of detail are the tools that distinguish props from big to small.

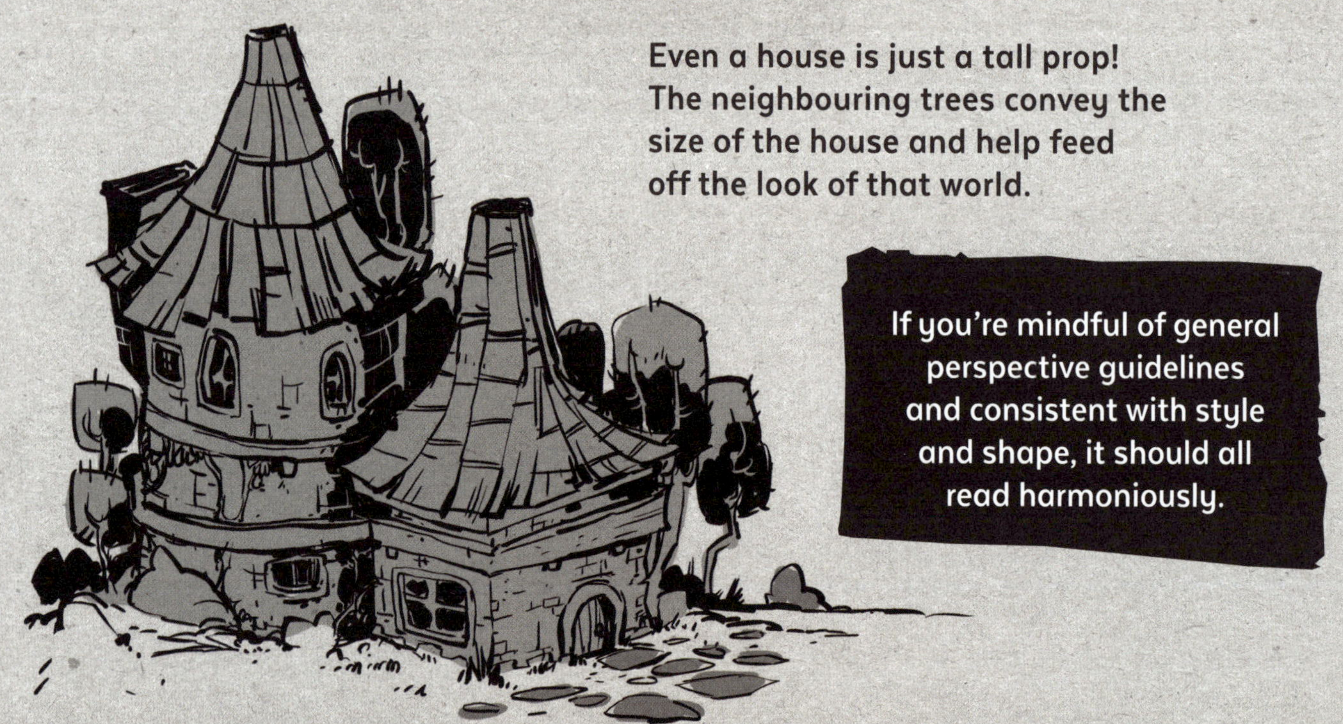

Even a house is just a tall prop! The neighbouring trees convey the size of the house and help feed off the look of that world.

If you're mindful of general perspective guidelines and consistent with style and shape, it should all read harmoniously.

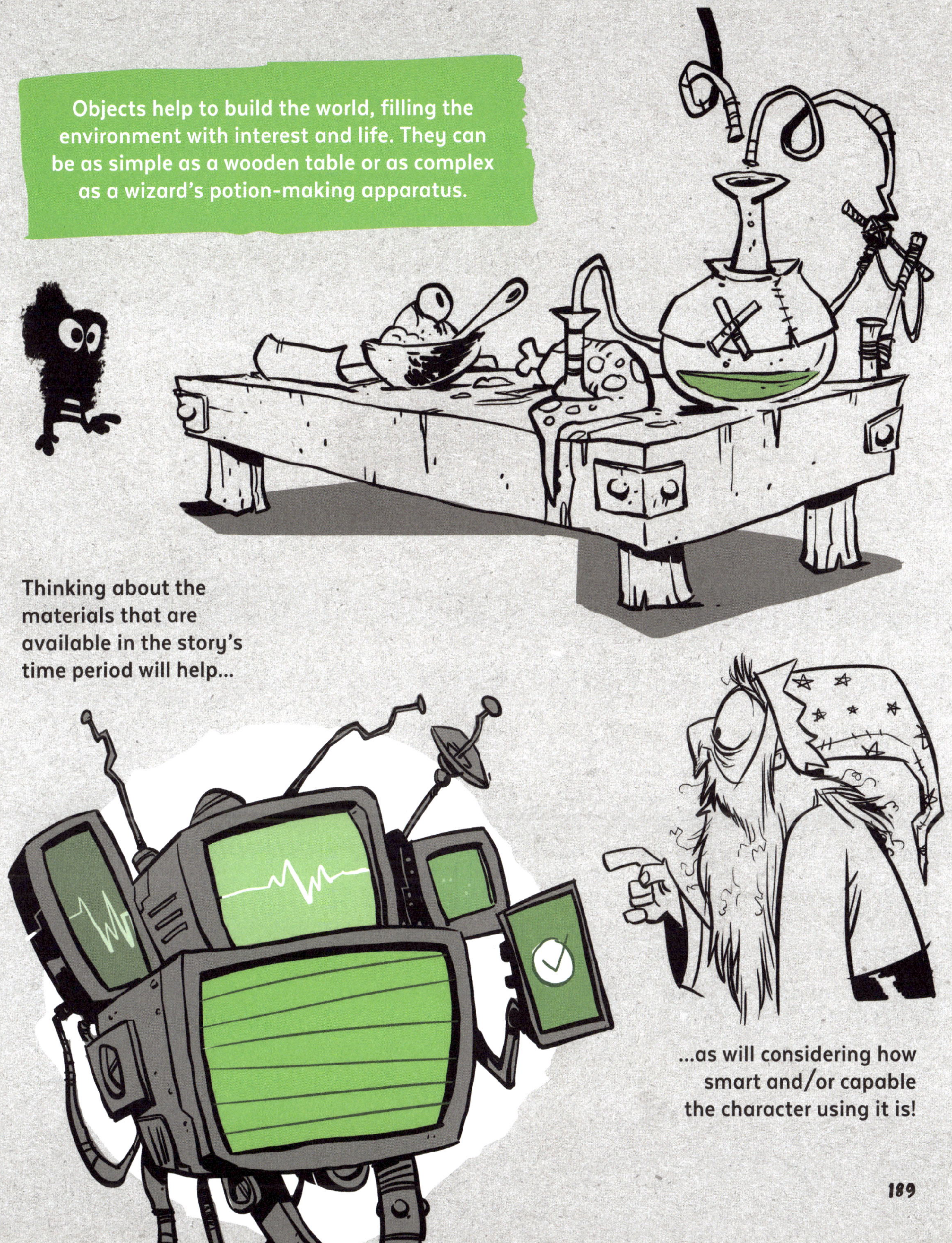

Thinking about the materials that are available in the story's time period will help...

...as will considering how smart and/or capable the character using it is!

Props can help to establish themes, ideas, and timelines. Basically, any part of the story behind your character or the objects propagating a scene.

Props can also be attributes - part of a character's character! This can include a character's quirks, such as a certain mannerism or habit.

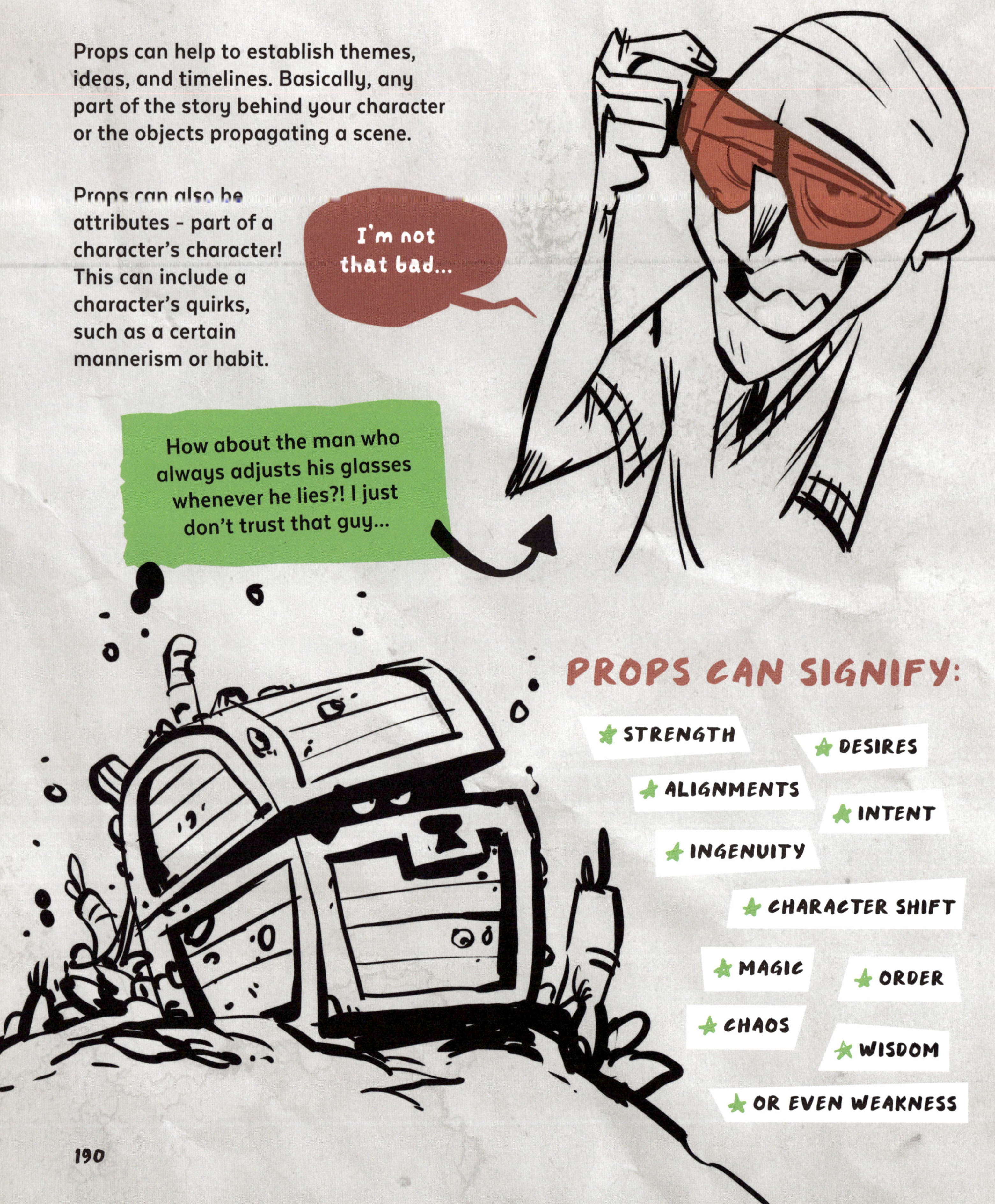

FIND THE PURPOSE:

⭐ Is the prop for filling out a scene? Whose scene?

⭐ Designing a baobab treehouse?

⭐ Could be a giant 200-page book that someone must finish by midnight?

⭐ Maybe just an old, crooked staff to carry the weight of an old, crooked man?

⭐ All living creatures will handle a prop in a way that reveals personality and story. It needs to be kept consistent or the character becomes weak or diluted. Like the hero's journey, how they become proficient in props or mannerisms should be purposeful choices.

TRY THIS!

Let's do a warm-up. Draw a prop to go on top of this pedestal. Is it old and worn? Funny? Gold? You decide!

Be mindful of the perspective (you're looking up at it).

You can complete this task by drawing over the image on tracing paper, or taking a photo/scanning it in to draw digitally.

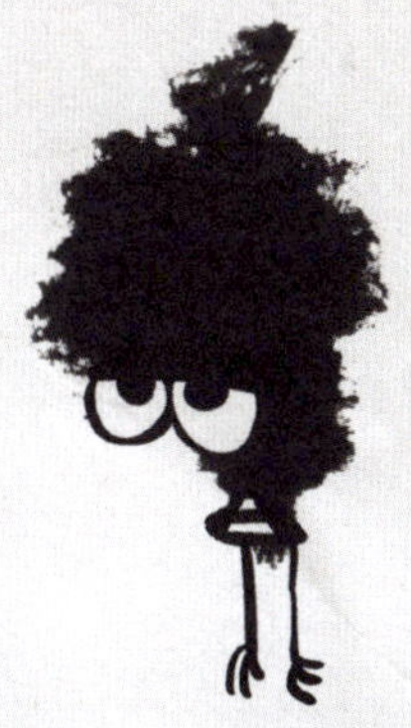

VEHICLES

For vehicles, start by drawing a trusly box to create various perspectives...

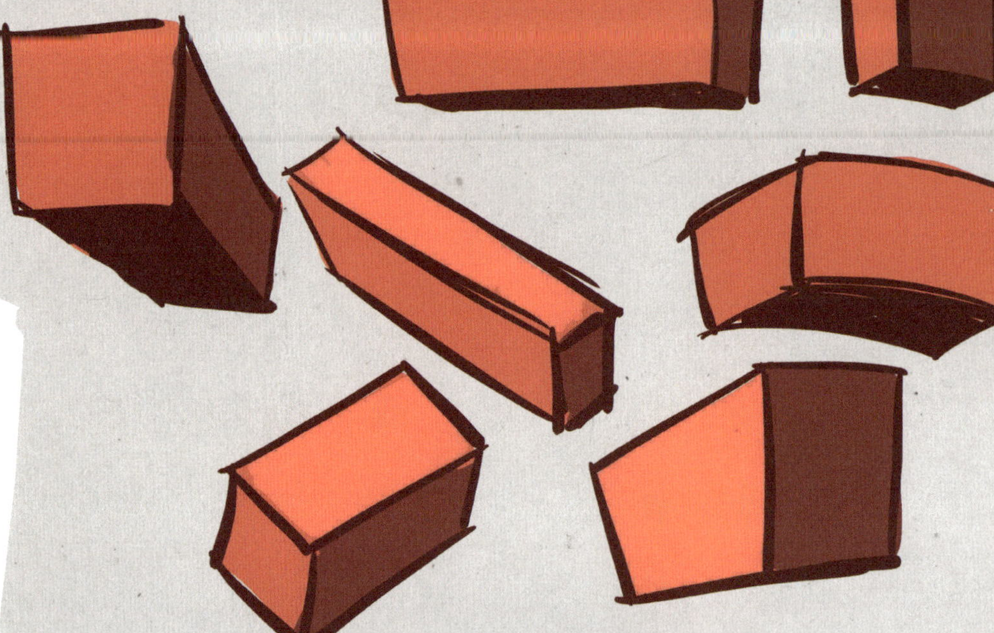

For tyres, draw two ovals and connect them to produce a basic wheel.

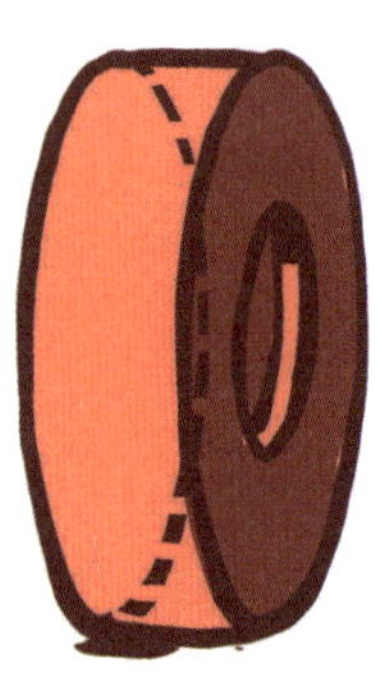

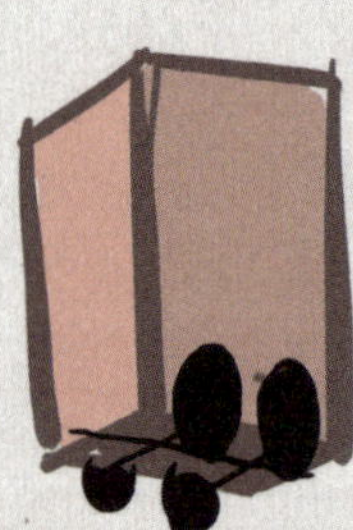

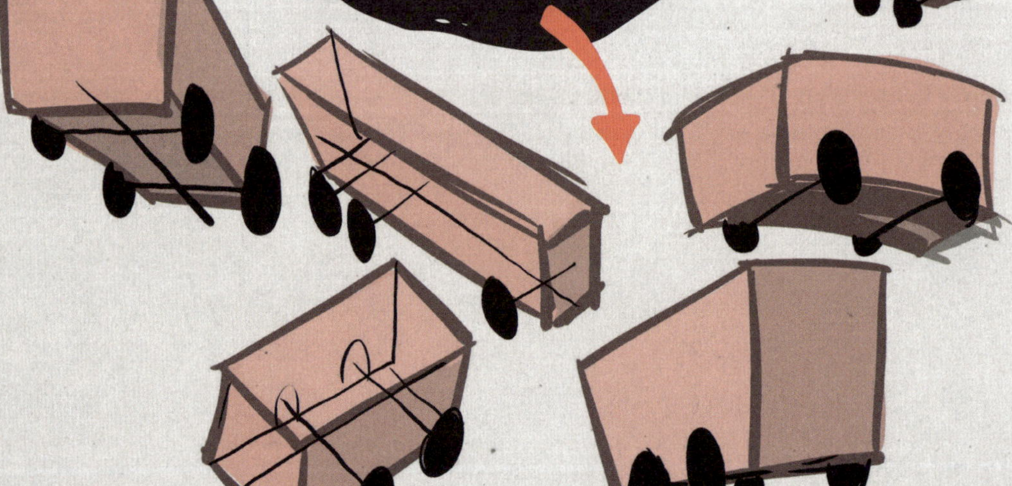

Feel free to experiment with the shapes. As long as they have headlights, windows, and tyres, you've got everything set up for creating interesting designs.

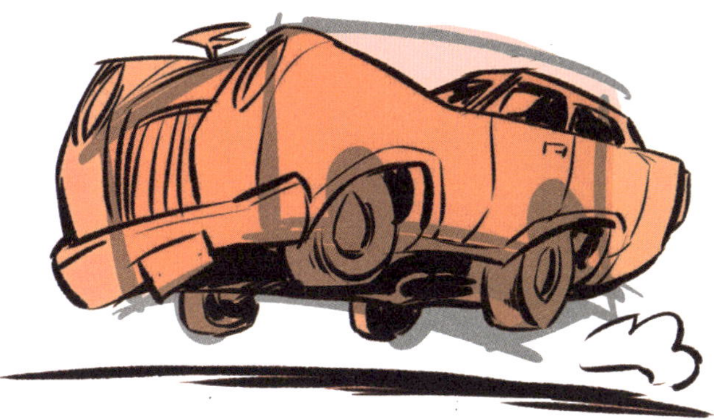

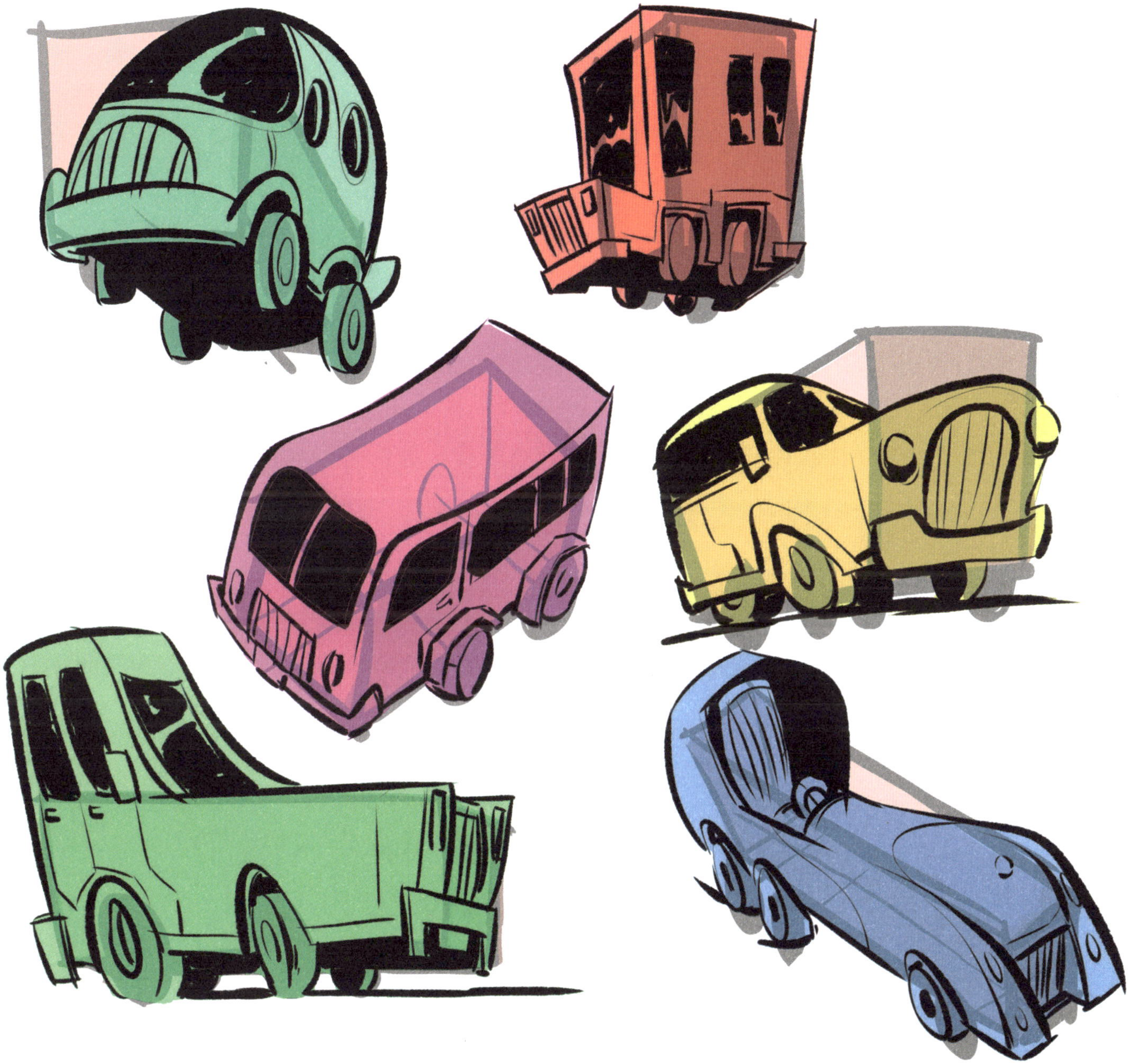

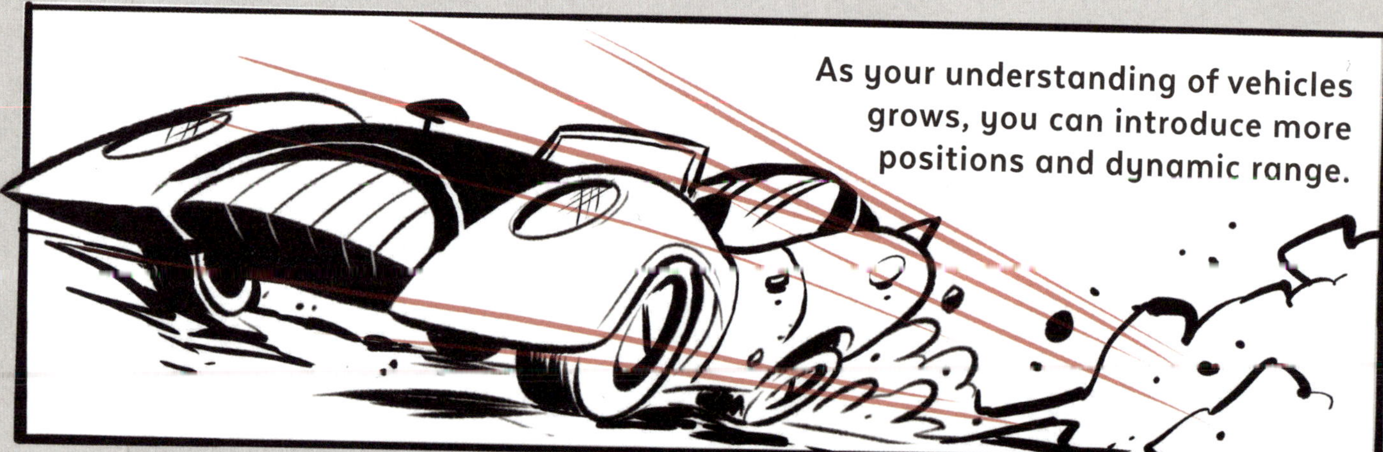

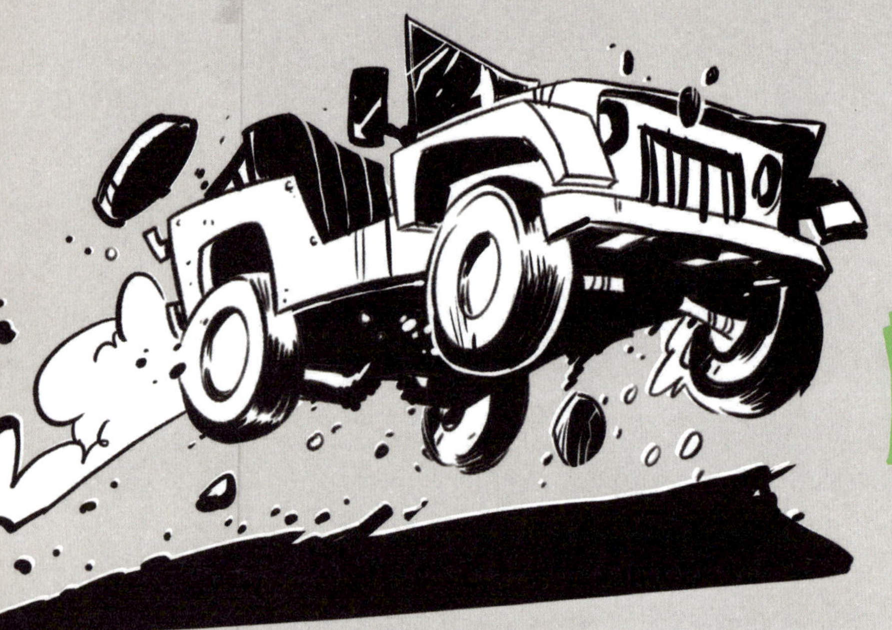

Cars can be all about design and/or action. They can lead a character to a scene, or act as a vital piece of the plot. Either way, hard edges, smooth curves, plus perspective is key!

A flying alien taxi can be instantly recognizable as a taxi given the right details, size relations, and colour choices.

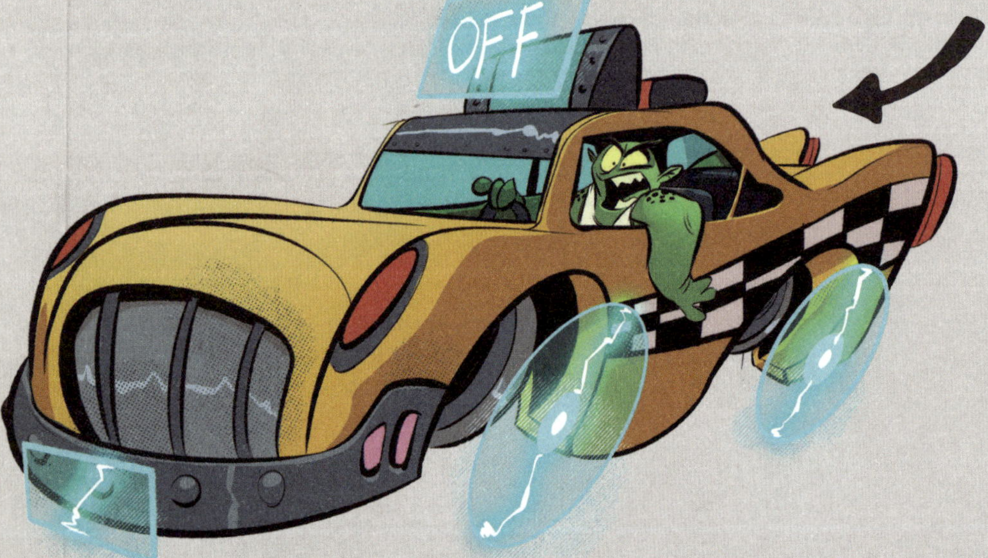

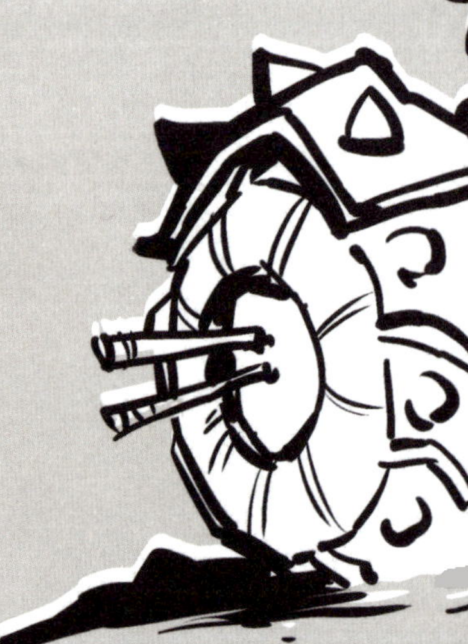

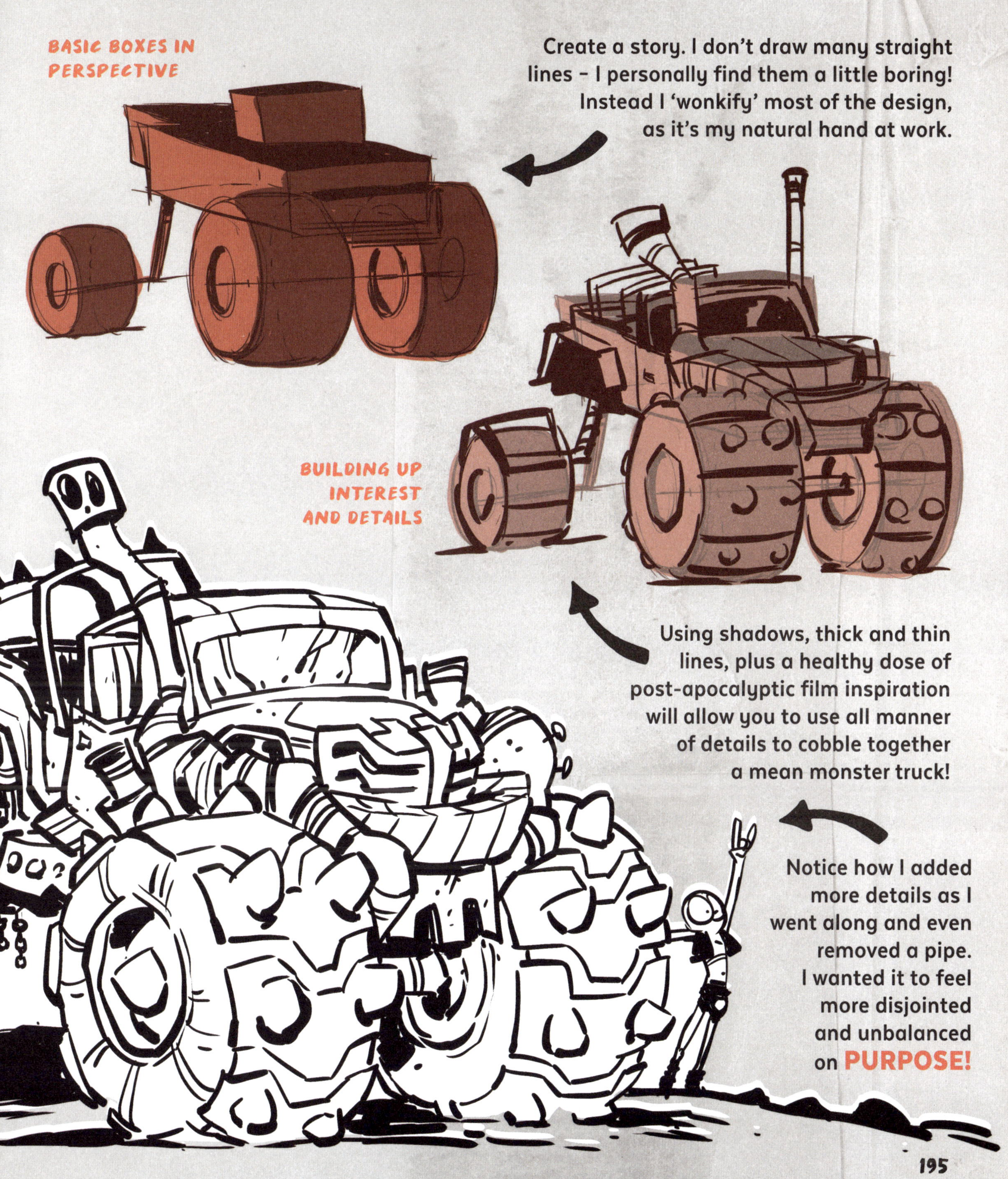

BASIC BOXES IN
PERSPECTIVE

Create a story. I don't draw many straight
lines – I personally find them a little boring!
Instead I 'wonkify' most of the design,
as it's my natural hand at work.

BUILDING UP
INTEREST
AND DETAILS

Using shadows, thick and thin
lines, plus a healthy dose of
post-apocalyptic film inspiration
will allow you to use all manner
of details to cobble together
a mean monster truck!

Notice how I added
more details as I
went along and even
removed a pipe.
I wanted it to feel
more disjointed
and unbalanced
on PURPOSE!

TIPS ON PROPS

I have no idea how a car works, nor a motorcycle or aeroplane, and don't get me started on warp speeds... If your design looks like it fits into the world around it, with colours, textures, and perspective, audiences will go with it.

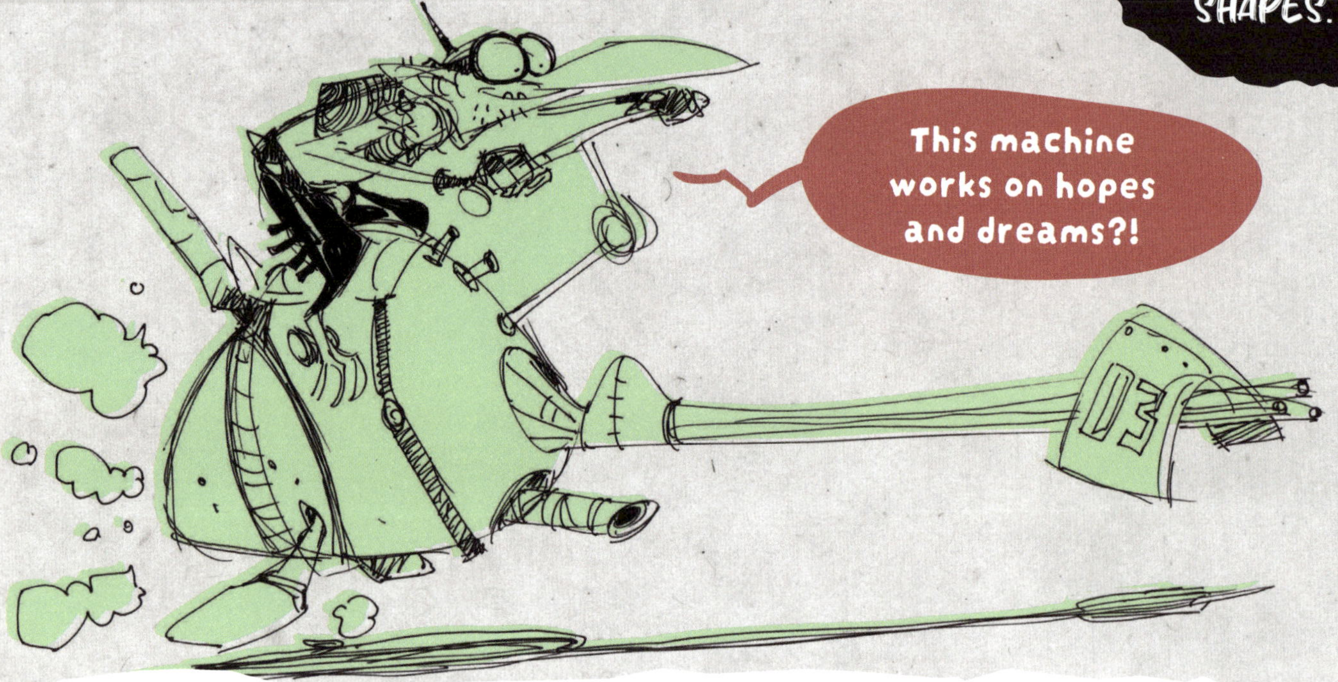

Growing in skill and confidence with prop design and creating something from nothing may seem overwhelming. Start small with real-world objects, finding their overall perspective and shapes.

As you gain control, introduce themes and story. Ask yourself questions about the object you're creating.

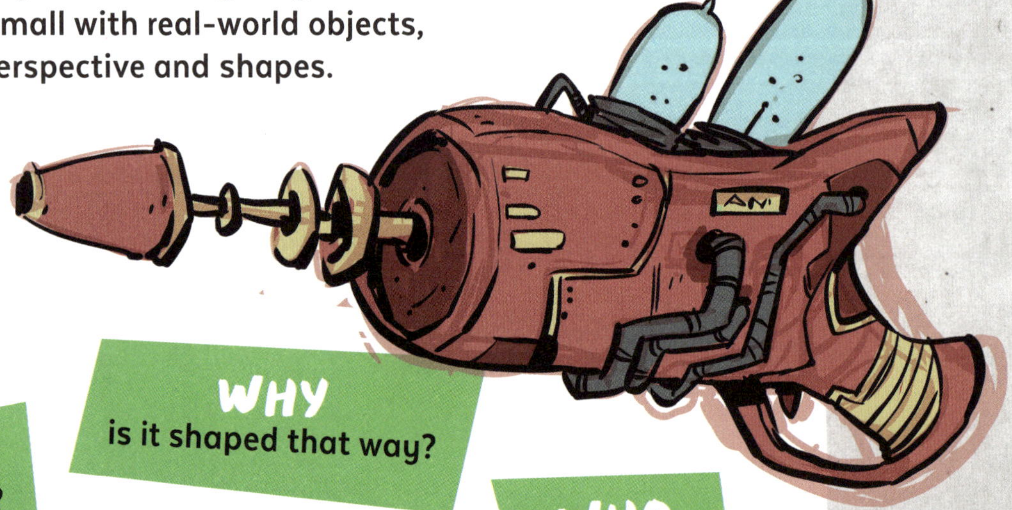

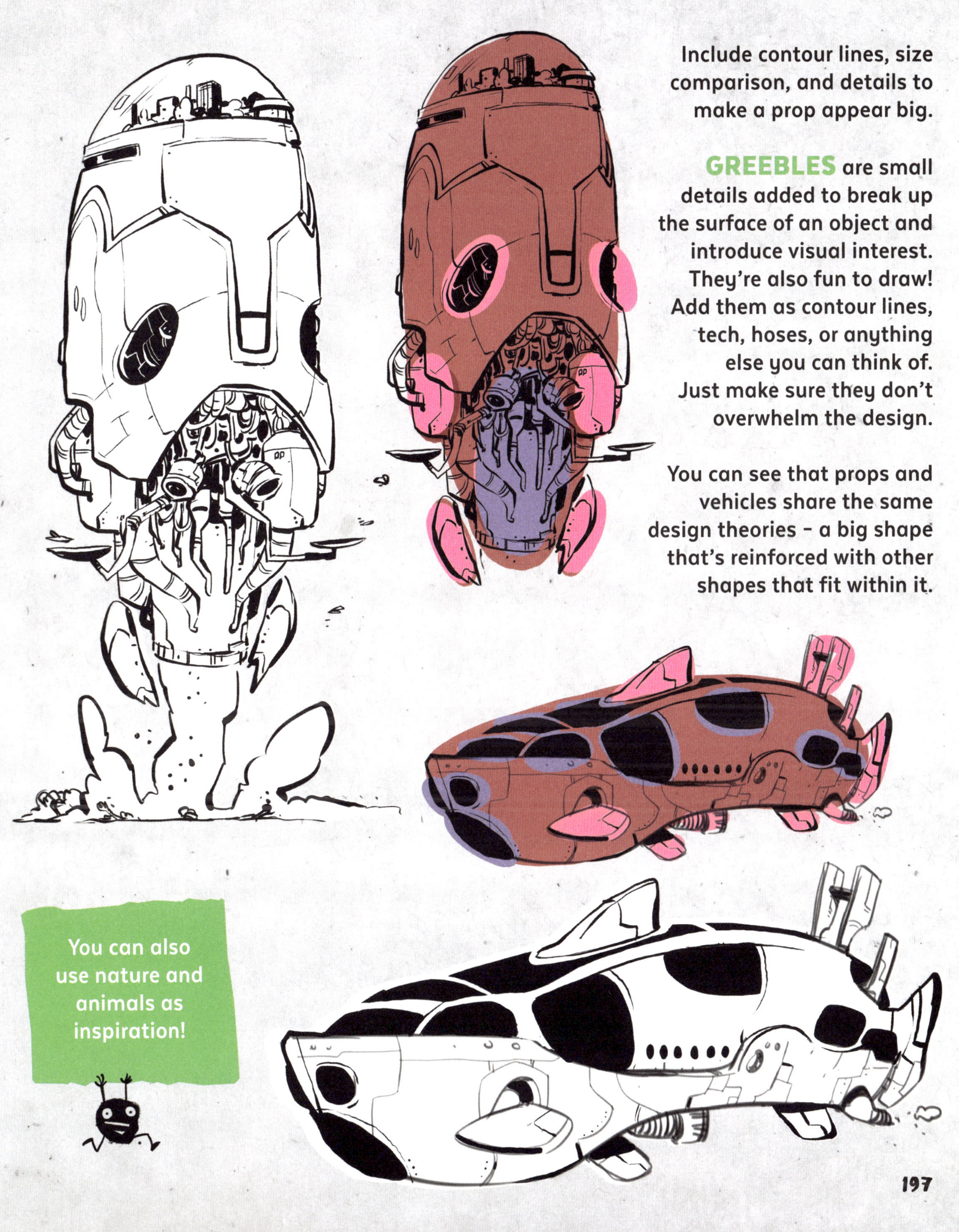

Include contour lines, size comparison, and details to make a prop appear big.

GREEBLES are small details added to break up the surface of an object and introduce visual interest. They're also fun to draw! Add them as contour lines, tech, hoses, or anything else you can think of. Just make sure they don't overwhelm the design.

You can see that props and vehicles share the same design theories – a big shape that's reinforced with other shapes that fit within it.

PROP EXERCISES

Trace over these, scan them, or take a photo to work digitally. Or download them (see URL on page 7).

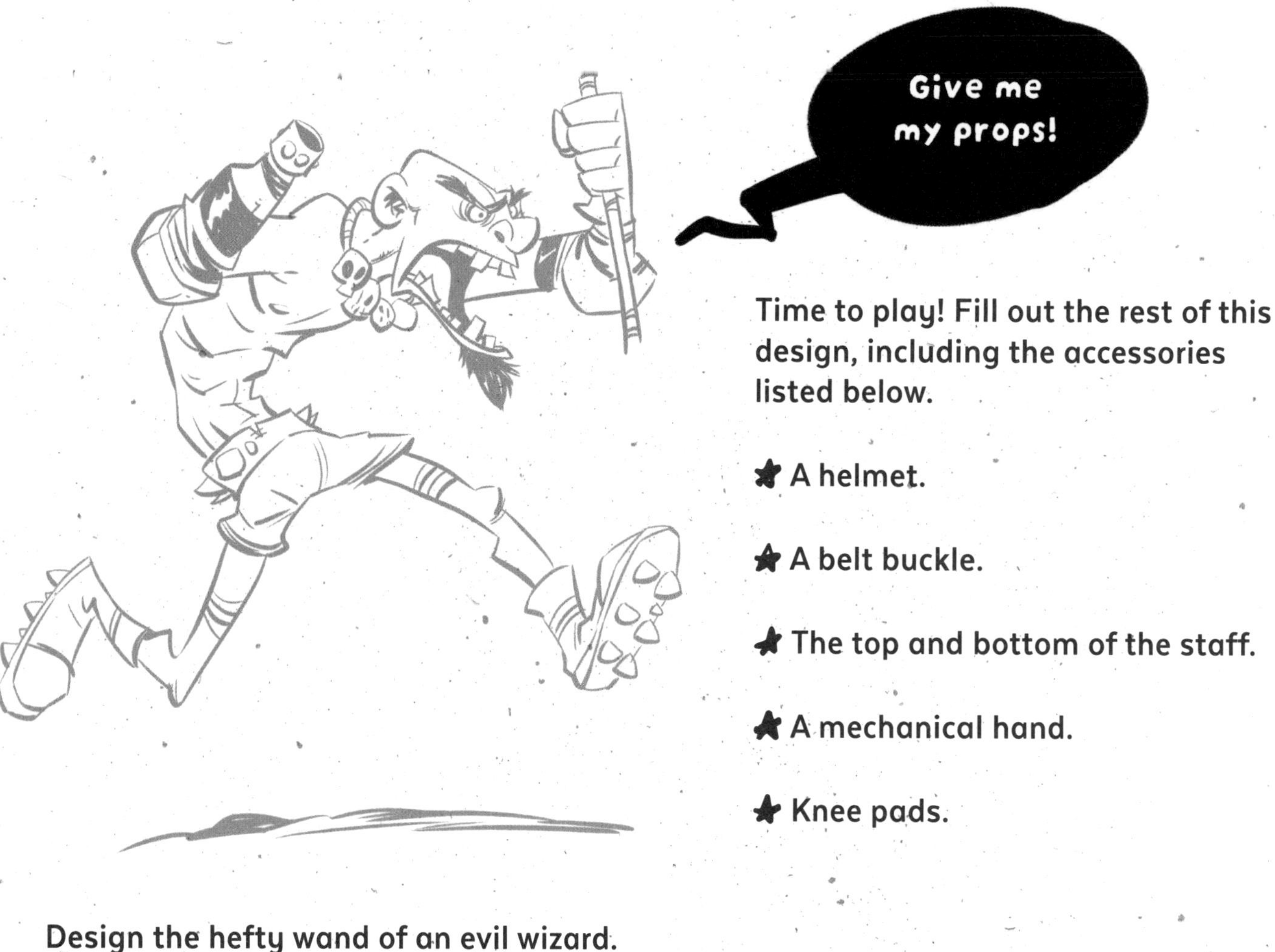

Time to play! Fill out the rest of this design, including the accessories listed below.

★ A helmet.

★ A belt buckle.

★ The top and bottom of the staff.

★ A mechanical hand.

★ Knee pads.

Design the hefty wand of an evil wizard.

Incorporate at least two tubes and
a lightbulb into a ray gun.

Build a gnome
home, starting with
this base shape.

Try to keep it
organic.

Think of two words to
draw from. For example:
cute & kittens
or
sword & ghosts.

Then design a banner.

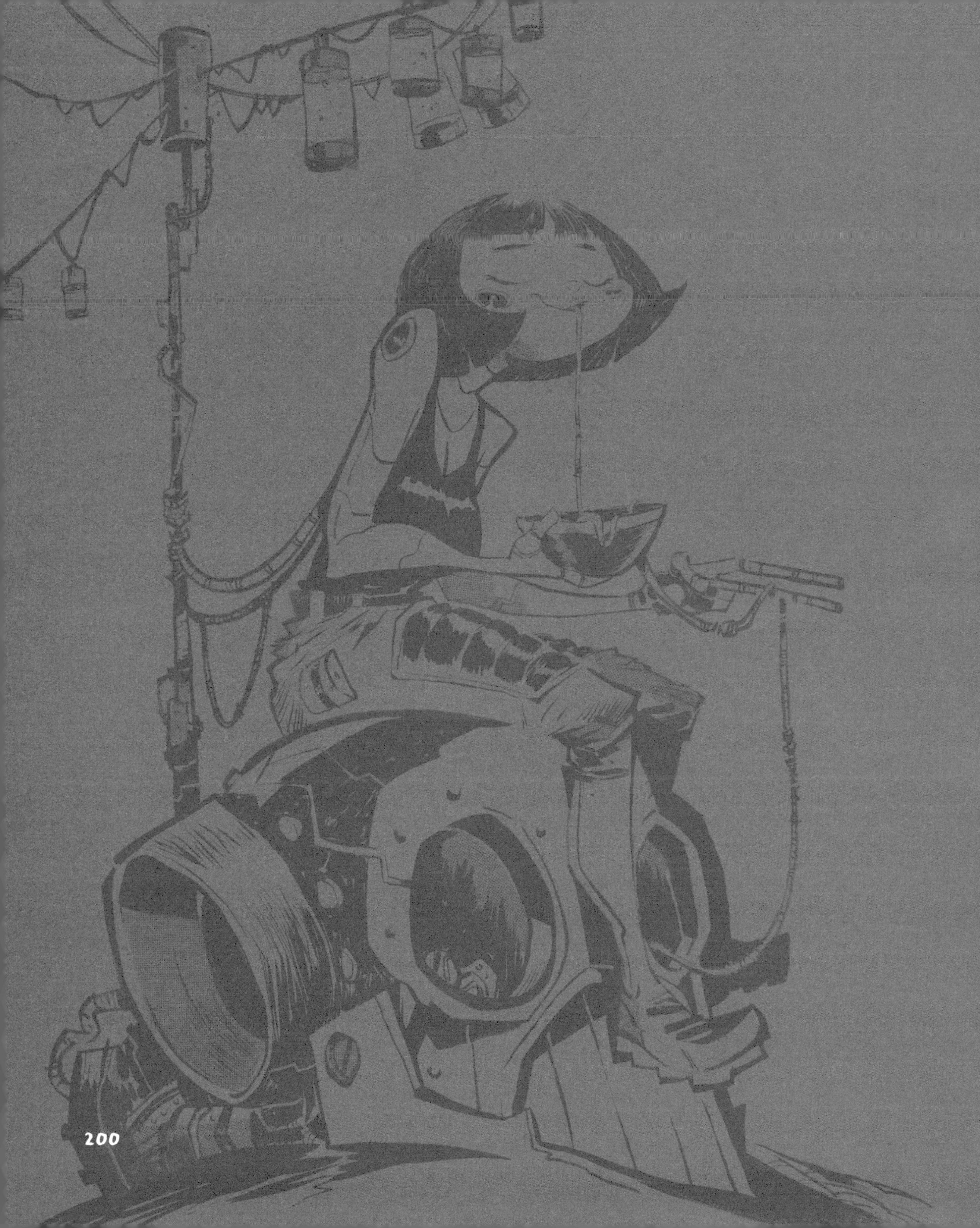

ENVIRONMENTS

ENVIRONMENTS

In every story, movie, TV show, or game, there is a need for believable and unique environments.

Environments are an opportunity to create a complete world. When done well, they provide the characters and story with a place that feels believable and lived in.

Environments can be boiled down to a few key ingredients:

★ Perspective (for believability).

★ Tone or line weight (for depth and atmosphere).

★ Colour (the world isn't black and white!).

★ Camera angle (for storytelling).

★ Composition (the relationships between elements).

★ Consistency (for world-building).

SOME ARTISTS WILL USE EVERY INGREDIENT LISTED, WHEREAS OTHERS, ESPECIALLY COMIC ARTISTS, MAY FORGO TONES OR COLOURS AND FOCUS ON LINE WEIGHT AND DETAILS TO CONVEY TONE AND DISTANCE. NEITHER WAY IS WRONG IF THE RESULT IS UNDERSTOOD.

Layout artists, background artists, storyboard artists, and illustrators all use environments to convey story.

STORYBOARD ARTISTS are story driven and concentrate on camera angle, quick iteration, and perspective line art.

BACKGROUND ARTISTS concentrate mostly on the finished rendered colour work after the other stages are complete.

LAYOUT ARTISTS create fully rendered black-and-white versions from storyboards for every shot.

ILLUSTRATORS do all these stages for production art, such as book covers, prints, books, and other media.

But all of them share the same process for visual storytelling: mood, location, and time.

MOOD: dramatic, creepy, cute, mysterious, fantastical, whimsical...

LOCATION: exterior, interior, a foreign land, a city or farm, a sci-fi prison on a far-off planet...

TIME: night, day, sunrise or sunset, the dark ages, feudal Japan, or turn of the century...

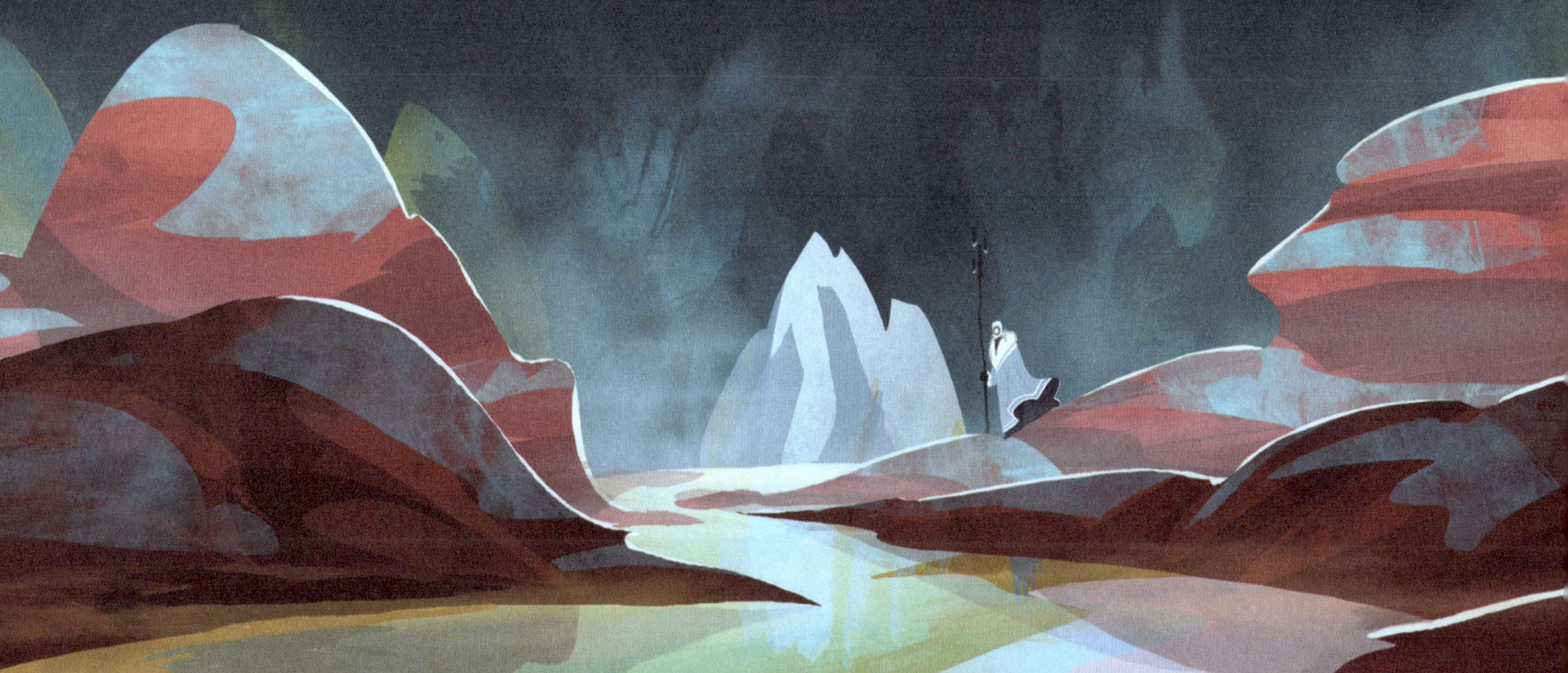

The first stage is **THUMBNAILS**. These save time to iterate and explore different compositions and options. Thumbnails should be rough and quick to create in comparison to fully rendered images, but should still provide enough visual communication (information) for you to use for later stages.

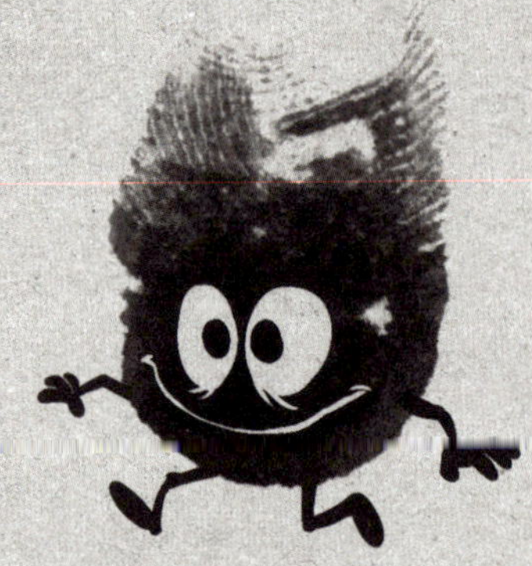

TONE THUMBNAILS

Tone communicates mood and feeling very quickly, but can get muddy fast.
Limit yourself to three to four tones at this stage to create strong contrasts and small scales.

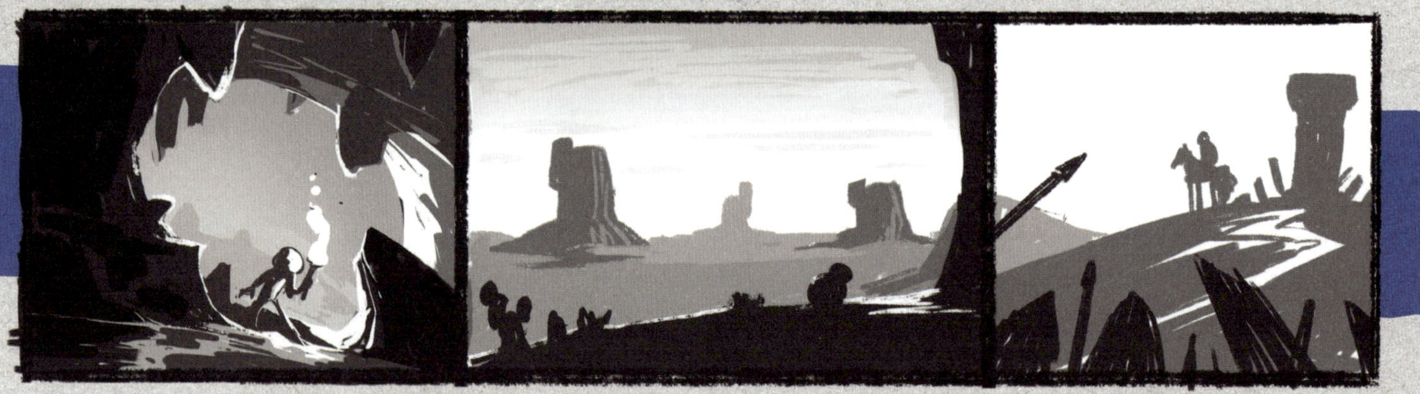

LINE THUMBNAILS

Line allows for details and quickly planning out environments. Take care to limit the amount of details to only the most important parts at this stage.

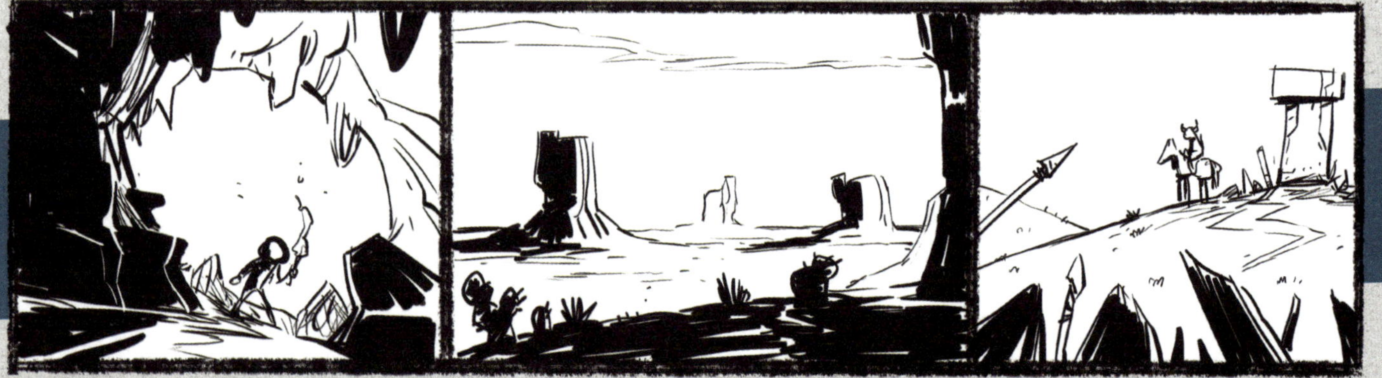

Artists will usually gravitate towards either line or tone, or sometimes both.
The needs of production or your natural direction will determine what to use.

Here's where we start to think about the camera.[*]

WORM'S-EYE VIEW is often used to signify the strength of the dominant shape, weakness for a small shape, or even to show the world from a child's point of view.

BIRD'S-EYE VIEW can show the vastness of an illustration or give context and location information as an establishing shot. This can be about information load!

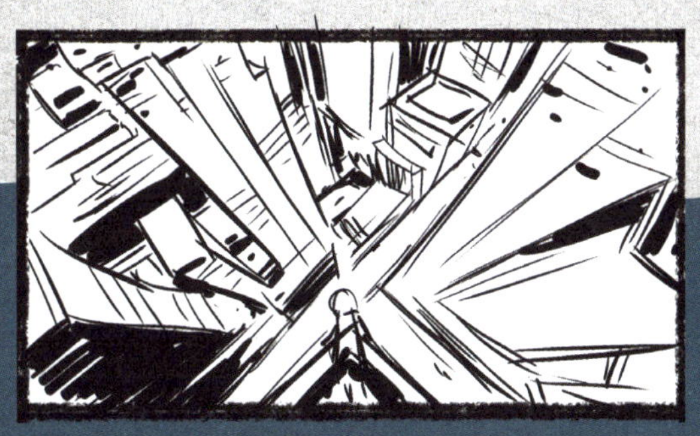

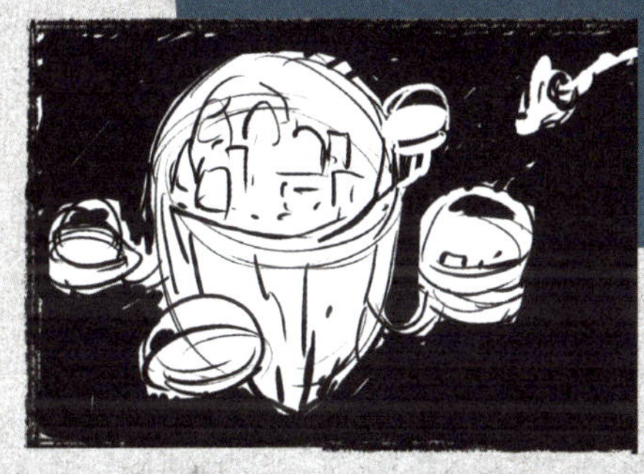

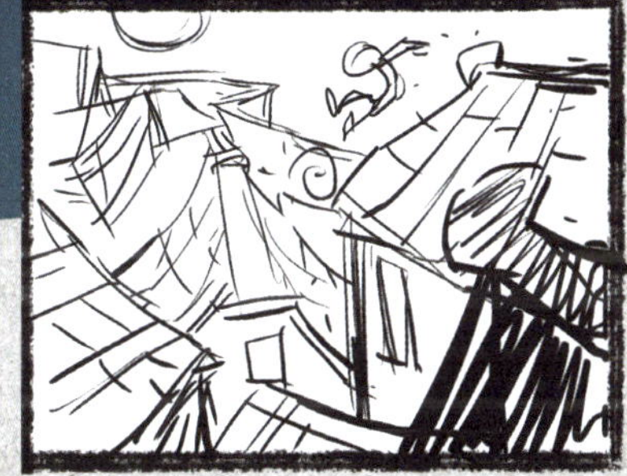

No matter which one you choose, remember the centre of interest, also called the **FOCAL POINT**. This should be the most interesting part of the composition.

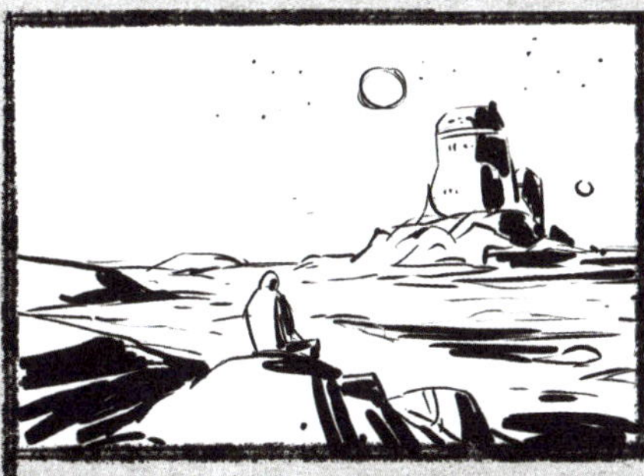

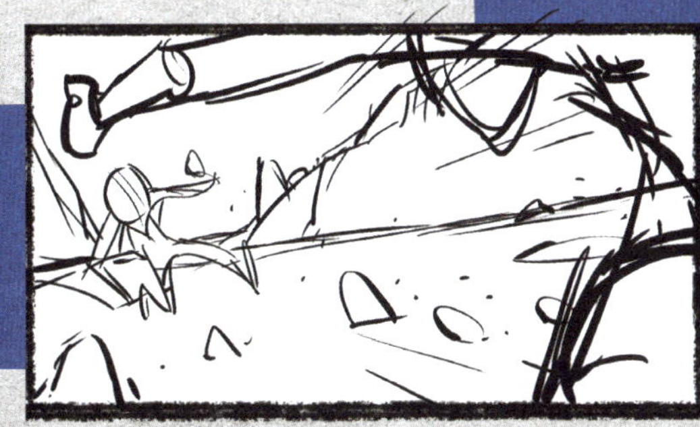

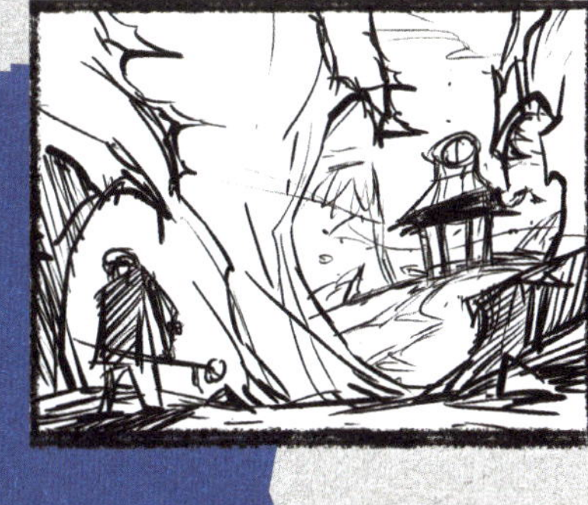

[*]This is not an all-encompassing list and, just like art, is all very subjective. Everyone will feel differently and every angle has been well subverted.

To create an establishing shot, start by sketching out thumbnails of your idea.

For me, it's undersea and alien, lit from below.

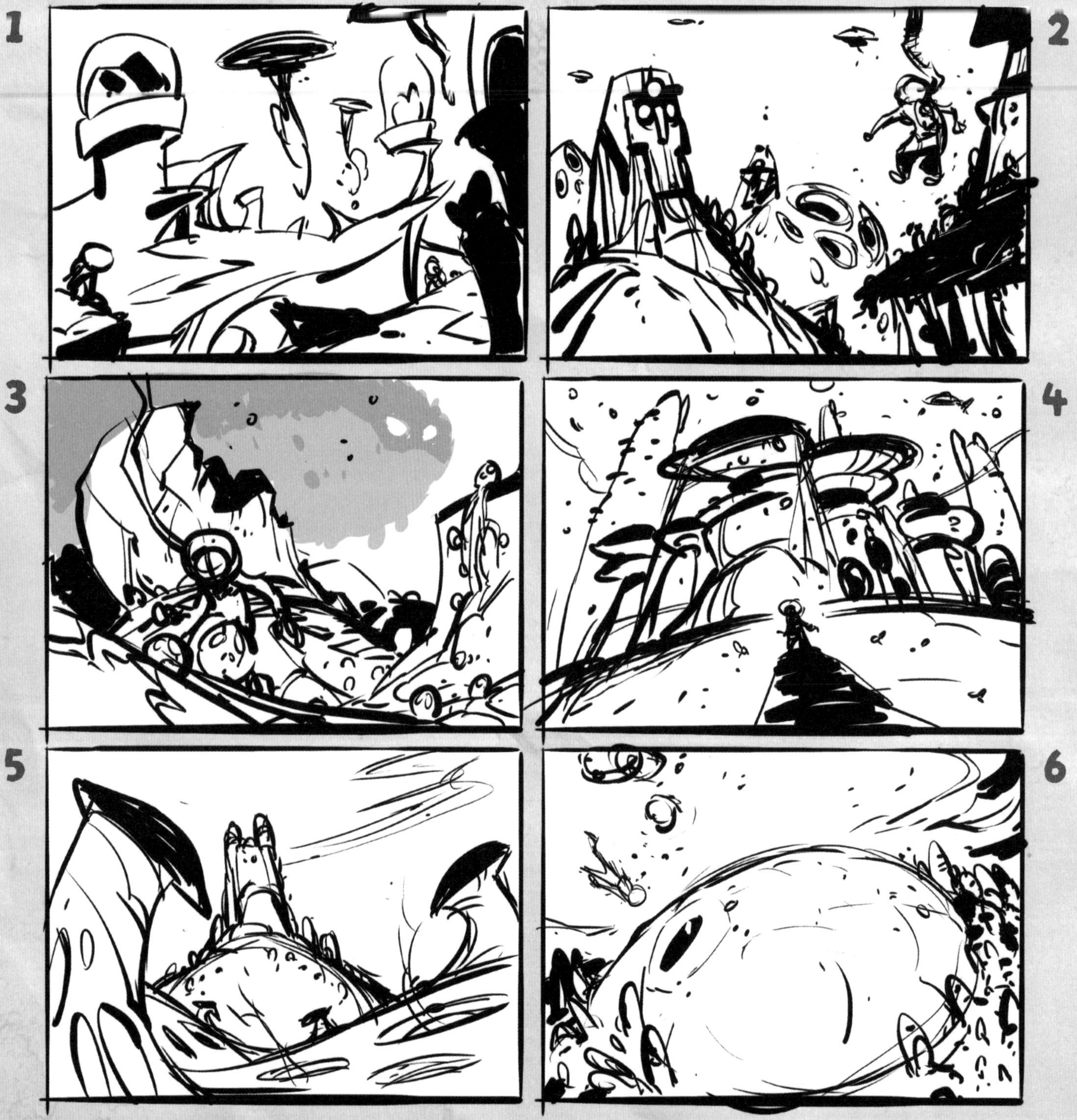

Next, choose your establishing shot. I've chosen thumbnail **1** because it introduces the environment well, which is the purpose of this exercise. Plus, I liked the alien jellyfish flying saucer creatures!

If this exercise was focused on story, I may have chosen thumbnail **3** to expand upon instead. This is because while it captures the environment, it's also a good vehicle for the story idea.

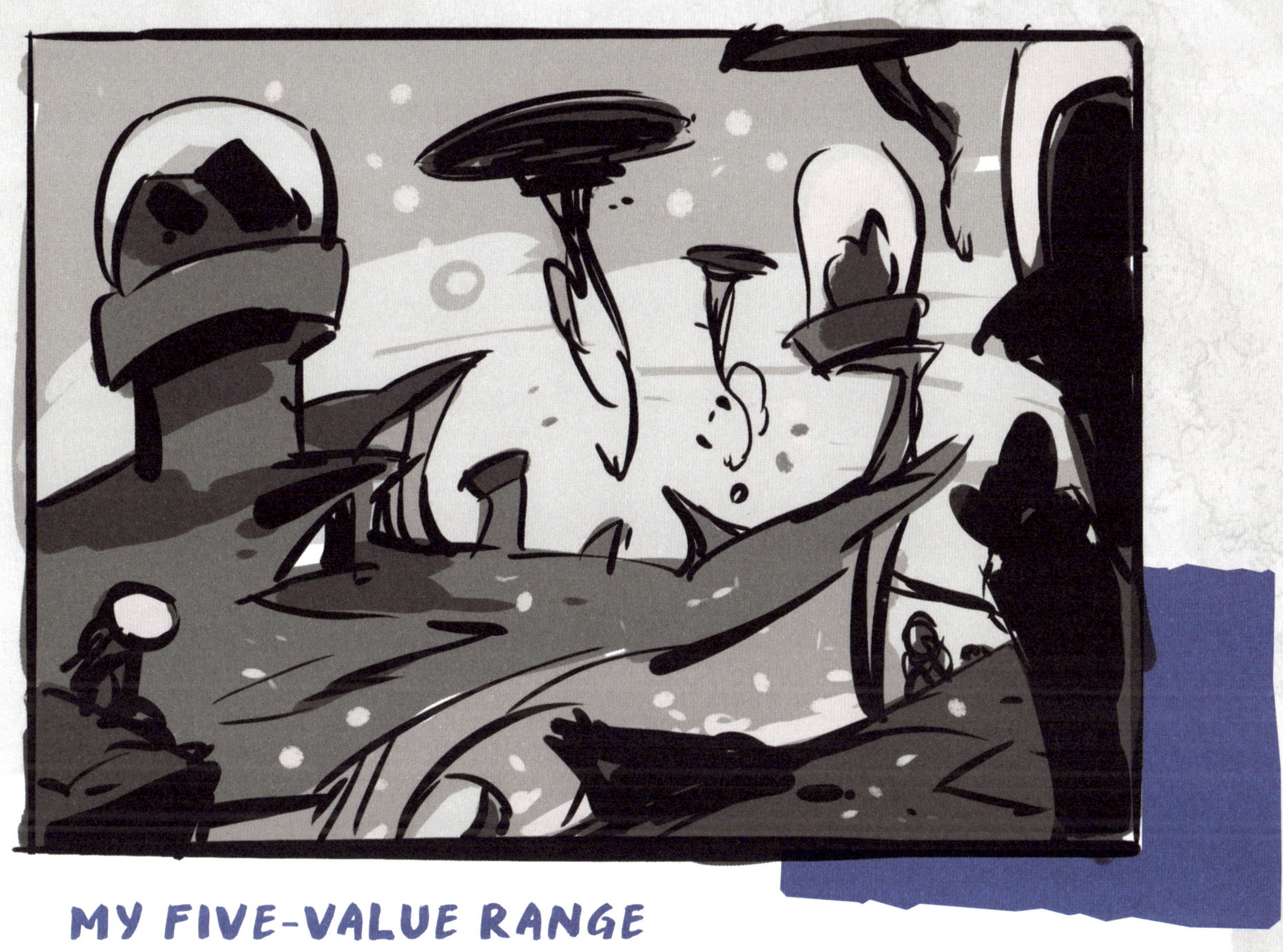

MY FIVE-VALUE RANGE

I included black because I intend to keep my line work intact.

A quick thumbnail value scale and first pass in digital. You can always create more than one thumbnail to try being subtler with gradients or to try out pencils, markers, or anything else you want to experiment with. I used a heavy hand to illustrate the changes in value to make them as clear as possible here.

After you've chosen your most successful
thumbnail, it's time to refine the design.

Some artists will keep working in tone while
they refine. If you're using line work in your
final image, you may wish to spend some
time refining the shapes and detail for the
inking stage, then choose to establish tones
and values after your design is finalized.

With this image, I've decided to
concentrate on the line work.

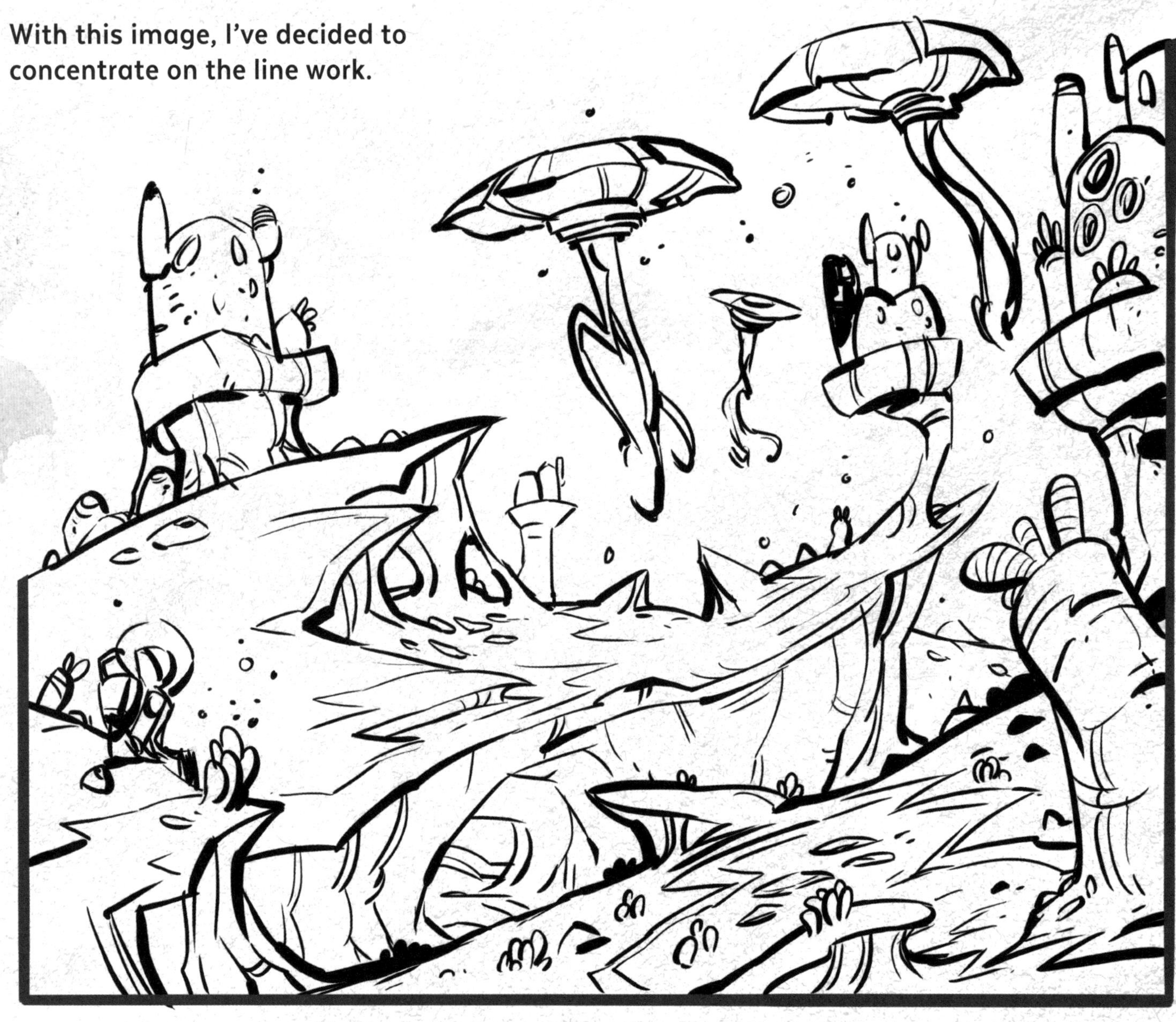

★ Create rhythm and flow to establish where you want the viewer to look. The jellyfish creatures have angular rocks pointing up at them to direct the eye and show their importance.

★ I left the character in silhouette for now. I intend to add a nearby light source to create contrast and interest.

★ Using overlap, varying line weights, and different amounts of detail helps to establish depth. I can colour the line work later to reinforce this.

★ I make use of shape repetition and try to stay organic within the theme of the alien environment.

★ I changed the building on the left as it was taking up too much visual space. I also removed the domes as they don't need them. Plus, it now makes the visitor look more out of place.

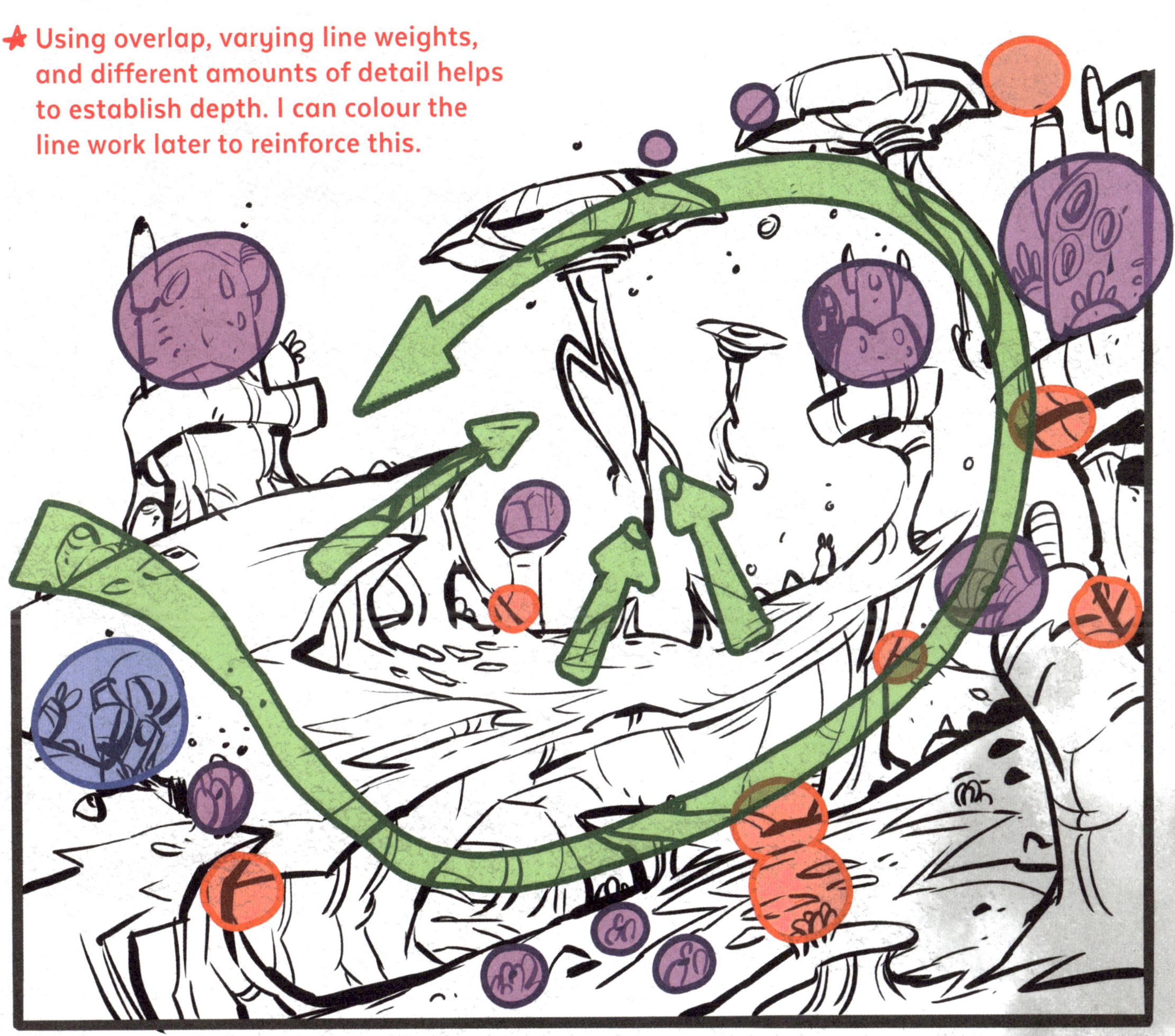

Adding the tones and value back over the finished lines, start making final decisions about what special effects you want to introduce. Here I have changed the background buildings and added more as a subtle backdrop. Never be afraid to change something that doesn't work just because you've already drawn it. Always be willing to do more work to achieve what you're after and never try to 'chrome a turd'.*

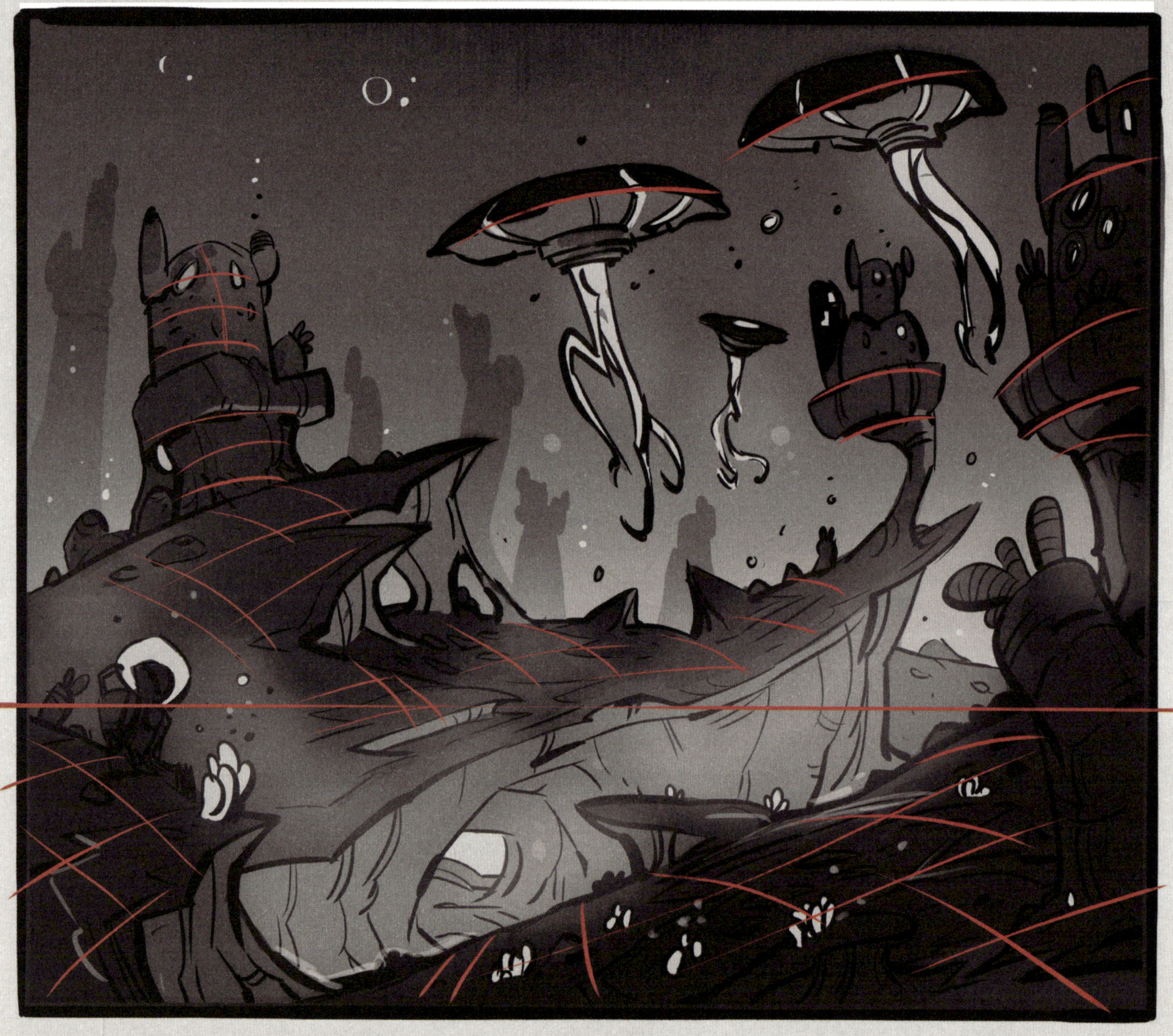

*Even if you render it pretty, it's still a turd!

Using colours and keeping the tonal values takes a lot of time and practice. I've made many mistakes over the years and I believe there is always something to learn from.

Fully rendering the painting takes even more time than maintaining the line work. The more you create art reminiscent of life, the more attention to reality it needs. Make sure to put in the work to maintain your style's consistency!

Don't be afraid to be bold and take big risks. You will learn from these challenges throughout your entire life as an artist.

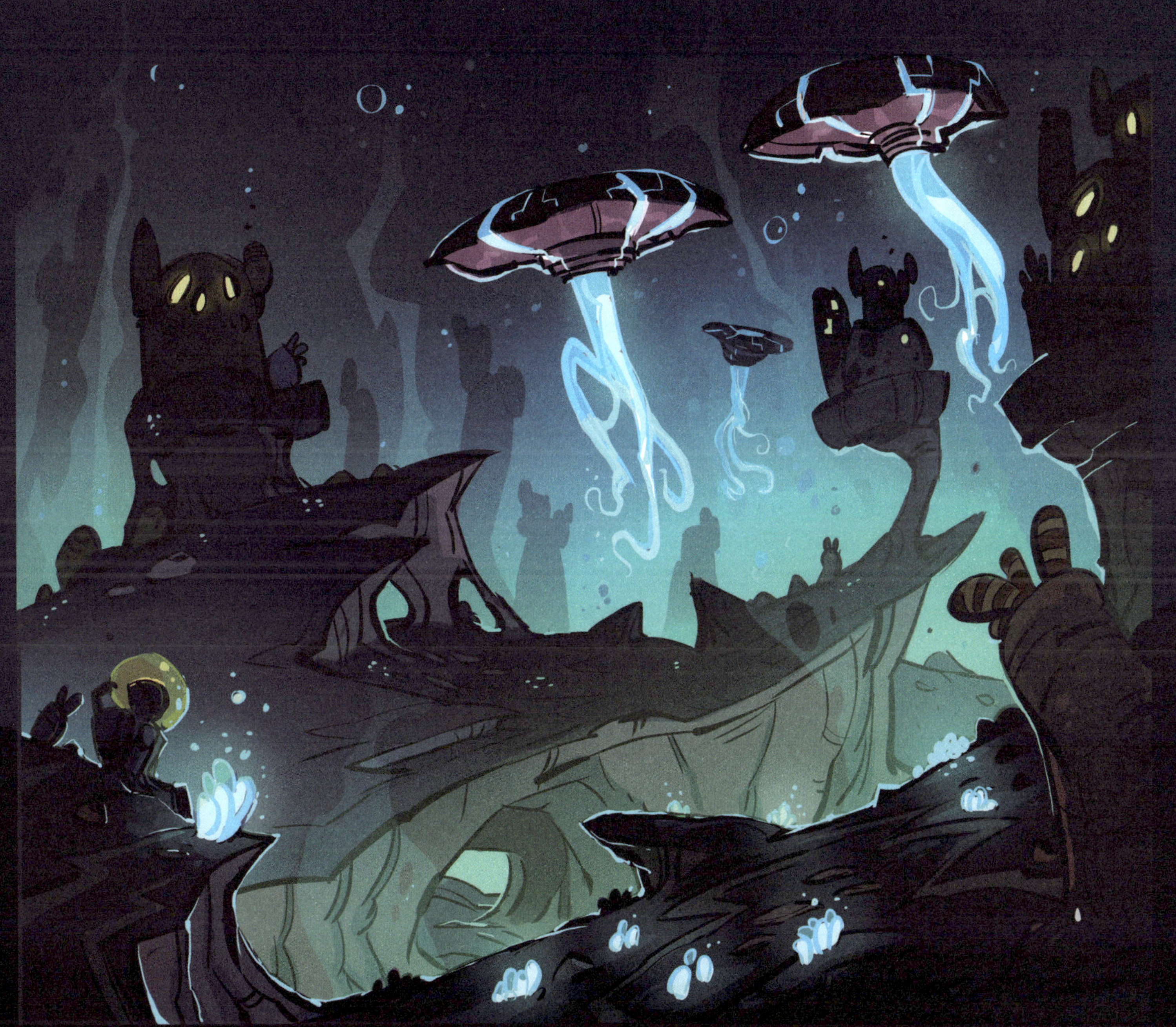

ENVIRONMENT EXERCISES

Trace over these, scan them, or take a photo to work
digitally. Or download them (see URL on page 7).

Create thumbnail scenes with a clear foreground, middle ground, and background.

Create an environment using line weight and/or tone.
Keep the character as the focal point.

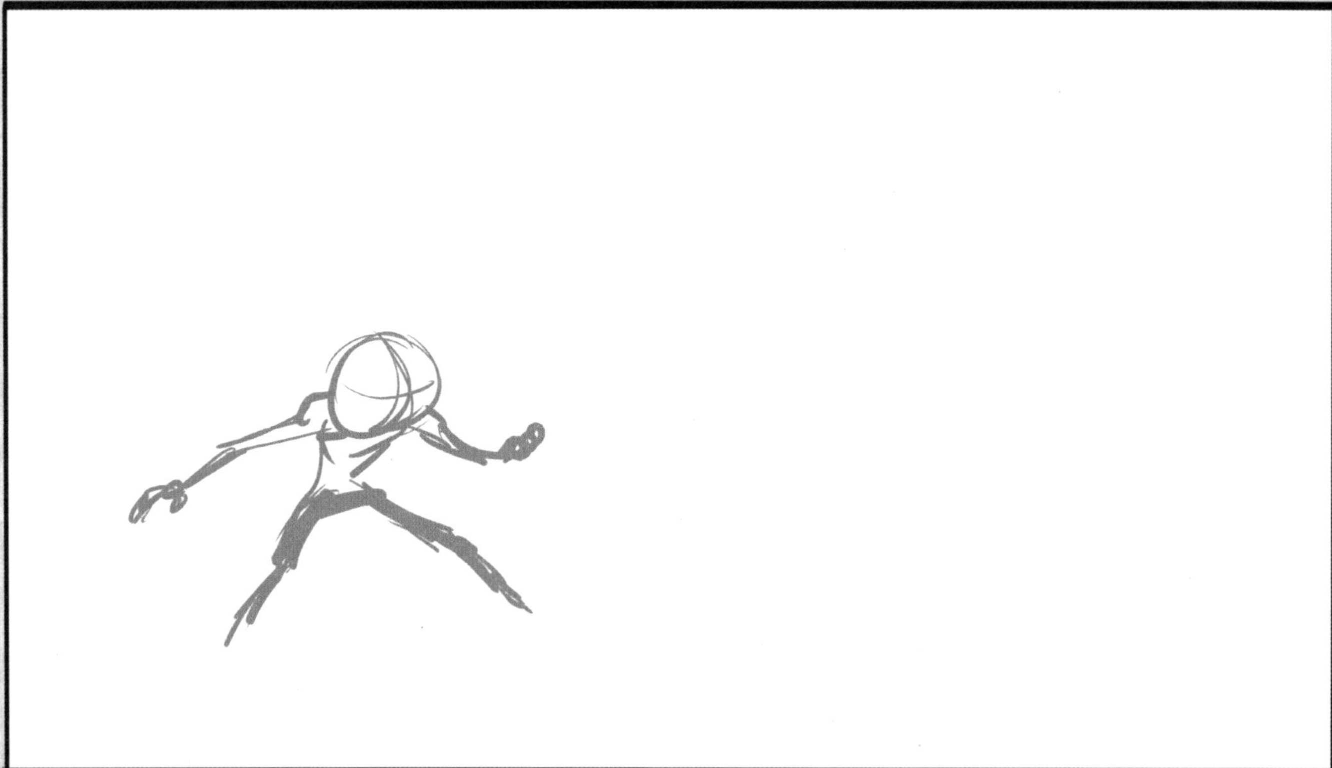

Create a line-only environment in an arctic setting.

Create a tonal layout in a desert setting.

Tone/colour each thumbnail to represent the time of day.

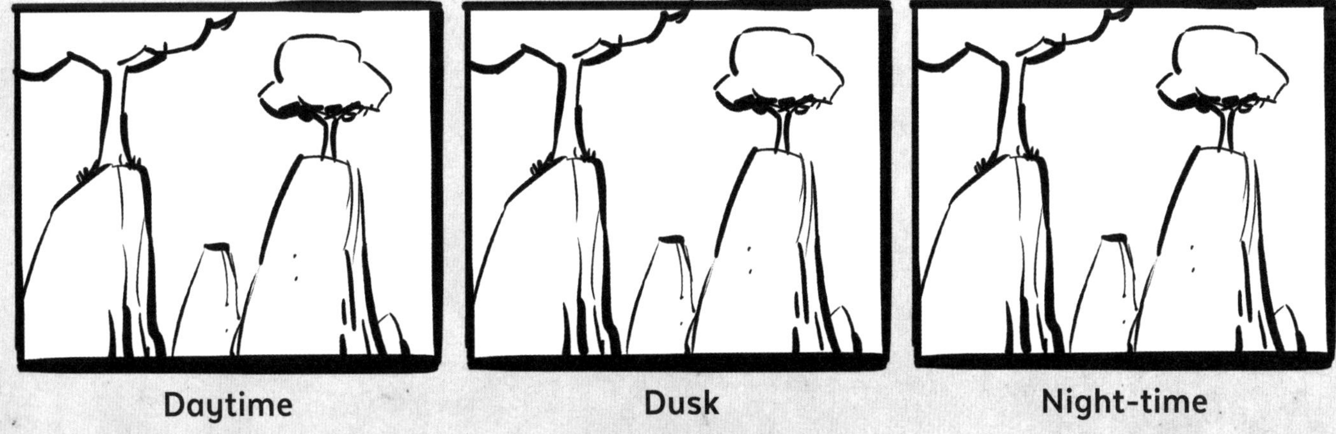

Daytime   Dusk   Night-time

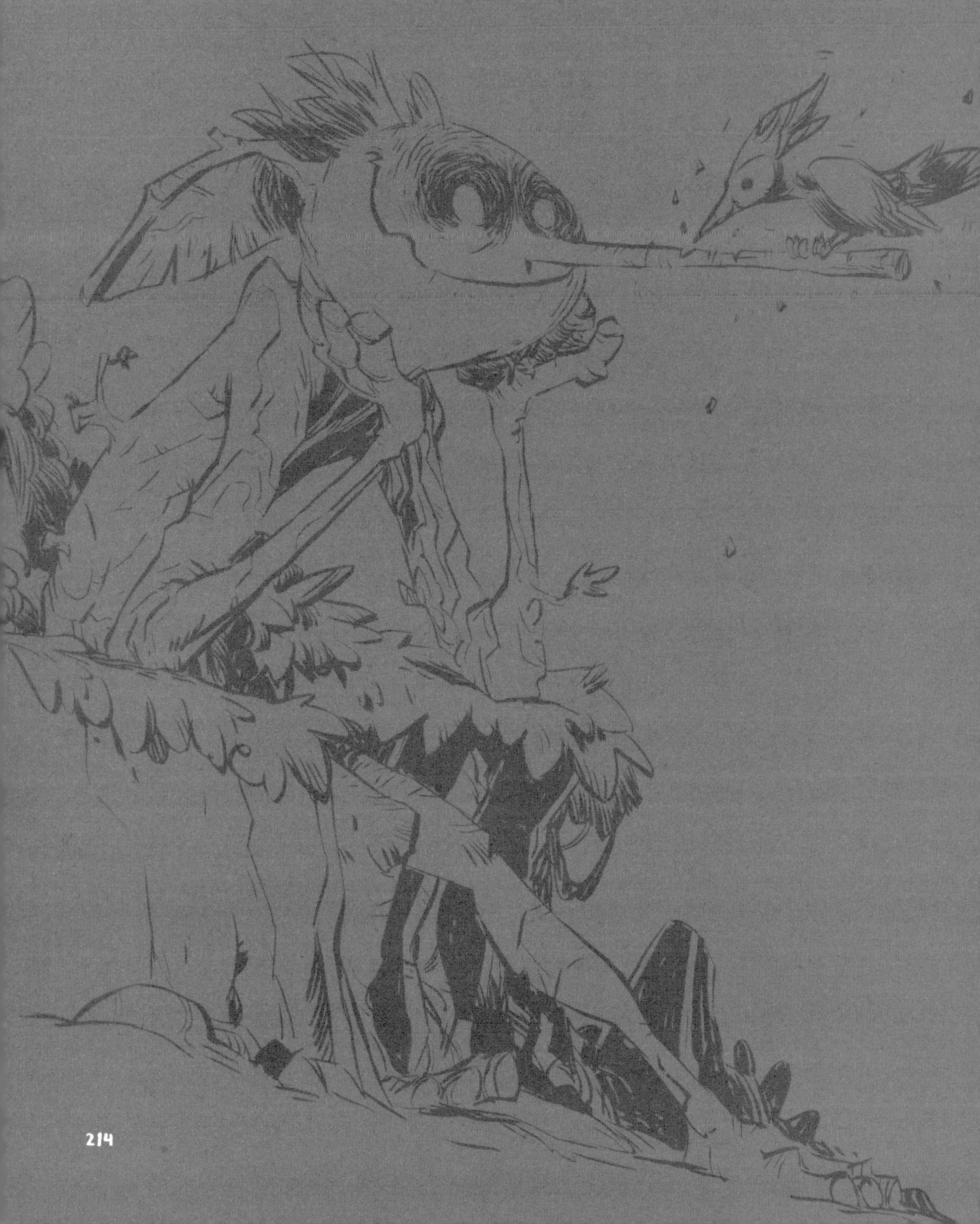

FINAL THOUGHTS

At thirteen I really wanted to be a drummer. My mother said it was too loud, so I found a piece of paper and a pencil instead. This is how it started.

I eventually went to community college and after a two-year degree, was accepted into a prestigious art school. But life challenges altered those plans and I couldn't go…
KEEP YOUR EYES ON THE PRIZE.

Several years and odd jobs later, I ended up at 3D animation school and had to take out a personal loan to pay my way through. My instructor told me I'd never be a character designer. I got my first job making 3D props for video games at twenty-eight.

Two years in, I asked to do concept art and they emphatically said no. I quit that day, even after they offered a bonus and pay rise to stay on as a 3D modeller. I moved out to Los Angeles, city of dreams…
KEEP YOUR EYES ON THE PRIZE.

In Los Angeles, I ended up working at a used game store selling the very games I'd worked on that holiday season. Continuing with my art education, I answered the phones at the art school to cover my class tuition. Again, an instructor told me I'd never be a character designer.

Nothing prepares you for starting over creatively and financially.
KEEP YOUR EYES ON THE PRIZE.

Two semesters of classes, answering phones, and selling video games led to my first concept-art job in Texas. We all got laid off nine months later…

I took a job in San Francisco with a big name in games, but the company went bankrupt within two years.

But I kept my eyes on the prize. Now there is a wall of my art at Jim Henson's Creature Shop. I've worked with Disney, DreamWorks, Blizzard, Sony, and Riot Games. I've art directed, been a lead designer, concept artist, and character designer for countless projects in video games, TV, movies, and board games. Now I'm writing books too.

I've taught art in places ranging from New Zealand to Mexico and have met amazing peers, students, and heroes all over the world because of art. I lived in Portugal when I started this book and I reside in Los Angeles at its finish.

I tell you this because I **NEVER** could have predicted any of these jobs, opportunities, or experiences when I was climbing the art mountain.

There is no one way to lead a creative life, but all paths lead somewhere. Your life can be full of adventure if you allow it.

BE SMART ABOUT YOUR TIME. IT'S THE ONLY THING YOU DON'T GET BACK.

BE KIND. WE'RE ALL IN THIS TOGETHER.

PERSEVERANCE IS THE BEST TALENT YOU CAN DEVELOP.

BE OPEN TO OPPORTUNITY.

EMBRACE CHANGE.

PROBLEM SOLVE.

AVOID COMPARISON.

WANDER AND WONDER.

I hope this book helps steer you towards more roads to wander and wonder. And even if it doesn't, use it as toilet paper, kindling, or to smoosh a bug. See? Problem solving...

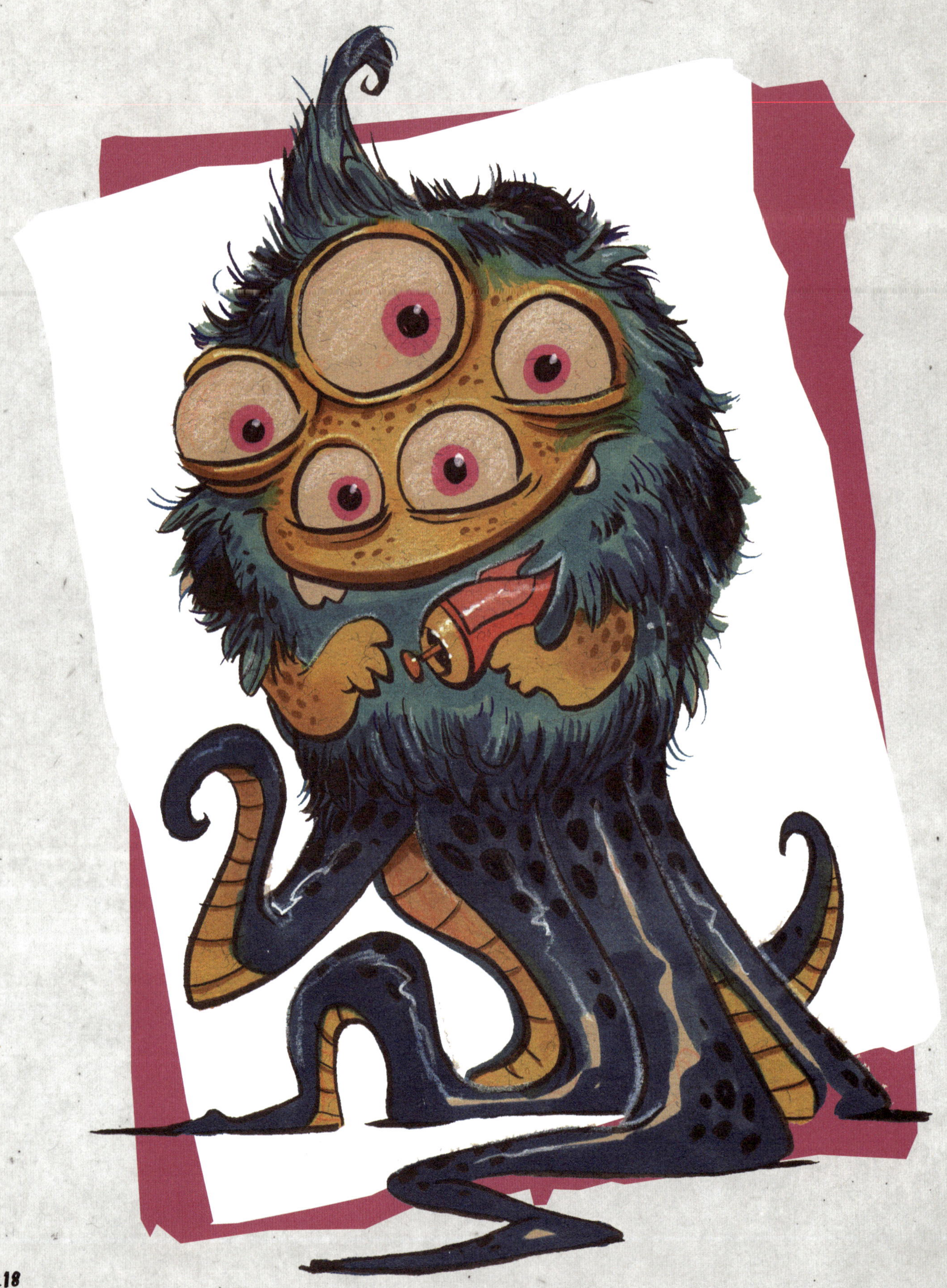

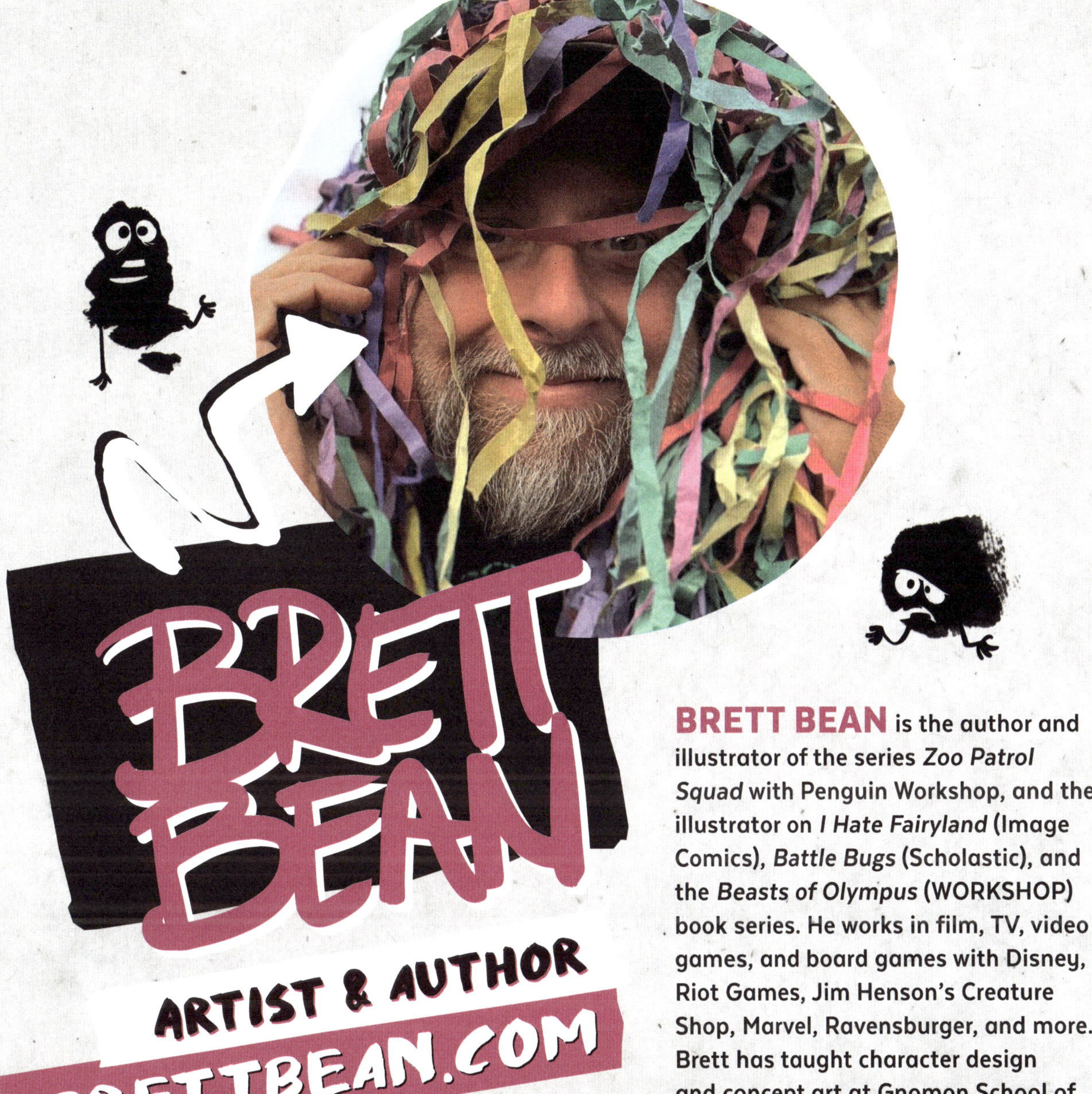

BRETT BEAN is the author and illustrator of the series *Zoo Patrol Squad* with Penguin Workshop, and the illustrator on *I Hate Fairyland* (Image Comics), *Battle Bugs* (Scholastic), and the *Beasts of Olympus* (WORKSHOP) book series. He works in film, TV, video games, and board games with Disney, Riot Games, Jim Henson's Creature Shop, Marvel, Ravensburger, and more. Brett has taught character design and concept art at Gnomon School of Visual FX, LAAFA, CGMA, and various workshops around the world. He loves board games, comics, original art, basketball, Tom Waits, and travelling.

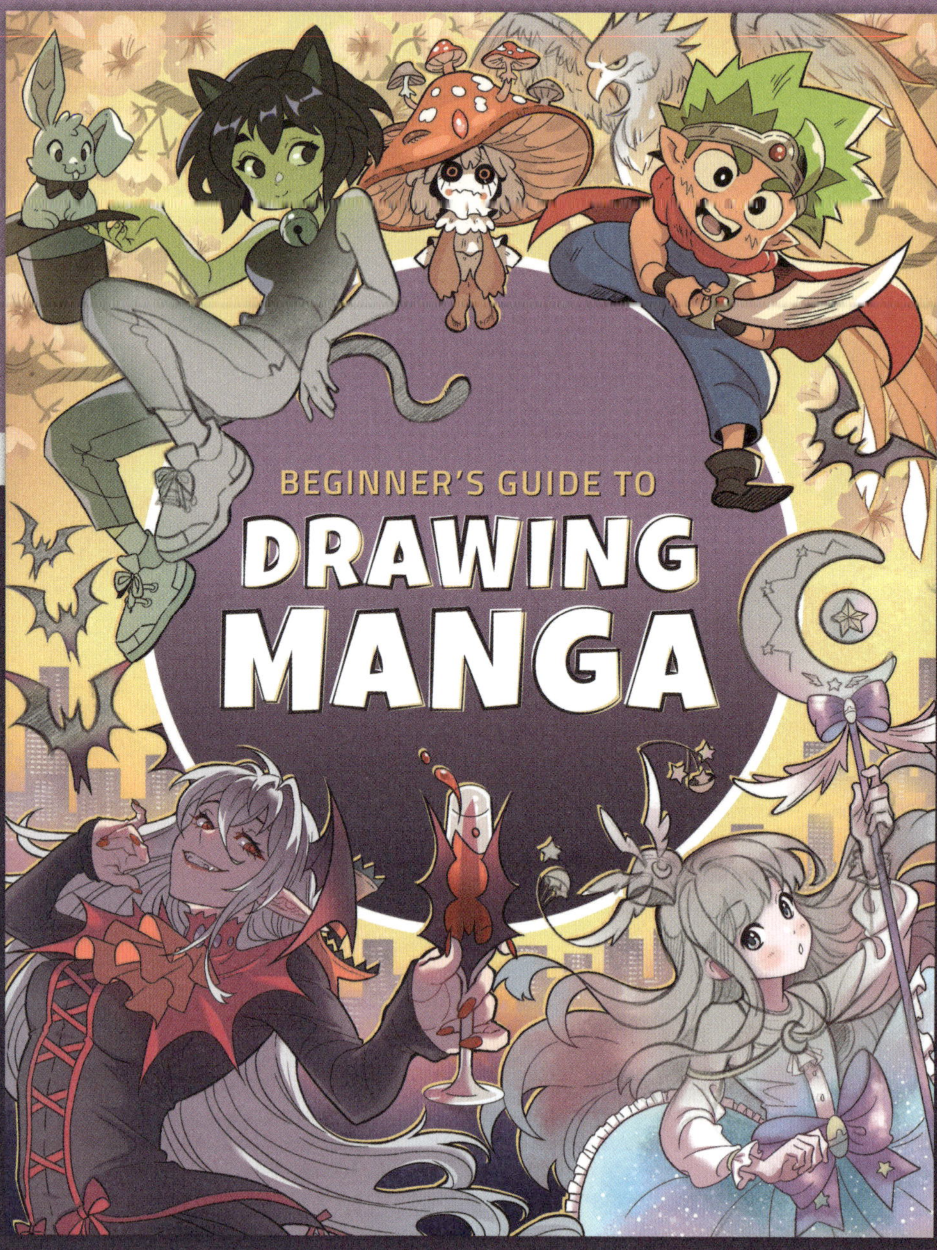

BEGINNER'S GUIDE TO
DRAWING
MANGA

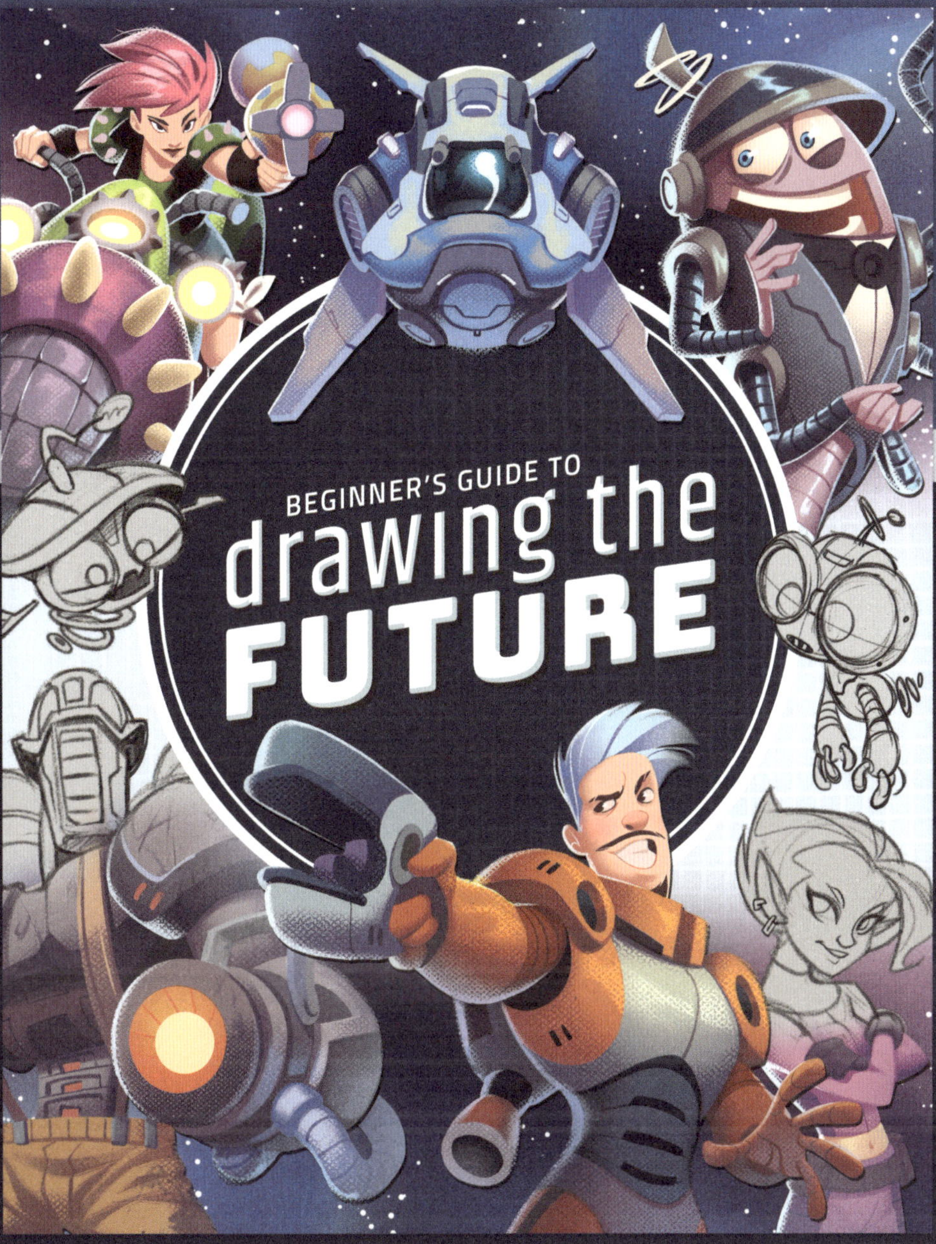
BEGINNER'S GUIDE TO
drawing the
FUTURE

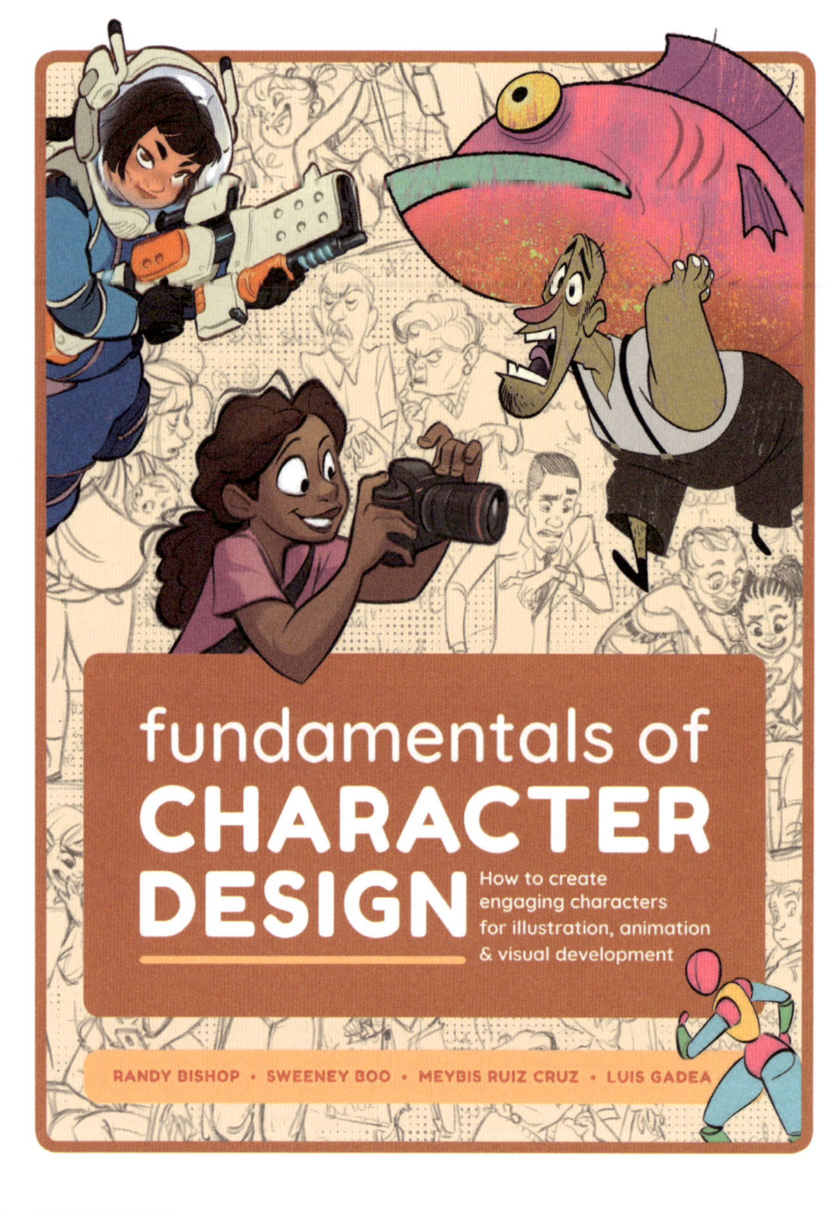

fundamentals of
CHARACTER
DESIGN
How to create
engaging characters
for illustration, animation
& visual development
RANDY BISHOP • SWEENEY BOO • MEYBIS RUIZ CRUZ • LUIS GADEA

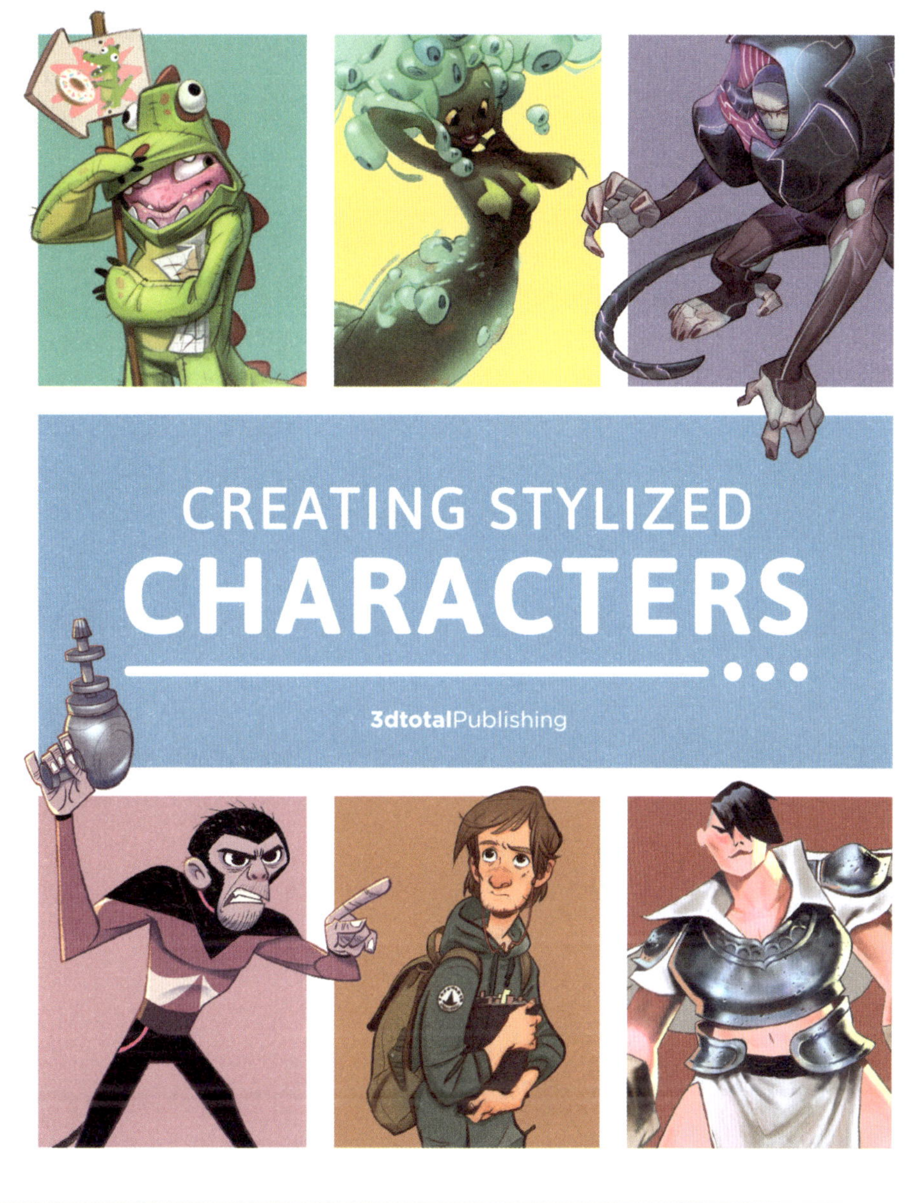

This beginner-friendly book delves into industry-essential aspects of the character development process, from real-world research, to thumbnailing, to exploring different genres, personalities, and styles. With multi-faceted tutorials and an introduction to key concepts such as gesture, colour, and expressions, follow the character development process with six talented artists and learn how they create interesting variations of an initial base character while maintaining the original character's core attributes.

Available now at
store.3dtotal.com

3dtotalPublishing

3dtotal Publishing is a trailblazing, creative publisher specializing in inspirational and educational resources for artists.

Our titles feature top industry professionals from around the globe who share their experience in skilfully written step-by-step tutorials and fascinating, detailed guides. Illustrated throughout with stunning artwork, these best-selling publications offer creative insight, expert advice, and essential motivation. Fans of digital art will enjoy our comprehensive volumes covering Adobe Photoshop, Procreate, and Blender, as well as our superb titles based around character design, including *Fundamentals of Character Design* and *Creating Characters for the Entertainment Industry*. The dedicated, high-quality blend of instruction and inspiration also extends to traditional art. Titles covering a range of techniques, genres, and abilities allow your creativity to flourish while building essential skills.

Well-established within the industry, we now offer over 100 titles and counting, many of which have been translated into multiple languages around the world. With something for every artist, we are proud to say that our books offer the 3dtotal package:

LEARN · CREATE · SHARE

Visit us at store.3dtotal.com

3dtotal Publishing is part of 3dtotal.com, a leading website for CG artists founded by Tom Greenway in 1999.